Fukuzawa Yukichi on
Women and the Family

The Thought of Fukuzawa
Volume 3

ADVISORY BOARD
Albert M. Craig
Anzai Yūichirō
Fukuzawa Takeshi
Hattori Reijirō
Sakamoto Tatsuya

EDITORIAL COMMITTEE
Helen Ballhatchet
Ikeda Yukihiro
Iwatani Jūrō
Komuro Masamichi
Nishikawa Shunsaku
Nishizawa Naoko
Yamauchi Keita

The Thought of Fukuzawa 3

Fukuzawa Yukichi

on Women and the Family

Edited and with New and Revised Translations by
Helen Ballhatchet

KEIO UNIVERSITY PRESS

The Thought of Fukuzawa, Volume 3
Fukuzawa Yukichi on Women and the Family
Published in commemoration of the sesquicentennial of Keiogijuku

KEIO UNIVERSITY PRESS
2-19-30 Mita, Minato-ku, Tokyo 108-8346, Japan

Unless otherwise noted, all the translations in this volume apart from the letters were first published by the University of Tokyo Press in either *Fukuzawa Yukichi on Education: Selected Works*, translated by Kiyooka Eiichi, 1985 or *Fukuzawa Yukichi on Japanese Women: Selected Works*, translated by Kiyooka Eiichi, 1988.

New and revised translations by Helen Ballhatchet.

Copyright © 2017 Keio University Press
All rights reserved
ISBN 978-4-7664-2414-0

Printed in Japan

CONTENTS

ACKNOWLEDGEMENTS 7
GENERAL INTRODUCTION BY HELEN BALLHATCHET 9
GENERAL NOTES ABOUT THE TRANSLATIONS 57

❖

PART I PUBLIC WRITINGS

A Message of Farewell to Nakatsu 61
An Answer to a Certain Gentleman's Inquiry
  about Female Education 69
On Japanese Women 73
On Japanese Women, Part Two 105
On Moral Behavior 139
On Relations between Men and Women 177
One Husband, One Wife, Together Even in the Grave 205
A Critique of *The Great Leaning for Women*;
  A New Great Learning for Women 209

PART II PRIVATE WRITINGS

Daily Lessons	287
Reasons for Sharing Some Old Coins with My Children	299
Selected Letters from Fukuzawa	305
Appendix: Two Letters from Fukuzawa's Wife	370

❖

APPENDIX

A Chronology of Japanese History, with Special Reference to Fukuzawa Yukichi and his Writings on Women and the Family	373
Further Reading	377
Notes	379
Index	419

Acknowledgements

First and foremost, I would like to thank Professor Nishizawa Naoko of the Fukuzawa Memorial Center for Modern Japanese Studies, Keio University for all the advice that she has so generously given. As well as helping with the translation, she has willingly shared her encyclopedic knowledge of primary and secondary sources related to Fukuzawa. In addition, it gives me pleasure to mention the generous grant from the Center itself that has made the publication of this book possible.

I would also like to thank Professor Janet Hunter of LSE and Professor Marion Saucier of L'Institut National des Langues et Civilisations Orientales for reading the first draft of the general introduction and making constructive comments. Thanks should also go to my editor at the Keio University Press, Ms Katahara Ryoko. All errors, of course, are my responsibility.

Helen Ballhatchet

General Introduction

Anyone who is familiar with the history of modern Japan will know something about Fukuzawa Yukichi (1835–1901). He spent the first half of his life in late Tokugawa Japan as a scholar of Western studies who participated in early official visits to the United States and Europe. He wrote books that introduced Western ideas on a wide range of subjects, as well as founding his own academy of English learning, Keiogijuku. After the Meiji Restoration of 1868 his academy developed into one of Japan's major private educational institutions. Meanwhile, he continued to write prolifically, encouraging debate about the domestic and foreign issues that confronted his country in a time of unprecedented change.

Women and the family are central themes in Fukuzawa's writings. They are important to both his understanding of the nature of civilization, and his arguments about the changes that were needed so that Japan could throw off its feudal past and become a strong and independent nation. His major criticisms of the Confucianism of the Tokugawa regime include its emphasis on vertical rather than horizontal relationships in families as well as in society as a whole, and the closely related subordination of women to men. Yet his record as a supporter of women has been questioned. For example, while he declared that marriage was an equal partnership between husbands and wives, he accepted the idea that in Meiji Japan, woman's place was in the home. There is also the intriguing issue of the extent to which he practiced what he preached when it came to his own family.

The purpose of this volume is to provide access to a key selection of Fukuzawa's public and private writings on women and the family, including fifty-three of his letters. Almost all of the texts apart from the letters were originally translated by Kiyooka Eiichi, one of Fukuzawa's grandchildren,[1] but these translations have been substantially revised and given more explanatory footnotes. The letters selected for translation here have been mainly chosen because they provide valuable insights into Fukuzawa's private persona, particularly with regard to his relationships with family members.[2] Each text, or collection of texts, is preceded by a short introduction of its own. The aim of this general introduction is first to provide the overall historical context, and then to introduce Fukuzawa's family background. Next will come an overview of the works that have been selected, an examination of the roughly contemporary response, and finally a tentative evaluation.

Women, the Family and Fukuzawa in Nineteenth-Century Japan

Fukuzawa's first extended exploration of the position of women in Japanese society, "Nihon fujinron" ("On Japanese Women"), was serialized in July 1885 in *Jiji shinpō*, the newspaper that he had founded three years previously. In the first six installments, Fukuzawa paints an overwhelmingly negative picture. Although he must have been exaggerating for rhetorical reasons, this portrait shows where he thought the main problems lay. From the Tokugawa period, he lamented, women of the samurai class and above have lacked the freedom to enjoy life, being mainly confined to the house, and unable to go outside without someone to accompany them. Even now, they have no personal property and therefore no responsibilities. The ideal woman is the wife who remains devoted to her husband however badly he behaves. Moreover, because of the double standard that denies sexual freedom to respectable women, they tend to suffer from sexual frustration. This has a severe effect on their mental health, and therefore on their physical wellbeing and that of their children. Even when young women are able to receive an education, this is of little use since they end up as wives who are expected to devote themselves completely to their household duties. As this situation is grounded in social custom, it will be extremely difficult to change.

As the symbol of this "social oppression"[3] of women, Fukuzawa fastened on *Onna daigaku* (*The Great Learning for Women*). According to *Jiji shinpō*,[4] his critical reading of this text began after he first came to Edo, around the age of twenty-three (twenty-five by traditional Japanese reckoning). He criticized *The Great Learning* in a letter to the former daimyo of Sanda in March 1870,[5] but first made it a public target in Part Eight of *Gakumon no susume* (*An Encouragement of Learning*) in April 1874.[6] It is attacked further in "On Japanese Women" and

Nihon fujinron kōhen (*On Japanese Women, Part Two*), both published in 1885. Finally, in 1899 he published a point-by-point rebuttal, Onna daigaku *hyōron* (*A Critique of* The Great Learning for Women) and his own updated version, *Shin onna daigaku* (*A New Great Learning for Women*).⁷

The Great Learning for Women was a moral primer for use in the education of girls that used *kanji* as well as *kana*. First they learned how to read it out loud, and then copied it as practice in writing.⁸ Although the Confucian scholar and botanist Kaibara Ekiken (1630–1714) was given as the author, and accepted as such by Fukuzawa and his contemporaries, it was in fact a shortened and simplified, probably plagiarized, version of *Joshi o oshiyuru hō* (*The Instruction of Women*), part 5 of Kaibara's *Wazoku dōjikun* (*Precepts for Children*). The Great Learning distorted the original by focusing on the duties of women after marriage rather than on teaching parents how to prepare their daughters for these duties. Moreover, while Kaibara considered that all humans were equally superior to the rest of creation and, like Fukuzawa, emphasized the joint responsibility of the husband and wife in maintaining the family, the basic message of *The Great Learning* was that women were morally inferior to men, and that wives should obey their husbands and their husbands' parents in all things.⁹

Fukuzawa was only interested in *The Great Learning for Women*, but in fact it did not normally exist as a single text. The first record of its publication, in 1716, was as the central part of an illustrated compendium known as *Onna daigaku takarabako* (*The Treasure Chest of the Great Learning for Women*). This became a bestseller and appeared in at least eleven editions during the Tokugawa period. It also appeared in other combinations, and in pirated versions. There were single text editions but these were cheap versions for poorer families.¹⁰

The Treasure Chest combined practical information about the tasks performed by women in all walks of life with the basic elements of cultural education. The practical information of a version published in 1800 included four full pages at the beginning with illustrations of women engaged in agricultural work ("Onna nōgyō no zu"). In the middle, the top third of each page of *The Great Learning for Women* itself was occupied by illustrated explanations of the techniques for making and caring for all types of clothing, including *tabi,* and of the occupations of low-status women in different parts of Japan, such as tea-picking and silk-worm rearing ("Sen no onna no shugyō no kazukazu narabi ni ishō no seijitsukushi"). The explanation of occupations finished with the message that being foolish, women should remain busy and focus on the afterlife; their path to success lay in having children, not in achieving material wealth. It also included observations designed to make higher-status women feel thankful. For example, sadness was expressed at the dangers faced by pearl divers, and at the occupation of the sex worker, which had existed since ancient times. The bottom half of the final section was divided into three. First came advice about how to become pregnant and behave during pregnancy in order to ensure the birth of a child with sound physical and mental characteristics ("Yotsugigusa"); then detailed instructions about the care of babies after birth, about breastfeeding and weaning, and a few pages on the treatment of older children with an emphasis on the need to be strict ("Shōni yōikugusa"); finally there was information about emergency health care ("Shōni kyūyō yakuhō"). The cultural part included illustrated extracts from *Genji monogatari*, a work that the real Kaibara, and other Japanese Confucian scholars, disapproved of. These followed the agricultural illustrations at the beginning. In the final section, the top quarter of each page was occupied by *Hyakunin isshu* (*One Hundred Poems by One Hundred Poets*, the 13th century anthology), and the quarter below this by an illustrated *Nijūshikō* (*The Twenty-Four Paragons of Filial Piety*, a classic from China).[11]

Fukuzawa used *The Great Learning for Women* as a convenient symbol of women's oppression, but it is not clear whether he was doing this because he really believed in its harmful effect or just because it would have been familiar to his readers. From his own life experience, he must have been aware that it presented a model of behavior that did not necessarily exist in reality. In fact, researchers have pointed out that *The Great Learning* was used for educational purposes rather than as a moral text. Emphasizing the importance of the additional material in *The Treasure Chest,* they have also suggested that its popularity should be taken as evidence of the growing number of women who were receiving a basic education rather than as proof of their indoctrination into lives of subordination to men.[12] On the other hand, even if teachers paid no attention to the meaning of *The Great Learning*, the precepts must have had some influence on the minds of their young readers as a standard of "respectable" behavior towards which they were expected to strive.[13] *The Great Learning* continued to be published in the Meiji period, and there were various attempts to update it. These will be examined later.

Of course, there was great diversity among Tokugawa women, depending on factors such as when and where they lived, their social status and their occupation. Since Fukuzawa was mainly interested in improving the situation of Meiji women of "the middle level of society and above," he referred to women of the samurai class when talking about Tokugawa Japan. They did not enjoy the extravagant lifestyle or influence of the "princess" daughters of shoguns and the other elite women that Sekiguchi Sumiko has written about.[14] Moreover, their lives were certainly more restricted than the lives of women in wealthier farming families or those in merchant families.[15] However, even among samurai, the situation of women differed as a result of factors such as the level of wealth, or indebtedness, of the *han*, and within a *han*, the rank of the family, ranks within a family and, of course, the personalities of those involved. Wives of household heads had a key role in the maintenance of the family, particularly if the household head died when there was no adult male heir. In addition, the poorer the household, the more important were the economic activities of the women within it.

Yamakawa Kikue (1890–1980) wrote a famous account of the lives of lower-ranking samurai in Mito *han* based on the recollections of her mother, Aoyama Chise, who had been born in 1857 and whose father was a scholar and teacher. The account gives clear evidence of the restricted life that Fukuzawa was to describe and criticize, for example in *Danjo kōsairon* (*On Relations between Men and Women*), in 1886. Women rarely went outside the house, and if they had a special reason to do so could not go out alone, but had to be accompanied. They had no social life with anyone apart from relatives, and did not know anything about what was going on outside the home. This included ignorance of political affairs and the reasons for the bitter conflict between two factions within the domain during which one of Chise's cousins actually died. However, women played a vital role in the life of the household, growing the food and cooking it, and producing everything the family wore, from spinning the yarn and weaving the cloth to sewing the kimono and *tabi*. Spinning and weaving could also be a useful source of secondary income. It was women who ensured the continuity of household traditions, by means of the instructions given by the wife of the household head to the wife of her eldest son.[16]

Fukuzawa emphasizes the negative effect on wives of the fact that samurai families had to ensure the continuity of their status and income by producing a male heir, or obtaining one through adoption. One result, he claimed, was the tendency to regard them as "borrowed wombs" (*hara wa karimono*)[17] necessary for the continuity of the family line rather than as members of the family in their own right. Another result was their lack of authority within the home, particularly with regard to child rearing.[18]

With regard to the latter, Fukuzawa's view is borne out by the fact that, as Ōta Motoko and others have pointed out, *The Great Learning for Women* focuses on a woman's duties as wife and daughter-in-law, and does not include any advice about child-rearing.[19] Even the *Treasure Chest* section on child rearing contained only limited advice. Tokugawa child-rearing guides by Confucian thinkers such as Kaibara Ekiken, Nakae Tōju and Yamaga Sokō were addressed to men, and Hayashi Shihei's late eighteenth-century guide was even called *Fukeikun* (*Instructions for Fathers and Elder Brothers*). These guides emphasized the importance of training children, primarily by example, from their earliest years and the harmful effects of parental over-indulgence. The focus was on inculcating correct conduct, primarily the loyalty and filial piety expected in a society governed by Confucian norms.[20]

Diaries kept by fathers belonging to late Tokugawa lower samurai families and analyzed by Ōta show that they were not only heads of household publicly engaged in service to the *han*, but were also actively involved in everyday domestic activities. These included childcare and the teaching of basic reading and writing skills to their own children, and even to the children of neighbors or friends. In addition, fathers had the major role in training their sons, particularly the heir, in the comportment and duties that would be expected of them as adults. When fathers had to work away from home, for example in attendance at Edo, wives could find it difficult to keep going without extra support from outside, but this was available because of strong family and neighborhood networks.[21] This situation suggests that men were the authorities in child rearing within the family, and that women were expected to follow their advice.

In late Tokugawa Mito, Chise received her elementary schooling with other girls in a small classroom run by the wife of a nearby samurai household and later, by herself, from a neighbor. Yamakawa reports that in Mito there was a tendency to regard anything beyond basic literacy as unnecessary for women. However, her father taught Chise how to recite Chinese texts alongside her brother, and there were other exceptions as well. After learning the basics of sewing at home from watching her mother, she also attended a sewing school run by the wife of an impoverished samurai in order to boost the family income.

Apparently the teacher's husband was extremely supportive, and frequently praised the work of his wife's pupils.[22]

Yamakawa states that "In raising girls emphasis was placed on the natural development of a spirit of self-sacrifice and submission."[23] This prepared them for their experiences as obedient daughters-in-law. Boys got preferential treatment, but were also held to higher standards of responsibility for their actions. But most of the women she portrays are highly competent and some are able to control the whole household through the force of their personalities. In particular, even though the second wife of the main Aoyama house did not have any children herself she was strong-minded enough to dominate the household, and force her stepson, the heir, to divorce four wives. Yamakawa also states that because of the high mortality rate, remarriage of samurai women was not unusual, despite being against Confucian norms. Even a childless widow who had been sent back to her family might be remarried to a widower and raise his children.[24]

Some of the evidence given by Ōta and Yamakawa shows that Fukuzawa's picture is over-simplified, as one might expect. In particular, it is clear that the relationships between husbands and wives could be close and harmonious. Samurai fathers had the opportunity to be intimately involved in family affairs because "male" work was not necessarily located outside the home. Moreover, as was mentioned above, they were expected to play an important role in domestic affairs. In fact, as Sekiguchi Sumiko suggests, it is likely that Fukuzawa's vision of the ideal family was influenced by the relationships in lower samurai families.[25] Although he did not grow up in a typical family since his father died when he was only eighteen months old, his mother made sure that the children knew about their father, and Fukuzawa made sure that this knowledge was passed on to his children.[26] The nearly two years that he spent from 1856 lodging with Ogata Kōan's family in Osaka during his second period of study at Ogata's private academy of Western learning may also have made a deep impression.[27]

As has already been mentioned, Fukuzawa fiercely criticized the double standard used to judge male and female promiscuity. He was also concerned about the fact that unlike contemporary Europe and America, there was no attempt to hide the existence of prostitutes and concubines. In the Tokugawa period, the latter were an acceptable way of ensuring the continuity of the family by increasing the possibility of producing male offspring. Yamakawa explains that wealthier samurai families in Mito might have one or more concubines, and that they were treated as being of lower status than the wife.[28] Fukuzawa would have had knowledge about this, possibly through his wife, since she was from a high-ranking Nakatsu family, and certainly from his contacts with Hōren'in, the elderly widow of a former Nakatsu daimyo. According to his autobiography, Hōren'in asked to meet him after hearing about his knowledge of Western customs, and specifically after being told that in Western countries men and women were regarded as equal, and monogamy was the norm. "This information was a revelation that moved her deeply, since she had suffered personally [from the opposite type of experience] when young." He adds that later, this encounter led him to reflect that "the theory of monogamy has a considerable, though hidden, appeal," which he gives as a justification for his seemingly hopeless fight against male promiscuity.[29] After their first meeting, he was given access to the female quarters of the daimyo's residence, which may be the basis for his negative description in *An Encouragement of Learning*.[30] Fukuzawa remained in touch with Hōren'in after the Restoration, providing temporary accommodation in the Keio compound at Mita for her and the rest of the Okudaira family around 1872, and even helping to organize her funeral.[31]

However, as Yamakawa relates, during the Tokugawa period pressure from relatives tended to stop men from becoming too promiscuous. This pressure helped to prevent the danger of a favorite concubine coming to dominate a household, but ceased to be effective when the traditional samurai family system collapsed in the changes that followed the Restoration. The increase in promiscuous behavior after the Restoration is also a problem that Fukuzawa refers to in *Hinkōron* (*On Moral Behavior*).[32]

During the Tokugawa period, the state tried to control sex workers by confining them to specific areas. The role of these "pleasure quarters" (*yūkaku*) and their glamorous inhabitants in the popular art, fiction and drama of the period is well known. Samurai were not meant to visit such places, although of course they did, particularly when they were stationed in Edo. The system of alternate attendance, which meant that daimyo had to move back and forth between their *han* and Edo, usually spending one year in each, meant that the proportion of samurai in the Edo population was unusually large, and predominantly male. The official wives of daimyo had to live in Edo, and high-ranking samurai stationed at Edo, such as Fukuzawa's father-in-law, were accompanied by their families. However, all other samurai had to leave their families behind. The temptation to visit the famed Yoshiwara must therefore have been strong, and even one of the attractions of attendance at the capital.[33] This is probably one reason why Fukuzawa's arrival in Edo triggered his interest in *The Great Learning for Women*.

Fukuzawa's criticisms of the situation of women in Japan were obviously influenced by his understanding of the situation of women in Western countries. He participated in three foreign trips made by Bakufu officials before the Restoration, in 1860, 1862, and 1867.[34] The members of the first embassy, to the United States in 1860, appear to have been surprised and disconcerted by the prominence of respectable women in public life, by the deference to women that formed part of gentlemanly behavior, and by their dress and behavior at a ball that was held to welcome the exotic visitors. Fukuzawa shared in this general surprise. His pursuit of Western learning in Tokugawa Japan had given him basic knowledge of science and technology, but political ideology, social institutions, and everyday human behavior were another matter.[35]

On his second trip, in 1862, he visited Europe. As well as buying books to study on his return, he tried as far as possible to find out about daily life by asking people questions and recording their answers in notebooks; he also kept a diary. These reveal, for example, that in Britain he witnessed female telegraph operators at work, and visually handicapped women receiving job training. In Britain, he must also have made inquiries about the sex trade because he recorded information about the reasons why women became sex workers, and about ways in which this might be prevented. Some of the reasons were economic: the high cost of living and the difficulty of finding work because of competition from men; some were moral, including "a love of extravagance" and male seduction.[36]

It is not clear why Fukuzawa made these inquiries, but the Embassy arrived at a time when the issue of prostitution was in the public eye. In the previous month, the government had published a report about the extent of prostitution at the garrison town of Aldershot and the need to prevent the spread of venereal disease through providing alternative sources of entertainment in the form of "soldiers' institutes." The Embassy actually visited the garrison at Aldershot, and the report was mentioned both in the House of Commons and in a letter to the London *Daily News* just after their arrival.[37] Later, Fukuzawa was to stress that while sexual morality in Western countries was not superior to that in Japan, respectable men concealed their promiscuity, and prostitutes and mistresses were ostracized from polite society.[38]

After this second visit abroad, Fukuzawa began to share the wide-ranging knowledge that he had gained of the West by writing a series of books that attracted great interest. The second, "supplementary," volume of the first of these was published after some delay in 1868, the actual year of the Meiji Restoration. It contained a definition of the family that Albert Craig has traced to a Scottish textbook on political economy by one John Burton.[39] In an implicit challenge to Tokugawa norms, Burton/Fukuzawa stated that the nuclear family was the basis of society, with no reference to the lord-vassal relationship. Consisting of husband, wife and children, with no mention of parents-in-law or concubines, it was an oasis of affection in a world of self-interested competition. Nations resulted from the gathering together of families that had a common origin in one family.[40]

Fukuzawa was not directly involved in the actual events of the Meiji "Restoration." The break up of the Tokugawa system that followed obviously had an impact on the life patterns and identity of women as well as men, and on the role of the family in society. Even before the Restoration social mobility had been growing, but now most of the barriers were removed. Marriage and career opportunities were no longer restricted according to birth. Family membership, including the need for samurai families to secure an heir, lost much of its public significance. As government policies developed, initially very much through a process of trial and error, and power became increasingly centralized, new legal, educational and occupational structures appeared that had direct and indirect effects on the lives of women and the nature of the family. In urban areas, starting with the emerging "middle class," girls as well as boys became increasingly involved in formal schooling in institutions apart from the family dwelling place; new forms of paid work were also located at a distance, in offices and factories. As a result, the lives of different family members became more disparate. In particular, the lives of men in non-traditional occupations began to revolve around the workplace. They had less time to spend at home regulating household affairs, and did not need to instruct their sons in the skills needed for hereditary posts. Over time, these changes obviously had an impact on women's roles, including the part they played in child rearing. Ideas about "love" (*rabu* or *ren'ai*) as the basis of marriage, and "the home" (*katei* or *hōmu*) as a center of stability and happiness for family members created by the wife/mother, attracted the interest of those who admired Western patterns of life.⁴¹ It was during the beginnings of this social transformation that Fukuzawa went beyond refashioning the information that he had found in Western books and began to express his own ideas.

It has been widely observed that Fukuzawa's writings on women fall into three periods. Hayakawa Noriyo has linked these to his major interests at these times. Figure 1 shows the texts from the first period that are referred to in this volume. Hayakawa points out that this was a period when he was concerned with Japan's survival as an independent nation. This required the revision of the unequal treaties and the development of a strong country populated by resourceful individuals.⁴²

Figure 1: Selected texts dealing with women and the family published in period one, the 1870s⁴³

1871 (1870 by the old Japanese calendar)	**"Nakatsu ryūbetsu no sho"** ("A Message of Farewell to Nakatsu")
1874	*Gakumon no susume* (*An Encouragement of Learning*), Sections Eight and Thirteen
1875	"Danjo dōsūron" ("The Equal Numbers of Men and Women," *Meiroku zasshi* 31)
1876	*Gakumon no susume* (*An Encouragement of Learning*), Section Fifteen
1879	**"Joshi kyōiku no koto ni tsuki Bōshi ni kotau"** ("An Answer to a Certain Gentleman's Inquiry about Female Education"), in *Fukuzawa bunshū* 2

The 1870s were a time when there was much public discussion (by men) about the path that Japan should take. These discussions were strongly influenced by knowledge of "Western civilization" gained through travel and through reading works such as those by Fukuzawa. His understanding of what was happening and what needed to be done can be seen in "Nakatsu ryūbetsu no sho" ("A Message of Farewell to Nakatsu"), a public letter of January 1871 (by the Western calendar) ostensibly addressed to a samurai of Nakatsu, his ancestral *han*.⁴⁴ It contains core ideas that formed the basis of his future writings. The most important one is the idea that free and independent individuals were the basis of a free and independent nation. In between individuals and the nation came the free and independent family, which was based on an equal partnership between a husband and wife. Their children had filial feelings for their parents and were loved and nurtured until they were old enough to become independent themselves.

If marriage was an equal partnership, it went without saying that both members should be faithful. A key feature of Fukuzawa's writings on women was his condemnation of male promiscuity and the practice of taking concubines. As his first reason he used the numerical argument, probably taken from Francis Wayland, that since men and women were born in roughly equal numbers, monogamy must be the natural state.[45] About a month after Fukuzawa finished his farewell message, however, the first Meiji Penal Code granted concubines the same status within the family as wives.

In the Tokugawa period marriage in samurai families had been strictly regulated, so that only one official wife was permitted. There had been no restriction on the number of concubines but, as was mentioned above, they were held to be of lower status than the official wife. In the Meiji period, the production of a male heir was less important, yet many of the men who had newly risen to prominence made no secret of having concubines. The first Meiji Penal Code, of February 1871 by the Western calendar, applied equally to everyone. It gave both concubines and wives similar status, as "relatives of the second degree," after the male heir, who was a "relative of the first degree." Presumably because of their role in preserving the family bloodline, it was a crime for both wives and concubines to have sexual relations with any man other than the husband; conversely husbands were not constrained in this way unless the woman was the wife or concubine of another man. The new household-register system that appeared soon after the Penal Code placed the wife of the household head after his grandparents and parents, and from mid 1873 also contained a space for concubines.[46]

Fukuzawa was involved in the first major public debate about the position of women in the new Japan. This took place under the auspices of the Meirokusha, a group of intellectuals who had come together in 1873 in order to spread their ideas in speeches and print. The members were all men who had first received a traditional Neo-Confucian education and then been exposed to Western ideas; many of them had experience of life in Western countries. This had affected their understanding of the universe, morality and human nature, and made them sensitive to the place of Japan in the hierarchy of "civilized," "semi-developed," and "primitive" nations.[47]

Before the periodical published by the Meirokusha began to take up the position of women, Fukuzawa had used their subordinate position as a familiar illustration when explaining the concepts of freedom and individual independence. In Section Eight of *An Encouragement of Learning*, which appeared in April 1874, *The Great Learning for Women* was invoked to illustrate that while independence and freedom required mutual respect, Confucianism taught the subordination of the weak to the strong by advocating the subordination of wives to husbands and mothers-in-law, and the practice of taking concubines. Here he employed the numerical argument again. The unequal relationship between parents and children that resulted from the one-sided focus on filial piety was also targeted. In Section Thirteen, which appeared during the Meirokusha debate in December 1874, he explained the damage caused by envy and gave the lack of autonomy associated with Confucian teachings as its cause. His main example was the destructive jealousy of the large groups of women, including concubines, who were forced to live together in the service of daimyo in feudal Japan. In Section Fifteen, which appeared in July 1876, after the end of the Meirokusha debate, he mentioned John Stuart Mill's refutation of the idea that women belonged in the home as an example of the fact that human progress required the willingness to question accepted customs.[48] This was a clear, if slightly misleading, reference to *The Subjection of Women*.[49]

The leading role in the Meirokusha debate about women and marriage was taken by Mori Arinori (1847–1889), who promoted monogamous mutual dependence as the norm in civilized countries and strongly criticized the situation in Japan: the practice of taking concubines, the way in which wives were treated by their husbands, and the double standard of sexual morality. He also drew attention to the role of wives in child rearing, and the importance of education in preparing them for this role. These were all themes that Fukuzawa had already taken up, or that he was to expand on in later writings. In addition, Mori proposed that marriage in Japan should take the form of a contract that required the willing consent of both partners.[50] He put this idea into practice in his first marriage in 1875, with Fukuzawa as the witness.[51] Tsuda Mamichi[52] and Sakatani Shiroshi[53] primarily supported Mori's position, while Fukuzawa expanded on his (or rather, Francis Wayland's) numerical argument against concubines, already given in "A Message of Farewell to Nakatsu" and *An Encouragement of Learning*. The existence of equal numbers of men and women in the world proved that monogamy was desirable. Men who were not willing to agree to this logic could go on keeping concubines or purchasing geisha, but should do so in secret. This should encourage a gradual change in attitudes through introducing a sense of shame.[54] He returned to this proposal in 1885, when he wrote *On Moral Behavior*.

As Koyama Shizuko has shown, the Meirokusha debate about marriage and concubines spread to the letter columns of newspapers. The majority of the contributors were in favor of monogamy, many drawing on the points made by Mori and Fukuzawa (in *An Encouragement of Learning* as well as in *Meiroku zasshi*). However, while some did focus on morality and the feelings of the wife, the major reasons for opposing concubines were that strong families were the basis of strong nations, and that the acceptance of concubines showed a lack of civilization that would harm Japan's international standing. There were also references to their role in ensuring the birth of an heir. When work on the Meiji Civil Code began in 1876, letters to newspapers, and at least one editorial, argued that the code should include withdrawal of official recognition for concubines.[55]

Concubines lost their official status in the new Penal Code of 1880, and it became no longer possible to enter them in household registers, but the change was mainly caused by government concern that failure to act on this would affect Japan's international status and therefore make it harder to obtain agreement from the Western powers for renegotiation of the "unequal treaties." The understanding was that the actual practice of having concubines was not affected by the legal change. In fact, in government and elite circles, there was still considerable support for their existence, if only to ensure the birth of a male heir.[56] Moreover, while there was now no legal case against unfaithfulness by a concubine, the unequal treatment of adultery by married women remained. The divorce provisions of the new Meiji Civil Code of 1898 preserved this inequality; nevertheless, they received an overall welcome from Fukuzawa in *A Critique of* The Great Learning for Women.[57]

Overall, the focus of the Meirokusha contributors was on the relationship between relatively affluent men and their wives at home, not on allowing women to enter the public sphere, through occupations that might give them economic independence, or access to the right to vote.[58] There was disagreement and uncertainty over the link between "equality" (*dōtō*) for wives within marriage and "equal rights" (*dōken*) for women in society as a whole.[59] Only Nakamura Masanao (1832–1891) came out clearly in favor of "equal rights," for educated and morally upright women only. The important influence of the mother on development of the child, both in the womb and after birth, meant that the quality of mothers would decide the future of Japan. Therefore it was essential to prepare daughters carefully for their role as mothers by giving them a moral and religious education. Men and women should be brought up in the same way, although the content of their education need not be the same.[60]

Fukuzawa did not write about women's education in *Meiroku zasshi*, or add practical efforts for women's education to his exiting involvement in education for men.[61] He made short-lived, small-scale arrangements to provide teaching for girls on the Keio compound at Mita, but these were centered on the needs of his five daughters. The first serious attempt, in 1876, involved providing accommodation for a female missionary so that she could set up a small school. However, this ended after about eighteen months. His views on the experiment can be partially seen in the second text from this period that is translated here. This is in the guise of a letter to a gentleman worried about the teaching that his daughter was receiving at the hands of Christian foreigners at one of the treaty ports. Fukuzawa criticizes this type of education because it does not prepare young women for their probable future as wives in Japanese-style homes. For example, they are not taught how to make Japanese-style clothes, which was admittedly a vital skill for women at that time.[62]

A similar arrangement was made around 1889 to 1890 with the first female foreigner to be employed by Keio. The three eldest Fukuzawa daughters were in the senior division, with the two youngest in the children's division. However, relations with the teacher were strained. Letter No. 48 shows that Fukuzawa became involved in a dispute about her dog, whose barking frightened his daughters. In between these two attempts to employ single foreign women as teachers, there was a period, from 1877 to 1881, when girls' names can be seen in the records of the elementary division of Keio. The three eldest Fukuzawa daughters were among the small number of girls being taught in the Keio elementary school during this time. However, the girls were taught separately from the boys. Their school day was shorter than that of the boys, and their curriculum was correspondingly narrower.[63]

During the 1870s, the original *Great Learning for Women* continued to be published, and there were seven attempts to update it. Nishino Kokai's *Kaika onna shōgaku* (*The Enlightenment Lesser Learning for Women*) of 1873 was very similar to the original, but admitted the need for more practical learning in areas such as arithmetic, childcare and hygiene.[64] By contrast, three years later, in *Kinsei onna daigaku* (*The Modern Great Learning for Women*), Doi Kōka began by stating: "There is no difference between men and women: all have the right to be free from restraint and control, autonomous and independent." The first double page of the book had an illustration of a small "Western" classroom with female pupils and a female teacher saying in English "Attention all."⁶⁵ In the same year he produced *Bunmeiron onna daigaku* (*A Civilized Version of the Great Learning for Women*), a point-by-point criticism of eleven of the sections of the original *Great Learning*, twenty-three years before Fukuzawa's similar treatment in *A Critique*. Doi also criticized the fact that there were no references to child rearing in *The Great Learning* even though childbearing for women was equivalent to military service for men. Women were subjects of the Emperor just like all other Japanese citizens, and should not put themselves below their husbands, as *The Great Learning* taught.⁶⁶ Doi went further than the members of the Meirokusha, but his approach was unusual. Reprints of the original *Great Learning* and less radical updatings continued throughout the Meiji period and beyond.

Figure 2: Selected texts dealing with women and the family published in period two, 1883–1888

1883	"Fujo kōkoron" ("On Female Acts of Filial Piety") and its appendix, "Fujo kōkō yoron," *Jiji shinpō*
1885	**"Nihon fujinron"** ("On Japanese Women"), *Jiji shinpō*; **Nihon fujinron kōhen** (*On Japanese Women, Part Two*); **Hinkōron** (*On Moral Behavior*).
1886	**Danjo kōsairon** (*On Relations between Men and Women*) and its appendix, "Danjo kōsai yoron"
1888	*Nihon danshiron* (*On Japanese Men*)

As Figure 2 shows, Fukuzawa's second, and most concentrated, period of writing about women and the family came in the mid 1880s. This coincided with a general increase in publications on these themes.⁶⁷ Women were also finding a public voice.⁶⁸ From the early 1880s, they had been speaking in favor of greater rights at meetings of the People's Rights Movement. They addressed audiences that included other women, who in turn formed their own networks for self-improvement. At least one of them, Kageyama (Fukuda) Hideko, had been influenced by *An Encouragement of Learning*. She later recalled the applause that followed a speech in which she recycled its ideas about human equality.⁶⁹ Inevitably their activities were criticized as unfeminine. In *On Japanese Women, Part Two*, Fukuzawa suggested that such criticisms were an overreaction,⁷⁰ but he did not actively support the participation of women in politics.

Women also wrote articles and letters, activities that became increasingly important as the government began to clamp down on public speaking, and particularly once women were banned from political meetings in 1890. In July 1885, just after the serialization of "On Japanese Women" began, *Jogaku zasshi*, the first major Japanese journal devoted to women's issues, made its appearance. It was edited by men, first Kondō Kenzō and from 1886 self-appointed women's spokesman Iwamoto Yoshiharu, but women writers played an important role. *Jogaku zasshi* was a Christian publication and had close links with the Tokyo branch of the Women's Christian Temperance Union, which was formed in 1886 and became a national organization in 1893.[71] While both of these shared Fukuzawa's goal of improving the position of women, however, their approach differed from his in some important respects. In particular, Fukuzawa did not support their campaign against the government system of licensed prostitution. *Jogaku zasshi* sometimes contained criticisms of Fukuzawa's views. These will be dealt with later.

Another way in which women attracted public attention from the mid-1880s was through the enlistment of the wives and daughters of the elite in "Rokumeikan diplomacy." This was part of the campaign for the revision of the "unequal" treaties that the previous regime had unwillingly signed with Western countries in the 1850s. Balls and other social occasions were held at the lavishly designed Rokumeikan in order to demonstrate to foreign diplomats that Japan had mastered Western social etiquette and therefore deserved to be treated as a civilized nation. It seems likely that Fukuzawa, like *Jogaku zasshi*, had reservations about these social activities. In April 1887, he even turned down an official invitation to a fancy-dress ball to be held by Prime Minister Itō Hirobumi, giving as his excuse "household affairs (*kaji no tsugō ni yori*)."[72] Later he criticized the extravagance of these events and the gap that they had created between the lifestyle of ordinary people and that of officials.[73]

As was mentioned earlier, in 1882, Fukuzawa had founded a newspaper, *Jiji shinpō*, to provide a stable outlet for his views, and for views that he wished to publicize.[74] General themes that occupied him at this time included Japan's relationship with the rest of Asia, and the nature of the promised constitution, including the role of the Emperor.[75] He was also concerned at the slow pace of social change and the tenacity of social customs, specifically at the difficulty of convincing former samurai like those he had left behind in Nakatsu of the need to revolutionize their way of thinking. They should stop relying on the security of the old system and become conscious of their identity as autonomous individuals responsible for their own livelihood, rather than as people whose lives were determined by inherited family membership. A sustained campaign was required, and since the nature of the family was central to his concerns, it is not surprising that a major target was the family, and the position of women. In particular, he had detected signs that far from slowly disappearing, the attitudes associated with the vertically oriented hereditary family system of the samurai, including the subordination of women, were actually spreading to other layers of society.[76] Moreover, although he probably approved of the introduction of Japanese-style sewing and other housewifely skills into the government curriculum for girls, he would not have welcomed the Confucian-based ethics classes that came in at the same time.[77]

In any case, the period from 1885 to 1886 saw Fukuzawa producing four substantial essays about the relationships between men and women, including standards of sexual behavior, and the role of women and the family in society. These were serialized in *Jiji shinpō*, and three were subsequently published. They were directed at both men and women of "the middle and upper levels of society (*chūtō ijō*)", the people who were most likely to have knowledge of Western ideas and lifestyles, and who he thought would provide a model for other Japanese to follow.[78]

The first of these essays, "On Japanese Women," began to appear in July 1885. On 11 April, Fukuzawa had given a speech on women's responsibilities, one of the themes of "On Japanese Women," at the hall he had built for speech meetings on the Keio campus at Mita. Between May and November there were five more speeches about women, two by Fukuzawa himself, and three by Keio graduate and *Jiji shinpō* journalist Takahashi Yoshio.[79] "On Japanese Women," and *On Japanese Women, Part Two* argued that women were not inherently inferior to men. He assumed that women should marry, and that the natural role of the wife was to run domestic affairs, but called for wives to be given autonomy within the home, and property that they could manage themselves. They deserved to be treated as equal partners by their husbands, not just as machines necessary to produce male heirs.[80]

Around this time, he also began to organize social occasions in the name of his wife and daughters, either for women only, or for both women and men.[81] Fukuzawa's desire to promote mixed social gatherings is not surprising since, like Burton, he regarded human relations as the basis of civilization, and even used the term *jinkan kōsai*, which literally means "human relations/intercourse," to express the Western concept of "society" in his early writings. Encouraging women's involvement in social gatherings was also linked quite naturally to the concern he had expressed in "On Japanese Women" about the social isolation of women of the middle and upper levels of society, and the argument of *On Relations between Men and Women* (1886) that the active participation of respectable women was essential to the development of civilized public discourse. These low-key experiments in socializing were completely different from the Rokumeikan model. In fact, it is likely that *On Relations between Men and Women* itself, with its advice that gatherings should be simple, was Fukuzawa's response to the interest in mixed-gender gatherings that was being sparked by the publicity given to Rokumeikan diplomacy.

The message of both *On Moral Behavior* (1885) and *On Japanese Men* (1888) was primarily for men. In *Tsūzoku minkenron* (*A Popular Discussion of People's Rights*, 1878) he had previously made an implicit criticism of the members of the People's Rights Movement for using the money that they had raised to fund visits to sex workers.[82] In "On Female Acts of Filial Piety" and its appendix, he had also criticized contemporary newspapers for praising poor girls who willingly became part of the sex trade in order to pay family debts. This was damaging not only because it encouraged high-minded girls in similar situations to see this as an honorable solution, but also because of the direct and indirect ways in which such attitudes created a favorable image of sex workers.[83] He had already described such women as "below human" (*ningai*) and called for them to be cut off from society until they had reformed.[84]

In *On Moral Behavior*, he directly targeted the self-indulgent promiscuity of men, particularly members of the elite and their methods of socializing. He was ambivalent in his remarks about the sex workers who were available to satisfy their demands, since without them unmarried girls and widows would be tempted to do so. However, as in his *Meiroku zasshi* essay, his solution was for Japanese men to learn from their Western counterparts that paying for sex was a shameful act that should at all costs be concealed. To achieve this revolution in attitudes, the status of women involved in the sex trade must be downgraded, so that they were seen as unfit for inclusion in human society. *On Relations between Men and Women* followed on from this with its proposals for mixed gatherings involving respectable women as an alternative to male-only meetings that employed geisha.⁸⁵ In *On Japanese Men* (1888), which is not included here, Fukuzawa continued his criticism of male promiscuity and suggested that it was necessary to lower the position of men as well as raise the position of women. Public rights could not be established in the absence of private rights, and private rights depended on the development of a sense of private morality within families. Public morality, too, could only develop in society on the basis of private morality.

Figure 3: Selected texts dealing with women and the family published in period three, 1896–1899

1897	*Fukuō hyakuwa* (*One Hundred Reflections by Fukuzawa*): **Number 20** is translated here.
1898	*Fukuzawa ukiyodan* (*Fukuzawa's Talks on Worldly Affairs*)
1899	**Onna daigaku hyōron** (*A Critique of* The Great Learning for Women); **Shin onna daigaku** (*A New Great Learning for Women*)

Fukuzawa's final phase of writing about women came in the late 1890s, when he was satisfied that Japan's victory in the Sino-Japanese War had secured its independence but uneasy about the militarism that it had encouraged, and worried about the influence of his ideas.⁸⁶ He was probably not overly concerned by government moves in 1890 to restrict women's political activities, for example by banning their presence at political meetings and even trying to keep them from the public galleries at the Diet. However, he must have been unhappy about the involvement of traditionalist Confucian scholars in the writing of moral textbooks for schools and the integration of Confucian-oriented stereotypes into new models of female behavior. For example, Hanabusa Tsuneo's 1889 update of *The Great Learning for Women*, *Meiji onna daigaku*, focused on women's duties as daughters, daughters-in-law, wives, mothers and patriotic Japanese, as well as giving detailed advice on matters such as ladies' deportment and their household tasks.⁸⁷

The state had given priority to secondary education for males and it was only in the 1890s that it turned its attention to nationwide provision for females. But the new girls' "high schools" (*joshi kōtō gakkō*) were for girls aged 12 to 16, and were therefore only equivalent to the first level of boys' secondary education. They were to produce "good wives and wise mothers" (*ryōsai kenbo*), women whose object was to serve their families and train their children to be obedient and patriotic subjects, not women who shared responsibility for the family with their husbands by looking after household affairs.⁸⁸

Fukuzawa did not agree with state attempts to teach morality. His view was that public morality grew from private morality, and that public morality should be taught by parents through the example of their behavior, not through school textbooks.[89] He did not make any public pronouncements about the moral message of the Kyōiku chokugo (Imperial Rescript on Education) of 1890. This echoed but did not entirely copy Mencius' Five Relations by urging the Emperor's loyal subjects: "be filial to your parents, affectionate to your brothers and sisters; as husbands and wives be harmonious (*fūfu aiwashi*), as friends true." However, until the late 1930s Keio did not copy the ceremonial recitations of the Rescript that became a requirement at government schools on all national holidays.

Inoue Tetsujirō, a pro-government scholar, was appointed to write an official commentary on the Rescript. He interpreted the expression "as husband and wives be harmonious" to mean "As long as husbands do not say anything that goes against reason or morality, wives should make every effort to yield to them and not oppose them thoughtlessly, while preserving their own chastity."[90] The second volume of the moral textbook that Inoue cowrote in 1897 stated that family morality was the basis of state morality because the family was like a little state. He extolled filial piety, a quality that was found only in humans, while parental love was something exhibited even by animals. As for the duties of married couples, "husbands show fondness (*aibu*) for their wives; wives act obediently (*jūjun*) towards their husbands. They must both maintain ties of intimate friendship (*shinmitsu naru jōgi*)." Being physically, mentally and intellectually inferior, the role of the wife was to assist the husband in his sovereignty over the family. In *On Japanese Women, Part Two* Fukuzawa had ridiculed the idea that men were yang and women yin as unscientific, suggesting that it had just been invented by men to justify their self-interested domination over women, but Inoue's textbook assumed its validity.[91] It is not difficult to imagine that Fukuzawa would have wanted to counter the views of Inoue and those like him.

The serialization of *One Hundred Reflections by Fukuzawa* in *Jiji shinpō* began in February 1896. Komuro Masamichi has suggested that Fukuzawa was restating his basic ideas about the essence of human civilization out of anxiety that only a few people had understood them. Over ten percent of the short essays were related to women and the family, with parts 20 to 25 on husbands and wives, and parts 26 to 31 on parents and children, and references to women in the sections on education and charity work as well.[92] Number 20, "Ippu ippu kairō dōketsu" ("One Husband, One Wife, Together Even in the Grave"), which is translated here, is interesting since he introduces the idea of free love, although he immediately says that it could not be adopted by the Japan of his time. In the next part, "Haigu no sentaku" ("Choosing One's Partner"), he urged people to consider hereditary factors, including the possibility of inheritable diseases, when choosing marriage partners. Issues raised in previous works such as the need for mutual respect between husbands and wives and the shamefulness of male promiscuity were revisited. Predictably, too, the section on parents and children emphasized the importance of neither side being dependent on the other without due cause, rejecting the official emphasis on the filial duties required of children.

Three of the other essays that dealt with women criticized the idea that they needed more rights in the public sphere. In Number 35, "Joshi kyōiku to joken" ("Women's Education and Women's Rights"), Fukuzawa declared that women's education was as important as men's, but that women had little need for specialist university-level studies since in most cases they would marry and spend their lives running the household and raising children. Those who wished to improve women's rights should focus not on education, but on curbing the promiscuous behavior of their husbands. This view of education brought him close to the limited academic objectives of the government's vision of women's secondary education. He continued this theme in the next part, "Danson johi no hei wa moppara gaikei ni aru mono ōshi" ("Men's Precedence over Women Is Largely a Matter of Outward Appearance Only"), where he claimed that inside the house, the wishes of mothers and wives already took precedence over those of sons and husbands. The improvement of women's rights was therefore largely a matter of reforming public behavior, not by changing the distinctive grace of Japanese women but by making men less arrogant and more polite when they addressed women. Apparently contradicting remarks in *On Japanese Women, Part Two*,[93] in Number 47, "Josei no aijō" ("Women and Love"), he suggested that according to Western theories, women's physique was dominated by their reproductive function, with the result that their thoughts and actions were governed by love, and the need to be loved. This being the case, in seeking greater equality for women, priority should be given to their rights to expect a partner in marriage to be faithful, and to remarry if widowed. Other rights were of secondary importance. *Fukuzawa ukiyodan*

(*Fukuzawa's Talks on Worldly Affairs*), which appeared two years later, similarly emphasized that it was not only the level of education that distinguished Western women from Japanese women, but also the public behavior of men towards them. Changing one would have little effect unless the other was also changed.[94]

Number 48 of *One Hundred Reflections by Fukuzawa*, "Jinji ni rimen o wasururu bekarazu" ("The Other Side of Human Affairs Must Not Be Forgotten") also needs to be mentioned. The topic was related to a series on emigration that had appeared in *Jiji shinpō* in January 1896, and built on Fukuzawa's reluctant acceptance of the sex trade as a necessary evil. He stated that the state of marriage brought a natural warmth to existence that could reconcile people to any hardship, including those that accompanied emigration, a way of advancement that the Japanese government was encouraging. Ideally, any unmarried emigrants should marry as soon as possible, but in practice there were too many for this to be feasible. As a desperate measure motivated by sympathy for their plight (*"ninjō sekai no kyūsaku"*), the free movement of prostitutes (*sengyōfu*) should also be allowed. He understood that this recognition of the human condition might smack of depravity, but Western nations behaved in a similar way by ensuring that troops stationed abroad had access to such women.[95]

In July 1898 the Meiji Civil Code came into effect. It has been criticized for institutionalizing the patriarchal family system, but in *A Critique of* The Great Learning for Women, which appeared in the following year, Fukuzawa was to welcome its divorce provisions, contrasting them favorably with *The Great Learning for Women*'s seven reasons, which included jealousy and talking too much.[96] However, as was mentioned previously, he ignored the fact that while any unfaithfulness by married women was grounds for divorce, the same was only true for husbands if the partner was married. Another factor that clearly concerned him around this time was the prospect of foreigners being free to travel anywhere in Japan once the rights of extraterritoriality granted by the "unequal" treaties were abolished in July 1899. He feared that they would form negative impressions about the level of civilization, especially in terms of sexual morality, unless there was a dramatic change in men's behavior.[97]

Fukuzawa completed his autobiography in May 1898. At the end he gave three things that he still wished to bring about. The first of these was "the gradual elevation of the moral character of the men and women of Japan so that we are worthy to be called truly civilized."⁹⁸ It was presumably in order to fulfill this aim that in August he tackled the project that had allegedly been on his mind since his first arrival in Edo forty years before, the systematic dissection and reconstruction of *The Great Learning for Women*. By mid-September he had finished both *A Critique* and *A New Great Learning*. The first was a point-by-point reply to the original *Great Learning for Women* that focused on the fact that even where the instructions were reasonable they required sacrifices from women but never from men. The second was Fukuzawa's advice to parents on how to prepare their daughters for their lives as responsible wives and mothers, and to daughters on how to perform these roles without losing a sense of independence.

Then, as now, there were those who wondered why it was necessary for someone who had played a leading role in the introduction of new ideas from the West to spend so much effort in attacking an outdated product of traditional Japan at this stage of his life. This issue will be dealt with later. In any case, the serialization of the two works in *Jiji shinpō* was delayed until the following spring because of the stroke that he suffered on 26 September. Before they finally began to appear they were heralded by a publicity campaign in the newspaper, and then accompanied by a series of articles on related subjects by prominent figures. They were published together in book form in November 1899 and sold so well that forty-eight editions had been printed by 1922. There was a special de luxe edition, perhaps designed as a gift for married couples. Fukuzawa died in January 1901, leaving behind five copies of the special edition signed and dated 1901 with the message "Men should read this too."⁹⁹ If asked, he would probably have extended this request to all the writings referred to here.

Women and the Family in Fukuzawa's Private Life

This section has two main purposes. First, as Nishizawa Naoko has clearly demonstrated, in order to understand Fukuzawa's perspective on women, it is necessary to look at the influence of his family background.¹⁰⁰ Second, since Fukuzawa was so free in his advice to other people, it is also important to examine the extent to which he was able to practice what he preached in his behavior as a husband, and as father to four sons and five daughters.¹⁰¹ The following is based on his autobiography and letters, some of which are included in this volume, the reminiscences of family members and students, and records of discussions and interviews with children and grandchildren.

Women played a strong role in Fukuzawa's own upbringing. He was the youngest in his family, with one older brother, who died when Fukuzawa was twenty-one, and three elder sisters. Hyakusuke, his father, had been a lower samurai of Nakatsu Okudaira *han* who was manager of the *han*'s finances at Osaka. When Hyakusuke died in 1836, Fukuzawa was only eighteen months old, so it is likely that he had no direct memories of his father. However, in his autobiography he writes that Hyakusuke's influence on the atmosphere within the family remained strong. Both the autobiography and "Fukuzawa-shi kosen haibun no ki" ("Reasons for Sharing Some Old Coins with My Children") build an image of him as a virtuous and unworldly Confucian scholar by inclination, and a strict but deeply loving father.[102] This pride in the "family spirit" (*kafū*) inherited through his father from the Fukuzawa lineage could be seen as contradicting Fukuzawa's support for the one-generational family.

After Hyakusuke's death, the family moved back to Nakatsu. Fukuzawa's mother assumed responsibility for the family until her eldest son, now technically head of the household, was old enough to take over. With some help from the children, including Fukuzawa, she performed almost all the household duties, since they were too poor to employ servants. He emphasizes that she was very considerate in her dealings with people of a lower rank, including beggars and outcasts, and patient in the face of his desire to leave Nakatsu and continue his studies after his brother's early death had put him in charge of the household.

In his autobiography, Fukuzawa states that the family did not have any strong ties of friendship with other members of the samurai community in Nakatsu, but that their life was happy.[103] Both in the autobiography, and in a letter to his only surviving sister written in 1899,[104] he suggests that the brothers and sisters never quarreled among each other. Even if this is exaggerated, family ties must have been close. After the Restoration, he brought his mother and his dead brother's only daughter to live with his wife and children in Tokyo.[105] Although he was still separated from his sisters, he kept in touch with them through numerous letters, and was always willing to offer support and advice.[106]

As well as having three sisters, Fukuzawa had several nieces, and five daughters of his own. He was also aware that the collapse of the feudal system left many other samurai, and the former head of Nakatsu *han*, with a great number of dependent females, including maidservants. Nishizawa suggests that one reason for his interest in the position of women was his resulting awareness of the vulnerability of women who were brought up in a society that did not expect them to achieve financial independence. She links this to Fukuzawa's decision to establish a tailoring and laundry service on the Mita campus in 1872 as a place of employment for women. He may also have helped his widowed sister-in-law, Imaizumi Tō, to become a professional midwife.[107]

Fukuzawa married Kin (1845–1924) in 1861, when he was twenty-six years old. She was over ten years younger, the daughter of a high-ranking family. Her father seems to have proposed the marriage in recognition of Fukuzawa's abilities. Their first son was born in 1863, and over the next twenty years, Kin went on to give birth to a total of four sons and five daughters. There were also two stillbirths, of a daughter, and of male and female twins.

Figure 4: Fukuzawa's sons and daughters

Sons	Ichitarō (1863–1938)	Sutejirō (1865–1926)	Sanpachi (1881–1962)	Daishirō (1883–1960)	
Daughters	Sato (1868–1945)	Fusa (1870–1955)	Shun (1873–1954)	Taki (1876–1970)	Mitsu (1879–1907)

Unfortunately, we know little about Kin, or about her relationship with her husband. She must have had a strong sense of identity. She insisted on changing first the sound of her name, from Kan to Kin, and then, after her marriage, the character with which it was written, from *kin/kane* (gold, money) to *kin/nishiki* (brocade). She must also have been a capable manager. As well as the normal tasks that caring for a family of this size would have involved at that time, Fukuzawa frequently received visitors and entertained a variety of guests. Apparently he referred to her respectfully as "O Kin-san," which was highly unusual for the time, and valued her contribution to the household. According to Taki's daughters, she had a very strong voice in the family. His third daughter, Shun, described how Fukuzawa hated dealing with money matters but sat down with Kin at the end of every month to calculate the household accounts. In addition, Fukuzawa told Shun's husband of his gratitude to Kin for her careful management of money. The fact that he did not have to worry about this had enabled him to focus fully on his work. He had invested money on her behalf so that if he died before her she would not become financially dependent on her children.[108] This accords with Fukuzawa's view that wives should have knowledge of their family's financial position and be able to survive financially even if widowed.¹⁰⁹

The letter in this volume that she wrote to Ichitarō shows Kin's concern for her husband.¹¹⁰ However, it is likely that she did not agree with all his ideas. For example, being from a high-ranking family, Kin had been brought up in a more formal atmosphere. Shun recalled how Fukuzawa disliked Kin's practice of welcoming him at the entrance to the house whenever he returned. To avoid this, he would go round the back and enter the house via the veranda that faced the garden. When she went after him in order to bow and say the traditional words of welcome, he would tell her not to behave so formally. This behavior seems to have continued for some time, until eventually she gave up. In fact, in an interview with a famous broadcaster, Tokugawa Musei, Taki, the fourth daughter, suggested that Kin probably did not understand her husband, adding that this was not surprising since few people did at the time. This possibility is strengthened by the fact that in another interview, when Maruyama Masao raised Fukuzawa's view that women should have some knowledge of economics and the law, Taki's response was that such matters were not discussed at home because of Kin's strong aversion to topics of this type. On this occasion, she also implied that there were problems in the way that her father treated Kin, although she did not give details.¹¹¹

According to Daishirō, Kin behaved in a reserved and obedient way, like a typical Japanese wife, and there were no disputes between husband and wife. By contrast, Fukuzawa behaved in a high-handed manner at home. According to Daishirō's sisters: "'Father went on about women's rights, but at home he had no scruples about always behaving exactly as he liked.'" Daishirō later added that both his mother and his sisters considered that for all his statements about equality between men and women, Fukuzawa gave priority to men. This is confirmed by a report that when Sato heard him talking to guests after the publication of his point-by-point rebuttal of *The Great Learning for Women, A Critique*, in 1899, she remarked to her mother, "'How hypocritical of him to say such things when he is always shouting at us.'" Daishirō comments that Fukuzawa's behavior at home is not surprising in view of his background, and the fact that there was no one in the family of similar or superior status to stop him.¹¹²

Koizumi Shinzō, who came to live on the Mita campus with his mother and sister when his father died, later wrote:

> ... Fukuzawa's children were his **Achilles' heel**. The same could be said of any parent, but it was particularly true in his case. As a father and grandfather he was indulgent beyond the normal boundaries of doting affection ...[113]

As this quotation suggests, Fukuzawa was actively involved with his grandchildren as well as with his children. This was particularly the case with the two sons of his eldest daughter, Sato, who returned home after the early death of her husband, despite her grumblings about her father's behavior, and refused to remarry even though Fukuzawa strongly urged this. Therefore, for almost all his married life he was surrounded by children.[114]

Fukuzawa's autobiography may be consciously idealizing the happiness of the family, but scenes described in some of the letters give a similar impression. Apparently, the parents shared the roles of caregiver and disciplinarian equally and did not use corporal punishment.[115] In education, he gave priority to physical development and general health over study, rewarding his children for perseverance in taking exercise rather than in academic work. There is evidence for this in his letters to Ichitarō and Sutejirō while they were studying in the United States.[116] As was mentioned in the previous section, in his writings he advised that morals should be taught by example not as empty rules, although "Hibi no oshie" ("Daily Lessons"), the elementary reading passages that he prepared for his two eldest children, are heavily moral in their content.[117] "Reasons for Sharing Some Old Coins" shows his desire to pass on to his children the ethical standards that he associated with his family traditions.

Fukuzawa may have been more openly affectionate with the children than Kin. Taki, who was looked after by a wet nurse when young, told Maruyama that she had no memories of being held by her mother. He talked with them during family meals and while travelling, for example. He walked around the garden with them on his back, and even did this with other people's children. During the period when he rode a horse in order to get about Tokyo, Taki remembered going to the stable around the time when he was due to come home. He would put the children in front of the saddle and ride around with them. Yamana Jirō, a Keio graduate, recalled the sight of Fukuzawa writing editorials for *Jiji shinpō* surrounded by noisily playing children. Yamana's view was that far from being irritated by the lively atmosphere, Fukuzawa found that it helped him. In fact, he was always ready to play with them, so much so that they just thought of him as their father, with little awareness of his importance.

Daishirō, the youngest, born when Fukuzawa was already forty-eight and only nineteen when his father died, recalled: "I saw my father as a good person, so I talked to him and asked him questions about everything, without feeling the need to hold anything back. He told me off sometimes, but I never felt afraid of him."[118]

In the autobiography, Fukuzawa states that he loved and valued all the children equally, the girls as much as the boys. However, since the eldest son would become the head of the family after his death, he would be left a larger share of the family estate, and any items that could not be divided equally. This egalitarian attitude is confirmed by the memories of the eldest daughter, Sato, as passed on by her grandson. Even in Japan today, younger siblings address their elder siblings respectfully as "*onīsan/onēsan*," meaning "elder brother/sister plus the title suffix '*san*,'" while elder siblings address their younger brothers and sisters more familiarly, by using their given names without "*san*." But Fukuzawa's children were all taught to use the given name plus "*san*," regardless of the age hierarchy. In other matters, too, the elder siblings were not allowed to lord it over the younger ones. Sato also recalled that once the children reached the age of being able to decide for themselves, Fukuzawa would allow them to do so, even if he did not agree. For example, before the birth of his youngest son, Fukuzawa had agreed to offer the baby for adoption to a childless friend if the baby was a boy and agreed to the arrangement. When the son, Daishirō, was asked for his opinion at the age of fifteen or sixteen, he said no.[119]

On the other hand, the sons and daughters were not brought up in the same way, or given equal opportunities. Of the sons, Ichitarō and Sutejirō, at least, received basic instruction at home from the parents, but the boys all graduated from Keio and Fukuzawa then paid for them, and two future sons-in-law, to study abroad. In the case of the eldest two, Ichitarō and Sutejirō, Fukuzawa intended this from the day they were born, although he worried about funding since this was before his many publications had guaranteed his financial stability.[120] It is clear from the letters that he sent them while abroad that he regarded this period as essential to make them truly independent beings, both in the sense of becoming psychologically self-reliant, and in the sense of being able to earn a living by themselves.[121]

By contrast, the girls were primarily educated at home. Nishizawa provides convincing evidence that Fukuzawa wanted his daughters to attend school, and even explored the possibilities of providing funds for them to study abroad.

Both Taki and her children also reported that it was the more traditionally-minded Kin, not Fukuzawa, who had the major role in deciding how the daughters were brought up. In any case, for most of the time teachers, some of whom were non-Japanese, came to the house to teach them subjects such as English, the piano, and traditional Japanese music and dance. As was stated in the previous section, Fukuzawa did make arrangements for them to study with girls of similar ages on the Keio compound, but these attempts were all short lived. In 1887, Fusa, Shun and Taki, then aged seventeen, fourteen and eleven, were sent to Kyōritsu Jogakkō (Doremus School), a Protestant mission-run boarding school for girls in Yokohama, but only for a short period. It seems that both parents missed them, and that Kin wanted them to be able to come back at the weekends, but the school did not allow this.[122] A criticism of Christian schools for girls that appeared in *Jiji shinpō* in July of the same year suggests that Fukuzawa had once again been dissatisfied at their failure to prepare their pupils for life as wives in Japanese-style households.[123] As for the daughters themselves, Taki later said that she had wanted more freedom, particularly the chance to study more, and seems to have been deeply offended when Fukuzawa was condescending about her attempts to read novels in English.[124]

Taki's children described Fukuzawa as an indulgent father to his daughters. Even though he supported the idea that women should be independent, he did not want to push his own daughters in that direction. They led sheltered lives. As was mentioned in the previous section, social gatherings were organized in the names of Kin and her daughters, but the guests were relatives of Fukuzawa's male acquaintances rather than members of networks formed by the women themselves. The daughters were all married between the ages of sixteen and twenty. Fukuzawa adopted one of the sons-in-law, and apparently would have liked to adopt at least one other, presumably so that it would be easier for him to keep an eye on the marriage. As was also the case with the sons, Fukuzawa and Kin searched for suitable partners but allowed the children to make the final decision. The strong-minded Taki was the only daughter to be active outside the home. Having become a Christian, she acted as chairwoman of the Tokyo YWCA from 1919 until 1942.[125]

However, despite the impression created by the idealized picture in the autobiography, and even by many of the letters, family life was not perfect. As was stated above, there seems to have been little, or no, intellectual understanding between Fukuzawa and his wife, and they probably disagreed over the education of their daughters. At home, he expected his wishes to be followed. Because of his position, and because he entertained at home rather than at restaurants or other public places, Kin was kept very busy, in addition to her twenty years of frequent pregnancies. While Taki seemed to have good memories of Fukuzawa at the stables, in the interview with Maruyama Masao she used an English word to describe her relationship with her parents, stating that she did not feel "intimate" with either of them, and was afraid that she would be scolded if she said something out of turn. This was particularly the case with her mother, because her approach was not logical ("*dōri ga nain' desu*"). The reason why Taki did not have arguments with her parents was not because she was content, but because she consciously avoided outright confrontations. As was mentioned above, her wishes for more education were not fulfilled.[126] It is not clear whether this unease was confined to Taki, or whether all the children experienced similar feelings, perhaps not as children, but when they entered adolescence.[127]

Independence was a central theme in Fukuzawa's life and writings.[128] After all, at Keio, Fukuzawa is remembered chiefly for his motto "*Dokuritsu jison* (independence and self-respect)". Fukuzawa's letters to his children, and those that mention them, show his affection, but they also reveal a constant struggle between this ideal that Fukuzawa stressed so unceasingly in public, and his privately expressed paternal feelings. It was hard for him to let them learn to become independent by making their own mistakes. This is particularly clear from the letters to Ichitarō and Sutejirō while they were studying abroad. Over and over again, he explains his own opinion in detail, but then states that it is up to them to make their own decisions.[129] He also wished them to maintain the record of unblemished behavior that he considered had been established by his ancestors,[130] and was aware that his position as an opinion leader would make him vulnerable to criticism if any family member drew negative attention.[131]

The strain of being the eldest son of such a famous father may have had a negative effect on Ichitarō, who appears to have suffered from low self-esteem, and possibly bouts of depression. It must have been particularly difficult for him since his nearest sibling, Sutejirō, was clearly more gifted. Although he was two years younger than Ichitarō, Sutejirō began to study at Keio at the same time and graduated half a year earlier. Moreover, while Ichitarō did not follow a fixed course of study in the United States or gain any qualifications, Sutejirō obtained a degree in civil engineering from the Massachusetts Institute of Technology. The letters also indicate that Ichitarō had problems with drinking, and something must have happened to drive his first wife away after only about six months of marriage.[132]

Finally, it is worth mentioning that the long-term servants on the Mita compound and the pupils and staff of the school seem to have formed an extended family. Daishirō remembered Fukuzawa's kindness to the family servants, and the fact that all visitors to the house were treated in the same way, regardless of their rank. This included both the gardener and Kanesugi Daigorō, the master carpenter who rebuilt and maintained the family house. He took these craftsmen on family holidays, showing Kanesugi famous shrines and temples so that he had the opportunity to see historical building techniques.[133]

Koyama Kango who was a student at Keio in the 1890s, when there were about 800 students, later recalled that "there was such a close atmosphere of friendship between everyone that it was like one big family," with Fukuzawa like "a loving grandfather." He was good at remembering all the students' names and showed concern for them if they became ill, even after they had graduated. His pre-breakfast walks, which could last up to two hours, were famous. He would creep outside while the rest of the family was asleep and bang a gong. This was a signal for any pupils from the on-campus dormitory who wanted to come. Students living off campus would join in as they passed by, and he would shout outside the lodgings of those who appeared to have overslept. Daishirō recalled:

> I think that the students felt really close to my father; they behaved quite naturally in front of him, with no sign of fear. Those who could not get home over the New Year vacation would come to our house every evening and happily play all sorts of games with us . . .[134]

The Texts as a Whole

Each of the texts printed here is preceded by a short explanation; problems such as inconsistencies will be discussed in the evaluation at the end of this introduction. The purpose of this section is therefore to draw attention to what the texts have in common. First, most were published after being serialized in *Jiji shinpō*. The published versions were given prefaces, but no other alterations were made. In other words, the installments were simply strung together with no indication of how they had originally been divided, although incidental references to the installment structure were retained. The installments are identified here, as was also Kiyooka's practice, because they show how the serialization process influenced the way in which Fukuzawa wrote. He often ended installments with a hook that would encourage his readers to look forward to the next part, and began a new installment with a reference to the previous one. On the other hand, the end of the final installment was sometimes abrupt, so that serialized works such as *On Japanese Women, Part Two* and *On Moral Behavior* lack proper conclusions. Kiyooka's translations lack the prefaces, but they are included here if they exist.

As should be clear from the previous section, Fukuzawa grew up in Nakatsu as a lower samurai, and in an almost completely female environment. It is likely that this made him sensitive not only to the injustices that arose from valuing family membership over individual ability, but also to the bias in favor of men, particularly when he arrived in Edo, where the samurai presence was predominantly male. Later, his conversations with Hōren'in in the women's quarters of the Nakatsu daimyo residence led him to believe that monogamy had an immediate appeal to most people in Japanese society, and particularly to female members of the elite, who had been forced to share their husbands with concubines.

By the time he met Hōren'in, he already had first-hand knowledge of the very different treatment of Western women in both the family and society as a whole. His reading of geography textbooks, Burton's *Political Economy* and other works further showed him that the position of women in a society was regarded as a marker of the level of civilization. When he wrote about women, a genuine concern for their happiness was therefore linked to an equal, or possibly greater, concern for Japan's reputation in the eyes of the Western powers. In addition, it is possible that when writing about women he was also criticizing the general attitudes of dependence that had been inculcated by the hierarchical structure of Tokugawa society. In that sense, explanations of how women's position could be improved can be seen as a way of promoting the need for everyone in Japan to cultivate personal independence and respect the independence of other people in order to lay the basis for a strong nation.

Fukuzawa's basic message was that men were not superior to women, and that they shared an equal position in the family, the basic unit of a society and a harmonious oasis of shared happiness and stability. However, his approach was fundamentally diachronic; he did not consider that men and women should, or could, immediately share exactly the same life opportunities or fulfill identical roles, whether within the family or outside. *An Outline of a Theory of Civilization* (1875) includes a utopian vision of "the tranquility of civilization," "when the whole world will be like one big family."[135] In *One Hundred Reflections by Fukuzawa* it is implied that this perfect state will include "free love," with autonomous men and women becoming involved in a succession of monogamous relationships, each of which would end through mutual agreement as soon as love faded. But this would not occur until far into the future. In view of the immediate challenges facing Japan, the need to maintain balanced development, and the great difficulty of changing established customs, his writings focused on explaining the historical circumstances that had led to the present situation, and the gradual adjustments that could be achieved in the short term. He was optimistic that changes could be achieved through progressive shifts in behavior. The setting of examples would do more to break the power of custom than formal education or alterations in the law.

First, therefore, Japan needed to build a "middle class" from the intellectually enlightened elements of Meiji society, who were to be found among the ex-samurai and the wealthier merchant and farming families. Marriage should be an equal partnership, and newly married couples should form independent families, living separately from their parents-in-law wherever possible. Divorce was undesirable, but a wife had the right to remonstrate with an unfaithful husband, or to remarry if she became a widow. The members of a family should be treated as individuals and tied together by mutual respect and affection rather than by vertical relationships in which the senior members expected unquestioning obedience from the junior members and offered nothing in return. Women should be given a fair share of their parents' wealth and needed to be able to earn a living in case their husbands died and left them without adequate financial means. However, even though women were capable of working outside the home just like men, in the present state of society it made sense for the duties of a married couple to be divided, with the wife taking care of household affairs. The main purpose of women's education should therefore be to prepare them for their household duties. Practical skills, such as the ability to make and repair Japanese clothing, must be taught, but girls should also receive basic training in financial and legal matters. Husbands should treat their wives as equal partners, giving them responsibility for household affairs, talking to them about their activities outside the home, and keeping them informed about their financial affairs. In "On Japanese Women" he referred to the emergence of arguments in favor of female suffrage, but did not adopt this as a cause. In any case, he did not want Japanese women to develop the same degree of "willfulness" that could afflict their Western counterparts.[136]

On the other hand, women's household responsibilities should not mean that they were confined to the home. They should have opportunities to visit the theater or make visits to beauty spots. Human beings were social animals, and social interaction played an important part in the civilization process. The involvement of women as well as men was necessary to the success of social gatherings. However, the women should be respectable members of the middle or upper levels of society rather than women with present or past links with the sex trade. As well as treating their wives as equal partners, he repeatedly emphasized that men should not be promiscuous, particularly since respectable women were not allowed similar freedom. While he realized that this double standard existed in Western countries as well, he feared that the open toleration found in Japan would harm its quest to be accepted as a fully civilized nation. It would be difficult to change sexual behavior at once, however. As a first step, men should therefore be encouraged to conceal their extra-marital sexual activities, so that they came to view them as shameful. This would require lowering the social status of prostitutes so that they were seen as less than human.

Fukuzawa explained his views using a combination of patient logic in the manner of John Stuart Mill, entertaining anecdotes, and ingenious analogies. Some of the latter are drawn from science, like the comparison between the joining of the sperm and the ovum in the embryo to the mixing of copper and zinc to produce brass. This is used in the fourth installment of *On Japanese Women, Part Two* to prove that mothers are more than "borrowed wombs." These scientific references, and his general preference for practical arguments over abstract theorizing, may be the result of his training in Dutch learning. He also makes various efforts to encourage men to put themselves in women's situation. For example, in the third installment of *On Japanese Women, Part Two*, he demonstrates the unreasonable nature of the demands on women made by *The Great Learning for Women* by altering the injunction against ever feeling jealousy so that it refers to men rather than women. Similarly, in the final installment he defends educated women from possible criticism for being assertive by showing that even the behavior of a comparatively soft-spoken man would be considered unsuitable if he was put into women's clothes.

Fukuzawa is well known for his criticisms of Confucianism.[137] However, in the writings presented here he also uses Chinese texts to support his arguments. The quotation that is most used in this way is "*Hito wa banbutsu no rei nari,*" which is taken from *Shang Shu* (*The Book of Documents*), one of the Five Classics. The full passage is as follows: "Heaven and Earth are the parents of all creatures; and of all creatures humans are the most fully endowed. The sincere, intelligent, and perspicacious among them becomes the great sovereign; and the great sovereign is the parent of the people."[138] Fukuzawa used this extract numerous times in his writings on women, as evidence for their equality with men. These, and other references to the Chinese classics as support for his points, as well as his general use of vocabulary derived from them, probably seemed a natural use of familiar language that would help his readers to understand and accept new ideas. They may also reflect the deep influence on his ways of thinking of the classical Chinese training that he received before beginning Dutch studies.[139]

The other quotation that he frequently uses is "*fūfu betsu ari* (distinction between husband and wife)," which appears in both *Mencius* and *The Book of Rites*. The latter also contains "*danjo betsu ari* (distinction between men and women)." In *Mencius* there is no clarification of the nature of the "distinction," but in *The Book of Rites* it is stated that men and women should not come into close physical contact, and that while men occupy the exterior, women occupy the interior. According to Watanabe Hiroshi, as pointed out by Sekiguchi Sumiko, the interpretation of this "*fūfu betsu ari*" caused problems in Tokugawa Japan, since marital relationships tended to be associated with "harmony" (*wa*) rather than distinction.[140] When Fukuzawa first uses this quotation, in "A Message of Farewell to Nakatsu,"[141] he does so approvingly, but this is because he interprets it as meaning that there are clear distinctions between one married couple and another rather than between man and wife. Although this was an unorthodox interpretation, it was not unusual at the time.[142] However, elsewhere, for example in the third and sixth installments of *On Relations between Men and Women*,[143] he takes the more orthodox interpretation and criticizes it because the emphasis on reserved behavior between marriage partners prevents the natural expression of affection. He links this criticism to the charge that Confucian scholars in Japan are too inflexible in their interpretations of the ancient texts. They are unable to adapt the teachings to take account of the great social changes that have taken place since they were first written. As a result, although society is now stable enough for women to be able to participate in social gatherings without any risk to their virtue, Confucian scholars are unable to conceive of any relationship between men and women that is neither chaste nor lewd.

The other major criticism of Confucianism is its one-sided morality. This is stated most clearly in *On Moral Behavior*, where he points out that while children and women are sharply criticized for any transgression, parents and husbands rarely receive any blame.[144] Linked to this is Confucianism's failure to demand that married men as well as married women should be monogamous. The reason is simple: Confucian scholars and commentators on Confucian texts are all male. As the lack of evidence for the yin-yang opposition shows, they "have been arbitrary in what they taught, focusing on how to make life easy for the men of their time without any thought for how this might cause difficulties for women."[145] Confucian teachings that subordinated women to men went against the ideal of human equality. Other one-sided teachings, in particular the admonition that women should value the parents of their husband over their own, violated natural human feelings. Paradoxically, however, it could be argued that when Fukuzawa bases his argument on natural human feelings he is probably influenced by the Confucian assumption that human nature is fundamentally good.

Contemporary Responses to Fukuzawa's Writings on Women and the Family

Fukuzawa was obviously not the only person interested in the place of women in the new Japan. As was shown in the second section, this was particularly the case during his second phase of writing about women, which coincided with a general wave of newspaper and magazine articles as well as books on this topic. However, his position as a well-known writer and educator, and his possession of a public lecture hall and newspaper, meant that his views easily attracted attention. Doi Kōka's criticisms of *The Great Learning for Women* in the 1870s went further than Fukuzawa's, and were more systematic than anything he was ready to provide until the late 1890s, but as Kaneko Sachiko points out,[146] it is Fukuzawa's views that were noticed, and have been remembered, because of the wide audience that he had created.

The overall response to the Meirokusha debate on women has already been examined. Of the texts in this volume, those that seem to have evoked the strongest response at the time were *On Moral Behavior*, *On Relations between Men and Women*, and the dual challenge to *The Great Learning for Women, A Critique* and *A New Great Learning*. Surprisingly, perhaps, a major critic in the 1880s was *Jogaku zasshi*, which also aimed to improve the position of women in Japanese society. It agreed with Fukuzawa that husbands should be faithful; that wives should be able to divorce them if they were not; and that women should not be forced to marry someone that they did not know, or live together with their parents-in-law. It also shared his vision of the happiness to be gained from family life if parents love their children, children respect their parents, and all love each other.[147] However, *Jogaku zasshi* was a Christian journal. Both opposed sex outside marriage, but *Jogaku zasshi* was not prepared to accept the sex trade as a necessary evil. It therefore ran an indignant response to the sixth installment of *On Moral Behavior*, in which Fukuzawa described prostitutes as social martyrs.[148]

On Relations between Men and Women seems to have attracted considerable attention, partly at least because hasty readers, or those who did not read it at all, assumed that Fukuzawa was talking mainly about relations between single men and women. Of course, it was also relevant to the one of the great stories of the day, the ballroom dancing of the Rokumeikan, which involved, or rather required, physical contact between elite men and women, regardless of marital relationships. At least six pirated versions were made. The one printed in Osaka even contained illustrations of Japanese men in suits and Japanese women in kimono eating together in Western-style dining rooms.[149]

Soon after the serialization ended, *Jogaku zasshi* published a response that summarized the series and agreed with the principle, but advised *Jiji shinpō* to give consideration to how social relations between men and women should actually be organized. Only after women, and then couples, had gained experience in interacting with each other should single men and married women, and finally single men and single women, begin to associate freely.[150] This shows how radical Fukuzawa's suggestion appeared to be. Three months later, the periodical was even more cautious. There had been a lot of debate about relations between men and women but it advised that close relationships between unmarried couples were unsafe unless belief in Christianity had given those involved the strength to maintain purity.[151]

In view of *Jiji shinpō*'s publicity campaign, it is not surprising that Fukuzawa's twinned final assault on *The Great Learning for Women* received wide attention in the press. There were two main responses to *A Critique*: puzzlement at the amount of attention Fukuzawa had given to a text written so long ago; and denial of his charge that *The Great Learning* was biased against women, the denial resting on the idea that since the author was writing for a female audience, it was only natural for him to focus exclusively on problems related to female behavior.[152] The serialization of *A New Great Learning* seems to have drawn less attention, apart from two lukewarm reviews in *Jogaku zasshi*.[153] *Jiji shinpō* made much of the decision of the principal of the Kyoto First Higher Girls' School to ban the book version, taking it as an early sign of the final confrontation between the forces of civilization and the old guard, which had lost the struggle in almost every area but was still staging a resistance against the new morality.[154]

Fukuzawa's writings on women therefore evoked short-term public debates, particularly among those who disagreed with him. Since his purpose was probably to encourage discussion of the position of women and men's behavior towards them as much as to gain acceptance of his particular views, it is likely that this brought him some satisfaction. Nishizawa has also shown that attention continued to be shown after his death. For example, in 1903, when Sakai Toshihiko (1871–1933), a leading figure in the emerging socialist movement, started *Katei zasshi*, a magazine for women, he acknowledged the influence of Fukuzawa on his views, and included *A Critique* and *A New Great Learning* in a list of essential books for the home.[155] On the negative side, a 1909 conference on *The Great Learning for Women* organized by Inoue Tetsujirō clearly showed that it was not possible to mention the text without dealing with Fukuzawa's criticisms. Three of the four main speakers reaffirmed the basic principles of *The Great Learning* but mentioned weak points. Although these weak points coincided with those mentioned by Fukuzawa, they treated him as an extreme spokesman for Western values of individualism and gender equality. Against this symbolic opponent, they set the Oriental / Japanese emphasis on factors such as the family system, the separate spheres of husbands and wives, and the duty of subjects to sacrifice themselves for the nation.[156] During World War II, Inoue supervised the publication of *The Great Learning for Women: A Newly Annotated Version*. The editor, Hirahara Kokudō, considered that the new edition was necessary to combat the corrupting influence of Western versions of female morality. Once again, even though weaknesses that he recognized in the text were all ones that had been pointed out by Fukuzawa, Hirahara singled him out for criticism because of his praise of Western-style freedoms for women and opposition to the spirit of self-sacrifice that was a special characteristic of Eastern morality.[157]

The most interesting near contemporary treatment of Fukuzawa's views is contained in *Joshi kenkyū (Women's Studies)* by Yoshida Kumaji (1874–1964), a future Tokyo University professor in education who specialized in the field of ethical training, particularly of girls. This appeared in 1911. The only Japanese studies of women that Yoshida paid detailed attention to were *The Great Learning for Women* and the critical updates of Doi Kōka and Fukuzawa Yukichi, but he also praised Fukuzawa's works on women of the 1880s for their role in raising female self-awareness. He contrasted Doi's focus on women's independence with Fukuzawa's desire to change men's behavior. He also pointed to ambiguities and inconsistencies in Fukuzawa's position. For example, at some points, such as his defense of a wife's right to be angry with an unfaithful husband, Fukuzawa seemed to be supporting women's independence. Yet his acceptance of arranged marriages suggested that he was also in favor of the family system, even though this placed the rights of the family, headed by the senior male or eldest son, above those of its individual members.[158]

All the responses above were from men, but women obviously knew of his views as well. Taki later recalled that married women would often come to ask for her father's advice when they had a problem,[159] and it is clear that women were among the large number of people who responded after his death in 1901.[160] A pseudonymous contributor to *Fujo shinbun*, a women's newspaper, even called him "the savior of the women of Meiji."[161]

In relation to the influence of his earliest references to women, we have the example already referred to of Fukuda Hideko modeling her People's Rights Movement speech "On the equality of man" on *An Encouragement of Learning*. With regard to the 1880s, the preface to the published version of *On Japanese Women, Part Two* and remarks in Letter No. 15, to Ichitarō in America, show that Fukuzawa himself considered that at least in the short term, "On Japanese Women" and its "sequel," *On Japanese Women, Part Two*, had made Japanese women more assertive.[162] In the book mentioned above, Yoshida Kumaji suggested that taken together, Fukuzawa's works of the mid-1880s marked a new period in the self-awareness of Meiji women. He also drew attention to Inoue Nao, an otherwise unknown woman who had produced what he called probably the first book by a Japanese woman on women's rights in 1886. In fact, she had republished (without attribution) "Nihon fujinron" along with four other works, under the title *Nihon fujin sanron* (*A Compilation of Texts on the Topic of Japanese Women*). She added a preface, in which she emphasized that improving the status of women was essential in order to improve Japan's status as a nation.[163]

For *A Critique* and *A New Great Learning*, we have evidence from two famous twentieth-century female activists who were born in the later Meiji period, Yamakawa Kikue and Ishimoto/Katō Shizue (1897–2001). In her autobiography, Yamakawa Kikue mentions being given a copy of *The New Great Learning* by an uncle when she must have been around ten years old. Her ethics teacher at the time had been emphasizing that once married, a woman should not leave her new family, even if she was dissatisfied with her life. "This had given me an uncomfortable feeling, and even though I did not really understand it properly, *A New Great Learning for Women* was like a breath of fresh air."[164] In *Women of the Mito Domain*, which was used earlier in this introduction to introduce the life patterns of samurai women in the Tokugawa period, she used two quotations from *A Critique* to criticize *The Great Learning for Women*'s teachings about divorce and the double standard of sexual morality.[165]

Ishimoto refers several times to Fukuzawa in her autobiography, calling him "a forerunner of the feminist movement." While Yamakawa's uncle gave her a copy of *A New Great Learning*, however, Ishimoto was given a copy of *The Great Learning for Women* itself in her grandfather's will. Like Yamakawa, she criticizes its teachings about divorce and its overall negative effect on women, calling it "the epitome of all I had to struggle against – the moral code which has chained Japanese women to the past." Fukuzawa's *A Critique* and *A New Great Learning* definitely established the "bourgeois view of feminism" and had a particular effect on women, "although quite aristocratic in temper."[166]

Phrases such as "bourgeois feminism" and "quite aristocratic in temper" indicate that Ishimoto was not completely happy with Fukuzawa's views. As Yasukawa Junosuke has pointed out, in his characteristically overblown way, Yamakawa also drew attention to Fukuzawa's limitations as a feminist in "Meiji bunka to fujin" ("Women and the Culture of the Meiji Period"), an article published in 1921. Here she considered that "progressive" thinkers of the "good wife, wise mother" era such as Fukuzawa were merely substituting the "feudal enslavement" of women with "bourgeois enslavement":

> Of course, as an individual, Fukuzawa was probably serious and fair-minded, but his protests were insignificant and could not have any effect since they did not take into account the basic causes of male-female inequality and only called for superficial reforms. This was only natural, an inevitable result of the level of society at the time, and Fukuzawa's own personal situation.

She also lamented that the bourgeoisie of her time, including women seen as progressive educators, still agreed with his views.[167]

In the letter to Ichitarō mentioned above Fukuzawa added:

> ... it is not unusual for a trend that attracts great popularity at the beginning to have no ultimate effect. I have **expected** this from the beginning and will not be particularly disappointed if it turns out to be the case.

In fact, while Fukuzawa's writings probably contributed to an unduly negative view of the position of women in Tokugawa Japan, and to the lowering of the social status of sex workers in the Meiji period onwards, it must be admitted that he was unsuccessful in turning prewar Japanese marriages into equal partnerships, and particularly in making husbands faithful to their wives. Those who expressed public approval of his ideas tended to be relative outsiders and critics of mainstream society. However, it is possible that a silent, but sizeable, number of women supported him.

A Final Evaluation

A final evaluation of Fukuzawa's works on women and the family should obviously go further than merely observing, or regretting, that their short-term effectiveness in stimulating debate did not translate into long-term substantive change. Although Yasukawa would not agree,[168] there also seems to be little academic point in judging his views according to the standards of more recent historical periods. This is especially the case since Fukuzawa's vision was based on a historical perspective that stretched back to the past but also continued into the future. The measures that he advocated were more likely to be goals that he thought were achievable in the short term, gradual steps towards "the tranquility of civilization" rather than ends in themselves.

Instead, this evaluation will look at some of the issues that have been raised regarding the texts translated here. The relation between these texts and other texts, such as those dealing with the institution of the Emperor, will not be dealt with.[169] Nor will there be any attempt at a detailed overview or critique of the many books and articles in both Japanese and English that have discussed Fukuzawa's views on women and the family.[170]

In general, it is agreed that Fukuzawa played a valuable role as a spokesman of the early Meiji Japanese "enlightenment." He criticized the vertically-oriented hereditary family system of the Tokugawa samurai class because of its fundamental bias against women. To replace it he introduced the contemporary Anglo-American model of the family as a social unit centred on a husband-wife partnership. On the other hand, he focused on the relatively privileged women who shared his social origins. Assuming that leading roles in the society of his time should belong to men, his main proposal for improving women's situation was to give them more control in the limited sphere of household affairs.[171]

In terms of the texts translated here, some attention should first be given to Fukuzawa's apparent obsession with *The Great Learning for Women*. It is not surprising that he paid interest to it in the late Tokugawa period, and even in his writings of the mid 1880s. But at that time he himself had written that it would be pointless to embark on a detailed criticism since "there is probably no one today who takes every word of *The Great Learning* at its face value. It is, after all, a general guideline for conduct, and in the present situation, for us to turn every detail into evidence to argue over would be childish and even make us the target of ridicule."[172]

It is therefore understandable that his decision to mount a full campaign against *The Great Learning for Women* over ten years later was greeted with puzzlement, as was mentioned in the previous section. Questions about its worthiness as a target have been raised more recently as well.[173] Yet even if *The Great Learning* was out of date, it was still widely available and its basic principles were still being proclaimed by establishment moralists such as Inoue Tetsujirō. Moreover, its very familiarity made it a useful vehicle for criticizing such ideologues. Koizumi Takashi has additionally suggested that Fukuzawa may have viewed it as a safer target than direct attacks on moral guidebooks that had received unofficial Imperial endorsement, such as Motoda Nagasane's *Yōgaku kōyō* (*The Elements of Learning for the Young*) and Nishimura Shigeki's *Fujokan* (*Female Paragons*).[174] In addition, when critics declared that it was ridiculous to criticize *The Great Learning for Women* for focusing on women's failings rather than men's, they missed the point. Rather than expecting the work to provide moral instruction for men as well as women, in focusing on its one-sidedness Fukuzawa was arguing first that Confucian moral teachings favored the strong over the weak, and second that women could not improve their situation by themselves. Men must change their attitudes and behavior as well.

There are also apparent inconsistencies that need to be addressed. Fukuzawa's basic vision, of independent individuals forming independent families with marriage as an equal partnership, is not necessarily followed through in what would now seem to be logical directions. For example, as Nishizawa points out,[175] there should be an inherent contradiction between the family as a horizontal one-generation gathering of individuals bound by ties of affection, and the family as a unit with a hereditary headship that lasts from generation to generation. Fukuzawa appeared to support the former, but did not oppose the hereditary family set-up of the Meiji Civil Code. Moreover, partly because of the influence of Galtonesque evolutionary theory, he also supported the idea of superior (and inferior) bloodlines (*kettō*) and family traditions (*kafū*) being passed down within families over time.[176]

Other apparent inconsistencies are related to Fukuzawa's understanding of gender equality. Unlike John Stuart Mill and Ueki Emori (1857–1862), Fukuzawa was lukewarm on the issue of female suffrage. He also supported the idea of separate spheres for men and women. However, it should be noted that in *The Subjection of Women* John Stuart Mill also saw separate spheres as a sensible arrangement.[177] The idea that household management was a full time occupation surely involved practical recognition of its heavy burden in an age without washing machines, vacuum cleaners or refrigerators, and before medical advances brought vaccinations and effective treatments for common ailments, drastically lowering child mortality rates. Fukuzawa did at least accept that women should be autonomous within the household, and have property rights. He also considered that husbands should be prepared to help their wives, particularly when there were small children, and that wives should know enough of the family's financial affairs to be able to stand in for their husbands in an emergency and even have some sort of skill that would enable them to earn money if necessary. He also recognized that there were professions that were suitable for women.

Another difficult issue is Fukuzawa's attitude to the sex trade. In *The Subjection of Women* Mill, as a Victorian gentleman, made no reference to sexual activity, apart from showing concern over the ability of married men to force "amatory relations," "the last familiarity" or "an animal function" on their wives.[178] By contrast, Fukuzawa openly regarded sex as a source of pleasure that was an important ingredient in a balanced life for women as well as men.[179] Over and over again, he also criticized the hypocrisy of the double standard of morality that allowed unfaithful husbands to expect their wives to be chaste, calling on men to show similar control. Of course, his "first step" in this direction, teaching unfaithful men to hide their activities in order to induce a sense of shame, was hypocritical in itself, and encouraged the stigmatization of female sex workers. However, this was a hypocrisy that he had learnt from the more "civilized" West. Moreover, he did at least recognize that the sex trade was created by the inability of men to control their desire as well as by the temptations offered by fallen women.

At around the same time as Fukuzawa's *On Moral Behavior*, in which he accepted prostitution as a "necessary evil," both Ueki Emori and Iwamoto Yoshiharu called for its abolition. However, they were not campaigning for legislation outlawing prostitution itself, but for the abolition of the government system of licensing prostitutes on condition that they underwent regular examinations for sexually transmitted diseases. Like many People's Rights leaders, Ueki Emori regularly consorted with sex workers, but he was the only one who supported political representation for women as well as men. In the late 1880s he was to go much further than Fukuzawa in his ideas about what women should be aiming for. In "Haishōron," serialized from 12 November to 17 December 1885, he did not criticize men at all, but said that banning licensed prostitution would safeguard the country's international reputation by allowing the government to deny any knowledge of prostitution in Japan. In addition, while prostitution would still exist, prostitutes themselves would not think that their activities had government support.[180] Japanese Christians like Iwamoto also campaigned against the licensing system, on the grounds that it implied government sanction of sinful practices. In November 1885 his magazine criticized reform-minded women for not protesting about the government's support of prostitution and men's treatment of women as tools and playthings. Like Fukuzawa, it criticized prostitutes as "sisters who are beyond the borders of the human world and literally falling into the world of beasts," but without calling on men to change their behavior.[181] Nearly eleven years later, *Jogaku zasshi* stated that prostitutes were like slaves, and were content to be treated as machines by men. They tempted men into immoral ways and spread syphilis.[182] In this context, Fukuzawa's untiring criticism of men deserves some recognition. However, as a leading article in the magazine of the Japanese branch of the Women's Christian Temperance Union complained, he did not support the Union's annual petitions to the Japanese Diet for the definition of male adultery to be broadened so that, like female adultery, it referred to all extra-marital sex, not just extra-marital sex with partners who were already married.[183]

Another problem, of course, is Fukuzawa's attitude to women's education, particularly considering his contribution to the education of men. Fukuzawa assumed that middle-class women would marry and be primarily occupied by household and childcare duties. They should be able to go outside the house for recreational purposes, but their education should prepare them for their domestic role. Academic study would be wasted. In accordance with these views, and perhaps also because of his wife's opinions, his daughters were educated mainly at home, and married husbands that he and Kin had selected for their acceptance or refusal before they reached the age of twenty. It seems as if Taki, the fourth daughter, wanted greater educational opportunities, but was refused. While Nishizawa Naoko finds various justifications for Fukuzawa's position,[184] it is still regrettable that he did not speak out in favor of higher education for those women who did not wish to marry early. After all, job opportunities for educated women were unlikely to appear as long as there were no women with the requisite education.

The refusal to allow Taki the same educational opportunities as her brothers is a symptom of the gap between the public Fukuzawa, spokesman of independence and self-respect, and the private Fukuzawa, husband, father, and head of the household. The picture of unblemished harmony that he paints in his autobiography is not entirely supported by his letters to family members or by the reminiscences of his children and grandchildren. Fukuzawa and his wife were strong characters with different upbringings. Their marriage was successful in the procreational sense, but it is likely that there was little understanding on an intellectual level. Kin certainly seems to have been more traditional in her views and this clearly led to some disagreements between them. It seems likely that she had a strong voice in the treatment of the daughters, and in the choice of topics for family conversations. However, it looks as if Fukuzawa expected the family to revolve around him. It was certainly the united opinion of his wife and daughters that his behavior at home showed a belief in the dominance of men over women. While his joy in his children and grandchildren is clear, there are signs that this affection was suffocating. It is obvious, particularly in his letters to his two eldest sons during their studies in the United States, that it was difficult for him to stand back and let his children develop as independent individuals.

Finally, there is the issue of Fukuzawa's real beliefs and motives. Most of the texts translated here originally appeared in *Jiji shinpō*. In his writing for the newspaper, Fukuzawa's intention was to provoke debate and push discussions in various directions according to the state of public opinion at the time. Compared to his stand on other issues, Fukuzawa's views on women and the family remained remarkably stable, even though some writers suggest that by the time of *A New Great Learning for Women* his position had become more conservative than it was in the 1870s.[185] But the question remains of whether his opinions on women and the family were influenced by expediency rather than being sincerely held. First, it is clear that they were influenced by his understanding of the social changes that Japan needed to introduce in order to "rise" to the level of Western civilization and become strong enough to preserve its independence. Second, it is equally clear that he did not want Japan to appear uncivilized to foreign visitors, particularly with regard to its standards of moral decency. However, the presence of both these motives does not mean that he had no genuine concern for the position of women, even if it was only for those who were qualified to join "the middle class."[186]

The issues of gender equality and work-life balance still trouble us today. Fukuzawa suggested that men needed to change as well as women, but "success" for both genders is currently defined according to stereotypes associated with masculinity. He recognized the importance of work within the home, but paid work outside the home is still valued more than unpaid domestic tasks, including caring for younger and older relatives. "Feminine" caring professions such as nursing, or elementary levels of teaching, receive lower status and smaller financial rewards than "masculine" executive positions in business and finance, regardless of their relative importance for society as a whole. In many developed countries, and particularly Japan, marriage and fertility rates are falling. With his evolutionary standpoint, Fukuzawa was aware that the proposals he made for Meiji Japan would not necessarily be suitable for future ages. If he were alive today, would he still be optimistic about the future of human civilization?

Helen Ballhatchet

General Notes about the Translations

1. Unless otherwise noted, all the translations apart from the letters are substantial revisions of translations originally made by Kiyooka Eiichi and published in either *Fukuzawa Yukichi on Japanese Women: Selected Works*, Tokyo: University of Tokyo Press, 1988 or *Fukuzawa Yukichi on Education: Selected Works*, University of Tokyo Press: 1985. The main purpose of the revisions has been to correct errors and make the translations closer to the original text. For example, explicit references to sex-related issues have been restored, and Fukuzawa's practice of repeating the same word(s) for rhetorical effect has been kept. For the same reasons, efforts have also been made to replicate the structure of the many complex sentences.

2. In new translations, and in revising translations by Kiyooka Eiichi, the editor has endeavored to use one English equivalent for each keyword. For example, in *Danjo kōsairon* (*On Relations between Men and Women*), *kōsai* has been translated throughout as "relations." In this particular work, *kankei*, which is often translated as "relations," has therefore been rendered as "ties."

3. Macrons have not been used for words such as "daimyo," "Keio" and "Tokyo" that are frequently found in English-language texts. Names of Japanese people have been given in the normal Japanese order of family name followed by personal name.

4. When Fukuzawa uses a word from a European language instead of a Japanese word, this has been indicated through the use of bold type.

5. All dates have been adjusted to the Western calendar, and all ages have been given according to Western reckoning.

6. Information in square brackets is basic information that has been inserted by the translator so that the text can be understood without recourse to the footnotes.

7. Readers should be aware that in Japanese, *shun/haru* (spring), and words related to spring such as *ka/hana* (flower, blossom) can have sexual connotations. To retain the ambiguity of the original, the translation does not always make this connection explicit.

8. Most of the footnotes are new to this edition. The editor is indebted to the

footnotes in *Fukuzawa Yukichi chosakushū* 10, Tokyo: Keiōgijuku Daigaku shuppankai, 2003. As far as possible, the source of quotations from classical Chinese texts has been given, and the context has been explained where necessary. The search facilities of Donald Sturgeon's Chinese Text Project (http://ctext.org/) have been of invaluable help in this endeavor. Where it has been necessary to quote from the *Analects* and *Mencius*, the editor has used the following translations:

The Analects of Confucius (Lun Yu). A literal translation with an introduction and notes by Chinchung Huang, Oxford: Oxford University Press, 1997.

Mencius. Translated and with an introduction by D. C. Lau, Harmondsworth, Middx: Penguin Books, 1970.

PART I

Public Writings

A Message of Farewell to Nakatsu

EDITOR'S INTRODUCTION

In late December 1870, Fukuzawa arrived in Nakatsu, the *han* in northern Kyushu to which his family had belonged. His main purpose was to fetch his mother and his late brother's daughter and bring them back to Tokyo. The letter to Yana Kihei of July 1869 that is translated in Part II (pp. 310–312) shows that he had been trying to get his mother and sisters to join him in Tokyo for some time. It was clear to Fukuzawa that his future, and the future of the country as a whole, Nakatsu included, lay in Tokyo. However, his family did not understand this new perspective. Their hope was for him to return to Nakatsu, where the rumor was that a prestigious role in the *han* administration awaited him.

This trip was Fukuzawa's first real visit to Nakatsu since the death of his brother fourteen years before. During this time, he had risen in prestige by becoming a direct retainer of the Bakufu, and travelled twice to the United States and once to Europe. Now he was an independent citizen, best-selling author, and principal of a renowned school of Western learning. He was at the forefront of the new Japan, while the higher-ranking Nakatsu samurai, his former superiors, were still struggling to understand what was going on. In fact, in his autobiography he relates that during his visit he was asked to appear before the *han*'s senior officials in order to advise them on the actions they should be taking in response to the changing situation. He also relates his later discovery that twice during this trip he had narrowly escaped assassination by xenophobic samurai, once by a relative in Nakatsu itself, and once on the return journey, while waiting overnight for the boat to Osaka.[1]

Fukuzawa's visit to Nakatsu occurred before the feudal order had been completely dissolved. Nakatsu's land had been returned to the Emperor, but the former daimyo retained his office under a different title; Nakatsu samurai continued to receive their feudal stipends. Although he did not know exactly how things were going to change, Fukuzawa wanted to prepare all those whom he was leaving behind in Nakatsu so that they could play their part as enlightened citizens of a strong and independent Japan. He therefore wrote, or at least completed, this message in the old family home in Nakatsu. He kept the first draft and gave a corrected version to Kuwana Hōzan, a senior *han* official. The document circulated in copied versions and appeared in print in March 1872, in *Shinbun zasshi*, an early Tokyo newspaper. Six months after this, it was even translated into English and published in a New York newspaper.[2]

As the footnotes show, the text is clearly influenced by Francis Wayland's *Elements of Moral Science*. It was written before Fukuzawa's first major publications of the mid-1870s, *An Outline of a Theory of Civilization* and *An Encouragement of Learning*, but many of his core ideas are evident. These include the important roles played by both women and the family in civilized societies since men and women are of equal worth. All human beings should be free and independent; a nation can only be independent if it is based on independent individuals in independent family units. In the ideal family, parents are joined to their children by mutual rights and duties. Above all, the basis of morality is to be found in the monogamous relationship of a husband and wife.

A Message of Farewell to Nakatsu[1]

To call human beings "of all creatures . . . the most highly endowed"[2] does not just mean that they are each equipped with ears, eyes, a nose and mouth, hands and feet; that they can talk, eat and sleep. It means that if they cultivate virtue by following the way of Heaven, enlarge their minds with the knowledge and experience appropriate to human beings, touch the things around them and associate with people, strive for their own independence and earn a living for their families — then, and only then, can they be called "of all creatures . . . the most highly endowed."

Although the Chinese and Japanese have shown little awareness of it since ancient times, the way of freedom and autonomy is an element in the inborn nature of human beings. At first hearing, "freedom" may sound like willfulness,[3] but this is definitely not the case. Freedom means to act according to one's own intentions as long as this does not hinder other people.[4] When fathers and sons, lords and vassals, husbands and wives, friends and their friends,[5] all allow themselves to carry out their particular intentions freely and without restraint, without hindering each other; when they each establish their own independence without imposing themselves on others,[6] then, since all human beings naturally act with correctness, no one will head in a wrongful direction. Misguided people who exceed the limits of freedom by harming others in order to benefit themselves are harmful to their fellow human beings. As sinners in the eyes of Heaven who are unworthy of human forgiveness, whether of high or low birth, old or young, they should be regarded with disdain and are deserving of punishment. In other words, freedom and independence are important; when their value is mistaken, no virtue will be cultivated, no wisdom developed, no family will be at peace, no *han* (*kuni*) will be secure, and there will be no hope for the independence of the nation. On the other hand, if every person is independent, every family will be independent; if every family is independent, every *han* (*ikkoku*) will be independent; if every *han* is independent, the nation (*tenka*) will be independent.⁷ Samurai, farmer, artisan, merchant, none [of the four classes in our society] should hinder the freedom and independence of any other.

The basis of morality is the relationship between a husband and wife.⁸ Husband and wife lead to parents and children, and to brothers and sisters. At the beginning of the world, when Heaven brought forth human beings, there must have been one man and one woman. Even now, when tens of millions of years have passed, the ratio must be the same.⁹ Moreover, since every individual, whether male or female, is equally a human being placed in between the Heaven and the earth, there is no reason to make distinctions as to their relative importance. Yet if we examine the customs of China and Japan, both now and in the past, no shame has ever been expressed at the fact that men keep concubines in addition to their wives, or that women are treated as servants or even criminals. Is this not despicable? If the head of the household shows contempt for his wife, the children will follow suit, by looking down on her and failing to value what she teaches them. Children who do not value what their mother teaches them might as well have no mother at all. They are no different from orphans. This being the case, since men go out to work and are rarely at home, is there anyone around to educate the children? Their situation is worse than pitiful.

In the *Analects* it says that there should be "distinctions between husbands and wives,"¹⁰ but "distinctions" does not mean that they should be separate from each other. In fact, a husband and wife should be joined by affection. If they were separate, like strangers, the family would not be at peace. Therefore, "distinctions" means "divisions" in the sense that this man and woman form one married couple and that man and woman form another couple; thus it must mean that there are clear divisions between each pair. However, if a man is supporting many concubines, and both the proper wife and the concubines have children, siblings will have one father but different mothers. It will not be possible to say that there is a division between different couples. Moreover, if one man has the right to have two wives, it is surely reasonable for one woman to possess two husbands.

I put it to the men of Japan: If a wife loved another man so that there were one woman and two men living under the same roof, would the head of the household willingly accept this situation and look after his wife's needs? Again, in the *Zuo Zhuan* [*Commentary of Zuo*]¹¹ there is a reference to the switching of consorts, meaning that men would exchange wives for a short period. The venerable Confucius was so concerned about the general deterioration of behavior that he wrote the *Chunqui* [*Annals of the Spring and Autumn Period*]. Mentioning now the barbarians and now the Middle Kingdom, he loudly voiced both praise and blame. Yet he had no word of censure for the exchanging of wives, choosing to pretend ignorance of the matter, probably because he was not overly troubled by it. This appears somewhat negligent to our ways of thought, or perhaps the words in the *Analects* about "distinctions between husbands and wives" should be interpreted in a different way. Experts in Chinese and Confucian studies must have opinions about this.

Filial behavior towards one's parents is only to be expected. We must do our utmost to devote ourselves single-mindedly to their service. But it is surely rather too heartless and mechanical to calculate that since children spend three years under the protection of their parents they owe them a three-year period of mourning.[12]

It is only too common for children to be criticized for being unfilial towards their parents, but all too rare for parents to be accused of lacking affection towards their children. Yet it is utterly misguided of those who have become parents to declare that it was they who brought their children to life, and to regard them as tools that they have made themselves or purchased with their own money. Children are gifts from Heaven and should therefore be cherished. When a baby is born, the father and mother should train it together. Children should be kept close to their parents until they are over nine years of age[13] so they can be guided in the right path by their love and authority. When they have a good foundation in learning, they should be sent to school and placed with teachers for instruction. In other words, it is the role of parents, their duty towards Heaven, to turn their children into proper adults.

When children reach the age of twenty or twenty-one, they are said to attain the age of majority. Since they are now capable of discretion, their parents can relinquish them without any second thoughts, leaving them to make a living by themselves and allowing them to go where they want and do as they like. However, as the path to be followed by parents and children does not change during life or even after death, children must not neglect their filial duties, and parents must not lose their natural feelings of affection. By "relinquish them without any second thoughts" I mean only that there must be no parental interference in a child's freedom and independence. Western books teach that once a child has reached the age of majority, parents may dispense advice but must not give orders.[14] This is an eternal maxim that all must think on.

Another point is to realize that while learning and the mastery of writing are obviously part of the training of children, teaching through example is more important; therefore, the conduct of parents must be correct. They may preach the correct path all they like, but if their actions are unworthy, their children will model themselves on their conduct and learn nothing from their words. This being the case, what will happen if their words are as incorrect as their actions? What can be expected of such a child when it grows up? Its fortune is even worse than an orphan's.

In some cases, parents have an upright nature and are aware of the importance of loving their children, but try to make them follow paths that suit the parents' interests without explaining the way of things. Such parents may seem to have done nothing wrong, but the truth of the matter is that while realizing the importance of love for their children, they do not know what this love consists of. In actual fact, they are sinners who oppose both Heavenly reason and humanity and lead their own children to the misfortunes of ignorance and iniquity. If a child has a weak constitution, there is no mother or father who does not worry. But since having a nature that is not worthy of a human being is so much worse than a physical shortcoming, why are parents so concerned about physical weakness and not about a weak nature? This should be called "the shallow benevolence of a woman"[15] or "the affection of a domestic animal."

People's natures differ just as their faces do. As societies develop there is a corresponding increase in wrong doers, and it becomes impossible for ordinary people working alone to keep themselves safe or protect their way of living. This being the case, the people of a nation (*ikkoku*) put up representatives, rules are established that take into account the relative interests of all concerned, and for the first time, society is run on the basis of laws that encourage good behavior and punish bad. These representatives are called "the government." The person at the top is "the head of the state," and those who assist the head are "officials." This is essential in order to preserve the safety of a nation and protect it from being regarded as inferior by others.

Although many different types of work are found in this world, none is more difficult than that of governing a nation. Since it is the Way of Heaven for people to be rewarded according to their efforts, the more difficult the work, the greater should be the reward. People who enjoy the benefits of being ruled by a government must therefore not resent the fact that the head of the state and the officials receive higher wages. If their laws are just, the sums that they receive are cheap at the price. Not only should people be free of resentment; it follows that they must also show respect to those involved in government. On the other hand, the officials and the head of state must not lose sight of the principle that each must labor in order to eat; they should be aware of the link between the degree to which they exert themselves and the degree to which they are recompensed. This may be the essence of the relationship between ruler and subject.

The above is an outline of human social relations, but two or three pieces of paper do not allow for a detailed understanding. It is essential to read books, and not only books from Japan, but books from China, books from India, and books from the various nations of the West. Nowadays there are said to be different schools of thought such as National learning,[16] Chinese learning, and Western learning, each with its own theories, and each one disparaging the others, but this is a ridiculous state of affairs. Learning is simply a matter of reading letters that have been recorded on paper, so it is not very difficult. Discussions about the strengths and weaknesses of different schools should come after the letters have been learnt; there is no benefit to be had from wasting time on empty arguments before this has been accomplished. If human beings apply the intelligence with which they are equipped, how much effort will it take to learn the languages of two or three countries, such as Japan, China, Britain or France? Is it not cowardly and unworthy of one's manhood to disparage a school of learning that one knows nothing about, and that uses letters that one cannot even read? Anyone who is to engage in learning should think of the interests of our native land rather than the strengths or weaknesses of different schools of thought.

Our nation has recently begun to trade with foreign nations, and it is possible that many of the foreigners are tricksters out to impoverish our nation and treat us as fools in order to make profits for themselves. This being the case, what will we achieve by extolling National or Chinese learning, longing for the ways of the past, disapproving of new methods, and letting ourselves fall into poverty and ignorance because we do not understand human affairs in other parts of the world? We will just be making these foreigners happy and playing into their hands. At this point in time, the only thing that foreigners fear is Western learning. We must gain understanding of the situation in the world through wide reading of the books of many nations, and enter negotiations with other nations on the basis of international law. In domestic affairs we must gain wisdom and virtue in order to extend the freedom and independence of the people; in foreign affairs we must use international law to proclaim the independence of the nation (*ikkoku*). Surely this is the only way to manifest the true greatness of Japan. This is my goal, and the reason why I stress the urgent need to take up Western learning alone, regardless of its strengths and weaknesses relative to National or Chinese learning.

I earnestly hope that both the samurai and people of Nakatsu, where I grew up, will view the world with fresh eyes and devote themselves to Western learning; that each will labor in order to eat, and achieve individual freedom without hindering the freedom of any other; that all will strive for virtue and wisdom and cleanse their natures of anything unworthy — all this so that they will come to understand how to keep their families safe and how to bring strength and prosperity to the land.

Who has no love for their native place; who fails to pray for the happiness of old friends? The time for my departure approaches. I took my brush in haste, and summarized what I have learnt from Western books so that I can leave something behind for your consideration.

Written on the night of 17 January 1871 (27th of the 11th month, Meiji 3 [1870] by the old calendar)

Under the broken window of my old house in Rusui-chō, Nakatsu

Fukuzawa Yukichi

An Answer to a Certain Gentleman's Inquiry about Female Education

EDITOR'S INTRODUCTION

After its first appearance in 1878 in a magazine published by Keio, this was reprinted the next year in *Fukuzawa bunshū* 2, a collection of Fuzukawa's writings. Fukuzawa purports to be replying to a father who is worried that a daughter whom he has sent to study under foreign teachers (probably female missionaries) will become estranged from Japanese society. He uses this format to express general anxiety about the effect of excessive Westernization on Japan's cultural identity and doubts about the utility of Western-style education for girls who were destined to run Japanese-style households. In the second installment of "On Japanese Women" he also refers to the use which women can make of educational opportunities, but his concern there is that education alone cannot improve their position. As long as their life after school is limited to household duties, it will have few long-term effects.

The education of the Fukuzawa daughters was discussed in the General Introduction. This "letter" was published eight years before three of the daughters actually spent two months as boarders at a mission school in Yokohama in 1887.[1] Nishizawa Naoko suggests that the "Western schoolmistress" whose curriculum is criticized in the 1877 extract from *Minkan keizai roku* is Alice Hoar. Hoar had arrived in Japan in 1875 as a missionary of the Ladies' Association for Promoting the Education of Females in India and other Heathen Countries in Connection with the Missions of the Society for the Propagation of the Gospel. Archibald Shaw, a missionary of the Society for the Propagation of the Gospel in Foreign Parts (SPG), the missionary organization for men to which Hoar's society was affiliated, was already living on the Mita compound and he introduced her to Fukuzawa. For about eighteen months during 1876 and 1877, Fukuzawa had allowed her the use of the second floor of his house, where she set up a small school for girls and lived with some of her pupils.[2]

An Answer to a Certain Gentleman's Inquiry about Female Education[1]

Dear ⎯⎯⎯⎯⎯,

You wrote to me about your daughter, whom you sent to foreigners at one of the treaty ports to study languages, mathematics, sewing, music and so on. On top of her daily lessons, she has been listening to lectures on Christianity. After two or three years, she seems to be making progress, but at the same time she has inevitably grown apart from both her relatives and her former friends. You are, quite naturally, extremely worried that she will consequently become an isolated and lonely figure.

At present, various arguments about female education are making themselves known in society. I myself have no definite opinion, but last year I wrote a little about my views in a volume called *Popular Economics* [*Minkan keizai roku*, 1877]. Since you may not yet have seen the work, I will quote from it here. On page 77 it says:

> ... For example, at the time of the Imperial Restoration, some Buddhists were so caught up in the political disturbances that they switched to Shinto and threw their [Buddhist] ancestral tablets into water or fire.[2] There were people who had heard that the teachings of the West were a little fashionable and therefore behaved as if they were superior disciples of Jesus, even though they had never read a Western book and did not even know a single word in a Western language. One can only say that their confusion was taken to unnecessary extremes. While some confusion was understandable, there were many people who lost their belief in the old before making any progress with knowledge of the new. They lost even their original sense of integrity, as if they were so empty within that they were floating in a state of weightlessness. One can only say that this was a pitiable state of affairs. In any case, people

AN ANSWER TO A CERTAIN GENTLEMAN'S INQUIRY ABOUT FEMALE EDUCATION

should not make radical changes in their beliefs unless these are accompanied by radical changes in their knowledge that enable them to make sound decisions . . .

On page 21 of the same volume it says:

> . . . In addition, recently a Western schoolmistress[3] came to Japan and founded a girls' school in order to show us the light of Western civilization and instruct the ignorant and untutored young women of Japan in a whole range of subjects, including not only literature and music but even cooking and needlework. Yet apparently the skills of this great expert in female accomplishments did not extend to cutting rolls of kimono cloth and sewing garments. In those countries, since the division of labor is widespread, making clothes is a task performed by specialists, and there is no shame if a woman does not know how to do this herself. Even so, this is not the case in our country. To learn how to embroider or make frills as those Westerners teach is no more than to master a useless pastime in Japan. It is much more important for girls to learn first how to sew a rice-bran bag, then how to make an undershirt, and finally how to cut a roll of kimono cloth and produce clothes for both men and women . . .[4]

As is stated above, Japan already forms a complete nation in itself, and accordingly has its own customs. If a nation has its own customs, each household must naturally follow those customs. This is a basic rule of human society. To measure how much wood to cut in order to make a new axe handle, you do not need to look any further than the handle of the axe that you are using.[5] To take a close example, imagine that you had a son who was already of marriageable age and were seriously thinking of possible matches. When searching for prospective brides, what sort of young lady would you look for? How would you respond to one of the educated young women who are so fashionable nowadays? She recites from the Bible every morning and evening, plays the piano, uses Western-style heaters because she has a poor opinion of Japanese-style heating, amuses herself with embroidery but relies on someone else to mend a sleeve that has come undone, dirties the tatami by treading on them with the bottom of her Western-style dress still muddy from the streets, and has such a high opinion of herself that she smugly looks down on relatives and older people as if they were inferior beings. Surely you would reject her. If you pay attention to such considerations, I feel sure that you will realize how your daughter should be educated. I hope that you will deem this an adequate answer to your query.

Respectfully yours,

8 February 1878[6]

On Japanese Women

EDITOR'S INTRODUCTION

This was the first work in Fukuzawa's second phase of writing about women and therefore his first systematic treatment of the topic. It appeared in *Jiji shinpō* in eight installments from 4–12 July 1885. Unlike the other serialized works translated here, it was not published as a single volume but was included in the collected works of 1898. Since this was published while Fukuzawa was still alive, this must mean that it had his approval. As in his other writings on the topic, his focus was women of "the middle levels and above (*shakai chūtō ijō*)."

The General Introduction to this volume discussed the connection between Fukuzawa's views and those of John Stuart Mill. In this work, Fukuzawa's strictures about the position of women in Tokugawa and early Meiji Japan, such as their general subordination and lack of property rights, are similar to those in *The Subjection of Women*. However, Mill considered that the emancipation of women would make society more efficient since they would be able to make a greater contribution. By contrast, in this work, Fukuzawa focuses more narrowly on the positive effect that improved conditions would have on women's mental and emotional wellbeing, and therefore on the health of their offspring. A more striking difference is the issue of sexual activity. Mill makes decorous references to the fact that husbands could legally rape their wives. Fukuzawa ignores this problem. However, despite worries that his frankness will invite censure, in Installment Four he exposes the unfair double standard according to which women could only seek and enjoy sexual satisfaction at the cost of their respectability, while men faced no such restrictions. Additionally, in Installment Five he explains that women's sexual frustration causes severe emotional and mental suffering, and even leads to ailments such as hysteria.

In this work, Fukuzawa's concern with the plight of Japanese women is justified by the need to improve their ability to bear strong, healthy babies in order to strengthen the Japanese as a race. This is not a constant theme in his writings on women, but he certainly considered that characteristics could be inherited through family lines.[1] The first six installments describe the negative situation of women in Japan. Lacking responsibility, they miss the fulfillment that results from exposure to the pains and pleasures (*kuraku*) of existence. Moreover, as the victims of "social oppression" (*shakai no assei*), they have limited chances of sexual satisfaction. Having equal physical, intellectual and emotional needs, all humans require similar amounts of stimulation and nourishment, but in women the emotional needs are both more developed and less nourished. Installment Seven contains solutions, including an end to the hereditary family system, complete with an ingenious way of creating new surnames for married couples. Installment Eight, which ends somewhat abruptly, criticizes women in the more traditional China and Korea, but also women in the West. However, Fukuzawa also looks forward to a time when all men and women will enjoy the same responsibilities and privileges.

On Japanese Women[1]

Installment One

On the subject of the improvement of the Japanese race, I am in agreement with methods such as mixed marriages with foreigners. Many people have written on this subject and we have frequently carried their views in *Jiji shinpō*.[2] Of course, we cannot embark on such a project lightly, nor expect immediate results. Since it is an undertaking that will, as it were, involve the whole nation for a hundred years, we must take up any and all means that might be effective and study their strong and weak points without regard to how long it might take.

Now, mixed marriages, the importing of new stocks of men and women from outside, should certainly be encouraged. This method I shall call the external-help method. Yet, one must not neglect the self-help method, too: that is, improving the physique of the men and women here already in Japan, and thereby producing more perfect children. For this purpose, one can consider a number of ways. One of them is to improve food and clothing; another is to pay attention to nutrition and the treatment of disease, in other words, proper health care. All these areas are important for racial improvement and will undoubtedly be effective.

However, there is one important topic which, in my opinion, is generally neglected by the whole of society; even in the higher circles of learned men it is not taken seriously. Therefore, in this article, I will ignore nutrition and the treatment of disease, and focus on the intellectual and leisure activities of women, which I propose to encourage as a way of improving their stamina. The purpose of my discourse being solely the improvement of the physique, when I discuss pleasure, I shall at times be touching on the animal nature of human beings. Since my description may make us appear no different from beasts, my words may seem questionable as public morality and therefore offend the narrow-minded moralist. However, because the spiritual and the physical are perfectly distinct affairs, I pray earnestly that my readers will take in my argument without any undue misunderstanding.

My idea for the improvement of our race through the self-help method is to enliven our women's minds and so strengthen their bodies that we obtain high-quality descendants. In recent years in our country, there have been many discussions on women. But most of them have dwelt on the need to compensate for their lack of education and judgment. Some have advocated instruction in reading or the arts to improve their spiritual well-being; others have encouraged physical exercise in order to stimulate both mental and physical growth. These are the common arguments of the advocates of Western civilization.

To me, these methods are not sufficient to ensure the true development of our women. Education in the style of *The Great Learning for Women*, that side product of Confucianism,[3] is simply out of the question, because the more one teaches it the more withering is its effect. It is nothing but a philosophy to oppress the spirit and, in the process, destroy the physique too. I am not even satisfied with the educational methods of the advocates of Western civilization. The reason is that even when women are instructed in reading and the arts or given plenty of physical exercise, that education is confined to the schoolroom. When they go home, they are treated as nothing more than the daughters of the house, and when they marry, they become nothing more than the ladies of the house.

All in all, people mold their lives out of the pains and pleasures of life. When their sufferings and pleasures are greater, their lives are that much more fulfilling. This means that any attempt to increase one's pains and pleasures will result in heavier responsibilities. For instance, in politics and other worldly affairs, suppose there is a man whose slightest move influences national affairs, and another whose words and deeds influence one village or one city. The former's responsibilities will be greater than the latter's, but so will his pains and pleasures. In the same way, if we compare a man in control of a million yen with another who has a hundred thousand, the difference in their responsibilities will be ten to one, and their pains and pleasures will also be ten to one.

Therefore, our pains and pleasures are borne out of our responsibilities; they do not depend on our education or lack of it. At times, when an unlearned man by chance comes into a position of responsibility, his bearing will improve, and even his speech, behavior, and personal features will change. A merchant might make a fortune and an official might obtain a surprise promotion, and at the time the fortune or promotion seems inappropriate. But it often happens that after some time, these men acquire dignity, and their appearance, too, changes, so that we are amazed to find them completely transformed. We shall have to concede that the advancement these men made was not the result of their studies at school, but of the education they obtained from their responsibilities in real life. Therefore, classroom training alone cannot enrich one's life and enliven the activities of both the mind and body; some sort of responsibility must also be provided. This has not only been proved by theoretical studies but it is also something that the general public takes as a matter of course even though they may not say so outright. Thus, the saying goes that the best solution for a young good-for-nothing is to give him a wife. In other words, if he is given the responsibility of managing a household, it will stimulate the activities of his mind and body. The proverb "Growing poor means growing dull" must be a description of both mind and body growing dull and lazy when responsibility is removed.

This being the importance of responsibility to a fulfilled life, let us examine the actual condition of women in Japan. They are given no responsibility at all. Just as in the saying "A woman has no home of her own anywhere in the world," in her infancy a female is cared for by her parents and brought up in a house that belongs to her father; in adulthood she joins someone else's family as a bride and lives in a house that belongs to her husband; in old age she is cared for by her children in a house that belongs to them. All the family wealth belongs to the head of the household; women can only share the benefits. In poor families, the poverty likewise belongs to the head of the household; the women simply share the hardship with him.

Some see a woman's responsibility as the handling of domestic affairs and the bringing up of children. But what are domestic affairs? The biggest item is clothing; the smallest item is the everyday food. Moreover, since the control of household finances is retained by the household head, the woman is only following his orders. The bringing up of children is no different.

It is natural that the work involving the raising and feeding of children should fall to the wife, but they are more her husband's children than her own. To give proof of this, during her pregnancy, if the husband prays for a male child, the wife too will pray for the same. This is nothing to be wondered at, but often this desire of her husband causes a pregnant wife much anguish. In extreme cases, if a female baby comes, the wife is ashamed on seeing her husband's displeasure; if a male child comes, the husband praises his wife and he may even give her a present as an award for her performance. Of course whether a child is male or female is something determined by nature, and it is foolish to wish for either sex. But that apart, to think of awarding one's wife for bearing a male child reduces her to a mere instrument for producing children. Such an attitude is highly insulting and deeply shameful.

As a result, when the child grows up the mother has no say in its education since the father makes all the decisions. This means that on top of being subordinate to a son once he is head of the household, she has no authority over his actions even when he is a child. If she has no authority, it follows that she also has no responsibility. And the conclusion is that women in Japan do not bring up any children of their own, they only look after the children of their husbands.

Installment Two

No women in Japan possess any assets. As the saying goes, a woman has no house of her own anywhere in this world; thus it is a natural consequence that there is no woman with her own savings. Sometimes, a father or a husband may give her some funds, but it will simply be a small amount for everyday use, not any large amount to be spent publicly for a purpose. As proof of this, one may note the scarcity of lawsuits on money matters in which a woman is either the plaintiff or defendant.

Since the Meiji Restoration, a new law has made it possible for a woman to be a household head or an owner of land or of public loan bonds, thus allowing her to possess movable and immovable assets.[4] However, custom dictates that a woman can only become the head of a household as a temporary substitute. As soon as she marries or adopts a son, her rights as the head of a household will be transferred to the new husband or son. Not only is it rare to see a woman hold legal possession of movable or immovable assets, but it is also not clear whether she has ownership rights to any of her personal possessions. A daughter from a good family who has married into another family might lose even the clothing and jewelry that she brought as a bride if that family's fortune declines. In an extreme case, the husband may be a dissolute and debauched man who empties his wife's closet and trunks, and in the end, contrives to divorce her. Still she has no recourse to complaint. These are examples of the utmost heartlessness and cruelty. Yet there is nothing that a woman can do about them.

Of course, the above examples are extreme cases, and I am not implying that all the wives in Japan are liable to experience such tragedies. As long as a nation exists and possesses a civilized society, its people are bound to have a fine set of customs related to family life. And yet, in this country, when a husband's affection cools, there is no means to restrain him, however cruel he may allow himself to be. As long as there is no law against such behavior and the way is left open, even if nothing actually happens, women will have no true peace of mind and their safety will be a matter of accidental good fortune. In other words, women rely on the good will of men: the security and destiny of the former lie in the hands of the latter.

The situation being as described above, it is simply natural that the position of women in society is low. They live quiet lives, eternally courting their men's whims. Their responsibilities are limited to food and clothing; they never extend their minds outside of their homes, their whole lives being spent within. When, on rare occasions, they go out and meet people, they are not treated as equals. For instance, at a Japanese-style party where both men and women gather, the honorary seats are occupied solely by men and women are forced to sit like attendants, regardless of what rank or age might dictate. A more conspicuous example is when women are seated with younger men who are relatives: they purposely instruct the young men to sit in the honorary seats and act as if to serve them. This is nothing but a reversal of the natural order seen from the normal ways of humanity. Confucius said, "Where there are chores, the younger brothers and sons render their services; when there is wine and food, the seniors drink and eat." If we borrow this saying to describe men and women in Japan, it becomes "Where there are chores, the women render their services; when there is wine and food, the men drink and eat."[5]

In this way, the women of our country have no responsibility either inside or outside the home, and their position is very low. Consequently, their pains and pleasures are very small in scale. Since it is the customs of hundreds and even thousands of years that have made them as feeble as they are, it is not an easy matter now to lead both their minds and bodies to activity and to vigorous health. There are animated discussions on the education of women. No doubt education will be effective. If taught learning and the arts, women will become competent in those areas; if they engage in physical exercise, their bodies will develop. But those attempts will only achieve a limited effect as long as they lead lives of confinement and feebleness. The results can be surmised even before they are begun.

I once compared the present efforts in schools for the education of women in Japan to caring for a dwarf pine in a pot and hoping it will grow up into the clouds. Cultivation is vital for trees and has an undeniable effect. If good quality fertilizer is applied and attention is paid to the levels of moisture and temperature, the pine will put out branches and leaves in profusion and their green luster will be enticingly beautiful. However, that beauty will not grow beyond the confines of the pot. One can never hope for it to tower high above us.[6] Admittedly, to rectify the sad state of women's utter ignorance, the use of school instruction and such means will not be in vain. A woman may become well versed in science or in book learning, even well informed in law. And such a woman may, in the classroom, vie with men very well. But when she returns home from school, what is the position she finds herself in?

At home, she owns no assets of her own, and in society she cannot hope for a position of any consequence. The house she lives in is a man's house and the children she brings up are her husband's children. Where would such a person, without funds, without authority of any sort, with no claim on the children she bears, and herself a parasite in a man's house, make use of the knowledge and learning she has acquired? Science and book learning will be of no use; worse still, her knowledge of law will actually be a liability, since society tends to regard any woman who discusses law or economics as asking for trouble.

Like machines, if discarded because they are not needed, knowledge and scholarship will rust away and fail to function when required. Therefore, when a woman who prides herself on her education marries into another family, she will come to resemble an ordinary wife, with nothing particular to attract one's attention any more. The knowledge acquired through education will be obliterated by the long hours spent in managing the household; at a stroke, the act of marriage will rob her education of all meaning. All the hard work expended at school will not even prove as effective as the care given the pine tree in the pot, because while the pine will preserve its lustrous green for years, the luster of school education cannot survive beyond the classroom.

On top of all this, the school education is influenced by Confucianism or Buddhism. Women are indoctrinated with the principles of womanly chastity and modesty through the constant drumming in of sayings such as "Women and small men are the most difficult to keep,"[7] or "To lack wisdom is virtue in a woman," or "The five obstacles and three obediences prove that women are sinful by birth."[8] The repercussions even harm the functioning of their ears, eyes, noses, and tongues. Yet some educators never realize the bad results of their methods. This only serves to hinder the healthy development of women's minds and bodies.

If this school education is so useless to our purpose, what are we to depend upon for developing more vigor in our women? I do not endorse every aspect of women's education in Western countries and have various objections apart from school matters, for example regarding relations between men and women. But any general examination of family life and social intercourse will reveal that women in the West do hold heavy responsibilities. There are women landholders and women household heads; even a married woman who stays at home may hold assets of her own without having to give control over to her husband. After all, power in human society is wealth; authority is engendered from wealth, and wealth is the springhead of authority. Therefore, it is not accidental that the women of the West, having wealth in many cases, also possess authority. If they have authority, they are free to dispose of their wealth; both within the home and in their dealings outside the home, they depend on no one but themselves.

Such customs, having been handed down from generation to generation, are now accepted by the general populace. Women are spared cruel treatment from the household head while at home, and if couples are able to preserve the essence of the marriage bond, there is nothing that the husband does that is forbidden to the wife. Women who excel in scholarship can make names for themselves; those with talent in worldly affairs may become renowned in their fields. The education they received in youth stays effective throughout their lives. Furthermore, in recent years, movements have appeared to campaign for women's participation in politics, and they are said to be gaining in strength day by day.

The responsibilities of Western women being heavy, their pains and pleasures, too, must be great. Under these circumstances, their minds and bodies develop naturally. My present wish is to let the women of Japan grow to be like the women of the West as the first step in their progress. We should not depend solely on what they learn in the schoolroom.

Installment Three

There is another factor that has greatly affected women in Japan, kept them constantly in gloom, made them over-sensitive, undermined their health, and finally made them as sickly as they are today. This is social oppression, which kept them from satisfying their sexual desires, confining them in hidebound customs. This problem is seen particularly among those of the middle levels of society and above. It is clearly noticeable, but since ancient times no scholar has discussed this problem. This is not because of a lack of awareness, but from reluctance to take up the topic since it encroaches on the embarrassing question of public morality. I, too, being a member of our society, wish to follow the social trend, but as a scholar, I cannot overlook something that I believe to be true. Moreover, as I announced at the start of this work, I intend to focus wholly on the improvement of our physique; that is, I have divided human life into two areas and will concentrate on the body only, leaving out the spiritual dimension. Therefore, I am not concerned with how public opinion will evaluate my efforts. If I can be sure that several hundred years after my death our women will be magnificent and the quality of our race will have improved, I will have no regrets.

Privately, I think that human life can be divided into three parts: the physical, the intellectual, and the emotional; together they make up a complete human being. Where there is life, there has to be nourishment to feed it. Physical life is nourished by food; intellectual life is nourished by mental discipline; emotional life is nourished by pleasure. It is easy to see that we should nourish the body with food, but the same stands for the need to nourish the intellect with mental training and the emotions with pleasure. Mental training is the food of the intellect, and pleasure the food of the emotions.

Food can be harmful when taken in excess, and when it is insufficient, starvation results. The phenomenon is the same in the case of intellectual and emotional nourishment. For instance, if you conscientiously exercise your mental powers, read books, study reason, and associate with good teachers and friends, or closely follow the trends in society and actually participate in them, your intellect will grow and become more powerful every day. This is because mental training nourishes the intellect. Yet when the process is carried out in excess, the mind will grow tired. The training will prove ineffective, and may even do such harm that finally one's mental power is totally undermined. It will be like overeating, which harms the stomach. The more one eats, the greater the harm, until finally the physique is totally destroyed. We can find proof in the scholar who works day and night, reading and studying, or the politician who gives his all to devise ways and means; finally their intellectual faculties are spent, and some become so unbalanced that they lose their sanity.

All this comes from lacking the intellect to regulate nourishment and from exceeding the limits of training. In contrast, if a mind that is accustomed to a certain degree of training suddenly gives up this daily schedule and neglects to function, it may become dull-witted and fatigued. This is due to the starvation of the intellect. Examples are scholars who give up their studies, politicians who leave the arena of politics, and active merchants or craftsmen who suddenly take retirement. I have evidence of men known for their brilliance in urban society who retired to the country. When they met up with their old associates a few years later, they were ridiculed for their slow-wittedness. This shows the debilitating effect of intellectual starvation.

The same is true of our emotions. Human beings are not made of wood or stone. The enjoyment derived from the beauties of nature, the joy bestowed by music and poetry, relaxation while smoking or chatting over tea, the delights of wine, love affairs and parties: all these are necessities of human life. When the emotions are nourished by these pleasures, human feelings find a balance, and the result is seen in our appearance and expressions. This is not only a source of happiness to the individual, but produces an air of geniality and grace that affects all those around.

The above are examples of proper nourishment for the emotions, but when someone overindulges in pleasure, the harm that results is exactly like that caused by overeating, leading to an emotional stupor. Nature-lovers who become mountain hermits, abandoning worldly pursuits, drunkards who fall unconscious, or couples who have fulfilled their sexual appetites to the extent that they weary of life and resort to double suicides: all these are problems caused by overindulgence in pleasure.

On the other hand, when some insurmountable circumstance prevents us from indulging in any of these pleasures, dejection accumulates and the suffering is even greater than the physical suffering that results from the lack of food. Some instances of this are profligates in cages, young ladies forced to lead the life of widows, men of wealth and position imprisoned for some reason and cut off from the enjoyment of nature, or habitual drinkers ordered to give up drink who become permanently sober. In all these cases, the resulting starvation of the emotions causes actual physical harm. Luster disappears from the victims' faces and vigor from their whole bodies. If the nervous system does not become oversensitive, they fall into a vacant stupor, just like those who have experienced excessive pleasure.

Even so, when one of the three aspects of human life is given more than enough nourishment it can lead to an overall balance, so that there is no ill effect even if other aspects are starved. Thus we have the sumo wrestler who receives physical and emotional nourishment, and experiences no discomfort as a result of neglecting intellectual food, and the scholar who forgets his body in his focus on knowledge but does not notice the lack of sustenance. Such men are lacking in one aspect, so that they favor two out of the three elements. As human life improves, such problems of uneven distribution will probably decrease. However, it seems likely that since the beginning of history, there have been more men partial to physical life than those inclined to the intellect. This is clear from the fact that Islam, which is based on sexual desire,[9] is still flourishing today, and from the prevalence of polygamy in Asian countries.

Similarly, even if we consider the functioning of the emotions, it can happen that when one of them is satisfied, no harm occurs if others are starved. For instance, gambling is basically an intellectual game, but we can temporarily class it with the emotions on the grounds that the purpose of the gambler is to gain money to buy other pleasures. If we then compare it with sex, the two appear to be of equal importance. Under the previous regime, sumo wrestlers and servants in daimyo households would increase their visits to prostitute districts if gambling was prohibited, while gambling would flourish in their common rooms if visits to prostitute districts were not allowed. The bosses of the common rooms usually reasoned that gambling was preferable to exposing the men to the diseases in the pleasure quarters. And thus it was customary for gambling to be publicly tolerated in those circles.

Supposing that all the arguments given above are true, I would like to ask whether among Japanese women, at any time, the three aspects of human life have been given equal opportunities to develop, whether the physique, the intellect, and the emotions have all been nourished properly, and none of them starved or overfed. Further, if their development has been uneven, which is most behind, and which most ahead? If the physical and the intellectual aspects are behind, leaving only the emotional aspect ahead, what kind of pleasures have been fed to it, and have these pleasures truly been enough to satisfy women's emotional needs? These matters must be urgently discussed.

Installment Four

Among the three aspects of human life — the physical, intellectual, and emotional — which is the most developed among Japanese women? The only possible answer to this question is "the emotional." The physique of women differs from that of men in its frailty. Some say this is a natural occurrence; others dispute this and claim that the difference evolved as a result of the customs of generation after generation. I shall ignore this issue for the present, but the frailty of Japanese women is clear. In addition, as was stated in the previous installment, it cannot be denied that the development of their intellects has also been slow because of the lack of opportunities for mental training. If the development of both the physique and the intellect is obstructed in this way, development will focus on the one remaining aspect, in other words, on the power of the emotions. But what opportunities are there for women to find emotional fulfillment?

If there is no doubt that pleasure is necessary for the nourishment of the emotions, what customs exist for nourishing the emotional life of women, and do they actually prevent emotional starvation? The only possible answer is to declare that the nourishment has been insufficient. From old times to this day, especially since the Tokugawa period, when both the government and religious ideology were used to establish a particular social order, it is clear that the pleasures apportioned to women of the middle class and above, rather than of the lower class, have been most pitifully meager. Only the most privileged of them have been able to give themselves up to the enjoyment of refined pastimes such as the contemplation of nature or the composition of poetry; those below them have been limited to the delights of music. In most cases, even this has been within the confines of the home, since neither outdoor activities nor the enjoyment of lively celebrations have been allowed. For those further below, the occasional visit to the theater, or the infrequent opportunity to have fun experimenting with clothes and hairstyles have been the highest sources of enjoyment. Lower still are women who have no freedom regarding clothing or anything beyond that. They have been ceaselessly occupied, serving their parents when young, their husbands and parents-in-law when married, and then caring for their children and supervising family affairs. Since women's emotions are particularly active, there is a possibility that depriving them of sufficient emotional sustenance will be harmful. In particular, I would like to make an issue of their lack of opportunities for sexual fulfillment and stress that to harm them in this particular way is most unfeeling.

Since ancient times, our country's laws have not forbidden polygamy. It is widely acknowledged that men of high rank and of wealth have supported many concubines, with the result that both the wife and the concubines have had to endure many lonely nights. For example, the feudal lord of a *han* would reside in Edo. When he returned to his own *han* every other year, he would take with him a few of his favorite concubines. His wife and all the rest of his concubines would be left behind in his Edo residence, guarding their empty bedrooms for the year of his absence.[10] But this practice was not confined to feudal lords. Retainers who were stationed at Edo, Osaka or some other important place, or made trips there on *han* business, were normally not allowed to take their families with them. Even among ordinary people, when men traveled on business, they practically never took their wives with them because travel was so inconvenient. In this way, a samurai would give priority to his public duties over his family, and a merchant would value profit and think little of separation from his wife. After that, hidden deep within their houses, wives and concubines could only spend their time in resentful contemplation of the lonely moon. Meanwhile, their menfolk did not skimp on visits to the pleasure quarters which they passed on their journeys. If news of these activities should waft homewards, this would simply add to the depressing atmosphere of the empty bedrooms.

There is an old saying about virtuous women not taking second husbands.[11] What is the meaning? My interpretation is that if a woman marries a man, she is honor-bound not to stray from the path of fidelity by having an affair with another man in violation of her marital vows. However, since ancient times, the general custom in our society has been that this saying forbids even the remarriage of a widow, and thus there is nobody who encourages widows to marry again. An elderly woman might be expected to endure widowed life. Yet if a beautiful girl loses her husband before she has reached the proper age of marriage and before fully experiencing sexual pleasure, even she will find that very few people close to her encourage a second marriage. On the other hand, if she herself declares that she will remain a widow for life, her relatives and people living near will unanimously express approval. The writings of Confucian scholars and the plots of novels and plays describe the "faithful wife" as being expected to bear extremes of emotional suffering that surpass the limits of human endurance.[12] But because they portrayed this terrible state as if the more the widow suffered, the greater was her honor, this eventually led to a general trend in society and even the women concerned have come to believe that this is how life should be. Having no means of voicing their frustration openly, they live melancholy lives with no outlet for their depression.

The contrast with the liberties that polygamy makes available to men is so great that the lives of men and women in Japan cannot be mentioned in the same breath. Men can sample pleasure wherever they go. At home, meanwhile, if a man is unlucky enough to lose his wife, he loses no time in taking a second, or even a third, one. Most shocking is when a man's close friends start negotiations for his next wife on the way home from the funeral of the previous one. In other words, a man of sixty or even seventy who gains a new bride feels no cause for shame. Women are to be pitied for their fate.

Some people may oppose my opinion on the grounds that nothing in our laws or our people's customs forbids the remarriage of a widow, and that it is clear that they are free to marry again, since some do so twice or even three times. However, I do not require many words to answer their doubts. All I need to do is ask them to compare the number of people among their friends and acquaintances who have brothers or sisters with different fathers or different mothers. Naturally, there are many brothers and sisters who share both parents, but there are also quite a number who do not. Some are sons of the former wife and some are daughters of a second or even third wife; some are children of one concubine, others of another concubine. It is not unusual to come across all sorts of variations. Yet brothers and sisters with the same mother but a different father are very rare.

Since there are no statistics to consult, it is difficult to make a firm assertion, but as a rough estimate, I think I would not be wrong in saying that the ratio of one mother and different fathers to one father and different mothers is around one to a hundred. Apparently, when the same ratio is measured in Western countries, the numbers are roughly even, and in some areas children with the same mother and different fathers are in the majority. And so, at a later date, when the relevant statistics for Japan have been compiled and my conjecture is discovered to be not far from the truth, it will be proved that Japanese women possess only one-hundredth of the freedom in marriage enjoyed by Japanese men. Since that is the shocking state of affairs, women in Japan are indeed to be pitied for their fate.

Installment Five

The physical harm caused by insufficient food is similar to the harm done by overeating. Pleasure is food for the emotions, yet the women of Japan are starving for this food. Unable to obtain satisfaction, most of them live lives of withered promise. The women of the middle and upper levels of society, in particular, face extreme torment since they are the least able to nourish their sexual desires. Trapped in the depths of melancholy, they are troubled by overwrought nervous systems and weakened constitutions. These tendencies have been passed down to their children and so to their children's children, resulting in their present situation: liable to express fear or the whole range of the emotions at the slightest disturbance; unable to withstand the least amount of hardship or physical discomfort. Even those said to be healthy give one the impression of being ill, anxious, fearful or sad.

Those who become ill suffer from a truly infinite variety of ailments, but to mention a few examples, headaches and the female afflictions that are colloquially known as "nerves" or "the gripes" are in fact illnesses such as nervous diseases, uterine disorders or **hysterie**.[13] They cause symptoms such as melancholia, a sense of isolation, anxiety, insomnia, irregular menstruation, and indigestion. Sometimes there are attacks of dizziness or sharp pain; the whole body gradually becomes devitalized, but no medicine is effective. Many patients endure long periods of absolute misery, half alive, half dead, until they finally succumb.

It is normal to entrust doctors with the treatment of an illness, but of course there is no hope that they will come up with the right idea. On rare occasions an experienced doctor might discover the cause of the illness by himself, and observation aimed purely at curing the disease should make it easy to exclude other possibilities. However, since social oppression does not allow the measures that are necessary to cure the disease, the most broad-minded doctor will be unable even to announce that the patient's disease is caused by sexual frustration. Therefore, he advises all sorts of treatments, such as a change of residence or a new form of entertainment or recreation, with the short-term object of affording temporary relief from the symptoms, and with the longer-term hope that this might transform the patient's mood. But there is only a small likelihood of success as they are all measures chosen in the absence of any viable alternative and the actual physiology of a patient cannot be deceived. The only hope is that the patient will not die half-way through, but will follow the natural aging process until she reaches frigidity and at long last her nerves settle down and the gripe attacks and headaches vanish.

If this sort of woman happens to become pregnant, it is absolutely obvious that there will be something wrong with the child. For proof, we have only to look back at the descendants of the lords of feudal times. The many concubines who were kept by these lords were not necessarily delicate from birth. However, nothing about their service in the inner quarters of the household could make them feel cheerful or lighthearted for they worried even if they were in favor with the master, and yet more if they were out of favor. They were prisoners in a hell that looked like paradise on the surface, covered in gold, jewels and brocade, their masters' favors as fickle as the weather. It was therefore clear from the outset that any child born in such an atmosphere would have both physical and mental problems. It is also said that if a woman remarries and has a child after a long widowhood accompanied by a degree of physical and mental deterioration, the child will in many cases turn out to be delicate. Seen from this angle, although people often point to the harm caused by early marriage, the harmful consequences of late marriage show that there is probably little to choose between them.

The cases cited above are just conspicuous examples, but neither the wives and concubines of feudal lords, nor widows who make late second marriages, are necessarily the only ones to be affected. We can only lament the fact that generally speaking women throughout Japan are plagued by similar miseries. Since their anxieties are passed on and therefore affect later generations, the result is that our racial development is being progressively impeded. From the beginning, doctors should have treated such matters as a health issue, but the principles of traditional medicine naturally tend to be identified with the moral teachings of Confucianism. Confucianism considers that rather than wishing for riches and spending heavily, we should wish for nothing and spend not at all. Accordingly, these doctors will not expound the need to increase stamina by taking in nourishment; instead they reveal the harm this might cause. They will only give instructions about restricting one's intake of food and drink, counseling light meals devoid of strong seasoning; those who do not follow this advice are accused of neglecting their health. Therefore, in the same way, when it comes to human emotions, far from mentioning that these can be nourished through pleasure, they talk as if it is our duty to renounce them. In particular, it does not occur to them that there is a need to find some way of soothing sexual desire. Just as they advise restrictions on food and drink, they believe that there is no reason why sexual desire should not be restricted, reduced, or even completely denied; their only concern is to warn against over-indulgence. Such a warning may be appropriate at times in the case of Japanese men, but to pay exclusive attention to men's overindulgence while ignoring women's lack of satisfaction reveals great medical negligence and a glaring betrayal of the basics of health care.

However, we should not be too surprised at the attitude of traditional medicine; after all, since the cause lies in ignorance, we cannot really condemn it. But I am unhappy that Western medicine, which claims to be pure scholarship and bases itself on the principles of truth, also neglects this issue. Or perhaps it is not neglect; it may be that even medicine based on truth is subject to control by social oppression, as was suggested in the previous section. Western medical books go into the type and quantity of food that is necessary to maintain physical health with great care and attention to detail. Yet the vital role of pleasure in nourishing the emotions is not addressed with the concern given to the familiar topic of foodstuffs. In particular, when it comes to women's sexual feelings, there is virtually no explanation of how these are related to the cause of ailments, to their treatment, or to general health issues. The few occasional references are warnings against over-indulgence in the soothing of sexual feelings, a tendency that is identical to the advice in favor of restraint voiced by traditional Japanese and Chinese medicine. To medical science it is obvious that physical harm is caused both by eating too much and eating too little, and the need to nourish not only the body but also the intellect is emphasized. Only in the case of food for the emotions is overindulgence criticized without equal concern for the harm caused by deprivation. What reason can there be? The concern for one and the neglect of the other are caused by nothing other than social oppression as a whole.

As I mentioned earlier, I, too, am a member of society and have no wish to become the target of public censure, but if I do not speak out, there is no knowing what might happen. Since I am luckily not a doctor myself, I will play the part of a loyal bystander and state what medicine dare not say. My only wish is to play even a minute part in the development of women. Readers are sure to have understood from the contents of this installment that my references to "pleasures" as nourishing women's feelings included all types of pleasure and, in particular, that they were not confined to the pleasures of sexual feeling. My reason for touching specifically on this issue was just that, since ancient times, it has been customary for society to recognize recreational activities such as instrumental music, singing and dancing as suitable for women but to maintain a deliberate silence with regard to other activities that are of comparatively much greater importance. Once again, my greatest desire is that readers will not mistake my intention.

Installment Six

In Western countries, the human body has grown taller, larger, and stronger compared with former times. For instance, suits of armor which were the right size for men of the past are too small for the men of today. By contrast, since the armaments used by the Japanese in the past all seem too large for us today, this suggests that we have become shorter, smaller, and weaker. It is likely that there is more than one reason for the gradual weakening and ultimate physical collapse of the families of the middle class and above during the over two and a half centuries of Tokugawa rule, and experts have advanced many theories. Of course, I do not disagree with them, but we must include as one very important item among the possible causes something which none of these thinkers has yet mentioned — whether or not women are free to indulge in pleasure.

Examination of the standards of living in societies from ancient times up until today makes it clear that the passage of time has brought improvements. People today enjoy better clothing and better food than previously, and their dwellings, too, are more adapted to human needs. In other words, basic living conditions have become less restricted as mankind has moved towards the present. Yet, when we look back at women's pleasures, it seems as if a gradual decrease has occurred in inverse proportion to the gradual increase in social order. Long ago, in uncivilized times, women in most courtier and samurai families learnt to read, understood poetry, played by moonlight, and amused themselves under the blossoms. There was scarcely any difference from men in their freedom to interact with society as they pleased.[14] Since interaction was free, it was natural for the feelings of men and women to be free as well, and there was no escaping frequent accusations of lewd behavior.

Some later scholars have been shocked by the extraordinary state of affairs in those days as a result of reading the love poems of the time,[15] but this is just disquiet caused by focusing only on the negative aspects. Detailed examination of the actual situation shows that women were able to maintain a vigorous disposition amongst all the lewdness. If we compare them with the delicate ladies of later periods, confined to the deep recesses of their dwelling places, we must admit that this state of affairs was an important merit of the time, on the grounds that it made the women both physically and mentally robust. Further, since men were also implicated in the lewdness, we cannot put the blame on women alone. We should not view this in the same light as the later behavior of men, when they looked down on women and made indulgence in lewdness a matter for themselves alone.

Even when the age of direct Imperial rule passed into the age of samurai rule, women's freedom was not violated, as it was in later times. Because it was a brutal and illiterate age, women must have experienced cruel treatment at times. But since this was just cruelty involving physical force and there was little that involved mental suffering, we can regard it as a clumsy way of restraining them. Women in those days were regarded as instruments, and it was clear that they would never be able to gain positions of honor in society, but while they were nothing more than instruments, they had a full allowance of freedom since they were not forbidden to mix with other people, or criticized for going outside. At times, wives and concubines would follow their menfolk to the battlefields, and some would even fight on horseback, or hole up in a castle in order to defend it. Active and unlettered, they normally had many opportunities for pleasure.

With regard to matters such as marriage, in particular, they were free to act as they pleased, and were never blocked by the [Confucian] teachings about moral duty of later years. Of course, there was no criticism if a woman remarried; moreover, even marriage to a former enemy seems to have caused no concern. It is said that [after his death,] Kiso Yoshinaka's [1154–1184] favorite concubine, Tomoe Gozen, married Wada Yoshimori [one of Kiso's enemies] and gave birth to Asahina. Oda Nobunaga's [1534–1582] sister married Asai Nagamasa and had three daughters. After Nagamasa was defeated by Nobunaga, she took her three daughters and became the wife of Shibata Katsuie. [Nobunaga's former retainer] Toyotomi Hideyoshi [1536–1598] killed Katsuie and took one of the daughters as a concubine. Takeda Shingen [1521–1573] defeated Suwa Yorishige, took his daughter as his wife and begot Katsuyori. In other words, the most bitter enemies would become allies and marry. Moreover, in order (so he said) to gain the support of Tokugawa Ieyasu [1543–1616], Hideyoshi seized his own sister [Asahihime], who was wife to a man named Saji, and presented her to Ieyasu in marriage. Saji killed himself in shame, but his former wife was only too pleased to become the lady of the House of the Tokugawa.[16] In later times, there have been those who criticized her. However, there have been many examples of men deliberately driving away one wife in order to take a second, and of the former wife becoming so full of angry resentment that she became ill or committed suicide. Surely, Hideyoshi's sister acted in just the same way by driving off Saji and marrying Ieyasu as a second husband. While neither type of action can be praised from an ethical point of view why should Ieyasu's wife, who lived several hundreds of years ago, always be the only one to get the blame? If she is to be blamed, there are a considerable number of men alive today who cannot be excused either.

My personal opinion is that the lack of freedom that cramps women's behavior dates from the Tokugawa period. After the defeat of the last opponents of the Tokugawa in 1615, Confucianism became a dominant influence, in conjunction with the gradual emergence of a settled order. Zealous attention was paid to its teachings about propriety. As well as clarifying the differences between high and low or noble and mean, restrictions were placed on the position of women; they were the main target of admonitions about correcting personal morality and exercising discretion in one's private life. Rough treatment such as violent abuse gradually stopped and women obtained freedom in terms of basic living conditions, but no attention at all was given to the issue of pleasure. On the surface, they wanted for nothing, yet underneath, their emotions were stifled; in the words of the saying, they were being smothered in cotton wool. The suffering was worse than that caused by violent abuse, with the result that their physique was harmed and they ended up as delicate as they are today.

The empty glitter of the teachings about moral duty has lasted for so many decades and centuries that the layers of emptiness have acquired substance. Therefore, any woman whose behavior fails to conform in every respect is immediately regarded with hatred and loathing. But in fact, this is the response of people who have forgotten the freedom enjoyed by women in ancient times, and who are therefore ignorant as to the real nature of our society.

When considering the reputation of Tokiwa Gozen [1138–c.1180], people assume that she felt anguish when her chastity was violated through her decision to serve Taira no Kiyomori, and therefore many sympathize greatly with her feelings.[17] However, I doubt whether this was really so. There was nothing particularly shameful about her action according to the standards of her day; the shame only existed in the eyes of Tokugawa teachers of moral duty, who inferred that being intimate with Kiyomori would cause her distress. In fact, she probably found it easy to behave in this way, thinking that there was nothing strange about it, but rather accepting the new relationship as perfectly normal, and being happy to save the lives of her darling children.

Thus, we must admit the clear truth that while in ancient times women enjoyed great freedom in pursuing pleasure, in more recent times they have had very little. However, as far as methods of obtaining pleasure are concerned, of course I do not long for the ancient times; I certainly do not expect women today to study the unrefined customs of many hundred years ago. But pleasures suited to those unrefined times naturally aided physical and mental development, and the effect was immediately passed on to the children and to their children's children. As a result, the Japanese people at that time were active and robust to an extent that we can only envy. If educated people are going to claim that the moral order of our society today is superior to that of ancient times, they must find some way of giving women a degree of freedom that is appropriate to the degree of superiority. As the moral order improves, what reason can there be for men to harm women by keeping freedom for themselves alone, despite the fact that in ancient times both of them were free? In the end, we must place the blame for this situation on the empty glitter of Tokugawa teachings about moral duty.

Installment Seven
In the installments that have been written so far under the title "On Japanese Women," I have laid out the following situation: Since women in Japan have neither responsibilities nor pleasures, we cannot expect them to develop strong bodies or minds, and if the mother's body lacks strength, the child's body will not be strong either. Therefore, as a result of the bad customs of the past few hundred years, our bodies have become so small and weak that they are inferior to those of our forebears, even though in ancient times basic living standards were more restricted. In other words, the prospects for our future development should be causing us rising anxiety.

I shall now examine how we can cut off these dangerous customs at the source, and therefore make women more active and robust in both body and mind. Of course, since the terrible state into which we have fallen is entirely the result of human, not natural, causes, the cure must also lie entirely in human hands. Moreover, because the roots reach down so far that they are at the very depths of our consciousness, it is essential to introduce major reforms and rebuild right up from the foundations. Major reforms of human affairs are often harder to carry out in practice than they are to picture in the mind or put into speech. Yet even though we are aware of the difficulty of carrying out reforms in the present situation, nothing will ever happen unless we first make the decision to open people's minds.

Our situation can be compared to that of a priest who draws a diagram as the first step in his plans for the construction of a great temple. It is absolutely clear that anything like the construction of a temple is way beyond the power of one priest to accomplish, and that the state of society is such that even if he asks for help he has no prospect of easy success. However, there are many cases where, sustained by his belief that the temple was required by Buddhism, a priest has ignored the immediate practical issue of feasibility in his determination just to complete the plan, whereupon it has finally been brought to completion by a later generation. If my efforts to cure the terrible state of our country's women today end only in a diagram, it is likely that I will invite both the dislike of thinkers of the old school and mockery of my daydreams from those who style themselves practical men. Yet I cannot suppress these little ideas of mine; all I can do is write down my daydreams and rely on a later generation.

In Japan, from ancient times, the custom has been to value the lineage of a family with a degree of fervor that is beyond comparison. This ancient preoccupation has led to the spread of the practice of adoption. As a result, most childless couples use the method of adopting sons and daughters in order to preserve the empty name of the family, even though the bloodline itself is going to die out. More outrageous is the fact that when such a family does die out, leaving no blood descendants, it is still counted as one family in the household register,[18] even if it is so poor that there is no property, not even a dwelling place, in other words nothing other than an (empty) family name. People that are not descendants are called descendants; households that do not exist are registered as households. This custom is so rarely seen in human societies that it has always bewildered experts and I have also long been aware of the problems that it causes. At this point, in order to reform the present situation and at the same time even introduce improvements, if I were to express my wishes freely, they would simply be as follows:

The foundation of the human family is the husband and the wife, since if you have a husband and wife this leads to parents and children, and if you have a husband and wife who are parents of children, the result is one family. However, if the child of a family grows up and marries, a fresh family should be established. Moreover, this fresh family should not be linked to the parents' families. This is because one half of the fresh family comes from one set of parents and the other half from another set of parents; that is, the offspring of two families have come together to create the fresh family. Seen in this light, when tracing the bloodline in order to name descendants, it goes against reason to mention the paternal side and ignore the maternal side. Moreover, if it is irrefutable in terms of mathematical logic that a fresh marriage produces a fresh family, it goes without saying that for the fresh family name, or surname, they should not choose only that of the male side, or take only that of the female side, but find a middle path by creating a fresh surname.[19]

For instance, as one way to show what I mean, an obvious solution would be that if a woman named Hake*yama* and a man named Kaji*hara* got married, they could form a fresh family named Yamahara; then if a *Yama*hara son married a woman named Itō, their name would be Yamatō. This would mean that a woman would not have to marry into the husband's family, and neither would a man become the son-in-law of the wife's family; being a true marriage of choice, the rights on both sides would be equal. Perhaps someone might object that if a couple meet with a misfortune and there is a second, or even third, marriage as a result of divorce or death, changing the family name each time will cause too many complications. In such a case, the couple could use their respective parents' family names and be addressed by an amalgamated family name when together. In other words, children would keep their parents' family name throughout their lives and changing the name of their own family every time they married would not cause any inconvenience.

If marriage rights are going to be equal, we must demand a law for insuring equal rights to assets as well. As human cultures advance, it is normal for wealth to lead to the emergence of various social rights. But even though it is an undeniable fact that sources of wealth are nothing other than a right, from ancient times until the present, women in Japan have possessed no personal property, and have lived exactly like parasites in men's households. To lack property is to lack responsibility. Since a lack of responsibility means the absence of any means of intellectual training, the hope that we can just wait for women to develop is clearly an empty one. After all, since it is man-made customs carried out over several thousand centuries that have brought them to their present state, to correct the situation now, man-made devices are needed that will lead them in absolutely the opposite direction. For instance, if it is going to be difficult for women to engage in wealth promotion at the moment because of their present state of physical and mental frailty, one method would be to arrange for all land and buildings to go to the female offspring when a parental estate is passed on to the children. Ownership of such assets would only be recognized if the signature was a woman's, and the signatures on public loan certificates could also be limited to those of women. Of course, even if we do this, men have such freedom of action in our society that there is a danger that women will be threatened into delegating their ownership, with the result that their possessions will be given up to men's arbitrary control. In practice, however, while there will be many cases like this, there will also be not a few that are different.

Since the Meiji Restoration and the abolition of the four [Tokugawa] status divisions, farmers and merchants have been exposed to the way of equality;[20] however, many of them are still unable to break free from the old ways, so that they reveal themselves to be subservient at heart. Even so, it must be acknowledged that, as an overall social group, commoners today have come to occupy a position of great importance. Therefore, even if women are given the sole right to ownership of land and property, there may be some who will withdraw of their own accord and not exercise this right; however, there is no doubt that the overall position of women will rise to a great height as a result.

The above proposals are the product of my imagination and I have never thought that they would be realized today; rather, I expect that they will give society a shock. However, even if they are the product of my imagination, there can be no easy way to destroy the logic of my argument; it will not be possible to do more than simply reject my proposals on the grounds that they do not fit the habits of this particular moment. At least, this is, again, my expectation. In fact, it is only time that determines whether or not a society adopts the logical course. Therefore, if something is of benefit to society and does not go against reason, there is no doubt that it will soon be put into practice. Accordingly, my wish is for the educated people in our society first to show agreement with my humble ideas, regardless of whether or not they will be easy to put into effect, and then try to apply just those aspects that have practical potential.

For instance, when taking a wife or giving a daughter in marriage, they should establish appropriate agreements, or if a child is born, they should pay minute attention to the distribution of personal assets. They should practice this themselves, and encourage others to follow suit. In addition, with regard to government-level matters such as the formation of the Civil Code,[21] my earnest desire is that moves should be made to deal with issues such as the inheritance and distribution of residential assets, the authority over ownership of the marital home, and the regulations governing marriage and divorce. As long as no great obstacles appear to disturb the present situation, we should set ourselves a target of one hundred years and progress, however slowly, towards the accomplishment of this goal.

In the various countries of the West, the laws and other arrangements concerning divorce are rigorous in the extreme, and therefore their civil codes will not permit instant separation. Not only is it impossible to reject a wife without sufficient reason; even if there is a situation that makes divorce virtually unavoidable, practice dictates that the first move after an application has been made should be to order a temporary separation. A notice of divorce will only be issued after a trial period of one to two years has proved that there is no possibility of reconciliation. Moreover, since both partners enjoy the same rights to divorce, a wife can publicly file for separation on the following grounds: first, if a dissolute and unfaithful husband has relations with another woman, for example, setting her up at home or in a separate hideout, and second, even when things do not go so far, if he behaves so heartlessly that it is equivalent to desertion, even though the wife is left under the same roof.

Of course, the countries do not all have identical laws, since although they share the same basic principles they differ in the details, as an examination of their law books will show. However, it is clear beyond doubt that both marriage partners have nothing other than equal rights.[22] How astonished the women of those countries would be to hear that according to Japanese practice, the right to divorce is held solely by the husband, and that the flimsy three and a half lines of a *mikudarihan* are enough to make an instant slice through a relationship that was meant to last into old age.[23] They would probably find this hard to believe even though it is the custom of a strange Oriental country.[24]

On the other hand, although laws in the various countries of the West are as strict as we have described, because affairs related to the true feelings of men and women belong to the most private inner realm of our lives, they cannot be completely subjected to law. Beneath the extremely rigorous legal provisions there lies an extremely generous freedom of application, and the practice of the law often presents unexpected results. It is essential for scholars who seek to evaluate Western law books to keep this in mind as they read. After all, if we temporarily leave aside the issue of whether a particular behavior is right or wrong, the fact that men and women have equal rights is not affected in any way by who is in the right and who is in the wrong. In fact, the basis of equal rights lies in custom, and when written laws are produced, this is just a way of reinforcing the power of custom.[25]

Installment Eight
If we reach the point where women regain their rights in marriage, rendering them equal to men, and further gain secure rights to ownership of their homes, so that they are no longer dependent on other people, the weight of their responsibilities will become many times greater than today, and their worries will also grow. However, this increase in worries will cause an equivalent increase in pleasures. If the result is an increase in their pleasures as well as their pains, there is no doubt that women will be more active in both mind and body. For example, if a housewife is in charge of her own property, she will either enjoy the satisfaction that results from prosperity and success, or incur the shame that results from impoverishment and failure. This will be a grave undertaking, but how much more enjoyable than the precarious existence of a lodger in the house that belongs to her husband, bejeweled in luxury one day and destitute the next? Moreover, if only women's rights could be restored, relations between married couples would naturally become much closer.

Up till now, even when a marriage has been happy, with the husband loving the youthful beauty of his wife, she has been abandoned without a second thought when her allure has lost its freshness. But it is not only women who lose their allure; this happens to men as well. Therefore, if men abandon the ladies who share their beds when they lose their allure, women should discard men when they lose theirs. Put this way, a marital relationship that lasts into old age seems unappealing, but close relations between men and women should not be maintained through affection alone; their love will only be fulfilled if an element of mutual respect is added to the affection. In our society, if a man uses money to obtain a concubine and later makes her his lawful wife, it very often happens that they cannot forget the time when she was a plaything, so that mutual respect does not develop and finally their love is destroyed. However, as long as a wife possesses the right to abandon her husband if the situation requires this, it is not necessary for her actually to do so. Since men have always had the right to divorce, this will mean that, both having the same rights, their feelings of affection will be mediated by their mutual respect and grow stronger.

Of course, it is not only in Japan that women are looked down on; it is an evil practice throughout the various countries of the East. In neighboring countries such as China and Korea in particular, women in families belonging to the middle and upper classes are confined within their homes and rarely allowed out. This cruelty is even worse than the treatment of Japanese women, and if we go behind the scenes and search for the innermost secrets, some aspects are beyond our imagination. For example, the number of widows in Korea is so great that any comparison with Japan is meaningless. The reason is that among good families in Korea, such as those of official rank, if the man to whom a woman has been betrothed dies, it is the custom for her to be counted as a widow and forbidden to remarry, even if the death precedes the actual wedding ceremony. In extreme cases, a girl might spend her whole life as a widow from around the time she was ten-years old.

This account makes the custom seem inhuman and calls forth our pity, but in actual fact it is not as inhuman as it seems. When willows in the street below dance in the spring breeze and even the young widow at her secluded window feels the quickening of the dead ashes of her heart, there are those on the sidelines who quietly sense the rising warmth and offer to find an outlet for these natural feelings. They are called "go-betweens." In Korea go-betweens do so well that they could virtually be said to be following a sort of profession, and no man or woman who calls for their services is ever left unsatisfied. Not only young widows but old wives who have lost their allure and are no longer attractive to their husbands, wives and concubines who have failed to win the contest for a bed-partner, heads of households who have been away for a long time and can no longer bear the lonely nights — since all are customers of the go-between, there is much clandestine toing and froing. However, convenient though this service is, the money that pays for it goes only to the go-between, so that neither the man nor the woman involved make any profit. Moreover, since neither side is able to specify who the partner is, it sometimes happens that the go-between makes a mistake, leading to indescribably embarrassing encounters and bizarre tales of how both parties beat blushing retreats.[26]

The above is just one item about Korea, but it will suffice to show the actual situation within that country. In fact, in almost all countries, while it generally looks from the outside as if they have strict teachings about moral duty, in practice it is extremely difficult to exercise control over the private aspects of people's lives. The text of a moral teaching is like the asking price of something that is on sale. The doctrine itself may be strict indeed, but those who are taught it may listen to half of it and carry out only half of that. This situation allows them to adapt the teaching to the state of society and enjoy the pleasures of life, just as someone buying a product might beat the asking price down to a half, and then down by another half, before actually finally agreeing to purchase. Because Korea is the sort of country where the asking price for Confucianism is extremely high, the people who listen to its doctrines beat the initial price down until it is extremely low; thus, the state of affairs described above actually exists.

On the other hand, in Japan during the Tokugawa period, when teachings about principles were clarified and social order became settled, doctrines concerning women were not as harsh as the empty [Confucian] teachings of neighboring lands, but the families of the middle and upper levels of society undertook to follow them to the letter, without allowing any leeway at all. It was just the same as agreeing to purchase a moral doctrine at the exact asking price. Therefore, since we hear that women in China or Korea are confined behind secluded windows, it may seem that women in Japan have much more freedom to indulge in pleasure. But in fact, it is the difference between haggling over a high asking price, and accepting a cheap asking price as it stands. It is likely that haggling a great reduction in the asking price will actually result in many times more freedom to spend as one wants.

The ideas that I have developed above should not be interpreted as an argument for Japanese women to adopt the lewd behavior of their counterparts in China and Korea. Moreover, while I deeply esteem the vigorous and unrestrained behavior of Western women, this is sometimes associated with chronic infections of willfulness and egotism. I do not wish to introduce anything that will raise the likelihood of such serious infections. In the various countries of the West, women are not trained in the ways of female virtue: they frequently make light of men; they are highly strung, both in body and mind, and their private lives are tarnished; uninterested in their household duties, they become dizzy social butterflies. Such behavior is no model for Japanese women.

To encourage women to behave without restraint owing to a dislike of men's lack of restraint is to counter violence with violence; if the confrontation is extended and ends in victory for women, we will merely have replaced one brand of violence with another.

There should be no need to offer further explanation, as my readers must have already discerned my humble opinion. To sum up, my intention is not to demand great sacrifices of men, nor to secure special benefits for women, but simply to achieve equality between them. That the freedom and pleasures of this world should be held in common by both men and women is a concept that is beyond dispute. Further, if something that is in limited supply is held in common by two parties, it is similarly beyond dispute that any attempt by one to own everything will lead to a reduction in the share of the other. If we were to ask about the situation regarding freedom and pleasure in Japan today, the answer would have to be that the balance lies in favour of men. As an illustration, let us examine the trends and customs of our society. There is practically nothing that women can do but men cannot, although there are countless things that are allowed to men but forbidden to women. Not only are they forbidden the right to possess property, as was discussed previously; in the case of every single action, even at the most trivial, everyday level, what is censured as immodest in women is praised as broad-minded in men; what is unsightly in women is not unsightly in men. In particular, we ignore the one element that is of the utmost importance among all the pleasures in nourishing the emotions. In other words, a man may taste the delights of women wherever he goes and single-mindedly indulge himself in drinking establishments and the pleasure quarters, while a woman must while away her youth shut away at the back of the house and has the right to remarry stolen from her before she even realizes it. There is no way in which any of this can be counted as equal treatment in human affairs.

Therefore, my aim is not to attempt to secure special benefits for women; my strong desire is merely to prevent one party from keeping all the pleasures that we should hold in common, so that both parties can enjoy and share them together. For instance, if men enjoy ninety-nine percent of the freedom to remarry while women have only one percent, all I want is for the men to return forty-nine percent and make the shares exactly even. Again, the basic purpose of my argument is not to plead on women's behalf so that they can fight with men over the possession of rights. My purpose is the improvement of the Japanese race. Since there is no point in relying on the women of today to produce a better quality of descendant, my overall idea is first to make them more active in mind and body and to this end, provide them with heavier responsibilities and greater pleasure.

If we disregard the mind, we are physically just a kind of animal. Imagine that the owner of a pair of dogs leaves the male free to run about and play to its heart's content while the female dog is chained within a kennel, given sufficient food but not allowed the relaxing company of other dogs, unable to play around in the green fields or to romp about on the snow. Worse still, even when she is in season, she is restrained and allowed no freedom. The result is an irritable temperament and deteriorating health, so that if she later chances to become pregnant, it is clear even to those like me who do not know how to look after dogs, that there will be something wrong with the puppies. If this is the case with a dog, why should it be any different with a human being? If those experts who are independent from the government cannot refute this story of a pet dog, they should immediately devote themselves to removing the chains from the women of Japan.

On Japanese Women, Part Two

EDITOR'S INTRODUCTION

This appeared in ten installments in *Jiji shinpō* over the period 7–17 July 1885, immediately after "On Japanese Women." The installments were published in one volume, with the addition of the preface, in the following month. Fukuzawa expressed his satisfaction about the response to both texts in a letter to his son Ichitarō dated 2 October 1885 (No. 15, translated on pp. 327–329).

Fukuzawa's explanation for publishing *Part Two* was that the style of "On Japanese Women" itself may have been too formal, particularly for easy discussion of the ideas in colloquial Japanese. This time he had therefore deliberately chosen to write more informally. *Part Two* is not, however, a simplified repeat of "On Japanese Women," and Fukuzawa himself states that he has not written about the negative results of having no personal responsibility in *Part Two* because it was covered in the previous part. *Part Two* contains more about the nature of marital relationships and the need to treat wives as equal partners. Fukuzawa also takes up Mill's point that the emancipation of women would make society as a whole more efficient when he talks about the effect that they should be able to have as half of the country's population.

On the other hand, *Part Two* is certainly written in a more colloquial style and with ingenious and entertaining analogies and anecdotes. An example of the former is the family tree in which husbands and wives are listed as different metals and their offspring as combinations of these metals. This is used to prove that the mother is more than a "borrowed womb," and that descent is not passed down through the male line alone. An example of the latter is the poignant description of a lonely wife as she waits for her husband, who is finally escorted home in a drunken state by the night watchman.

In the first three installments, Fukuzawa demonstrates the power of custom (*fūzoku*) to prevent people, even victims, from becoming aware of injustice and the need to change. The only difference between men and women lies in their reproductive organs, and yet the Confucian worldview, symbolized by *The Great Learning for Women* and including the yin/yang dichotomy, has been manipulated by the former in order to justify their dominance over the latter. In Installments Four to Seven he emphasizes the unhappiness of women and the generally negative effects of the present situation. The next two installments contain advice about how women can assume an active role within the home and in society as a whole with the support of men. In the final installment he responds humorously to an imagined rebuttal of his views.

On Japanese Women, Part Two[1]

Preface

The ten installments of "On Japanese Women, Part Two" that were recently published as editorials of *Jiji shinpō* received a warm reception. Not a few ladies and gentlemen sent us articles in a similar vein. Then about seven days ago, we were highly amused when a certain gentleman visited our offices in order, as he said, to express his displeasure with the series. He had been reading each long installment, highly satisfied with the arguments and style, but then disaster struck. Apparently, his wife had made repeated requests for new summer kimono in this summer's color, dark blue. He had mounted a steady defense on the grounds that summer clothes should be white, and that the very idea of dark blue was ridiculous. Unfortunately, the serialization of "On Japanese Women" had overturned the battle stations and the previous evening his wife had won the argument. As he left the house that morning, employees from Echigoya[2] were delivering the material that his wife had ordered. His mortification knew no bounds.

Whether those who read it respond favorably or unfavorably, we hope that this volume will attract the attention of many people and we wish to know the public response. That is why we have brought the ten installments together as one volume and made it available to both male and female readers.
Nakamigawa Hikojirō,[3] 24 July 1885, *Jiji shinpō*

Installment One
We have been publishing a series of editorials under the title "On Japanese Women" in *Jiji shinpō* for the past few days. We trust that many people have read them. But we fear that the style used was a little too formal and that though our readers might have followed it without difficulty, it may have caused problems

when they wanted to talk about it. Therefore, this second part is being presented in an informal style, with *hiragana* [Japanese syllabary] added to Chinese characters. As this new piece is an attempt to explain the same subject in an alternative way, there may be some overlapping with the first part. We hope that you will forgive this as resulting from the writer's lack of talent and inability to write well.

In the first part, I stated that society should afford women both the same rank as men, and the same rights, including property ownership. My arguments were logical and convincing and should not have been viewed with suspicion. However, for many hundreds of years it has been acceptable for men in this country to act according to their own desires, without paying any consideration to women. However perfect my logic, men will not readily concur, and even though women would benefit directly from my proposals, there may be some who do not welcome the new ideas. In their sorry state these women resemble the pet nightingale reared in captivity that does not care to fly out of its cage, or the domesticated horse that, of its own choice, comes back to its stall. Even if the birdcage and the stall are miserably confining, the nightingale knows only bird feed and the horse is accustomed to the taste of fodder. Unaware that they are born to sing amid the blossoms or gallop through the fields, they do not grasp the true misery of their position.

"Know thyself." This is an old saying in the West, meaning that it is vital for people to understand their circumstances in life. For instance, for women, it is very important to realize their position in life in relation to men. The only real difference between men and women lies in their reproductive organs. Even in this respect, the difference is only in their structure and function; it is not a question of one being more important than the other. As for the other parts of the body — ears, eyes, nose, mouth, arms, the functions of the limbs, the proportions of the internal organs, the number of bones and the circulation of the blood — every minor detail of the body is exactly the same in both men and women. The workings of the mind are also the same. There is nothing in men's activities that women cannot do. As civilization advances, it is not unusual for women to take up employment. In America, for example, there are women working as telegraph operators and in similar skilled positions. Some women become medical doctors and there are many women who are secretaries in commercial companies or even government officials. And it is said that in certain types of work, women are more efficient than men.[4]

In Japan, the difference is just that women have not yet been given the chance to try. Or is it that there is no use in trying because our women are incapable? If that is the case, I must declare that Japanese women were not born incapable; there is a cause that makes them so, and our first duty is to remove that cause. Whatever theories one might try to produce, since all human beings are fundamentally the same throughout the world, no logic can argue that Western women are capable but Japanese women are not. Since it is evident that the differences between Western women and Japanese women are caused by differences in customs, we should change our customs and adopt those of the West as quickly as possible so that our women will also become capable of contributing their fair share. Both men and women should now strive for this goal.

It is an irrefutable fact that men and women do not differ in their physiques or in the workings of their minds, and that they are equal beings. When human beings are called "of all creatures . . . the most highly endowed,"[5] this means that both men and women are the highest of creation. When it is said that without men neither countries nor households could exist, it should also be declared that without women there could be no nations. As to which should be rated as more important, we know of no reason to say that either one is above the other in importance or nobility.

Confucianism characterizes men as yang (positive) and women yin (negative); that is, men are like the heavens and the sun, and women are like the earth and the moon. In other words, one is noble and the other is humble, and there are many who accept this idea as a law of nature. But this yin-yang theory is the fantasy of the Confucianists and there is no need to take it seriously. Its origins go back thousands of years to uneducated and illiterate times when men briefly surveyed all things between the heaven and the earth. Whenever they found two things that seemed similar, they would take it upon themselves to name the one that seemed to be stronger and more active yang, and the one that seemed to be weaker and more passive yin. For instance, the heavens and the earth looked very much like the ceiling and the floor of a room. One was low and trampled on by people's feet, while the other was high and beyond reach. Therefore the heavens were termed yang and the earth yin. The sun and the moon are both round and shining; one is very bright, even hot, while the other is less bright. Therefore, the sun was yang and the moon yin. This is the level of the logic behind this theory, and we today should regard it as no more than childish nonsense.

In other words, there is no basis for this theory. Even so, people constructed dual categories of thought in their minds and placed things that seemed slightly superior in the yang section and things that seemed a little inferior in the yin. Then they would think up various ideas to liven up their nonsensical theory. That was all. Therefore, there never existed any such distinctions as yin and yang dividing women from men. The idea itself being fictional to begin with, there was no basis for applying it to men and women. But some scholars of Confucianism despised women for some reason and assumed that they were inferior to men. As a result, they placed them in their mental category of yin. It caused women no end of trouble to be labeled as yin according to a theory explaining the relationship between the sun and the moon and the heavens and the earth, which had nothing to do with women at all. They were nothing less than victims of the Confucian scholars' ignorance and lack of education.

Suppose now, we ourselves make up a new theory in jest, declaring that women are gorgeous and full of life. Their decorative jewels shine and twinkle like the stars and the sun; their faces resemble luxuriant flowers under a spring sky. It is not that men have no beauty, but when compared with women, they are somehow reserved and quiet; their bony limbs are like withered trees and their firmness is like the great earth. We should then implement this as a theory, classing women with the sun and the heavens as yang and placing men with the earth and the moon as yin. This shows the unreasonable nature of the yin-yang argument. No one in the civilized world should allow such nonsense to be talked of today.

Installment Two

As yesterday's article ended on a light note, today we will return to the serious discussion of why Japanese men treat women so poorly. After we have listened to men's arguments I will explain why they are unreasonable.

The Great Learning for Women declares:

> The five worst maladies that afflict the female mind are: discord, discontent, slander, jealousy, and silliness. Without any doubt, these five maladies infest seven or eight out of every ten women, and it is from these that arises the inferiority of women to men. A woman should cure them by self-inspection and self-reproach. The worst of them all, and the parent of the other five, is silliness. Woman's nature is passive (yin). Yin, being of the nature of night, is

dark. Hence, as viewed from the standard of man's nature, the foolishness of every woman prevents her from understanding the duties that lie before her very eyes, from perceiving the actions that will bring down blame upon her own head, and from comprehending even the things that will bring down calamities on the heads of her husband and children. Nor when she blames and accuses and curses innocent persons nor when, in her jealousy of others, she thinks to set up herself alone, does she see that she is her own enemy, estranging others and incurring their hatred. Lamentable errors! Again, in the education of her children, her blind affection induces an erroneous system. Such is the stupidity of her character that it is incumbent on her, in every particular, to distrust herself and to obey her husband.

We are told that it was the custom of the ancients, on the birth of a baby girl, to let her lie on the floor for the space of three days.[6] Even in this may be seen the likening of the man to Heaven and the woman to Earth; and the custom should teach a woman how necessary it is for her in everything to yield to her husband the first, and to be herself content with the second place.[7]

The purpose of the above section is to enumerate the five infirmities peculiar to women as evidence that they are inferior to men and must therefore obey men in everything. But when men examine women, they are bound to discover infirmities, and symptoms not found in men. The cause of the infirmities clearly lies in teachings derived from Confucianism. *The Great Learning for Women* is a compendium of those teachings, and its basic message is as follows:

A woman must rise early in the morning and retire late at night, with no naps during the day; she should drink wine and tea only sparingly and stay away from performances of music or drama; until she has reached the age of forty, she must even refrain from going to crowded shrines or temples. Further, a woman must show discretion when exchanging words with her husband's friends and with young men. Visits to her parents' house, let alone other people's houses, should not be frequent; in fact, she must not go anywhere without her husband's permission and the same should apply to writing letters and sending presents. All she needs in the way of clothing are garments that are not soiled but clean: colors and designs that attract people's attention are to be frowned upon.

In addition, because a woman has no particular lord, she should regard her husband as her master, obey all his orders and not disobey him in the least; a wife should revere her husband as the supreme being. On the other hand, a husband can get rid of a wife whenever he pleases if he invokes the Seven Reasons for Divorce; in other words if a wife fails to obey her parents-in-law, or to bear children; if she is promiscuous or shows strong feelings of jealousy; if she develops a serious illness; if she is talkative; or if she shows a tendency to steal. To put it another way, promiscuity in a woman is strictly prohibited, but there are no constraints on men. They can take as many concubines as they wish without being labeled promiscuous. A man is only considered to be promiscuous if his abominable behavior goes beyond having a full supply of concubines as well as a wife. Such behavior might cause him some problems, but the rights regarding those seven reasons for divorce are held only by the husband; the wife has no right to divorce at all. Moreover, not only is a wife unable to divorce her husband for promiscuity; she is not even allowed to be angry or resentful. Women must never give way to jealous thoughts. Their only possible response is calm and quiet remonstration.

If a woman follows this teaching faithfully, she has no freedom to choose when to get up or go to bed, or what to eat or drink; she is denied the pleasures of music and the theater, cannot dress up, and is prevented from going outside the house or from making friends. On top of all this, there is no telling when her husband may have the notion of divorcing her. She is said to be the mistress of a household, but in the uneasiness of her position she resembles someone walking on thin ice across a bottomless pool.

Seen from the wife's perspective, a husband is able to get his own way in everything, as if he were a lord. He is in the enviable position of being able to control what happens both inside and outside the house. Even if we accept men's view of women as vastly inferior, women are still human beings. If they have the feelings of normal human beings, how hard it must be for them to feel at ease when their life is so full of pain. After all, both men and women agree that mustard is hot and sugar sweet. However much forbearance a woman shows in enduring the bitter hardships of her life, she cannot alter the ways of nature, and we should not be surprised if her true feelings break free. At times, she may fail to be compliant and obedient; she may show anger and resentment, or even give vent to her jealousy with words of abuse. But there is nothing strange in this behavior since it is a natural response to the actions of the husband. Therefore, it is surely completely unreasonable to blame the woman without investigating the circumstances. It is like neglecting a horse, and then cursing it when it becomes bad tempered. The bad temper is not a result of the horse's disposition; it is a problem caused by the owner's heartless treatment.

In the same way, it is not unusual for stepmothers and stepchildren to quarrel. This is ascribed to the heartlessness of the mother or, alternatively, to the disobedience of the child. But surely there is no preordained reason why a stepchild should be inherently disobedient. Which establishes the relationship, the mother or the child? Since small children are innocent, it is obviously the behavior of the mother that will determine whether the relationship is good or bad. For this reason, the general consensus of society is to blame the stepmother rather than the stepchild.

Similarly, where men and women are concerned, since it is always men who establish relationships and therefore determine whether they are good or bad, it is men who have made women what they are today. It is therefore hard to see how they can put the blame on women. If men in Japan understand about horse rearing and are confident in judging between stepmothers and stepchildren, they should be prepared to reconsider their attitudes to women.

Installment Three

In our society, we are very thorough in censuring lewdness on the part of women, and in admonishing them against jealousy. Of course, lewdness is despicable and intense jealousy is ugly to behold. We are in complete agreement that both men and women should show restraint in these areas. However, what is the point of admonishing only women in minute detail and acting as if such behavior by men can be ignored? There is a deep reason for this which people have not talked about since ancient times, but we must bring the matter to light now, even though it is rather embarrassing for men.

From the very beginning, both the teachings of Confucian scholars and the Japanese versions of their teachings, including *The Great Learning for Women*, have been produced by men. And these men have been arbitrary in what they taught, focusing on how to make life easy for the men of their time without any thought for how this might cause difficulties for women. It is like a conference of people who cannot drink to which members have invited confectioners rather than liquor merchants, or a gathering of people who love drinking where many motions for drinking parties have been passed. It is natural for many unbalanced and self-serving rules to emerge in such situations. However, when one stops to think, it will become clear that there is not the slightest difference in the sexual desire felt by men and women, and that they have equal capacities for jealousy. Even so, men have been accustomed to licentiousness for hundreds and thousands of years until it has almost become part of their nature. If there was any attempt to discipline their behavior or impose restrictions now, their jealousy would be wild beyond our imagination—like the raging of a hungry tiger. Even that Kabuki scene of Kiyohime at Hidaka River would be nothing in comparison.[8]

In the newspapers these days, stories of wives going on a domestic rampage because of the thriving state of the pleasure quarters are rare. On the other hand, we frequently come across news of a man with a knife bursting into a room and injuring a woman, all because he has sent himself into a frenzy over groundless suspicions. Men are quick in temper and fiercely jealous, as easily aroused as an obsessed lion.[9] In fact, suppose we were to borrow one paragraph from *The Great Learning for Women*, reversing the references to male and female so that it reads like the passage below. Would men accept the precepts obediently? No one in Japan will need any prompting from us to understand that there would be no chance of this happening:

> Let him never even dream of jealousy. If his wife be dissolute, he must expostulate with her but never either nurse or vent his anger. If his jealousy be extreme, it will render his countenance frightful and his talk repulsive and can only result in completely alienating his wife from him and making him intolerable in her eyes. Should his wife act ill and unreasonably, he must compose his countenance and soften his voice to remonstrate with her; and if she be angry and listens not to his remonstrance, he must wait over a season and then expostulate with her again when her heart is softened. Never set thyself up against thy wife with harsh features and a fractious voice.[10]

If the men of Japan were ordered to follow such precepts, they would certainly be highly unsatisfied and might even become so angry as to declare that such a suffocating life was not worth living. If men would find no reason to live such a life, the same must go for women as well. Someone who can find no reason for living might just as well be dead. To establish a precept that you yourself cannot tolerate while ordering women to do so is equivalent to treating women as if they were dead. This is cruelty at its most extreme.

Everyone will agree that lewdness and jealousy should not be approved. But when such behavior is criticized, women alone are singled out for severe blame, while men are not penalized in any way. This is bizarre. It is claimed that men are easygoing, and that they do not develop feelings of intense jealousy. But that is wrong. The truth is that men want to limit the chance to indulge in lewd behavior to men alone. They feel jealous at the idea of such behavior in women and therefore censure it. At the same time, men are irritated when women show jealousy because of a man's lewdness and therefore censure this too. In other words, men have shown great ingenuity in devising precepts to insure their liberty.

We could retract our insistence a little and admit, reluctantly, the claim that men in our present society seem to have a diluted sense of jealousy. But this does not mean that it does not exist. Men are in truth masters in jealousy. But having thought up all sorts of devices to bind women, they are completely secure and occasions when they might feel jealous are rare. In other words, their good behavior is just skin-deep. If you let a dog run about free, you run the danger of being bitten, but if you chain it up, there is no need to be on one's guard. Present-day women have been chained for some time, and that is why men show few signs of jealousy. The fact that men have reached the point where they are free from jealousy should be taken as evidence of their extreme heartlessness.

In attacking this very heartless and unreasonable attitude, we will not need unfamiliar theories from the West. We will use Confucian teachings to render the flaws visible. The Sage uses the expression "like-hearted considerateness" (*jo* 恕), which is written by combining the characters for *like* (如) and *heart* (心).[11] It means that the consideration that one shows to the hearts of other people should be like the consideration one shows to one's own; in other words, we should guess that anything that is difficult for us to bear is equally hard for others, and should therefore act with restraint. This is a wise teaching of the Sage that has made a deep impression on us. Then, how is it that in the process of applying the Sage's teachings to society, women were ordered to bear hardships that men cannot bear? It appears that there has been no attempt to apply the way of like-hearted considerateness [, reciprocity in other words,] to relations between men and women.

The truth must be that the Sage himself was a man, and people who handed down his teachings were also men. Since men were in the majority, they forgot to account for women and applied the way of reciprocity only to relations between men. Moreover, conveniently for them, women are docile and obedient, even when put in an unreasonable situation. They must have decided that other men would like to take advantage of this as well. Thus, assuming that others' minds worked as their own, they spread this self-interested teaching widely. This has put women at a great disadvantage. Men have completely monopolized the benefits of this precious teaching of the Sage, leaving women to suffer as a result.

Once men have abandoned the precepts of reciprocity in their relations with women, there are no limits to what they can do. This situation is not limited to love relationships. In the case of rights over property as well, men alone are qualified for ownership and women are no better than hired hands. Again, interactions with the outside world have been monopolized by men, and they have declared themselves masters of their households, claiming to be "foremost" in the parlor, the bedroom, and even every corner of the kitchen.[12] Faced with the smallest infringement on their rights, they shout "Outrageous!" to their families with regard to private issues, and "Obstruction!" to outsiders with regard to public ones. The same objections have been made regarding these very editorials, "On Japanese Women," which we have been publishing for the past few days. However, such objections have been limited to men because if we count all the complaints about outrage and obstruction and boil them down, it is unfortunately clear that the only outrage is suffered by men and the only obstruction is to men's right to act as they please.

So what can be done, given that one man does not make a family and that a nation relies on the cooperation of both the men and the women? We are not suggesting anything unreasonable to the Japanese men of today. Since they have been accustomed for so long to acting as they please, we will not attempt to impose restrictions without any warning. We should be prepared to accept a man's desire for a new wife immediately after the death of the previous one; if he is very inconvenienced with only one wife, though it is hard to admit it, we cannot prevent him from keeping a concubine under strict secrecy; if he is attracted by the spring fragrances coming from those fascinating [pleasure] quarters, some enjoyment of the "flowers" will have to be tolerated too. In fact, the question of relations between men and women should not be discussed too lightly. In a certain area in America, we are told that a group known as Mormons is enjoying some prosperity. Such being the trend of the world, we too cannot form inflexible arguments of stone or iron that ignore human desires.

But the fact remains that anything disagreeable to men is equally disagreeable to women. If men have secrets, women should also have secrets. If men enjoy "the flowers of spring," women should be allowed to amuse themselves under "the autumn moon." To be as strong-willed as stone or iron, or to be as easy-going as running water: such decisions are the choice of the man concerned (This problem will be discussed in a future article). For the present, let us be satisfied either way, as long as both men and women are given equal chances to be like one or the other.

Therefore, we are not attempting to say anything difficult. We are simply providing a commentary on the concept of reciprocity, which has been well known in Japan since ancient times. Our wish is to make its teachings applicable to women as well as men. Our hearts will be satisfied when men cease to force upon women what they themselves do not want to accept.

Installment Four

So far we have discussed various subjects with frequent references to passages from *The Great Learning for Women*. That work is a manual of moral precepts, but no one expects that society will actually function according to its every word. As was stated in Part One, the Sage's teachings are like the prices given to goods at a market before bargaining begins. Just as customers actually haggle and beat the prices down to half or even one-third, there is probably no one today who takes every word of *The Great Learning* at its face value. It is, after all, a general guideline for conduct, and in the present situation, for us to turn every detail into evidence to argue over would be childish and even make us the target of ridicule.

We shall therefore turn from our detailed examination of *The Great Learning for Women* itself to the spirit behind all the teaching of the sages that have influenced people and shaped social customs. In fact, we will pick up those elements that are often talked about or practiced in an attempt to describe the true state of our women today and free them from unhappiness. By so doing, we hope to contribute to both the vitality of the Japanese family and the power of the nation.

Of all the assumptions of our society, the one that most humiliates women is expressed in the saying that goes "The purpose of taking a wife is to have descendants to carry on the family line." The effect this saying has can be understood if we compare it to "The purpose of buying a rice cooker is to cook rice." This implies that if you are not going to cook rice, you do not need to buy a cooker; in other words if you do not want descendants, you have no need for a wife. The true purpose of marriage should be for a husband and a wife to live together in harmony and love, helping each other and being helped in turn, enjoying the greatest pleasure and happiness in life. But here nothing of this rule of nature is mentioned. The only purpose of marriage is said to be having descendants and carrying on the family line. This falsehood is the starting point of all evils. The wife who bears children is no different from the cooker that boils rice; she is just a piece of equipment. Just as any cooker unfit for boiling rice can be thrown away, any wife who does not bear children may be divorced. If a pot can take the place of a cooker, then a concubine may be just as useful as a wife. Even if a kitchen has a rice cooker, no one minds having a number of pots besides. Similarly, there are no objections to having one legal wife in the main part of the house and a number of concubines elsewhere. All this shows how the bodies of women are treated as pieces of equipment.

From this attitude stems the common saying about "the borrowing of a woman's womb."[13] The meaning is that any child born into this world belongs to the father and not to the mother. This is similar to stating that this year's rice was born from the seed of last year's rice and was not produced by the soil, which was just a borrowed resting place. What a surprising degree of ignorance and illiteracy!

If we study human physiology to investigate the truth of reproduction, we will realize that it is not possible to decide whether a child originates in either the man or the woman. The ovum lies concealed in the female body while the sperm is in the man. The sperm by itself cannot grow into a child and neither can the ovum. The two must come together to form an embryo that grows in the woman's body and is nourished by her blood. The mechanism of the whole procreation process is mysterious and beyond the knowledge and understanding of human intelligence, but to describe it by means of an analogy, it is like mixing copper and zinc to produce brass. It makes no difference whether copper and zinc are called the mother or the father; in any case, the two metals must be melted together and mixed into one in order to produce brass. Therefore, it is impossible to decide whether copper is the basic material with which zinc is mixed or zinc is the base to which copper is added. Even with the help of a theory that lacked all reason, it would not be possible to insist that brass is basically copper that has borrowed from zinc rather than being basically zinc that has borrowed from copper. On the other hand, if such an unreasonable theory was accepted, and people were to claim that women's bodies were borrowed in order to produce children, it would not be possible to refute the reverse argument, that it was men's bodies that were borrowed. Alternatively, if we abandon the analogy with brass and return to the widely held identification of men with seeds of rice and women with the soil, does the seed borrow the soil or the soil borrow the seed? No firm verdict is possible.

However, if we look for evidence rather than theorizing, it is clear that both physically and temperamentally, right down to the last detail, a child resembles partly its father and partly its mother. Even hereditary disorders are inherited as much from the mother as from the father. Beyond any doubt, therefore, a child is equally a part of both parents. Those who ignore this and talk about the womb being borrowed are just looking for any pretext to devalue the role of women. This may work in times of barbarism and ignorance, but in the present age of civilization, we should not permit such sterile and impractical thinking.

And yet, in our society, there are people who loudly proclaim that the womb is borrowed; that the purpose of marriage is to have descendants; and finally that wives unable to bear children should be divorced. And no one seems to take exception. Some men are taking advantage of this silence to openly indulge in illicit behavior with no attempts at discretion: they take one concubine, then exchange her for another; marry a woman on a whim, and then divorce her equally on a whim. However, these self-indulgent goings on do not have the slightest effect on their reputation in society. Obviously, the basic cause of such behavior is, as was mentioned before, the evil custom of regarding the female body as a piece of equipment. However, the fact is that women are human beings and "of all creatures . . . the most highly endowed," just as men are.

Since women are not, in fact, insentient pieces of equipment, what are the likely feelings of a wife in such a position? She does not grieve if she is divorced, nor resent the presence of many concubines. Whether her husband amuses himself with his concubines, whether she is divorced or even murdered, the cause lies in the husband's lewd and reckless behavior. The wife can feel herself to be pure and innocent, with no need to hide from heaven and earth in shame even if she were to die. This is proof that women are human beings and "of all creatures . . . the most highly endowed."

But when her thoughts turn to the roots of where and how her husband developed these ideas and came to act in this way, despite being exactly the same as women in the circumstances of his birth, then a wife's resentment becomes unbearable. For the precious human body to be treated like a piece of equipment is a humiliating insult, since it means the destruction of honor and dignity and is therefore equivalent to death. At such times, women must keep their minds firm as a rock, and call a halt to men's self-indulgence, even at the risk of their lives.

Installment Five
The idea that a woman's womb is not "borrowed" should already be clearly understood. In other words, when a child is born, half of its body is inherited from its mother and the other half from its father. The child is neither entirely like its father nor entirely like its mother, but somewhere in between. To continue the previous analogy, it is the same as producing brass by mixing copper and zinc, or type metal by mixing lead and antimony. It is clear at a glance that brass and type metal are neither copper nor zinc nor lead nor antimony; they are types of metal falling somewhere in between them. If we further mix the brass and type metal, yet another type of metal will be created. Each time we increase the degree of mixing, there is a corresponding decrease in the proportion of each ingredient. The same logic governs the process by which one generation of people produces the next. Therefore, if we were to think of copper and antimony as men, and zinc and lead as women we could draw up the following family tree:

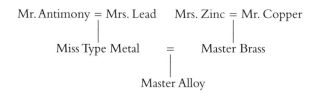

In other words, the fact that the womb is not "borrowed" is a truth that no one can deny.

The next conundrum we must consider is the line of descent to which Master Alloy belongs. His mother, Miss Type Metal, is fifty/fifty antimony and lead; his father, Master Brass, is composed of equal amounts of zinc and copper. Therefore, since Master Alloy has inherited a fifty/fifty share on one side and equal shares on the other, the only way in which we can describe him is to say that he is the grandson of four grandparents and the son of one mother and one father. If we calculate the proportions of each forebear in order to find his physical composition, it is absolutely clear beyond either doubt or argument that he has inherited twenty-five percent each from antimony, lead, zinc, and copper or fifty percent each from type metal and brass.

Despite this, the strange fact is that since ancient times the custom in Japan has been to conceive of the family (*ie*) as something that is passed on from father to son. Women have been treated as if they are completely outside the process, so when a family has no son, the daughter is made to marry the child of another family, who becomes an adopted heir; if a family has no daughter either, both a boy and a girl are brought in from outside. This is because even though the real bloodline might die out, as long as the family name itself continues, people do not feel concern. Therefore, in the case of Master Alloy from the family tree above, suppose that his family name is "Anti," this name will be passed down generation after generation. Daughters will not be counted as inheritors of the blood line and as generation succeeds generation, the blood link with the ancestors may just thin out, or even be completely cut off and leave no trace; all that will remain is the practice of seeking a male to carry on the name.

Females derive no benefit from this state of affairs; in fact their misfortune is beyond comparison. The only daughter of a rich family, for instance, should be able to inherit the house, the storehouse and the money on the death of her parents. But she is forced to find a husband for adoption as the heir, give him all her fortune, and greatly bemean herself by serving him as if he were her lord. This is equivalent to offering one's fortune to another and then entering his service by way of thanks for his graciously agreeing to accept it. This is a misfortune for the woman, and a grave accounting error.

The origins of this grave error can be found in the feudal times of old. If a samurai distinguished himself through great deeds, he would be granted a fief, and also a name that carried rank and status. The custom was for this fief and name to be handed down to his descendants, so that as long as there was a son, however weak he might be in body or intellect, he would become his father's successor, take over the fief as his father had before him, and swagger around in just the same way too. As a result, the family would pay the utmost respect to "the master's vital public duties" and constantly praise them to the skies. For his part, the master of the house would feel very pleased with himself and assume a domineering attitude as if to say: "It is the public duties which I perform that keep you all in the lap of luxury! In truth, both my wife and children are a terrible burden; all I need is a son to succeed me, and a second and possibly third just to be on the safe side. My wife and daughters mean nothing to me; it is out of pity that I look after them." In truth this is false feeling that flies in the face of human emotions, but samurai were too proud to admit this because they were meant to "act as if they had full stomachs even when they were starving." This has ended up as the custom in ex-samurai families throughout the country and spread even among commoners, so that the absurd situation has arisen where bad behavior towards women is seen as proof of masculinity. Men despise and look down on their womenfolk, becoming abusive regarding matters that they themselves know are not important. Worse still, they publicly scold women in order to gain other people's good opinion. These are the acts of madmen, but in a world of deceit, deceit is valued. Accordingly, there are enough other madmen to be impressed by this sort of behavior, on the grounds that it is evidence of strict traditions of family conduct. The result is a society founded on error.

Since these preposterous practices have continued for several hundred thousand years, it is difficult to see what can be done. However, we are no longer in the age of feudalism. One act of prowess with a spear does not lead to a hundred years of prosperity; husbands and wives can form their own separate units and establish separate households. They should spend their lives cooperating with each other, sharing their own lineage and their own property. In other words, they should not only live together, but live together as equals.

To put it another way, if a man takes up a post as, for example, an official in government service, he may somehow take on the airs of a samurai of old and even his family might view him with respect. But an official is no more than a man working for his monthly salary; it is no different from any normal way of earning a living. The same should apply, or even more, to farmers and merchants. Why should men act as if they are more important than their wives and children just because they are earning a living? No man can manage a household properly all by himself. It is true that many women of Japan today are lacking in accomplishments and knowledge of the world, but such ineptness is not uncommon among men either. At any rate, even with women in the state they are at present, can men alone manage the household affairs without this having a bad effect on their ability to earn a living? Are women really such a nuisance that their absence does not cause any problems? If it does have a bad effect, and if their absence does cause problems, this shows that men cannot manage by themselves but need to work in cooperation with their wives. In other words, if husbands and wives need to act together in order to maintain a household, what reason might there be for the husband to assume all the authority and treat his wife like a serving maid?

Whenever a husband insists on putting on airs, using bad language and treating his wife like a lowly serving maid, then she has no alternative but to call him a man servant in turn and address him as if he had been hired for labor. But that would be against the behavior proper to any personal relationship, and also far from the way of a husband and wife at home, and the feelings of love and affection that they should share. Any person with normal feelings, who knows proper behavior and understands the Way, is aware of our fundamental duty as human beings: Power over household affairs should be shared equally between husband and wife without any need to put one above the other; property should be held in common, or there should be an agreement about how it is divided; finally since the household is the responsibility of the couple themselves, they should follow whatever way suits them and hold each other in mutual love and esteem. The time has come for us to sweep away the customs of the old feudal period, when it was so important to maintain the family line that every step was taken to ensure that there was a male heir and women were accordingly reduced to nothing.

Installment Six

Our discussions on the status of women do not mean that we are acting on their behalf in order to force a showdown with men. In fact, it will also be to the advantage of men to make women into competent adults, because that will greatly increase the strength of both individual households and the nation. Even if a household contains one husband and one wife, if the wife is in effect equal to nothing, the household will be supported by the strength of the husband alone. From a wider perspective, women comprise half of Japan's total population of thirty-seven million people. If we discount this eighteen and a half million on the grounds that women are useless, this will not only halve the population, but stunt the strength supporting the country by one half as well. In other words, women have become so weak that they are inferior to men both in body and mind. Of no use to either the household or the country, they are also so frail that the children they bear are unlikely to be robust either. The quality of our racial stock is declining, and eventually the Japanese people will develop a reputation for having the worst physique in the world. Is this not a lamentable state of affairs? Since this is just punishment for the suffering imposed on women for so long, those who care for their households and their country, and fear for the condition of future generations, must give careful consideration to this matter.

As was pointed out in Part One [Installment Two], women today do not possess any property or home of their own; they are more or less lodgers in men's houses, and because they have nothing serious to worry about, they have no opportunity to increase their intelligence. To have wide contacts with people and to worry about financial matters will quicken the workings of the brain, but how can those who live their whole lives with no social life or financial responsibilities obtain any practical intelligence? To find fault with women for their lack of intelligence is like commanding mountain folk to swim in the ocean. If such people are to be made to swim, they must first be shown the ocean and allowed to grow accustomed to it. (As this issue has been discussed in Part One, we will not give it detailed treatment here.)

During the long peaceful years of the Tokugawa regime, all the institutions in society were well organized and people were strictly disciplined in both their manners and conduct. As the target of these rules, women were confined to the house with no amusements permitted; even marriage, such a vital issue for women, was taken out of their hands. At the present moment of time, households of the middle class and above may not be following the exact wording of *The Great Learning for Women* as referred to above; however, on reaching the proper age, a daughter will marry into another household in obedience to her parents' choice of a "good match" and even if the husband turns out to be a man without feelings or discernment, she will simply have to bear her fate. Even if she weeps about this on visits to her parental home, there will be no sign that they are really listening. She must return to her husband's home in tears and spend months and years in sadness until finally she becomes an invalid, half alive and half dead. Nothing that she sees or hears will interest her; nothing that she eats or drinks will taste good to her. Thus in melancholy she will spend the rest of her pitiable life.

Relations between a man and a woman are of essence most private, and should not be revealed to other people, even at the risk of one's life; moreover, personal considerations of individual taste are involved. Yet parents, from thoughtlessness or low morality, may try to match their daughter with a relative, regardless of the age difference, in order to strengthen the closeness of family ties; alternatively, if there is a proposal from a rich family, its high social standing may lead them to try forcible persuasion, without considering the mental and physical attributes of the man in question. If the daughter refuses, they will scold her willfulness. Such parents are fishing for profit with their daughter as bait. Any parent with principles would be extremely reluctant to turn a daughter into a prostitute or send her into service as a concubine, since they would see this as a despicable action.[14] But to force an unwilling daughter into a relationship is no different from selling her into prostitution, even if it is labeled as a marriage on the surface. It is hard to imagine more cruel behavior.

If a daughter cannot reveal the depths of her gloom to her own parents, how much more impossible will it be for her to tell her parents-in-law? Since her anxieties can find no release, she somehow loses her freshness; noticing this, her husband finds her even less attractive than before. As a result, he turns his eyes away from home and looks for pleasure to the "spring flowers" [of the pleasure quarters]. He may even get so tangled in their branches that his health is damaged and his household destroyed. Such instances have not been rare in history and still occur today. Not only do they bring unhappiness to women; they do not bring any advantage to men either. The only result is an increase in overall misery that benefits no one.

Even in less unfortunate cases, when a couple is getting on fairly well, the man in a normal household will act as if he is the lord and his wife is a vassal. Whenever the husband sets out or returns, the wife will see him off or welcome him back with great deference and ceremony.[15] When the wife goes out, the husband shows no interest beyond expecting her to submit details of her destination. (Perhaps he is behaving in an honorable way and observing the precept that calls for "distinction between husband and wife."[16] In that case he is carrying it so far that it is comical to watch.) On the other hand, when the husband leaves the house he does not reveal his destination and it is not clear when he will return. Left behind to look after things at home, the wife waits, and even delays the start of the evening meal. If he is very late, she reluctantly prepares the food and sits down all alone. She has half-heartedly cleared away the remains of her silent supper and the winter night grows late. Then there is a knock on the door accompanied by the voice of the night-watchman: her husband has returned, looking somewhat under the influence. When asked for details of where he has been since the morning, and what he has been doing, he simply answers, "Business," or "A post-meeting celebration."

My personal opinion is that there must be times when a husband feels highly satisfied with the way things are going, and times when he is greatly unsettled after making a serious mistake. But since he finds it almost impossible to confide in a woman, he will reveal neither the good news nor the bad. Convinced that whatever might happen she does not need to know, he will keep her away as if it is not her concern. His intention must be to adhere to the old precept against listening to women or allowing them to take any action. Admittedly such stoic behavior is appropriate, and even praiseworthy, from a man's point of view, but how can a woman be expected to endure it without feeling dissatisfied? In Western countries, wives are not only consulted by their husbands in relation to domestic and other matters; they say that if a husband broke a promise to eat with his wife without a good reason even once, loud dissatisfaction would result. We should count ourselves lucky that Westerners still do not know the situation in Japan. If the truth ever became widely known and the women actually saw it with their own eyes, they would probably label Japan as a living hell for women.

It might be true that the women of Japan have been accustomed to living in hell since ancient times, but since we are all born into the same world, human feelings must be the same, regardless of East or West. Even though there are no outward manifestations of misery or dissatisfaction, it is clear that deep depression lies under the surface of Japan. An ancient saying states that when a great king is about to appear, purple clouds will rise over the area. Presumably the idea is that if a hero's inner virtues are powerful enough, they will influence the universe outside him and be seen in the sky. If the virtues of such a monarch manifest themselves as a purple cloud, the misery and dissatisfaction of Japanese women should cause black clouds to cover our islands, with the darkest patches hanging over households of the middle levels of society and above.

Installment Seven

In the previous installment, we gave the general picture of what happens when men cause women to suffer through their individual arrogance. In brief, since the man robs himself of the strength of the person who could act as his right hand, it does not only lead to the unhappiness of the wife; there is no benefit for either the country as a whole or for the individual household. By increasing the level of misery and dissatisfaction in this way, men are pointlessly weakening the whole nation. Today we will clarify what this means by discussing familiar examples from everyday life.

When the head of a household swaggers about, he makes a fine sight. It is almost as if the master would have no reputation without this show of swaggering; it grows in proportion to his outward manifestation of authority. But there is one thing that is beyond the control of any man, however impressive his reputation: the length of his life. In particular, since it is customary for there to be an age difference of from five or six to ten years in most married couples, it is a sad fact that husbands leave their wives and children behind when they depart this world. If a husband lives to a very old age, he will have nothing to regret. However, if he has the misfortune to die in middle age, it will be hard for him to escape the law of cause and effect since this will be the day of retribution for his everyday wrongdoing.[17]

Left behind will be a young widow and small children, and the household will be completely in the dark. Even the household account books do not show clearly whether the family is in the black or in the red and they seem to have both loans and debts. They become involved in negotiations with an entirely unknown party who claims that their house and land have been mortgaged and that the eviction date is very soon. Moreover, according to another account book money has been lent, but when they press for repayment they are told that there is a mistake in the accounts; the borrower has a counterbond signed before the husband's death, so the matter has been settled. And so on and so forth. Since there is no way in which the wife and her children can deal with the situation, they must request the help of relatives or friends of the deceased and hold a meeting to settle his estate.

The widow turns the house upside down and brings out not only the account books with details of income and expenditure, but old bonds related to debts and credits, new bonds, land certificates, public bonds, ledgers of loan repayments, and even all the paperwork from the double-lock drawers, such as correspondence and drafts of correspondence that her husband had secretly hidden away, even from his family, while alive. Her only recourse is to reveal all of this at the meeting, admit that it is completely beyond her understanding and ask those present please to confer on her behalf about what should be done. What an incredibly unsettled state of affairs!

In the aftermath of her husband's death, the widow automatically becomes head of the household and must also take sole charge of the children. Yet, despite having this role, she does not know whether they are rich or poor, and since she lacks this knowledge, she does not know whether their life will be easy or difficult either. Directions from a third party will tell her either to rejoice in gratitude at the news that they are well-off and can have an easy life, or to face the threat of poverty and reduced circumstances with sadness and humility. This can be compared to a person who laughs or cries on demand. Such a person cannot even decide if the bath water is at the right temperature without external help: if someone says that the water is hot, it will feel hot, but if someone else says that the water is lukewarm, it will feel lukewarm. If the deceased was aware of this embarrassing situation, would he feel joy or the reverse? It is inconceivable that it would be pleasant for him to watch this from his grave.

Even more unpleasant is the way in which the relatives and friends take advantage of their opportunity to investigate the management of the household. They may stick their noses where they are not needed and give directions to the wife and children; partly out of boredom they might open papers that were treated as confidential by the deceased; they might just read what a document said without knowing the circumstances at the time; or they might even jeer secretly among themselves that now at last they realize that the deceased was such and such. Even though he is no longer alive, it is a very regrettable state of affairs.

As long as our world stays at its present level of intellectual and moral development, there will not be one among us who does not have some secret. It is only by concealment that we can maintain surface appearances. Secrets should only be shared by husbands and wives, parents and children. Even if it is not a misdeed such as the theft of a sheep, a son conceals for his father, and a father conceals for his son (though it is true that many people try to prevent both sight and sound of matters that husband and wives should show and tell to each other).[18] Nevertheless, while the scenes that followed immediately upon the death of the master of this household — the revealing of all his secrets, the misinterpreting of his deepest thoughts, the resultant mockery — were unspeakably shameless, it must be admitted that all of this was caused by his lack of discernment while alive.

Similarly, when it comes to financial gains or losses, matters can become so confused that it is hard to find a solution. On the news of the death of the head of a household, yesterday's friend turns into today's enemy; respectable relatives, and even blood-brothers, behave like strangers. There will be disputes over who should inherit the estate, or between the main house and branches of the family; a younger brother born of a different mother might claim his share, and even a long estranged uncle might suddenly stake an unwarranted claim. Finally everyone ends up in court with the result that the assets go up like smoke, leaving behind nothing but social ridicule. Such instances were certainly not unusual in the past and even right now, it is likely that there are many households in the midst of this type of confusion.

Situations like these have various origins, but it is not unusual for the unsatisfactory ending to be the entrusting of the household to outsiders. This is because after her husband's death the lady widow finds herself unfamiliar with the affairs of the household of which she is a part, having been kept in ignorance because her husband normally despised her. The dead may regret this as they dwell in the other world, but regrets from the other world can serve no purpose.

If such husbands had listened to our advice while alive, they would have realized that women deserve respect. If a wife is treated seriously, so that she and her husband really are ranked as equals, they will develop the custom of talking to each other with honesty and affection about both public and private matters, not only taking equal charge of the settlement of material assets but also sharing their minds. In those circumstances, even in the unhappy event of the early death of its head, the household will still have bright prospects and need not fall into darkness. While one thing leads to another, the children will grow out of infancy and the next generation will shine forth. In other words, this is how succession should occur in an independent household. The many reverse examples that have occurred since ancient times should be seen as natural retribution for men's foolish inability to treat women as competent adults. That is why to respect women does not benefit women alone, but is also to the advantage of men.

Installment Eight

We therefore have no need to go further into the fact that when a household contains both a husband and a wife, it is supported jointly by both of them and there is not the slightest distinction of rank or importance between them. It should be obvious that women do not need to stay at home all the time just because they are women and that they should be able to go out at will and associate confidently in mixed society. They should also pay attention to domestic and outside events, rejoicing over the good and grieving over the bad and keeping both their minds and bodies active. Now is the time for women to realize that they own not only half of what is in their houses, but also half of Japan itself, to change themselves so fundamentally that they will never again fall even one step behind men. Unfortunately, however, after hundreds and thousands of years of unrelenting suffering at the hands of self-centered men, women's bodies have weakened and their mental capacities have shrunk, with the result that any quick revival will be difficult.

Therefore now is surely the time for a big contribution from men. This is because even though their uncivilized state made them unaware of their errors, men's forebears are the ones who caused the present imprisonment of women, through their unreasonable behavior over many hundreds of years. Accordingly, it is the duty of their descendants to atone for their wrongdoing by behaving more carefully and devoting themselves to efforts to raise women until they reach a level equal to men. It is possible that the government will pay special attention to this area in the drawing up of the Civil Code, so that there will be much that is of benefit to women.[19] But however civilized the code, if the people themselves are not civilized, it will have no effect. Therefore, Japanese men, particularly those who have knowledge of civilization, must prepare to accept a great responsibility and be conscientious, first as regards their own actions and then in encouraging other people.

The points that must be observed are not at all difficult: When a baby girl is born, do not neglect her from infancy because she is a girl, but love her and care for her in the same way as a boy. As she grows up, pay attention to her physical development first, but give her an academic and artistic education that is in no way inferior to that of a boy. Give her freedom to meet people and make friends, and provide her with basic knowledge of both domestic and worldly affairs. If the family has property, a girl's share should be equal to a boy's, and she should be allowed to manage it herself. However, besides all this, the most important thing is to train her in one accomplishment so that she will be able to support herself in the future, because if a woman has a special accomplishment together with some property of her own, she will never need to depend on a man and will therefore naturally acquire a spirit of independence. In other words, we should not rely solely on school education for a girl, but should also take pains to educate her about both domestic and worldly affairs.

Well, if there were many such women today, men would marry them and be truly happy. But since women in Japan now are all clumsy, inexperienced, and careless, just like the deprecating set phrases used by parents at their daughters' weddings, their husbands must always help them and guide their temperaments. This is obviously unnecessary in Western countries today, but a very important point concerning the treatment of wives in Japan. As has already been mentioned several times, there should be no distinction in the household between husband and wife, but besides this, no pains should be spared in encouraging a wife to take part in the management of the household and to keep up with events and trends in the world outside.

According to one expert, although it is true that when bringing up a child, parents must always play with it and never glare, they should not take advantage of its ignorance to tell ridiculous stories. Instead, they should respect a child as an individual and even while playing, should not allow any distortion of reason. For instance, even in the case of a popular portrayal of thunder, after a brief explanation of the picture, say to the child, "This picture is fun to look at, but it is all make-believe. Thunder is not made by drums in the sky, and there is no thunder demon wearing a loincloth of tiger-skin.[20] Thunder is really caused by electricity, the same as the power that makes telegraphy work. When you grow up, you will learn about thunder." In other words, parents should always be ready to use even small things like this as an opportunity to talk about important matters in an interesting way.[21] If this is the case with children, it must be doubly clear that one should never take advantage of a wife, who is already much older than that.

Although it is the custom to instill total humility and modesty in women from childhood, there are some who are quick to make sense of complicated matters and understand reason. If evidence is required, it often happens that despite being so docile and reserved that nothing was heard of her while she was married, a woman takes complete command after she becomes a widow. She brings up the children and manages the household affairs; she handles relations with relatives and society at large; but above all this, she single-handedly takes control of the family business so that things prosper even more than when her husband was alive. In such a case, the woman involved has always been capable, but during her husband's lifetime she was permanently cooped up, so that she was unable to develop her natural talents. These only emerged after her husband's death exposed her to experience of the world outside.

Who is responsible for the fact that these talents did not appear during the lifetime of the husband? In other words, it is wrong to assume that a woman is beneath one's notice just because she is unassuming in her words and behavior. Even if she seems to be slow-witted, one should talk and show her things, in other words act like her teacher. Then, after she has heard serious explanations of a wide range of matters, including those not related to household affairs, she should be allowed to make judgments about their relative merits and demerits. On occasions it will become possible for husband and wife to enjoy debating and arguing with each other, and as they gradually become used to this, there will be a smooth transformation from "foolish wife"[22] to "wise lady" until the wife becomes the first person the husband turns to for advice. In fact, this is what we think should happen if a husband respects his wife.

Installment Nine

To know that wives should be loved but not realize that they should also be respected is a malignant but widespread tendency in Japan that is hard for even "good" families to avoid. In fact, even among those who call themselves scholars of Western civilization, there are some who, on this point alone, find the old Japanese and Chinese ways to be basically more convenient and become indignant when there is any mention of equal rights for men and women. These men are not monkeys wearing crowns but Confucianists made of metal who have been gilded with civilization on one side only. They show either the back or the front, depending on which side serves them best.

When a husband and wife are at home, the husband naturally wields greater power. He secretly looks down on his wife because of her docile speech and behavior, and assumes that it is either useless or troublesome to seek her advice. He never discusses anything with her other than everyday matters such as food, drink, and clothing. Even if his wife happens to express a doubt concerning an issue that she thinks is important, he will brusquely declare that it is nothing to do with her or simply laugh instead of answering. This leaves the wife with nowhere to turn to. If even her husband does not listen, who else will have the patience to talk with her? As a result, she has no chance to take control of her life. And yet, her husband is not cruel or hardhearted. The marriage is a very happy one; he loves her deeply and since he provides her with ample food and clothing, she is able to live in comfort. Since almost all the requests that she makes are granted, she is allowed to go out and wants for nothing. In the eyes of the world it probably looks as if she has nothing to complain about. However, this would be the misjudgment of a shallow observer; we ourselves cannot commend the situation.

Food and clothing by their nature satisfy our physical, not our intellectual, needs. However carefully we look after the needs of the body, if we neglect the intellect, it is no different from bestowing affection on dogs and cats. Even if one serves a pet dog all the courses for a formal meal, or dresses a cat in brocade, this is evidence of love, but not respect. In the same way, a husband might take great care to ensure that his wife wants for nothing in terms of food and clothing, even wrapping her in luxury, as the saying goes; but if he shows not even a whiff of respect and fails to value her intellectual capacities, we shall have to say that he is viewing her in just the same light as a dog or a cat.

Then, what do we mean by "respect"? It is to treat a wife as a competent adult and give equal rank to both marriage partners; to talk to a wife about everything and ask her advice about everything. If a man fully respects his wife's intellectual capacities, in times of prosperity man and wife will share the wealth, and in times of need they will share the poverty. Even though they hold both wealth and poverty in common and always show each other the deepest devotion, there may be occasions when their opinions about matters involving either the household or the world outside differ and arguments ensue. It may not be desirable for couples to have arguments, but if the cause lies in their valuing each other, it must be admitted that this feeling is very different from the one-sided affection that leads to the showering of fancy food and clothing on a wife as if she were a dog or a cat.

This is not directly related to our theme, but recently there has been talk about a National Diet for Japan.[23] In essence, the National Diet will be a place where people from throughout Japan can participate in the running of the nation, conferring upon, and making decisions about, both government laws and income and expenditure. The point is that since the nation is owned by all the people, there is no reason why government officials should take sole charge of political affairs; it is quite appropriate for the people to join them too. For thousands of years, it has been the custom for the people to be kept down by the government. They may appear ignorant because they have lacked even freedom of speech and action. But if leaders in our society encourage them to take the right path, they will become perfectly competent adults and perfectly able to give advice about the running of our nation. To love the people and rule them with benevolence is the old way of running the nation, but benevolent rule alone is not sufficient for the civilized world of today. The people should be valued as well as loved; they should be given a rank that allows them to participate in national affairs. In other words, the essential point is for the government and the people to join forces together so that they can support the nation together. The government and the people are agreed on this point, and it is said that a National Diet will be realized before many years have passed.

While we are impressed by this admirable situation, there is a need for a general balance in human affairs. Accordingly, as we prepare to bring fairness to the running of the nation by opening a National Diet, I would certainly like to inquire whether or not we already have fairness in the running of the households of the people. In fact, if we were to analyze the links within households by comparing the men to the government and the women to the people, and ask what type of government was being adopted, it would be impossible to decide between tyranny and despotism. Men's refusal even to give women information about income and expenditure, while themselves dealing with the family property in any way they see fit, is equivalent to government seizure of the rights to private ownership. Their refusal to allow women any say in matters within or without the house, on the grounds that they should be seen and not heard, resembles government attempts to silence the people by banning discussions. Worse still is that men take their fill of pleasure, indulging in immoral pursuits themselves, while depriving women of freedom by shutting them inside, thereby causing them to become depressed and even suffer physical harm. This is no different from government by force, when the people are oppressed in the cause of greater wealth, and the peasants are exposed to extreme cruelty. Even men who happily do not take things so far, and profess themselves devoted to their wives, just bestow affection and toy with them, as if they were dogs or cats. This is the same as a politician skilled in making fools of the masses.

Now, when our National Diet is opened, those who attend will include representatives of both the government and the people, but all will value fairness highly, so it is likely that they will act fairly during debates about national affairs. However, the embarrassing truth will be that their households are in a state of tyranny or despotism. If asked about the situation where they come from, they will have to reply that at home they hold a monopoly of the power, ruling by force with the authority of a regent. While accustomed to running their households without reason or law, they propose to run the nation through fair debate. It is true that since a household and a National Diet are separate entities, such marvels might be feasible. But seen from the outside, there is a serious imbalance, as if beings from many little hells were gathering in one great heavenly hall to preach the benefits of Buddhist salvation and rebirth in Paradise. Therefore, we would like to establish household diets along the lines of the National Diet, and grant women the right to participate in household government.

Installment Ten

We have already argued at such length throughout the two parts of "On Japanese Women" that we fear that our readers may be bored, but the fact that there has been little public opposition must be because the logic leaves no hole to be attacked. On the other hand, the human mind is not governed by logic alone. The logic may be so convincing that initially there are no objections, but it may be that there are at this very moment educated men or scholars who are in the process of producing objections on the grounds that in the real world things do not act according to plan and there are many obstacles in our way. It might seem sensible to wait for their opinions to appear and then reply to them, but if their objections resemble those that we have long been expecting, there is nothing to be gained from listening to them. For this reason, we will experiment by producing our own objections and having an internal dialogue about them. We shall then request the judgment of those who have been educated in the old school.

Our objections will not look to *The Great Learning for Women* and other old-fashioned sources for support, but will voice new opinions, as follows:

> We are very much impressed with the contents of "On Japanese Women." It is truly excellent to suggest that since men and women are basically equal, they should be treated in the same way; in other words that we should encourage women to be active both mentally and physically until they reach at least the level of women in Western countries today. However, when it comes to publicly promoting this idea and producing opportunities to put it into practice, is there not reason for concern? Even the author of "On Japanese Women" must be well aware that Japanese women today are lacking in both wisdom and judgment. When people without wisdom and judgment hear something new or see something unusual, they become so fascinated

that they do not give themselves time to savor the full benefits at its core. They become so carried away by the novelty that there are inevitably some who mistake the original meaning and end by turning it completely the wrong way up.

Already we find some young ladies who have learnt their letters, perhaps at school, and can manage some broken speech in a foreign tongue. Though they do not even know how to hold a needle, they behave as if they are the only ones who know anything and look down their noses at everyone who is senior in age, including their parents. They make uncalled for attempts to join in the discussions at gatherings of many people, or worse still, present the shocking spectacle of a young lady making a speech.[24] As a slight precaution we are now in the process of devising ways to reform this malignant behavior. At such a juncture, how might they react on reading a discussion of women that is so different from the Chinese and Japanese classics? They will assume that it justifies their behavior, and their tendency to welcome anything novel without properly digesting it will grow until it knows no bounds. Therefore, even though the message at the heart of "On Japanese Women" is truly admirable, far from helping them, its fame at this time will, on the contrary, disrupt their morality.

Even if we are challenged about whether or not we considered such issues, it will be easy for us to answer, for we had problems of this order in mind from the beginning. The first problem given is that the content is good but they fear that readers will misunderstand; in other words just that it is not clearly written. In that case, the offence lies with the writer's lack of skill, and we can only beg instruction from the critics. However, when it comes to scolding young ladies who have learnt their letters for using foreign words, we must point out that this is not confined to them, since there are many men whose chatter includes broken phrases in Western languages. We very much regret that young ladies do not know how to hold a needle, but it is extremely embarrassing to see men who are only too willing to talk but do not know how to hold a writing brush and must ask for assistance, not only when composing complex opinion pieces but even when writing a letter.

Further, while it is hard to accept the behavior of young ladies who believe that they know everything and look down on their seniors, we should criticize men much more severely. For what reason do men today show disdain for women older than themselves? At a party or a gathering of relatives, the men take better seats than the women, regardless of age. While the eating and drinking is going on, they do not assist the women, but rather expect the reverse. Moreover, they do not lift a finger upon the arrival or departure of a woman, but take it for granted when a woman kindly takes care of their outer garments and such. Is this anything less than atrociously ill behavior?

Worse still, although all those moral teachings say that we should serve our father and mother and respect our elders, no one rebukes the unruly and irregular behavior of sons who push their mothers aside and take the seat of honor, nephews who treat aunts as their inferiors, and younger brothers who put themselves before their older sisters. This situation suggests that in the case of mothers, the injunction to serve one's father and mother means not that she should be respected, but merely that she be cared for. According to our way of thinking, this behavior is bad enough to be questionable according to the moral standards that we value, even though ordinary people ignore it as a matter not worthy of attention. This being the case, complaints about the immodest arrogance of young ladies today do not stand up to comparison with men's behavior, and those who rebuke them are merely taken aback because there is a slight difference from time-honored customs.

Anyone who doubts this should imagine what would happen if we took the meekest and most self-effacing man we could find, dressed him in female garb and thrust him in among the women's seats, but let him keep to his normal speech and behavior. This fake woman would look down on the other women and call attention to herself; moreover, she would show no reserve on meeting a man, using unrefined language, moving without grace, drinking, smoking, and even making unnecessarily loud tapping noises when filling her pipe.[25] If the atmosphere were to heat up, she might even forget about appearances and allow the other guests to catch a glimpse of her legs. Everyone present would be really shocked at such behavior in a woman, indicating their disgust through looks and secret gestures. In the same way, while society today would rebuke the immodesty of any such young lady and show its disapproval through using the colloquial term "tomboy," by comparison with the meekest man, even one judged to be a wet drip, we would have to say that a tomboy is far more restrained. Even if a young lady and a man exhibit the same speech and behavior, the same degrees of politeness, the former will be rebuked because she is female, and the latter will escape censure because he is male. We must conclude that these standards are unfair.

There are no discrepancies in the logic of the above, but let us make a slight concession and imagine that misunderstandings caused by the publication of "On Japanese Women" have led to the appearance of rowdy women who act disgracefully and are completely out of control. Even in such a case we would be reluctant to withdraw our arguments. This is because to raise women to a position equal to men is essential for both every household and the nation; once we have begun, we must not worry over minor setbacks. There may be rowdy women, but alongside them will be those who are not. As time passes, the true value of our ideas will naturally become understood, and things will calm down.

The situation is similar to that of thirty years ago, when we opened the country and started trade with foreign countries. In the beginning, there were many problems of various kinds. Even the merchants who participated in the trade were not from good families but were all a rowdy lot. The situation was so bad that we wondered if we would not have been better off if we had never opened the country. But as time passed, the people gradually became accustomed to interaction with foreign countries and gradually learned its guiding principles; the rowdy lot gradually disappeared and people of true value came to associate with foreigners. In other words, the worries caused by the minor difficulties that occurred soon after the opening of the ports did not justify the losses that would have been caused by closing the country again. Similarly, therefore, even if there is faint disquiet about the initial craze that might be sparked off by the novelty of our discussion of women, this cannot provide a reason for abandoning our purpose.

On Moral Behavior

EDITOR'S INTRODUCTION

On Moral Behavior appeared in ten installments in *Jiji shinpō*, Nov. 20–Dec. 1, 1885 and was immediately published in one volume, with a preface. In "On Japanese Women" and *On Japanese Women, Part Two* Fukuzawa had referred to the different standards of sexual behavior expected of men and women as an issue of gender equality. In *On Moral Behavior*, however, as well as implicitly criticizing the womanizing of Meiji oligarchs such as Itō Hirobumi, he returned to an idea that was briefly raised in his *Meiroku zasshi* article in favor of monogamy. Men could not be expected to control their sexual urges, but they should at least be encouraged to regard their promiscuity with shame through learning to hide it.[1] A major reason for this proposal was concern for Japan's reputation in the eyes of the West. As was mentioned in the General Introduction, *On Moral Behavior* is one of Fukuzawa's more controversial works. At the time, he was criticized for advocating the concealment of prostitution rather than a ban. More recently, he has been accused of showing more concern for Japan's standing with the Western powers than for the actual position of women.

In the first installment, Fukuzawa states that his aim is to reevaluate standards of private behavior in Japan since there are now outside standards for them to be measured against. In the second installment he describes the Tokugawa origins of the present lax attitudes to male sexual behavior as samurai were transformed from warriors to bureaucrats. Confucian teachings included moral guidelines for the behavior of subordinates, but by definition this excluded the behavior of men towards women.

In Installments Four through Eight he criticized the openly lax sexual morality of the present. Geisha were indispensable to most social gatherings, and had become willing to act as sexual partners as well as entertainers. For financial reasons, it had become harder for young men to marry, and this meant that prostitutes were increasingly necessary. The sexual promiscuity of older members of the elite set a bad example to young men of ambition. Meanwhile, women saw becoming a concubine as a way to success, and selling themselves into prostitution to help family members as an honorable act. In Installments Three and Ten he counseled that Japan must follow the example of Western countries. In other words, the solution was not banning prostitution, since this would cause social chaos, or a call for sexual restraint, because this would have no effect. Concubines, and wives who were originally concubines, should not be treated like respectable women. Those who were involved in the sex trade, either as geisha or as simple prostitutes, should be ostracized and disparaged. Men should only visit them in secret, and in time, the habit of secrecy should lead to improved behavior. He ended abruptly with the suggestion that stopping compulsory syphilis inspections for licensed prostitutes might have a similar effect to his recipe for social ostracism, by making men avoid them out of fear of infection.

On Moral Behavior[1]

Preface

Many aspects of the moral behavior of Japanese men fall below the standards desirable both for our society itself, and for our relations with foreign nations. Those who share my views find this a constant cause of anxiety, but at the world's present level of civilization there is no chance of correcting the faults of men's inner nature in this regard. Instead, my wish is for men to recognize the indecency of their immoral behavior for what it is, and therefore take steps to conceal it. To my despair, however, there are none who even advise caution, while the majority are oblivious.

Careful examination of the unvarnished moral behavior of men in the East and West is likely to reveal that there is nothing to choose between them. While all gentlemen of high morals must lament this fact, at least if everything is concealed, there is room for forbearance. However, to my eternal embarrassment, in the case of our nation alone it has been the custom from time immemorial to have no qualms about leaving everything in full view.

While there must be many gentlemen who share my feelings, it is not pleasant to speak of these things, and it is therefore tempting to avoid making any public statements, even though one secretly harbors deep concerns. I too would greatly prefer to avoid controversy by observing an eternal silence, yet this is not possible. In particular, recently transport throughout the world has become extremely quick and convenient, so that we cannot know when foreigners will learn of the real conditions here, or what criticisms they will make. It occurred to me that if I advised caution before we faced any strong objections, so that there was some debate among the Japanese about our moral behavior, and a slight improvement in the honor of male society, this would be of some help in protecting us from disdain. Accordingly I spent several days hurriedly writing this piece and had it serialized in the *Jiji shinpō* from 20

November until 1 December in the hope of encouraging caution. Our existence as Japanese is no longer a matter of concern for other Japanese alone. We must accept responsibility in the eyes of the whole world for every word and action, for every single movement. Fellow countrymen in your multitudes, can you accept this responsibility without shame?

Recorded by a *Jiji shinpō* writer in the *Jiji shinpō* office in Nihonbashi Minami, Tokyo, December 1885

※

Installment One
"Nation" is the word used to describe the unit formed when human beings group together. Therefore, to say that a nation is rich or poor, strong or weak, means that its people are rich or poor, strong or weak. A place where poor and weak people have grouped together is called a poor and weak nation; a place where rich and strong people have grouped together is called a rich and strong nation. If the name of a nation depends on whether its people are poor and weak or rich and strong, the same will apply to their wisdom or foolishness and virtue or lack of virtue, so that there will be both nations that are wise and nations that are foolish, nations that are virtuous as well as nations that lack virtue. In all these cases, the relative value of each nation is decided according to what its people say and do.

During the *sakoku* period [1639–1859, when our nation had little contact with the world outside], its poverty or richness, strength or weakness, knowledge or foolishness, virtue or lack of virtue were all confined within its borders, and people could only evaluate themselves by carrying out mutual comparisons. When it came to deciding the relative value of the people when they were grouped together as a nation, there was nothing else to place it in relation to, and so even though it did have a relative value, there was no way in which this could be determined. It was only possible for individuals to establish the relative value of the nation by evaluating themselves on their own terms. However, now that the doors are open and we are enjoying friendly relations with the people of civilized nations, our nation's relative value can easily be weighed on the scales of the rest of the world. Even the smallest differences will be so openly apparent that there will be no way of concealing them. In particular, when the old ways of the *sakoku* period are revealed and viewed in the light of the growing tide of civilization, our wealth and strength may turn out not to be wealth and strength, our wisdom and virtue may turn out not to be wisdom and virtue; it may even happen that matters that were formerly viewed as lacking in wisdom and virtue will come to be valued for having them after all. This being the case, our task is to shape the worth of the nation by bringing together the worth of the individuals within it, and ensure that there is nothing to embarrass us when we are evaluated in the eyes of the world. To this end, we must first widen the sphere of our observations, and each resolve to develop a thorough knowledge of the nature of poverty and wealth, strength and weakness, wisdom and foolishness, virtue and lack of virtue in the civilized world. This is exactly what scholars should speak about. But because there are many possible observations to be made, my purpose here is to briefly give my opinion regarding one small but familiar topic, the issue of moral behavior. The title of this series of articles is therefore "On Moral Behavior."

As was shown above, it is only logical to maintain that the relative value of a nation depends on the relative value of each individual. The only way for people to accumulate worth in a society is to perfect both their public and private behavior and allow the evidence of every single action, however small, to accumulate. To illustrate, it is like time shown on the face of a clock: the seconds add up to minutes and the minutes to hours. In just the same way, it is possible to watch as the smallest of actions group together to form someone's personal worth.

Now, the Western phrase for "public behavior" is **public morality**, and it involves everything related to interactions in human society. Examples are: showing the utmost loyalty in performing one's patriotic duty, devotion to government, and efforts to benefit the people and profit the nation. These all result from concern for interests outside the sphere of the individual and the family. To perfect one's public behavior is to die for one's nation, to exert oneself for other people, to suffer in the public interest and share the pleasures and pains of the people. On the other hand, "private behavior" involves all activities that one performs for one's own benefit, and is known as **private morality**. Examples are: the relations between husband and wife or children and parents, and personal matters such as rising and going to bed, eating and sleeping, and leisure pursuits. These are all activities that have absolutely no connection with the public sphere. It is because they concern the private sphere that they are classed as private behavior.

The purpose of this series of articles is purely to discuss private behavior. Therefore it will first be essential to examine the nature of private behavior among the Japanese people from the past up until the present day and the nature of private behavior at this very moment. At the same time, it will be necessary to examine the standards used in observing and making comments about other people's private behavior in the past, and what standards are in use today. In the process, the relative value in the eyes of the world of the people of our nation, and therefore of the nation itself, will also become clear.

In past ages, Japan too was not excluded from the history of barbarianism found in other nations of the world. Nothing was as highly valued as the art of war, and those of superior strength in body and mind were so involved in fighting that they were rarely at home, and so they had no time to consider their private behavior: "Fathers acted unlike fathers, sons acted unlike sons, husbands acted unlike husbands, and wives unlike wives."[2]

Men tramped across mountains and rivers, and if at times they suffered hunger and thirst, there were also times when they gave themselves over to victory celebrations, eating and drinking till they could hold no more. It is clear from the records of the civil wars during the period of Ashikaga rule [1336–1573] that on expeditions far from home samurai would not only sample the pleasure quarters, but engage in violent acts, forcing themselves upon young girls and turning the wives of their enemies into concubines. Even today, people whose occupation prevents them from having a settled home such as captains of ships, sea voyagers, traveling merchants and soldiers, do not have a strong sense of the need to show restraint in their private behavior. While there are times when they refrain from indulging their desire for wine and women, there are also times when they allow themselves to let loose completely. Of course, since these occupations do not permit a normal life, involving danger and even the risk of death, it is not surprising that when the opportunity presents itself they give themselves up to pleasure in compensation for their pains, just like the samurai of the civil-war period. We should not submit them to wholesale blame but view them with sympathy, because, after all, it is their occupations that make them so. For their part, while the samurai of the civil-war period were truly guilty of the acts of violence described above, they were not completely without any sense of morality. A promise was as hard to overturn as a mountain; a life was as easy to throw away as a speck of dust. This martial spirit with its emphasis on duty and self-sacrifice contains much that has impressed those of later generations. But sad to say, because their thoughts were focused only on fighting and military strategy, they did not understand the significance of private behavior, and since they did not understand its significance they felt no shame in violating its rules. They did so openly, showing satisfaction rather than guilt.

It is said that Toyotomi Hideyoshi [1537–1598][3] once invited a missionary from Spain[4] to his castle in Osaka to hear his explanation of the teachings of Catholicism. Hideyoshi showed his joy, and expressed no doubts about any of the teachings except one, the commandment that said that a man could only take one wife. Hideyoshi expressed his dissatisfaction by openly declaring, without any hesitation, that he would be unable to keep such a rule. This episode should be seen as evidence of Hideyoshi's candid and carefree nature and the general fact that the military leaders of those days neither understood the significance of private behavior, nor felt any guilt about ignoring its rules. In other words, it is clear that the tendency of the people in the civil-war period to pay little attention to private behavior was an inevitable result of the atmosphere of the time.

Even today, any general examination of the customs of the Japanese will show that as far as private behavior is concerned, the past traditions of the ancient samurai still hold sway. Since Japan still calls itself a fighting nation, power is in the hands of military men; since the words and actions of military men are held up as a model to all, it is only natural that these customs are followed, regardless of whether they are good or evil.

Installment Two

Ashikaga rule gave way to the regimes of Oda Nobunaga [1534–1582], Toyotomi Hideyoshi and finally, to the Tokugawa. The long years of unrest ended and a period of peace came to the land. With the establishment of the carefully organized feudal system with its hereditary stipends, the samurai and their military leaders no longer went on expeditions or fought battles, and those who had once been the most active members of society became those with the least personal freedom. In former years, they had spent their lives outside, buffeted by the elements, with only a few days at home every year. While those left behind longed for them to return, they went on their expeditions to enemy regions and faced no restraints on their behavior as they celebrated victories by drinking and reciting poems under the autumn moon. But now all was changed. They were assigned to live in feudal castles or in residences that were appropriate to their rank, and their normal bureaucratic duties required them to sit in the *han* administrative base dressed correctly in formal robes and headgear. The bloodthirsty exploits of the past were replaced by flowery words, and they could not even go out whenever they wished, but only if they were on official business. Their situation was so restricted that they resembled beasts that had been captured in the wild and confined to cages. In other words, the policy of the Tokugawa government was to control the feudal leaders and their samurai by imposing the outward observance of protocol, and thereby restraining their rough nature. To borrow the words of Confucius, "One is supposed to govern a state with the rituals [propriety]."[5] Leaving aside consideration of the wisdom of such a political strategy, the taming effect of this life of protocol was so great that when the first generation gave way to the second, they seemed on the outside to have been transformed into extremely mild-mannered and refined gentlemen. However, they could not shake off the active and carefree disposition that had been passed down from their ancestors, and the financial freedom that came from the wealth that accrued to their rank only served to feed this spirit. Behavior that had once been active and carefree now became selfish and willful and was also very difficult to control.

Since interactions in the public sphere were restricted by protocol and therefore gave them no enjoyment, their private dwellings became places where they turned their willfulness to the pursuit of unbounded pleasure. While there were differences in degree, men of families high in the feudal scale, at the top those eligible to be appointed Shōgun and at the bottom daimyo, *hatamoto* [the Shōgun's immediate retainers] and the chief retainers of daimyo, all shut themselves up in their own little kingdoms and gave themselves to the pleasures of the flesh. To give one or two examples of their pastimes, they would build gardens with lakes, buy rare birds and exotic flowers, and enjoy performances of Noh, the tea ceremony, songs, dance and music, even horse riding and hawking, all within their residences without ever venturing outside. But the most popular pastime was womanizing, and they were willing to spend any amount to buy beautiful women. Noble families would keep several dozen concubines, and would therefore have dozens of children. It was not unknown for two infants to be born on exactly the same day and the same hour, not as twins from one mother but from two different mothers, so that it was difficult to decide which was the elder and which the younger. Shōgun Tokugawa Ienari [1773–1841] had fifty-one sons and daughters; Ieyoshi [1793–1853, his second son and successor] had twenty-seven. Similarly, it was not unusual for daimyo to have thirty or forty children.

One can easily imagine the deplorable state of private behavior in such households. A glance would show that even if the teaching regarding the father acting like the father and the son acting like the son was understood, the principle according to which the husband should therefore act like the husband and the wife like the wife was not.[6] In other words, in the past men who belonged to military families had enjoyed an active life unrestrained in either mind or body with no awareness of the morality of private behavior and no qualms about behaving in a bold and impetuous way. When the peaceful times of the Tokugawa period began, they were unable to shake off the old habits that they had inherited, and even if they were clothed in refinement on the outside, their lack of regard for the morality of private behavior showed resemblances to the civil-war period.

Such being the state of affairs, one might assume that those belonging to families high in the feudal scale would have lacked discernment in all aspects of private behavior and been rough and ill mannered in every respect, but this was definitely not so. After the peace of Tokugawa rule was secured [through the defeat of Hideyoshi's son at his castle in Osaka] in 1615, the teachings of Confucian scholars gradually became known. In particular, almost all members of samurai families were raised under the influence of Confucianism, with the result that there were none who lacked reverence for the Ways of "benevolence, dutifulness, observance of the rites [propriety] and wisdom" or the need "to be good sons and good younger brothers, loyal to their prince and true to their word."[7] From morning to evening, Confucian scholars taught their pupils to be good sons to their parents and obedient to their seniors. Their doctrine was based on correct conduct and sincerity and truthfulness in all situations, with no distinction between public or private behavior. As a result, significance was actually given to private behavior and emphasis was placed on acting with restraint even when alone. These developments were due to the peaceful state that society was now in, and the well-ordered nature of civilized life was a great contrast to the civil-war times.

Unfortunately, however, examination of the nature of Confucianism reveals that its instructions are all aimed at those who are of junior status and in a weak position, while it has only vague warnings for those who are of senior status and in a strong position. Children were taught filial behavior but parents were not informed of their duties; the young were ordered to perform hard labor, but the old were not expected to give anything in return. The basic principle was for young people and children to be loudly scolded, but for their seniors and the elderly to escape any blame. When this principle was extended to the relations between men and women, the result was the same. In other words, because men are strong but women are weak, the blade of censure was normally directed at women. They were taught to be mild mannered, ordered to show self-restraint, prohibited from meeting people and from engaging in talk. Worst of all, joy was shown if they were without learning or ability and therefore servile in their attitudes. Since such qualities were regarded as feminine virtues, eventually they were even robbed of the precious chance to acquire an education.

On the other hand, men lived in a world of unrestricted comfort. They bore not the slightest duty with regard to women; at the most their only duty was to keep them alive and provide them with food and clothing. If they felt love for them, it was only the sort of love that one feels for a plaything; if they felt affection for them, it was only the affection that one feels for something that is familiar. In their interactions with women there was no trace of respect, and this gave result to the custom of respecting men and despising women.[8] As a result, however self-indulgent those who belonged to high-ranking families were in satisfying their lust, however violent and ill mannered they were in their relations with women, the public morality and customs of the time meant that there was no one to reproach them for their lack of virtue. On the rare occasions when there was someone who reproached them, the censure did not focus on the proper relations between one human being and another but on the correct way in which to handle such weak vessels. You would hear exchanges such as the following: "X threw out his lady wife in a fit of anger." "What a shame, for she is young and beautiful. He will come to regret this some day;" and "Young Y sold his horse in exchange for a concubine." "Which affords more pleasure — a horse or a concubine?" The tone of such remarks clearly showed that the speakers despised women and did not regard them as equal members of the human race. This being the case, under the peaceful feudal rule of the Tokugawa period, life may slowly have become more civilized and teachings about private behavior may have looked as if they were gradually becoming more severe. But in the most important area of private behavior, relations between men and women, these teachings seemed to be without effect. The failure of the most dignified nobles and gentlemen to show any shame regarding their immoral behavior, and the equal failure of anyone to reproach them, must be seen as the fault of Confucianism.

Although the thousands of books on Confucianism seem to cover every conceivable topic, I have never heard any mention of the principle that there should be one husband to one wife, or that since there are equal numbers of men and women, they should have equal rights. On the contrary, there are a great many references to respecting men and despising women. In making this distinction between high and low it is taken for granted that the one who is placed high can amuse himself with the one who is placed low as if she were nothing more than a weak vessel; therefore there is no point in hoping for any improvement in men's behavior. As a result, my opinion is that the only way to correct the present behavior of Japanese men is to control the carefree and impetuous spirit that has unfortunately been inherited from the samurai of the civil-war period, and to be open about the failings of Confucianism.

Installment Three

In the previous installment, I declared that in order to correct the present behavior of Japanese men it is vital to control the carefree and impetuous spirit that has unfortunately been inherited from the samurai of the civil-war period, and to be open about the failings of Confucianism. This is because in my view, there are certainly reasons for being dissatisfied with the present behavior of men in our society. It is my earnest desire to return them to the correct path by removing all traces of this deplorable state but, as is the case with all declarations of this kind, I must admit that it is easier said than done. In other words, in this world of ours, to put pressure on people with forceful arguments while knowing that your efforts will be futile is equal to putting pressure on those who are lame in order to get them to run. Your attempts will not only be fruitless; the lame people may end up so upset as a result that they will even stop the efforts to walk that they have been making up till now. I do not wish to use the sort of methods that would put a lame person into such a state of despair.

Now, any examination of the behavior of men in Japan today will clearly show that the majority fall into the same category as people who are lame. Accordingly, I will not require men of this kind to return to the correct path immediately. I am willing to take a sympathetic attitude to their past misdeeds for the moment, but I have three requests to make of them for the future: that younger men cease to imitate the immoral behavior of the older men who preceded them; that if they cannot prevent themselves from committing immoral acts, they treat them as the most delicate aspects of their private behavior and therefore keep them so secret that no indecent rumors escape; and that they become aware of those aspects of society that they had not seen as indecent up till now, and keep their distance from them.

By suggesting that people who commit immoral acts should secretly conceal them I will displease those who stand up for righteousness, since it is equivalent to taking refuge in outdated customs. They will take a forthright attitude, and declare that the only way to correct immoral behavior is to rectify it from the roots upward: "There are only two paths, the correct and the non correct."[9] "Those who are subject to the morality of human beings, who are 'of all creatures . . . the most highly endowed'[10] cannot contemplate the acceptance of indecent behavior; there is no reason for allowing it whether it is public or private, seen or unseen." I basically hold to the same principle and cannot offer anything that will counter the force of their argument. But examination throughout history of both the natural working of human emotions, and the abilities that people gain through education, shows that it is extremely difficult for human beings to maintain a state of perfect moral behavior. Admittedly, there are some who are so slow and sickly in mind and body that they lack either the energy or the need to commit immoral acts, and some who are active and healthy and know how to commit these acts but have the strength of character not to do so. However, efforts to demand better behavior from those who remain once these two types are excluded will be as ineffective as efforts to make someone who is lame go faster, no matter what arguments are used to reproach them.

In this world of steady change, there being few who are feeble in mind and body and hardly any who possess moral courage, society has, as it were, thousands upon thousands of people who are lame. Since there are not even any teachings that make clear why to be lame is to be at a disadvantage and to warn about the need to be careful, I do not expect much from this type of person at the beginning. The first step is to erect a respectable front to improve the outward appearance of society by concealing all traces of immoral behavior. The second step is my own outlandish dream that a time will come when the pretense will turn into reality and moral behavior will actually return to the correct path. We can only hope that this result will be achieved several hundred years into the future.

The present state of affairs clearly shows that sexual desire is one of the main urges in everyday life, so that to control it is extremely difficult. The urge can be so strong that men are ready to throw away whole fortunes or even risk their lives. It brings the individual a feeling of the utmost pleasure or pain, on a level so personal that it can be neither discussed nor brought up for discussion. Nothing is shown on the surface, so that despite the infinite variety of sensations both inside and outside the body, and the infinite gradations of pleasure or pain that result, there is no way in which anyone's actual experience can be understood by anyone else. This means that any comments by an outsider must be highly sympathetic. Therefore, my object is to not to involve myself directly in anyone's personal affairs and work to correct behavior at an individual level, or even worse, expose these same affairs to the standards set by a cold and unfeeling man of virtue. I have a great dislike for such preaching. My only wish is that people will take greater care and build deeper ramparts of privacy, for the sake of the outward appearance of society, and as a matter of personal protocol. I sometimes hear the claim that as civilization and enlightenment progress, private behavior will improve, producing a society of men of pure and unstained virtue who will fulfill their marital duties by being faithful to their wives, thus presenting a picture of unblemished beauty. But if the present state of progress is to be called "civilization and enlightenment," I can only say that I have no hope of our ever reaching a morally pure society.

Any comparison of Japan with Western nations will show that the latter are several steps higher up the ladder, but if we get a clear look at people's private behavior by exposing the most personal levels and going below the ramparts of secrecy, we are likely to discover that they are not necessarily as civilized on the inside as their level of civilization might suggest. It is more a matter of the ramparts being so steep that it is difficult to see what is going on. This being so, at our present level of civilization we do not have, as it were, the **chemical** power to purify private behavior, only the **mechanical** ability to put it out of sight and sound by containing it within deep ramparts. In other words, since we cannot hope to change the actual state of affairs, the only course is to cover things up so that no odors are able to escape. This process leaves much to be desired and there will be some who express indignation, but we are living in a world that is governed by the standards of Western civilization and enlightenment. Any failure to keep in step will make one person fall behind the other people or put one nation out of joint with the other nations. Just as the proverb says, "If you can't beat them, join them," everyone must keep in step and imitate the prevailing trend. With regard to the case of moral behavior as well, if the people of America and Europe truly followed the doctrine that they uphold by guarding the principle of one husband one wife with pure hearts, there would obviously be no question about our imitating this trend. Yet even if the actual truth is that there are few whose private behavior is without a blemish, and that in fact most of them are just skilled at keeping their blemishes secret by concealing them, the wise course is still to imitate the trend, even though it is one of concealment. This is because we Japanese, too, are part of this world of civilization and enlightenment and wish to preserve the honor of our nation by assuming the mantle of progress. Surely it is blindingly obvious that the difference between concealment and openness is equal to the difference between beauty and ugliness or heaven and hell. Thus, our only choice is concealment.

Confucius said, "When [the gentleman] makes a mistake, he is not afraid to correct it,"[11] and in normal circumstances, it is considered virtuous behavior not to conceal one's errors but to be open about them. But the case of moral behavior is slightly different; regardless of whether one is able to improve it or not, the principle of concealment must not be forgotten even for a second. This is the fine line that marks the distinction between humans and beasts; the only reason why I find myself reduced to proposing this resort to secrecy lies here. I beg the understanding of the advocates of righteousness.

Installment Four
Customs that date back hundreds or thousands of years cannot be easily shaken off. The people of a country do not suddenly perceive the errors of the public morality that has taken root in their minds. The opening of the treaty ports followed by the restoration of Imperial rule caused an upheaval on a scale never before experienced in our history. Changes did not occur only in government: in areas unrelated to politics, from folk customs, education, and methods of production to the details of clothing, food, and housing, the old ways were abandoned in favor of the new, as if Japan was being completely recreated. Witnesses from other countries were not the only ones to be astonished; even

we ourselves have been unable to believe how and why the transformation has occurred.

Yet, although it looks as if nothing old remains to be seen, when we turn our eyes to the moral sphere and observe the state of private behavior with particular attention to men's moral behavior concerning women, we discover, to our amazement, that it is just like Japan was before the country was opened, since nothing has changed at all. Moreover, in the past the ranking of the feudal system was accompanied by rigid protocol so that even though members of the higher ranking samurai families and the richer commoners became involved in the ugliness of immoral behavior, the ugliness was blockaded within so that no trace could leak out. However nowadays, since the restraints of rigid feudal protocol have been abolished along with the ranking system, moral behavior is completely uncontrolled, like a horse that has lost his bit and been set free in the fields of spring. He prances among the flowers, gambols between the willows, licks at the tender young leaves when he finds them, but kicks around anything less tasty such as dry grass.[12] Active and carefree, his impetuous nature is exposed in broad daylight to all eyes and none of his movements are hidden. The pedigree of this horse dates back past the long peace of the Tokugawa period to the civil wars several hundred years ago; his forebears showed no concern regarding moral behavior, nor did they ever receive any instruction in this area. Even in these days of Western-style civilization, he cannot shake off the impulses that he has inherited. He puts his lips to Western-style food, and clothes his body in Western-style garments; both his words and actions seem rooted in Western-style ways. But in his preservation of the old Japanese attitudes to moral behavior he is similar to a language expert who has lived in a foreign country for so long and learnt the language so thoroughly that he appears to have almost completely forgotten his native Japanese. Yet this same man mumbles his native language when he talks in his sleep. It must be that the language that has been passed down to him from his ancestors for over a hundred thousand years has penetrated so deeply into his memory that even though it appears to be forgotten, it will come back to life in his dreams, when it is beyond his conscious control. Similarly, we must conclude that the reason why Japanese men who live in civilized times wish to preserve only those old attitudes that involve moral behavior must be because in this respect alone, they still have not woken from yesterday's dreams of carefree impetuosity.

Let us have a look at how some of those prominent figures respected as gentlemen of high virtue in Japan today enter into marriage. Among them are men who say that it is foolish to inform one's parents before marriage, or that it is impossible to stay by the side of the wife who was selected by one's parents in former days; they run around searching for the "spring fragrance" of a glamorous beauty. Others, tiring of the "fading blossoms" at home and "the branches" heavy with growing children, decide to abandon them. Of course, since a man should stand on his own feet there is no reason why he should consult his parents when choosing his partner for life, and I would never reproach such behavior; however, a man who is independent enough to stand on his own feet in marrying should also be independent enough to make his own living. Despite this, there are outrageous tales of men who rely on their parents to fund all their everyday needs and yet expect to choose their wives entirely by themselves. Again, while there may be no reason for a man to pay any thought to the faithful wife whom he married long ago at the orders of his real or adopted parents, if he simultaneously forgets to pay any thought to the emotional and financial outlay that his adopted parents expended in providing for his everyday needs and even his education, we have no choice but to call him an anti-social egoist.

At a stroke the Imperial Restoration abolished the feudal rankings so that everyone became equal. Daimyo, members of the Imperial court, samurai, farmers, artisans, and merchants: since all were of equal rank, they were free to marry whomever they wished, regardless of status. It is truly splendid for men of high status to marry the daughters of lowly townsmen or farmers. As well as giving this my complete approval, I am convinced that it is an essential feature of civilization and enlightenment. However, the daughters of townsmen and farmers include all kinds of women, and while I do not want to discuss differences of appearance or ability at present, what about those who wish to discuss the issue of money before they discuss marriage itself? The object is not to measure the respective wealth of both the families involved. The girl's family is known to be poor from the beginning; since she has no "possessions" apart from her body, the marriage is arranged by agreeing a sum of money based on the value assigned to this possession. Of course, the word used for money in such cases is not necessarily "price." There are all sorts of euphemisms such as "the cost of the *trousseau*," "various allowances" or "a formal loan," but the fact of the matter is that the marriage will only be agreed if money is put on the table. In other words, we have no alternative but to say that marriages are being bought and sold. Moreover, in such cases marriage is probably not the first time that such a woman has been involved in discussions about money, since it is likely that she has already been whoring,[13] either openly or in secret. This is clearly not a marriage, but the buying out of a contract with a brothel. Whatever the origins of such a woman, whether she was born in the city, in a village or to an ex-samurai family, to take to wife a woman like this is to form an utterly illicit bond, since to buy or sell a marriage is uncivilized.

Most women who are known as concubines in Japan today were obtained through this method of marriage. Some live in the family residence, while others are housed separately; some rise from the position of concubine to become proper wives and live in triumph like the heroines of a rag-to-riches story. Where this has happened, my hopes will be met if it is possible to present a respectable front to society in general. This can be done by keeping secret the existence of concubines, or wives who rise from the position of concubines, and concealing them from public knowledge; when they are already wives and cannot be concealed, we can reduce their participation in society, even if this is inconvenient and regrettable, and thus endeavor to prevent them from attracting attention. I will not try to expose people's private affairs by penetrating beyond this point, since I highly dislike such attempts; my only desire is to encourage people to conceal what is going on by showing restraint and remaining silent, in order to improve the habits of society. But unfortunately, the men who I am talking about here are so impetuous and lacking in concern that they have no idea of the importance of being secretive about these matters. For instance, when two gentlemen talking together mention a third party, it is very common for one of them to remark, "Did you know that A's concubine . . . ?," but their intention is not necessarily to slander A or show their contempt. Worse are those who let slip remarks about "**my concubine**" doing such and such or that the house she has been set up in is like this or that, all without the least sign of embarrassment. Worse still are the men who take such pride in the total number of their concubines, both those they have living in the family residence and those whom they have housed separately. In their practice of inviting people to the dwelling places of the latter, as if to flaunt this pride, they are similar to men who take guests to their stables to display a horse that they have raised.

I have some personal knowledge of the conditions in civilized countries and have also heard people talk about them and read books. There are many things that could be said about what goes on behind the scenes, but I have yet to find any example of a country that exposes everything in broad daylight, as Japan does. I cannot bear this shame, for it reveals the unenlightened nature of the people of my country.

Installment Five
Concerning the moral behavior of Japanese men, one of the points that I have been advocating is that they must wake up to the indecent and immoral nature of behavior that they have taken for granted up till now, and begin to avoid it. When it comes to actual examples of this behavior, there is no need to give fresh warnings about adulterous acts since they call forth universal disapproval, but there is one group of people whose truly indecent behavior has been taken for granted by ordinary members of society, who overlook and ignore them. I mean the geisha.[14]

In the years before the Imperial Restoration, geisha already existed in commercially flourishing areas such as the big cities of Tokyo, Osaka, and Kyoto, but their profession was to play music, sing, and dance, or at the most to look after the guests at drinking parties and liven up the atmosphere. It was only rarely that gossip was heard of their becoming involved in obscene behavior, and in fact they had their own ways of keeping order among themselves. As a result, the few who did act licentiously were ostracized or, even if not publicly driven away, quietly withdrew of their own accord. However, since the Restoration, these customs have been more or less abandoned and if we take Tokyo for an example, it now has no less than one thousand geisha and over twenty places that are known to be their haunts. I have made efforts to find out about both the public goings on when they look after clients at restaurants and teahouses, and also their inner secrets. My only reason for not revealing them here is that I do not really wish to expose these matters to the light of day. However, my information is that the profession of today's geisha is not limited to encouraging drinking by providing musical entertainment. It would seem that the majority are only too ready to accede to the demands of their guests, and that not one has never sold her favors.

According to an expert in medical hygiene, inspections for syphilis in areas licensed for prostitution such as Shin Yoshiwara have largely made it possible to prevent the harm of contagion,[15] but they are only carried out in publicly licensed districts. As long as the geisha in other parts of the city are left as they are, the best way to describe the situation will be to compare it to the proverb about driving the tigers away from the front gate but leaving the back gate undefended from the wolves.

I will not attempt to ascertain whether it is the demand for geisha that appears first and produces a supply, or the supply that appears first and produces the demand. In any case, ever since the Restoration, the custom of inviting geisha has been steadily growing throughout society to the extent that in both small and large gatherings, whenever drink is offered, geisha must also appear. Geisha have not only come to feature virtually as part of the menu at banquets; they form such a vital ingredient that one could even say that a banquet without geisha is not fit for a gentleman. For example, a man situated at the upper levels of society who is deeply involved in affairs of state, a dignified paragon of virtue, is said to have invited dozens of geisha to help to enliven a feast at such-and-such a banqueting hall yesterday, so that the main guests departed greatly satisfied. Tonight he is meeting such-and-such a group who are up from the provinces at such-and-such a restaurant, and since an order has been sent out for geisha it is clear that it will be a splendid occasion. Once a trend like this has become established in the popular imagination, it cannot be gainsaid. Geisha are invited to every gathering, from merchants' negotiations about loans of money and receptions held for companies, to student meetings and get-togethers of friends or relatives. Most shocking are discussions of temple business held by monks. When a room full of men with shaven heads reaches the height of drunkenness, the sight of the crimson hems of the geishas' kimono flashing among the confusion of black robes has to be seen to be believed.

The reason why geisha originally became an indispensable part of the parties held by Japanese men of this type was not only because their sexual favors could be purchased. Since geisha are experienced in helping guests to have a good time together, without them it is much harder to make a success of gatherings at restaurants or of occasions when arrangements are made to deliver food to someone's residence. As a result, there are situations when their presence is essential. However, consideration of their true identity makes one wonder what part of society they really belong to, and how they should be judged in the eyes of civilization. As was mentioned above, most of them are willing to supply the demands of those who wish to purchase sexual favors for money, and whatever general name they may go by, any woman who sells her favors in response to these demands must be classed as a type of whore. In the Western language they are known as **prostitutes**, the most numerous inhabitants of the most contemptible regions of the civilized world. Not only will gentlemen refuse to go near them in public; "to be in company with" one of these whores by mistake at an enjoyable gathering in a civilized country would give all the ladies and their male escorts the same sensation as [the virtuous] Boyi when he felt as if he was "sitting in mud or pitch while wearing a court cap and gown." The indignation they felt as they spurned her would be similar to the scorn Boyi felt for "improper sights" and "improper sounds."[16]

There is no point in talking about these matters with those influenced by Ancient Learning[17] or men who behave impetuously; neither is there anything to be gained by warning those talented men of the floating world[18] who behave as if they are connoisseurs of the pleasure quarters. But there are also men who set their hearts on Western civilization from a young age, have had contact with gentlemen from there and frequently visited the actual countries. Since they should have personal experience of the organization of Western societies, one would expect them to understand all about it. There are also those who have spent long periods studying abroad, and many prominent men who have made trips for the specific purpose of observing the living conditions and customs of the West. Yet, when these men come home and are once again exposed to the Japanese atmosphere for a while, they easily succumb to its influence and become connoisseurs of the pleasure quarters. As for their behavior at very grand drinking parties when the geisha play music, sing and dance, I find it hard to believe that they show a [pure] nature like that of Liu Xiahui [720–621 BCE],[19] and are never troubled by lewd talk or disconcerted by indecent games, remaining unruffled in the presence of people both drinking, talking, laughing, yelling, even lying down and sleeping, or with a hundred geisha undressing nearby.

Regardless of whether they have visited Western countries, prominent men like this must have some close friends among people from there, and they probably write to each other once in a while to explain what they have been doing. Such a letter might go as follows:

> On such and such a day last month, I joined together with some like-minded people to inaugurate such and such an association, which we have been planning for some time in order to benefit both the people and the country itself and serve the interests of public morality. Many gentlemen from both

the government and the private sector attended and after greetings from Mr. A and a speech by Dr. B, we held a banquet . . .

So far, so good, but how should the writer continue? After mentioning that they invited *x* many geisha to liven up the atmosphere, and describing how the music, singing and dancing created such a pleasant atmosphere that all the guests became thoroughly drunk and went home highly satisfied, will he then add a few words of explanation just in case, since a foreigner might not understand the meaning of "geisha"? For example:

> Originally, as their name suggests, geisha were women with a profession that involved particular skills, or *gei*, but recently their customs have changed greatly. They have made a step forward and are now willing to supply the private demands of their clients by selling their favors either temporarily or on a regular basis. When gentlemen in the upper reaches of our society have public or private meetings and organize banquets either big or small, they always invite geisha to look after everything, so that guests and geisha share boundless pleasure among the ruins of the feast.

My guess is that however close a friend the foreigner he is writing to might be, he will not add such a clear explanation. Rather, my belief is that his inner voice will prevent him from doing so. Although there is no need to be uneasy about talking with other Japanese men about amusing oneself with geisha at a banquet, to mention it to a foreigner is somewhat embarrassing. But if it is a matter that must by all means be kept secret from the members of civilized countries, it is not clear to me why within Japan alone no embarrassment is involved. Individuals achieve high honor and weighty reputations by building them up little by little, and the same is true of nations. Only a thoughtless person who knows nothing of himself or of his country would consider that such little matters are of no account.

Installment Six

If we leave the society of the geisha in order to examine the enclaves within which *shōgi*[20] are licensed to operate, we will find that the latter are unashamedly engaged in the business of whoring, and that the areas officially termed pleasure quarters (*yūkaku*) are haunts of whoring, regions that do not form part of the everyday human world. There are few people now who are interested in discussing the merits and demerits of the *shōgi*, and the view of those who are known as moralists is obviously that we would be better off without them. Yet the human world does not function solely according to morality, and if we were to divide human nature into two halves, one half would be human, but the other half would be animal. In other words, the human part resembles a man wearing clothes, and the animal part a man wearing nothing at all. If it were possible, as the moralists wish, for the rational, human, part of the mind to control the workings of the irrational, animal, part of the mind, everything would go perfectly, but no example of this has ever been seen. In that case, if it is really impossible to prevent the animal part from working, we must accept this situation and cease to fight against it. Thus nowadays, even among the most narrow-minded people, there are none who talk about eliminating *shōgi* at the roots, on the grounds that the most beneficial policy will rather lie in finding ways of preventing the worst consequences. In particular, the advance of civilization has sharply increased the gap between rich and poor, causing a proportionally sharp increase in ostentation. The poor are so poor that they cannot provide for a wife; the rich are so occupied with their desire for ostentation that they do not have time to marry. Everywhere this has produced multitudes of bachelors and the need for *shōgi* as a means to satisfy their sexual appetites. In truth, if the gap between rich and poor were not as sharp as it is, if society was constructed so that both the upper and lower reaches contributed a reasonable amount of labor in return for a reasonable amount of money, and everyone was able to maintain a household, we would have an ideal situation and the need for *shōgi* would greatly decrease. However, this is impossible to achieve in reality because it runs against the overall direction in which society is moving.

At present, one man earns between 20 to 30 *sen* [0.2 to 0.3 yen] and 40 to 50 *sen* per day, at least in the cities; in the countryside, it is often not even half of that. If we take account of holidays and days when the weather prevents work, this amounts to less than 10 yen a month, and 5 or 6 yen in most cases. This is barely enough to cover one man's food and clothing expenses with nothing left even for drinking. There is no way in which it would be possible to provide for a wife as well, so if any man who has married despite this is unlucky enough to have a child, the whole family will simply be driven to starvation. On the other hand, in the case of the upper reaches of society, ostentation is an inevitable fact of existence. Its evil presence is particularly evident in the countries of Europe and America, since acceptance in high society requires the maintenance of outward appearances in the form of magnificent clothes and food. In particular, marriage is a great event in the life of both men and women, but it is not something that can be undertaken lightly. The wedding itself requires considerable expenditure, and afterwards living expenses are bound to multiply as a result of the changes in the style of living that are needed to procure a reputation for the family. In any case, most men have no choice but to bear the hardships of bachelorhood.

Another factor is related to the recent advance in educational methods, which has caused remarkable development in the mental capacity of both men and women. This has given them what might be called a high awareness of their dignity, but in financial terms they are clearly poor, and if a poor person seeks to marry, the choice of partner is limited to someone equally poor. No young man or woman of learning, whatever school they attended, no matter how outstanding their literary talent or other accomplishments, will be able to find a marriage partner better than the daughter of a backstreet trader or the son of an alleyway artisan, unless their talents or accomplishments can be turned into enough money to provide them with a comfortable lifestyle. With their level of education, they think to themselves, they cannot be expected to accept such an unrefined girl as a wife, or endure a husband who is an ill-mannered lout. "I may not have any money, but compared to my real worth, the difference between lord and vassal is as nothing." Their situation resembles that of a foolish and impoverished member of the aristocracy who clings to his title and decorations even though no one takes them seriously. Such a man, too, will have no choice but to remain a bachelor. Therefore, it is true that as civilization and enlightenment continue their gradual advance, there are small signs that people are coming to value intellectual pastimes in place of physical desire; however, at the same time, enlightenment is increasing the number of bachelors, with consequences that are presenting real problems. The only solution is an unpleasant policy of desperation: reliance on the services of *shōgi* to preserve social order.

Suppose we were successful in abolishing all *shōgi*, so that there were no signs of them left. The effects would be horrific. For instance, if some time in the near future all the pleasure districts in Tokyo, including Shin Yoshiwara, were banned and on top of that strict controls on whoring were enforced throughout the city, so that a complete blockade was imposed, what would happen? Within a few months, it would undoubtedly prove impossible to control the animal desires that filled the city. On the surface this would be manifested in the licentious behavior of children of good family; below the surface, lonely widows would consent to sex.[21] There would be outbreaks of rape and adultery, kidnappings and elopements, and explosions of conflict in place after place. The result would be an irreparable disruption of social order. In fact, we must surely admit that the only reason why such terrible situations have been avoided up till now is because of the efforts of *shōgi*. Their profession is most contemptible and unsightly, and unpleasant both mentally and physically for the women involved. But in view of the way in which society is organized at present, not only are we far from being in a position to be able to abolish this profession, it is in fact the only means by which social order is being preserved. That is to say, regardless of the actual purpose that women have in mind when taking it up, without them social order would immediately be disrupted. From the point of view of society, if we judge the end results of their efforts rather than considering who is performing what, we must define the *shōgi* as someone who serves society through her suffering.

While his metaphor may sound a little far-fetched, a certain Western scholar once called prostitutes **martyrs** of a corrupt world.[22] **Martyr** is a word for people who sacrifice their lives for the principles of a religion or doctrine, in other words, people of benevolence who offer themselves up in order to lead others to salvation. In Japanese terms they are people on a par with the Buddhist leaders Shinran [1173–1263] and Nichiren [1222–1282], who clearly did nothing less than sacrifice their lives in order to spread the teachings of the Buddha and to bring peace to all living things, sleeping on grass with a rock as a pillow, even enduring the sufferings of exile and being sentenced to death.[23] These **martyrs** achieved virtuous deeds that are of great worth; however, at this very moment *shōgi* are saving us from the danger of terrible situations that would easily occur without their presence; their purpose is different, but in terms of the effect on society, the value of their virtuous deeds is neither more nor less than the virtuous deeds of Shinran and Nichiren. Since they advance the safety and happiness of the world through their suffering, they should be called **martyrs**. I wish not to abolish them but to keep them, and I have an idea about how this should be done. My idea will be explained in the next installment.

Installment Seven

In the previous installments I have presented strong arguments regarding the essential role of *shōgi* in our present state, and I assume that my readers agree. However, their profession is utterly contemptible and unpleasant; it can only be described as a practice embraced by those who have rejected the laws of human morality and who are therefore no longer human. Any woman who takes up this profession has forfeited her honor as a woman, and any man who amuses himself with such women has abandoned his reputation as a man; having fallen below the lowest levels of human behavior in each other's company, they are sharing the illicit pleasures of animal passion. Therefore, even though there are a multitude of reasons why this practice cannot be prohibited, in a world of civilized human beings we must take care to conceal it as thoroughly as possible. A metaphor used in the previous chapter implied that clothing served to hide the indecent nature of the body. Clothing does not remove the indecency, but whenever it is worn, the indecency has no visual effect. In the same way, although concealing the evidence of whoring will not actually remove its indecency from society, the effect can be easily understood if we compare the visual effect of wearing clothes versus not wearing them.

In Western countries too, the number of prostitutes is very large and their services are enjoyed with enthusiasm, but civilization has reached such heights of display that nothing is revealed to the public eye. Even if a glimpse is revealed, no mention will pass any lips or reach any ears. In the beauty of its outward appearance society displays the assurance of a noble lady showing off her garments. If someone looking for the inner reality strips off the garments and looks at what lies beneath, unexpected blemishes may be revealed, and the indecency may be such that the eye turns away. Yet the eye of civilization only evaluates the beauty or vileness of the garments, ignoring what may lie beneath. In other words, civilized societies owe their beauty to the fact that the many public women (*shōgi*) are unseen, and the flourishing pleasure areas are invisible.

On the other hand, if we turn to Japanese society, the situation is exactly the opposite, for there is nothing that imprints itself more on the eyes and ears than *shōgi* and the pleasure quarters. In Tokyo, for instance, it is beyond the power of words to describe the boisterous scenes as the pleasure quarters in different parts of the city compete with each other to make the strongest impact. They display this and proclaim that, and if more is needed will plant flowering trees and place lanterns even outside their gates.[24] Occasionally *niwaka* festivals are held, when the women of the quarter parade around its streets [in floats], playing music and dancing.²⁵ Many songs mention "Edomachi and Kyōmachi beautiful as flowers," and while some poets write 31-syllable Japanese *tanka* in praise of the deep emotions that are evoked, others express elegant feelings in Chinese verse.²⁶ In other words, rather than seeking concealment, the pleasure quarters seem only to fear being unknown.

Since the pleasure quarters are organized so as to accommodate such openly boisterous scenes, men in search of pleasure can seek it equally openly, and with no feelings of embarrassment. People probably remember hearing that in the early years of the Tokugawa regime, many daimyo and samurai frequented these places, on horseback or in palanquins, accompanied by great numbers of attendants. Of course, since we live in a less sumptuous age, nowadays there is unlikely to be anyone who will summon a group of servants to attend him when he goes to purchase the services of a *shōgi*. But respectable gentlemen and high-minded students who are such conspicuous visitors in their rickshaws, how they describe the deep emotions of one pleasure quarter and explain the enjoyment provided by another, how they mock the failures of other visitors and crow about their own triumphs, how they preen themselves, how they drool in envy! If you suddenly catch the sound of their boisterous chattering as you pass, you might think that some hot-blooded young men are reenacting the pleasures of the hunting expedition that they had enjoyed the day before.

Since amusing oneself in the pleasure quarters is a respectable activity in Japan, they are often used as a meeting place for business gatherings, the settlement of disputes, parties for the reunion of old acquaintances, assemblies of aficionados of literature and the arts, and even for discussions about politics or secret talks about one's past career, all on the grounds that the atmosphere of these sacred enclaves will somehow help to liven up the proceedings. Serious men who have taken care over their appearance, older men with grey hair who are leaning on their canes, they all go to these meetings with a calm and dignified air. In the same way, when leading men come to the capital from the provinces for a month or so of sightseeing, first they tour the brick buildings of the main street of the Ginza and the famous temples and beauty spots of Shiba, Ueno, Asakusa, and Mukōjima, then they view the facades of the various government buildings and courthouses. Next on the list should be the factories and schools, but even at the cost of postponing the inspection of these important buildings, they must have a try at the delights of the Yoshiwara, since this will give them tales that they can tell for the rest of their lives. To fulfill their lifelong dream of visiting the capital but miss this one delight would be as disastrous as forgetting to buy souvenirs as presents for the people left behind at home. In other words, the value that they place on a visit to Yoshiwara equals the beauties of Ueno, Asakusa and Mukōjima and far exceeds the importance of factories and schools.

Once established, customs cannot easily be defeated. They can force good into evil, and right into wrong. If they can blur the distinction between good and evil, right and wrong, it is not surprising if they can also turn ugliness into beauty. It is customs dating back to the civil-war period and feudal society that have prevented the people of Japan from seeing the ugliness of the profession of the *shōgi*, or from being so embarrassed that they want to conceal their trips for entertainment at the pleasure quarters. However, if they take a look at the civilization of the world with a fresh mind and consider our nation in the light of its relations with this civilization, they should become aware that the time of the civil wars and of feudal society is long gone, and that the Japan of today is a civilized nation. It should equally be clear that if there is anything lacking in the state of our civilization, part of our duty as citizens is to make up for that lack. This being the case, if the prostitute is treated as a secret aspect of human affairs in civilized nations, we must imitate this and make it secret in Japan as well.

Let us reflect on the eye-catching buildings that are put up in the brothel districts, the cherry trees that are planted, the displays of lanterns and the *niwaka* parades, the lively sound of the music that can be heard playing from all directions. This all serves to attract the attention of people near and far. Instead of hiding the ugliness it spreads a shrill invitation: "Here is the paradise of animal pleasures! Honored guests from all parts, in other words, beasts in your multitudes, come and play your brutish games, indulge your brutish desires until you want no more." Of course, there are a great number of such animals in the West as well as in the East, and in the face of this reality, I am not particularly embarrassed by the behavior of the Japanese, only at the shrill voices of invitation and the blatant lack of concealment (In what can only be an attempt to keep this ugliness below the surface, I have recently heard tell that the shrill hawking of Yoshiwara guidebooks has been banned from the streets of Tokyo).[27] If educated men actually share my feelings and agree with my ideas, that will be all to the good. On the other hand, their feelings and ideas may differ from mine, and at the worst, there may be fellows who wish to carry out these immoral acts themselves. However, they are entitled to their opinions. Let them expound their ideas without holding anything back and I will also hold nothing back when I reply. My only wish is to clarify the distinction between right and wrong. Since these matters are clearly misdeeds, just as stealing is, they should be clearly prohibited by government law and the law should be enforced throughout Japan; however, given the corrupt nature of human emotions, a prohibition of that nature would threaten social order, and therefore we must try to conceal these matters rather than prohibit them. Since this will be so difficult to achieve that it is beyond the power of government legislation, we must accept this task as the private responsibility of the most senior members of our society. It is essential for them to accept this burden, and direct all their energy to achieving this end. This is why I am calling on educated men in particular to pay attention.

Installment Eight

Japanese men today do not show restraint in their private behavior. Ignoring the rules of matrimony, they pay money to go-betweens in order to obtain live-in or live-out concubines. In extreme cases, they cannot even reveal the past career of the woman who is termed their legal wife, but have to obfuscate. As has been explained in previous installments, they do not recognize the ugliness of geisha and *shōgi* for what it is and have never been embarrassed about amusing themselves in their company. Readers should also have realized that this indecent social practice originated in the civil-war period and did not become a custom until relatively recently, in the feudal period. This being the case, since our civilization has been advancing and the remains of feudal customs have been disappearing, one would expect that the younger generation, who are the products of this more civilized world, would have a higher sense of values with regard to moral behavior. However, there are few signs of this. While it seems exceedingly strange that what one would expect to happen does not, there is in fact an entirely convincing reason that is linked to the trend of the times.

Taken on average, the words and actions of most members of younger generations are cast in the molds of the generations that preceded them; with the exception of those born with outstanding abilities, it is virtually impossible to gain independence from these set patterns. Since the same is true of moral behavior, the model that younger men imitate is the easily available one presented by their seniors, and inevitably this is as true for the unpleasant as for the pleasant aspects. Unfortunately, the older men of society today belong to the generation that experienced the political upheavals of the Restoration twenty years ago. These upheavals affected their moral behavior to an extreme degree, so that they developed habits that they have never been able to shake off. Even now, there are many who are reluctant to reveal the past careers of their wives or who are inconvenienced if people ask for the addresses of their live-out concubines.[28] Given these examples, younger men assume that moral behavior is too trivial a matter to have any effect on the value in which an individual is held, and although they frequently indulge in quite shocking escapades, it does not lose them face in the eyes of their seniors and can even have the effect of making the relationship closer. If one listens to what the old men say, it seems to have a clear internal logic, for they stress the importance of correct behavior in human affairs at all times, and are extremely strict with regard to moral teachings, even lamenting the decline in the morality of the younger generation. However, when the topic changes to the everyday moral behavior of the individual, tales revealing their shameless acceptance of licentiousness fall in an unceasing flow from their lips. There is such a gap between the rigid correctness of the moral instructions and the fluid opportunism of the accounts of everyday behavior that it is almost as if two different people are talking. It is therefore not surprising if the younger men, whose blood has not yet cooled, rashly decide that immoral behavior is not in fact governed by moral teachings and lose all sense of embarrassment.

It is likely that a father who drank too much when he was young will warn his sons about drinking, while one who has pockmarks on his face will make sure that his children are vaccinated against smallpox. The mistakes and misfortunes experienced by a father give him the desire to prevent his offspring from suffering in the same way. However, these scruples are limited to family members, and the older generation does not show a similar kindness to younger people in general. If a man used to be a heavy drinker and is still unable to give up drinking, he will not criticize the fact that there are many people who like drinking. Similarly, if a man has pockmarks on his face, it does not concern him if his friends are also pockmarked. But at the bottom of his heart, it is not only a lack of criticism or concern, but of misery liking company and like attracting like: while he knows that he should not welcome the existence of fellow drinkers or people with similar disfiguring marks, he is secretly happy that there are many who share his predicament. In other words, there is a reason why older men do as they wish and make no attempt to restrain the immoral behavior of the younger generation.

Similarly, there is a group of talented men who are usually well versed in reading, skilled writers, and good at managing affairs. This is an age in which knowledge of Western civilization is valued, and some of them would at first sight be taken for scholars whose knowledge of this civilization makes them useful people. They have even learnt how to read a Western language or actually travelled abroad and associated with prominent foreigners. They have a logical approach to political affairs and discussions, and put this ability to good use both in writing and in taking action. However, any enquiry into their true nature will reveal the fact that they have not freed themselves from the confines of Chinese learning. The problem is not only that they look ridiculous when their discourses on civilization or their actions reveal the Chinese underpinning behind the facades of Western-style modernity. Their Confucian principles would be acceptable if they belonged to the Neo-Confucian school of Cheng-Zhu, with its rigid attention to personal cultivation. But whatever school of Confucianism they belong to, they are guilty of unspeakable levels of misconduct. In their drunken orgies they amuse themselves in the pleasure quarters, guzzling away in the brothels without a shred of embarrassment, as if these were normal activities. Even in the ways of marriage, the basis of human morality, they show no commitment, but occasionally set up live-out concubines, and regularly install them at home. Of the many types of immoral behavior that can be found in this world of sin, none is allowed to go untasted. Moreover, far from planning to conceal their misdeeds by keeping them secret, when with friends they talk with pride of their debauchery and dissipation, and even in front of larger audiences they think nothing of using vulgar language to proclaim their familiarity with the pleasure quarters and their success as sexual adventurers. They resemble nothing more than barbarians running wild and naked through the streets.

There are those who complain about the improper effect caused when men of the lower levels of society go about wearing little clothing;[29] little do they know that there is a group of talented men in the upper levels who are naked in their disregard for propriety, however splendidly they might try to dress. When it looks as if the conversation may become high-minded, these men prevent it by changing the subject. They talk about national affairs with a geisha in their arms; they discuss the world situation while gulping down saké from extra-large cups. In this way, they divert attention from their immorality by deliberately light-hearted and indiscreet remarks, and successfully deceive society, so that no one inquires into their guilt. Instead they are regarded as gentlemen and scholars, conscientious politicians, and forgiven because of their social position.[30] It is therefore not surprising that many younger men are deceived by their light-hearted and indiscreet remarks and proceed to take the wrong path. And so these men of talent not only destroy themselves; they also ruin the lives of other people's children. They are nothing other than worms eating away at the moral foundations of society.

It is said that Xie An [320–385], [the famous statesman and poet] of Jin Dynasty China, often took courtesans with him to amuse himself in East Mountain[31] and that the literati of the country all wished to follow his example. But while Xie An's behavior may have been acceptable in the barbarous days of Jin China, if today's men of talent decide to pattern their behavior on him, the civilization of the nineteenth century will not allow such open indecency, nor will it tolerate the trumpeting of such indecent opinions. Moreover, who would entrust the fate of the nation to a drunken womanizer who finds pleasure in cuddling **prostitutes**? This is not only my complaint as a Japanese, but also something that will be opposed by public opinion throughout the world.

When these men of talent are censured for their immorality, their ultimate excuse is always that they must behave like this in order to participate in social gatherings. One can question whether violating the ways of matrimony in order to socialize is acceptable conduct, but even if we ignore this for the moment, we must realize that by "participate in social gatherings" they probably mean inviting geisha to dinner parties or visiting brothels. Social gatherings require interaction between the hosts and their guests. Therefore, if immoral behavior is involved the sins have surely been committed knowingly by both sides in the interaction, so that no excuses can be allowed. The conclusion must be that these men's minds are still immature, so that they know of no pleasures besides those of the flesh, and can barely engage in relaxed conversation or put on a temporary show of liveliness without the help of wine and women. In view of this, we should surely feel pity for them rather than distaste. Therefore, in order to lead younger men to the path of correct behavior and prevent them from going astray, we must first stop older men from being so carefree in their conduct, and endeavor to drive it home to the men of talent that even if they are unable to mend their ways, they must be more discreet and observe the principle of secrecy.

Installment Nine

In my private opinion, the morality of Japanese of the upper levels of society is in no way inferior to that of members of other civilized nations. In their sense of honor and feelings of compassion, in the virtues of loyalty, filial piety, honesty, courtesy and humility, they are in no way below the average of other nations, and may even be superior. This is not only my personal belief, but something that is acknowledged by others as well; only when it comes to moral behavior are there many points that cannot be discussed without pain. My view is that this negative tendency on the part of Japanese society as a whole had its origins in the civil-war period and the formation of feudal society, and was then exacerbated by the failure of Confucian teachings to take such matters seriously, but this argument has already been covered in previous installments. It is ultimately this tendency that has led Japanese of the upper levels of society to have such a weak sense of shame when they are guilty of immoral behavior. However, because this situation is peculiar to Japan, and therefore not found in other civilized nations, more explanation is needed.

If a woman ignores the fact that she has equal rights with men and becomes someone's concubine, or sells her favors for money as a geisha or *shōgi*, she has adopted a profession that reduces her to the lowest levels of human existence and places her outside human society. However, from ancient times, the tendency in Japanese society has been such that these actions did not earn particular contempt. In fact, as sayings such as "from no family to bride of a top family" indicate, it is possible for a concubine to rise in society and finally gain the rank of official wife, and even for her child to end up as the heir and successor, so that she gains both high status and respect as the mother of the next head of the household. This is the reason why service as a concubine is seen to be as lofty an ambition for a woman as a post in government for a man. Similarly, it is true that a woman who sells her body to become a *shōgi* is thought to be in an unpleasant situation. Such women are said to be drowning in a sea of suffering like the bamboo leaves that dip despairingly into the river water. Yet in many cases, the woman herself feels no deep sense of shame, and far from feeling contempt, those around her feel pity and may even secretly admire her. This is because she leapt into this sea because of family misfortunes, in order to buy medicine for her ailing parents or to save her husband from some disaster; in other words, it is often the pressure of circumstances that eventually forces a woman to offer her body for sale.[32]

Moreover, since ancient times official histories of Japan, novels and plays have featured both true and fictional accounts of these matters, but none of them have drawn on the principles of human morality to portray either concubines or *shōgi* as contemptible. There are innumerable examples: Tokiwa Gozen [1138–c.1180], the mother of Minamoto no Yoshitomo and Yoshitsune, and Shizuka Gozen [1165–1211], a concubine of Yoshitsune;[33] Tora Gozen [1175–1238?] and Shōshō, concubines of the Soga brothers;[34] Akoya, the concubine of Kagekiyo;[35] Komurasaki [of the Yoshiwara] and her lover Gonpachi;[36] Miyagino [of the Yoshiwara] and her sister Shinobu who took revenge [on the samurai who killed their father];[37] and Okaru, who agreed to be sold [to the Gion pleasure quarter in Kyoto to raise money for the vendetta of the forty-seven *rōnin*].[38] They are all wise and steadfast, and some are of such a high quality that they have been included in scholarly compilations of the lives of wise and steadfast women.[39] When ordinary women and girls read such novels or see plays of this type, the plots naturally become topics of conversation, and naturally influence their ideas, encouraging them to look up to these women as heroines rather than down on them as figures of contempt. The result is that when the occasion arises, some will offer to become concubines, while many feel that there is no need to feel shame even if one has to sink so low as to become a geisha or *shōgi*. This is why it is not unusual to find daughters of good families working as prostitutes in Japan although this would never happen in any Western country.[40] Accordingly, as prominent men who initially amuse themselves with whores only to satisfy animal desires gradually increase their knowledge and gradually become familiar with these women's overall situation, they discover that some of these inhuman beings have human feelings, and that there are even lotuses blooming in the mud. Even if there is only one such woman in a million, she lights up the realm of whores and creates an excuse for the womanizers to continue their dissipation and debauchery.

On the other hand, the custom of respecting men and despising women is so deeply imprinted in the hearts of Japanese people that it cannot easily be washed away. In extreme cases, a woman may rate herself so low that rather than just witnessing a man's debauchery in silence, she actually offers assistance and knowingly gives him freedom to act as he pleases. For instance, in wealthy and high ranking households now, as in the past, if a husband shows signs that the delights offered by the marital bed are not enough to satisfy him, it is not unusual for his wife to persuade him to obtain a concubine, even if she herself has not yet entered her autumn years. In response to her show of persuasion, he puts on a show of declining, and after they have gone back and forth in this way several times, her urging turns into an entreaty, and the husband finds that he has no alternative but to consent. Society praises the wife for living in harmony with her husband's concubine and she therefore gains a reputation as a paragon of the female virtues.

These situations are not limited to wealthy and high ranking households. In families that are completely normal, even if a violent and abusive husband is so dissipated that he is completely absorbed in his enjoyment of geisha and *shōgi*, his wife continues to look after the affairs of the household and is unable to object. If she dares to create waves by protesting, social opinion will side with her husband, and no one will support her. If men feel affection for women and therefore allow them some freedom or show them some respect, they will be mocked for being a soft touch, reviled for their stupidity, and even ostracized. By contrast, women who do not censure male debauchery are praised for their wisdom. Since women are human beings just like men, and have the same rights, it is hard to understand why they can only obtain a reputation for wisdom if they exceed the bounds of stupidity by not only showing affection for men but also condoning their reckless dissipation. However, since this state of affairs results from the dictates of public opinion, there is nothing we can do about it. Since this is a custom that has gone on for hundreds or thousands of years, women do not know how to give voice to their dissatisfaction either, but merely resign themselves to their unhappy lot, reluctantly assume a brave face and force themselves to find some comfort in the midst of their suffering. "The hunt for sexual pleasure is part of men's nature; only the most unsophisticated women would object." Other than giving voice to their powerlessness with remarks such as these, they leave matters to occur as they will. Accordingly, men have no need to fear any criticism from within their households, while outside the home they have the occasional good fortune of finding lotus blossoms in the mud. The general trend of society is tranquil, since no eye sees the blatant ugliness and no ear hears the trumpeting of indecent opinions. It is impossible to hope that today's men will begin to behave morally unless they have the strength to do so of their own accord.

Installment Ten

I have already filled a number of installments with my observations concerning the moral behavior of Japanese men and have explained both their shameless acceptance of licentiousness, and the causes behind it. However, this explanation will be of no more use than a historical record unless we can use it to find a remedy. Therefore, in this installment I will conclude by giving an overview of the solution. This does not lie with the government, but solely with the endeavors of progressive people in Japan, and it is therefore they, and only they, to whom we can turn. Fortunately, many members of the upper levels of society possess the true spirit of civilization. Since they have shaken off the evil practices of Ancient Learning and also refused to imitate the ways of the shallow men of talent, they know their own value and worth. Even to my knowledge there are many able men whose value and worth can be brought together to give the country value and worth and form the backbone of the nation. Accordingly, I am confident that it will not be difficult to achieve my humble purpose.

With regards to my aim, if someone were to ask at the outset what I would really like to achieve, it would be to make all the men in Japan completely flawless, so pure and innocent that they gave as much value to behaving morally as they did to life itself. However, since I am fully aware that such a goal is completely unattainable in this world of sins, I am prepared to concede a little, and ask that even supposing men actually do indulge in immoral behavior, they do so in secret, and make sure that everything is concealed so well that it does not reach the eyes and ears of society.

There are many possible methods of concealment, but above all they must aim to be as skillful in their devices as the civilized men of Europe and North America. I will therefore leave aside my great desire of correcting men's hearts, even though I do still hope that in some cases, the practice of putting on an appearance in order to conceal reality will actually turn what was the appearance into reality. In other words, I hope that this desperate policy will result in the emergence of some truly pure people. However, what is most urgent at this point is to devise ways to restrain the activities of people who indulge in immoral behavior by putting obstacles of some kind in their way.

My suggestions are twofold:

First: To ensure that women who are basically concubines are not treated in the same way as the average lady. Whether they began as concubines and rose to become legal wives, or were called wives from the beginning but were only married after the transfer of money, all women who gained the position of wife as a result of any kind of financial dealing must be regarded as concubines, and prevented from enjoying the same honors as genuine ladies. Some may argue that a wife shares the honor of her husband, or that even if a wife was originally a concubine she is still a wife, and should be no different from any other. I would like to ask such people how they would reply to the following: Suppose there was a man who had formerly lived as a concubine in return for money. (I have no idea whether male concubines exist or not, but let us suppose that they do.) If he later acquired wealth and station, or was adopted into a family of wealth and station, would society accord him the same honor and standing as a genuine gentleman? I am convinced that this would not happen. In other words, there can be no difference between a male and a female concubine. Since both have equally distorted the principles of human morality by selling their favors, if the man is ostracized there is no reason for not treating the woman in the same way.

Second: Whether she be a *shōgi* or a *geisha*, any woman who works as a whore, either publicly or on a private basis, must be excluded from human society and barred from human company. It does not seem proper to openly designate particular areas as brothel districts, but since they have been an accepted part of society since ancient times, it would be difficult to abolish them immediately. They can be implicitly allowed rather than forbidden, but should have the same position in society as *eta* [outcaste] villages in the feudal period,[41] and the men who take their pleasure in them should be prepared to observe the utmost secrecy, like the womanizers of those times, who would occasionally visit shabby *eta* dwellings and purchase the services of the women called *onnadayu*. (*Onnadayu* were *eta* girls who would beg for money in Edo in return for singing and playing the *shamisen*, and would sometimes sell their favors.) In addition, geisha who are whores should obviously not be allowed to attend gentlemen's banquets. If entertainment in the form of music and singing is part of the banquet, geisha who are skilled in such accomplishments, and nothing more, should be invited to perform either in an adjoining room or at the back. Whatever excuses they might attempt to make, those who are called gentlemen of achievement, leaders of society, should not be at liberty to converse and otherwise amuse themselves with whores at a banquet. On the other hand, each individual is entitled to have freedom in the private sphere and society would not tolerate the exposure of private acts to thorough inspection.

For a few close friends to meet and have a night out together when there are no holds barred is one of the pleasures of this life, and if they are men who are used to the pleasures of the flesh we cannot expect them to give this up of their own accord. If they really require the services of geisha, we cannot prevent them from amusing themselves in a brothel district. All we can ask is that they act with restraint and observe the principle of secrecy. In other words, I am not being unreasonable in my requests.

If we call on our powers of imagination, what results are these two suggestions likely to have? First, considerable damage will occur to the reputations of *shōgi*, geisha and also concubines, so that even though they belong to the world of human beings, other people will cease to see them as individuals in their own right. As a result, as a group they will lose all honor and status, and therefore it will naturally happen that even those who previously wished to join them of their own accord will now endeavor to avoid them. Moreover, since it is likely that the first women to develop this dislike will be girls from good families who have received a certain degree of education, the realm of whores will seem emptier and there will no longer be any flowers blooming in the mud. The only remaining women will be members of the lower levels of society who have no learning, virtue or sense of shame, and may even resemble hideous she-devils. Men of the floating world will feel slightly revolted at the thought of being in their company, and it is likely that gentleman of the upper levels of society in particular will feel shame at the mention of geisha, *shōgi*, and the practice of providing separate residences for concubines, and even hold back of their own accord. Alternatively, if they are compelled by circumstances that prevent them from holding back in this way and actually indulge in immoral behavior, the result should be that they will keep up appearances by doing all that they can to conceal their transgression and present an unspoilt reputation to the world. These are the methods that I have devised for restraining men's hearts by putting obstacles of some kind in their way

My understanding is that whores in Western nations have fallen into such a desperate plight that they do not care what happens to them, have no thought of gaining acceptance in normal society, and no contacts with their relatives or childhood friends. They rove around in search of food, drinking heavily and living day by day, with no plans for the morrow. In their rowdy behavior they resemble nothing so much as good-for-nothing maidservants who can find no permanent employment. This being the case, ordinary men find it difficult to approach them and even if they do so are careful not to let their guard down; those without wisdom or strength do not even dream of indulging in immoral behavior.

As a matter of fact, it is undesirable even for residents in the realm of the whore to be so devoid of knowledge and morals, and so contemptible in their words and actions. On the other hand, it is pointless to hope that people who have already abandoned the ways of human morality will be of great virtue. That being the case, one way of dealing with the problem is to abandon them to their contemptible state and rely on the stench that this state produces to drive away all men of the upper levels of society who think of approaching them. I therefore hope that it will be possible to reduce whores in Japan to the level of their Western sisters.

Some people regard the system of inspecting whores for syphilis as a public good, but others take a different point of view and argue that the system has the opposite effect, on the grounds that inspections serve to reassure womanizers about the consequences of their indulgence in immoral behavior.[42] It might therefore be better to abolish the law and use the fear of catching syphilis from *shōgi* to act as a deterrent. This may sound ruthless, but it makes extremely good sense. My proposals for efforts to maintain secrecy, and for the downgrading of the social position of whores in order to prevent gentlemen of the upper ranks from approaching them, are not exactly the same but the goal is similar to that envisaged by those who wish to abolish inspections for syphilis.

On Relations between Men and Women

EDITOR'S INTRODUCTION

This was serialized in eight installments in *Jiji shinpō* from 26 May to 3 June 1886, and published immediately afterwards as one volume, with a preface. Having deplored illicit sexual relations between men and women in *On Moral Behavior*, Fukuzawa explains here the important role in society of gender relationships that are not focused on sexual activity. Once again, he uses arresting analogies and entertaining descriptions to keep the reader's attention. The series, or at least the title, seems to have had an impact. Four different pirated versions have been found, three dated 1886 and one dated 1898, and there were responses, for example in *Jogaku zasshi*. (See the General Introduction, pp. 46–47.)

In the first four installments, Fukuzawa explains the problem. Human relations are the basis of society, but in Japan they are limited to men. Yet throughout nature, male and female are drawn together and find happiness and harmony in each other's company. There are two types of relations between them: the emotional and the physical. Both are important and pleasurable, and one is not necessarily dependent on the other. Moreover, males and females choose their own sexual partners for reasons that cannot be understood unless they are ascribed to emotional rather than physical factors. The emotional aspect is especially important in humans, yet Confucianism has focused only on the physical aspect, and the need to restrain it.

In the last four installments, Fukuzawa explains that the custom of separating men and women has become a form of social oppression. Women have no place in the public sphere, being completely isolated in their homes. Society is deprived of their potential contribution to overall harmony, and men are deprived of the enjoyment that women's company could provide. In the private sphere, while most parents give their children the opportunity to accept or reject the marriage candidates that they have selected for them, lack of social experience hinders sensible choices. Moreover, even if a match is successful society does not allow couples to express their affection, and relations with other people, even parents-in-law, are therefore stilted. Men take refuge in illicit affairs and women become infatuated with stage performers. Fukuzawa declares that the solution is to allow social gatherings of men and women and ends strongly by vowing to defy social oppression.

The serialization of the work was followed by an "Appendix" ("Danjo kōsai yoron") in four installments, from 23 to 26 June. This is not translated here, but it gave practical advice to both women and men on how to converse with each other despite their different levels of education and experience. Fukuzawa encouraged husbands to talk to their wives about their work, and women to develop the ability to handle their own finances and even earn a living. Women should also have their own social circles rather than depending on their husbands for all opportunities for social contact. Finally, there was no need for ostentation in social gatherings.

On Relations between Men and Women[1]

Preface

Social relations are essential in the human world. Society cannot exist without social relations, and humans will disappear without society. Therefore, we do not need to spend a lot of time explaining their importance. But examination of the way in which the Japanese people have behaved since ancient times shows that they used to be ignorant of the value of social relations and that it was very common for people to live in isolation from each other, and to enjoy doing so. Even though the recent fascination with the customs of Western civilization has at last made people realize that social relations should not be neglected, they are only permitted among men, so that women are not yet involved. Thus, the idea of anything involving both men and women is, of course, out of the question. If a man and a woman are not husband and wife, they are not permitted to see each other, converse with each other, or socialize with each other. As far as human affairs are concerned, this leads to a great many indescribably complex and troublesome problems. In fact, there is no greater misfortune that could befall a nation. Since it is an issue that causes me constant concern, I have drawn wide attention to it by writing "On Relations between Men and Women" and serializing it in successive issues of *Jiji shinpō*. Here I have made the text easier to read by bringing all the parts together into one volume so that those who sympathize with my aims can understand what I wish to say. It will give me much happiness if you are kind enough to read my words.
Dictated to Nakamigawa Hikojirō at the *Jiji shinpō* building in Nihonbashi, Tokyo, 4 June, 1886.

※

Installment One

Since the long-awaited introduction of the principles of Western culture into Japan, our people have gradually come to realize the importance of human relations. Recently we have seen a growth in socializing based on links between relatives, friends, and between those who share the same field of business, the same province or school of origin, or the same ideas, either by holding regular meetings or by organizing occasional parties. I rejoice to see human relations developing in this way but even so, it is regrettable that only men are involved: while relations are possible between one man and other men, the only link between one woman and other women is their solitude. Moreover, in addition to solitude among women themselves, relations between women and men are virtually nonexistent, to the extent that if they happen to occur they are regarded with suspicion and invite censure. Since this is not a positive sign in terms of the degree of civilization, it is evidence that we cannot yet be proud of Japan's level of development. As a result, I find reasons to be both optimistic and pessimistic at the same time. It would take a large book to explain why relations between men and women are so important that their existence can further the happiness of the individual, the family, and even the whole nation, while their absence causes indescribable sorrow and anxiety. At this point, however, I will give an outline of the matter in the editorial columns of this paper over the next few days and ask our readers to give their advice.

It is hard to discern what the Chinese meant to convey about the disposition of men and women by describing them as yang and yin respectively, because the meanings of these words are so vague. Examination of works by Confucian scholars shows that when yang and yin are applied to the nature of men and women they symbolize qualities such as strength and weakness, wisdom and foolishness, brightness and darkness, implying that men are strong, wise, and bright, while women are weak, foolish, and dark. This theory is often used as an excuse for respecting men and despising women, but since it is obviously a delusion that is not supported by any reliable evidence, there is no reason why it should be accepted.

If we therefore turn to Western theories, we can use a simile borrowed from a scientific phenomenon, and compare men and women to positive and negative charges of electricity. In other words, we can say that there is a similarity in so far as like (positive and positive or negative and negative) repels like, but unlike (positive and negative) attracts unlike. Anyone who has studied the elements of physics knows that if positive is brought close to positive or negative to negative they will push each other away and never get near, but that if positive is brought close to negative, they will immediately come together and cannot be separated. Similarly, if a man comes close to a man, or a woman comes close to a woman, they will not feel linked by deep feelings of tenderness, and it is almost as if they are repelling each other, but if a man and a woman come close, they immediately grow near to each other and feel affection, as if there is some eternal emotion involved. In other words, we can actually observe like (men and men or women and women) repelling like, and unlike (men and women) attracting unlike. (An explanation about the meaning of "emotion" in this context will be given later on; it should not be taken to mean physical desire.)

The emotion that leads men and women to grow close to one another is not normal only among humankind: birds and beasts, plants and trees, anything that has life, is the same. When birds and beasts form groups, there will always be male and female pairs. When plants or trees cluster together, both types will be found in close proximity. When birds and beasts are in pairs, their voices are harmonious and their movements show their joy. Since this is the case with animals, despite their not being perfect specimens of evolutionary development, it should be even more so with humankind, "of all creatures... the most endowed."[2] When a man and a woman come near, it is like the peaceful breeze of a spring day; their hearts are filled with such calm that they could overcome any violent instinct; their spirits are completely in tune with each other. The subtle changes that occur once they are close resemble what happens when positive and negative charges of electricity are brought together and achieve a state of balance. A familiar example from real life would be a meeting or party involving men of the upper classes. If there are women present, it somehow calms the atmosphere: nothing escalates into violence or winds down into silence; it is possible to have fun without losing control, talk without arguing, and in some inexplicable manner everyone feels infinite pleasure. This is something that is so widely known that I am always hearing people remark on it.

The above was mainly about men since it was an example of what happens if there are women at a gathering of men, but if a gathering of men becomes harmonious because women are there, the reverse should also occur, so that a gathering of women will become harmonious because men are there. Therefore, if men are present when women are meeting, the predominant emotion will be a pleasurable calm, and as long as the men chat or joke pleasantly and do not ruin the atmosphere, for example by referring to matters that are taboo among women, every remark and every jest will bring joy to those around them. In fact, conversation and jesting are not needed; like the scent of a southern wind, just the presence of men will be enough to dissolve discord among women. Some men love women so much that they claim that the female body has a special perfume, which they call "heavenly fragrance." In physiological terms, too, since there are differences in the constitution of the bodies of women and men, it is quite conceivable that there is some special effusion. Whether this is sweet or foul smelling, however, what gives the air around women a "heavenly fragrance" is simply the loving hearts of men. Moreover, it is clear beyond dispute that if women produce a heavenly fragrance, the same must apply to men. That is, if women feel the scent of a southern wind when they are close to men, even if the men are just within sight, so that no conversation or jesting can be heard, they must be sensing some heavenly fragrance.

Thus, in human life, the greatest and the most important connection is that between men and women: when they are together, there is harmony; when they are apart, there is discord. The positive and negative consequences that arise from the extent to which men and women are free to be together or apart have an incalculable effect on both individuals, families, and society at large. Despite this, from ancient times up until the present, scholars of the East, whether experts in Japanese or Chinese learning, have paid no attention to this vital issue. Since it is they themselves who are responsible for this neglect, scholars have committed an unpardonable sin.

Installment Two
In the last installment, I gave a general outline of the way in which the emotions of men and women become harmonious if they are near to each other; now we shall examine what happens in the opposite case, when they are kept separate. This will be sufficient to demonstrate the importance of connections between men and women with even greater clarity.

Setting human beings aside for a while to look at the birds and beasts, we mentioned before that when their voices are harmonious and their movements show their joy, the group contains both males and females. But if we divided a pack of several thousands of dogs into two, with one half all males and the other all females, what would happen? Even if they were given enough food, rather than just being unhappy it is likely that they would howl, or even harm each other. If this is the case with dogs, chickens will be the same, and cows and horses likewise. Wild horses are friendly when living together in herds containing both mares and stallions, but if someone who owns only stallions lets them loose inside an enclosed space, they are certain to begin fighting among themselves. This should be sufficient observation of the key aspects of their natural temperament.

While human beings are above cows and horses or chickens and dogs, the natural temperament of men and women is just the same. As evidence from the feudal [Tokugawa] period we have the rough behavior of the male servants and retainers of daimyo, who were housed communally at Edo in quarters known as *orisuke beya* and *kinban goya* respectively. Their language and conduct were almost always in unspeakably bad taste. Yet these men had been brought up in the territory of one domain or another, or were samurai in the service of a daimyo, and while they had been living at home, away from Edo, they had not behaved like ruffians. Even so, as soon as they arrived in the city and formed groups composed entirely of men, their nature changed: some gambled and quarreled over the results, while others gave themselves up to drinking, and then argued or fought. The relations between them seem to have lost almost all signs of what we would regard as human. There could only be one cause: the fact that there were no women among them.

An example from today is the bad taste shown among fellow residents of sumo stables, while the particular strictness of the regulations governing soldiers and sailors is presumably necessary in order to control their moods. In the case of individuals as well, customs from ancient times in Japan have dictated that older men who have a reputation for upright behavior should have hardly any relations with women that involve conversation or entertainment. The only way in which they can satisfy their desires is by moving one step down from relations at this refined and upright level, and indulging in immoral behavior in the pleasure quarters. If they are unable to bring themselves to behave so indecently because they find the idea to be so unspeakable, they will have to resign themselves to having no outlet for their frustration. Thereupon in many cases, unless they ruin their health by escaping into alcohol, they develop hearts of stone, turn their backs to the world, and become known as weird eccentrics. Therefore, while there are many reasons why Japanese men who marry late, and even those who are already married, tend to fall into indecent ways in the pleasure quarters, the fact that there are few opportunities for men and women to enjoy social relations of a refined nature is clearly an important contributing factor. Since bad taste is such a feature of our society, only a man who is born with strong control over his mind and body can hope to behave in an upright manner throughout his life, with no reason to feel shame before either heaven or his fellow man, and without losing his calm despite the ups and downs of this world.

If the above is evidence of the disastrous consequences of separating men from women, similar harm must be caused by separating women from men. As a good example of what happens, there is the extreme case of the women who were communally housed in the residences of the various daimyo in the feudal period. Great numbers of women were confined together, regardless of rank, within the daimyo's private quarters (*okumuki*).[3] They were never allowed to go out, and could not speak with men unless there was an official reason for doing so, while strict household codes of conduct prohibited all conversation or entertainment involving men, with penalties for any violation. In extreme cases, the whole year might go by without their catching even one glimpse of a man in the distance. While they might appear very well mannered on the surface, many aspects of their actual words and actions were horribly indecent. In places where they could be seen, they assumed elegant airs, but when grouped together inside, where no restraint was necessary, each word and act of these beauties would normally exhibit such extreme lasciviousness that any man who secretly saw or heard them would feel so embarrassed in his hiding place that he would unconsciously begin to sweat. Not only were their words and actions lascivious; the thoughts behind them were full of insincerity and viciousness, and lacking in feeling for other people. In fact, they might be described as completely without feeling, for one could never expect them to make efforts to sense the joys and sorrows of other people. These women had been pledged to what was known as "lifetime service," beginning to serve in the daimyo's residence as virgins, and growing into adulthood and then old age in the same place. They developed quite unique and unusual dispositions, seeming to combine kindness and cruelty, timidity and decisiveness, so that it was very hard for any bystander to sense their emotions. It is a widely known fact that even if elderly virgins of this type left the daimyo's residence for some reason and joined everyday human society, they were unable to grow out of the ingrained customs of their former lives; only a few were able to find enjoyment in the human relations associated with running a household and being a normal member of society.

Of course, given the great length of the two hundred and fifty years of Tokugawa government and the high number of the three hundred feudal lords, there must have been some wise ladies among those who served in the *okumuki*. But just as one swallow does not make a summer, they were too few to conceal the facts about the majority. From my observations, it is perfectly appropriate to call the *okumuki* of feudal times the equivalent of a women's *orisuke beya* or *kinban goya*. In other words, the cause of these disastrous consequences must lie in the great mistake of separating women from men, putting them in women-only groups, and preventing them from enjoying the summer breezes of male-female relations.

Installment Three

The failure of scholars in the various countries of the East, both now and in the past, to discuss the benefits to be gained from the connections between men and women, despite their vital importance, is not a simple matter of neglect. Whenever scholars have chanced to refer to the issue, in most cases their aim has actually been to act against these benefits, which is nothing short of a sin. But now, after several thousands of years have passed, we are so accustomed to the lack of refinement that results from segregating men and women, that we take it for granted; any sudden attempt to trigger discussions about it would be certain to startle everyone and lead to much dissatisfaction. That being said, although it is an issue that cannot easily be broached either in speech or writing, nothing can be solved until we do so. Therefore, I intend to fly in the face of public opinion and openly refute the teachings of the ancients.

To begin with, the ancients appeared in the ancient, barbarian age, producing teachings suitable for barbarians that must have served a function at the time and were known as teachings of public morality [Confucianism]. As society advanced and knowledge grew, the scholars of subsequent ages should have embellished and improved these teachings by adding various explanations, so as to make them appropriate to the atmosphere of the various times. It is of the utmost regret that instead, they just stubbornly preserved the ancient sayings to the very letter, without any attempt to adapt them to practical use.

Barbarians must have had minds that worked simply and without sophistication, like country bumpkins today, or children, so that they were not able to deal with matters that involved many variables. For instance, their eyes perceived black and white, and their tongues sweet and sour; in other words, in their understanding anything that was not colored white was black, and anything that did not taste sweet was sour. Their minds, too, perceived good and bad, right and wrong, drawing a straight line between them and guarding it rigidly, so that something that was not good had to be bad, and something that was not right had to be wrong. They were unaware that infinite gradations exist between these opposites. Therefore, great sages of the time who were laying down teachings, being aware of the way in which people thought then, realized that no one would understand involved explanations and produced instructions in extremely simple language. For example, they said, "There are two ways and two only: benevolence and cruelty;"[4] "Profit first and righteousness later;"[5] "The gentleman etc; the small man etc."[6] The tone suggests that they are declaring that behavior that is not benevolent must be cruel; that those who talk about profit cannot know anything about righteousness; and that anyone who is not a gentleman must be a small man. While these principles are so simple and straightforward that they are doubtless suited to childlike barbarians, it is now thousands of centuries since the sages passed away and society has been continuously advancing. Yet the scholars of more recent times have preserved their teachings as if they were carved in stone, without any attempt to improve them. In addition, by distorting the principles they have carried the debate to extremes, causing many errors in the human affairs of advanced society. To my sorrow, even in the evaluation of people's words and actions, I have observed that they have consistently failed to permit any flexibility, with the result that anyone who is not filial is unfilial, and anyone who is not loyal is rebellious.

The above illustrates the narrow outlook of scholars over the ages. Therefore, when presenting explanations about the connections between men and women, they have similarly drawn on traditional methods, saying that the sages of old taught that there should be "distinction between man and wife,"[7] that "men and women should sit apart"[8] and so on, interpreting the words literally and advising people to observe these teachings for thousands and tens of thousands of years. But when the lively progress of human affairs means that events do not turn out in accordance with their counsel, they tend to become inwardly angry and declare that these are signs of moral breakdown. Their minds contain only two ideas — chastity and lewdness — without any allowance for the slightest flexibility, so that anyone who is not chaste is lewd, and anyone who is not lewd is chaste. They lack awareness of the wide space, the infinite gradations and nuances, that divide chastity and lewdness. This has been the great misconception of scholars over the ages; once accepted, this delusion unfailingly releases the myriad evils of human society.

Allow me to explain the gist of my humble opinion: There are basically two kinds of relations between men and women. If we were to name them, they would be the emotional and the physical. The latter, as the description indicates, involves physical contact between males and females and occupies a place of extreme importance among all human pleasures. However, when one goes a step further and observes the relations between men and women as a whole, examination of the details, both surface and hidden, makes it clear that the ties do not end with the physical. In particular, as human culture gradually advances and the area requiring mental activity extends to the point that people develop a complex mental life, the emotions also grow in range and complexity and relations between men and women are no longer limited to the physical. They grow to involve the mutual exchange of ideas and literary or artistic pursuits, conversations or meals together. Even if this is similar to relations between members of the same sex, a subtle and mysterious effect resulting from the attraction of opposites means that every word and action on the one side will evoke emotion in the other, so that something that would evoke no response between people of the same gender may cause pleasure just because those experiencing it are male and female. If they both noticed even the smallest change in expression, it would overwhelm them, awakening indescribable but limitless emotion. To describe the sensation to someone else would be an impossible task, similar to that facing a highly sensitive painter who, moved by a magnificent landscape, tries to capture the subtle appearance of every fallen leaf or every rock. In other words this summer breeze that spreads its fragrance whenever men and women meet is what we call "emotional relations."

The above shows the depth of emotional relations. Although physical relations are also important, they are not necessarily associated with emotional relations; there is an enormous distance between the two, each having its own particular effect. In fact, careful examination shows that the effect of the former is dramatic but limited, while the effect of the latter is gentle but wide-ranging. Any inquiry as to which is more important for the pleasure and happiness of human society could not be met with a simple reply of one rather than the other, because both are of the greatest importance and neither can be spared.

The need for both emotional and physical relations is linked to the fundamental nature of men and women, but in spite of the clear distinction between the two, scholars through the ages have dismissed this need as of little importance, and have failed to make even a single reference to it. They have confined their opinions to the physical, giving themselves no leeway to reflect on the emotional. Having been presented with the instructions of the ancient sages to maintain proper ties between men and women, they have assumed that "ties" means physical relations, and that "maintain proper ties" means the prevention of lewd behavior. Accordingly, they have used many different combinations of words to say or write that men and women should not come near to each other, and that even husbands and wives should not appear to be on intimate terms. Although in reality this prevented the crucial development of emotional relations, they named it a principle of public morality. When it was proclaimed to governments, it was made into law, and when it was taught to the people, it turned into manners and customs. In addition, complacent in the midst of the evil custom of respecting men and despising women, they have aimed the main thrust of public morality at women alone and submerged them in the depths of depression, while at the same time depriving men as well of the pleasures of emotional relations. Thus, the fact that society today lacks compassion and refinement, and that the advance of civilization has been delayed, is the responsibility of scholars who have lacked the insight to realize the distinction between emotional and physical relations and declared that the latter are the basis of all connections between men and women. A word or comment from a scholar leads generations into error. Try as I may, I cannot hold back my resentment at the ancient learning of China and Japan.

Installment Four
The fact that emotional relations and physical relations can thrive independently of each other and that one does not necessarily accompany the other is clearest in the case of advanced peoples. Yet close observation of the characteristics of living things reveals the existence of emotional as well as physical relations not only in the most barbarian and primitive of races, but even among birds and beasts. Everyone is aware that whether domesticated or not, male and female animals are happy together. According to some people, this is because being together strengthens sexual desire and the resulting pleasure leads to feelings of

intimacy. This may sound reasonable, but it has also been pointed out that since animals have mating seasons, outside these seasons they will not experience any physical desire at all. In addition, if two or three stallions are kept together in a stable, they are sure to fight among themselves, but a stallion and a mare that are placed together will always be peaceful and extremely contented, even if they do not mate. If the closeness between male and female animals really comes from love in the sense of physical relations only, their affection should disappear outside mating seasons, and mares and stallions stabled together should behave as fiercely as stallions stabled with other stallions. The fact that this is not the case informs us that harmony among birds and beasts does not necessarily result from physical desire; it is the difference in sex alone that allows the effective communication of feeling. Perhaps we should admit that birds and beasts can have emotional [as well as physical] relations.

Moreover, even in the case of birds and beasts and barbarian peoples, all males and females exercise choice in finding partners for physical relations. Humans normally base their choice on bodily appearance, but this is not the only criterion. They can experience a mutual attraction related to their dispositions that is so subtle that it cannot be described; for example, ugly men sometimes take beautiful women as their wives, while ugly women sometimes marry handsome men. As the saying goes, "There is no accounting for tastes." In the case of birds and beasts, it is not possible for us to appreciate the finer points of appearance and disposition, but it is clear that individual preferences must be involved. In other words, loving and hating are not governed by reason. If the connection that leads males and females to feel close to each other was simply physical for either humans, birds, or beasts, why would appearance and disposition be so important in searching for a mate; why would feelings of loving and hating develop for no reason? Why, in fact, are both humans and animals so sensitive in this regard if this is not the sign of a different factor? We should accept the power of affection to draw male and female together as proof that physical desire is not everything.

The above concerns phenomena that are normal for both humans and animals, but something more remarkable can be found if we look only at humans. As was mentioned before, among birds and beasts physical desire occurs during fixed seasons during the year, but this is not the case for humans. Yet the basic nature of the human body suggests that the onset of desire is seasonal after all and that the only difference is that while birds and beasts have a yearly cycle, in humans it is monthly. In women, the menstrual cycle begins every month as the egg leaves the ovary; this is a sign that the body is ready to conceive, in other words that this is the time for the onset of desire. However, sensory perception in humans has developed to such a high degree that the emotions have also become varied and complex. Unlike birds and beasts, which are controlled by instinct alone, humans have occasionally been able to go against instinct and become free of its control. Repetition of this practice over many generations has turned it into human nature, so that people have overcome the cyclical occurrence of physical desire and now experience it without reference to bodily rhythms. This is the explanation of the science of evolution;[9] if it is without error, humans already have the ability to control their instincts, and this has enabled them to overcome the onset of desire. Those who have the ability to overcome something should also have the ability to forget it. To be free to take something is to be free to reject it as well. Or, expressed the other way round, physical desire in birds and beasts is so strong that it controls them, but the same cannot be said for humans. If we accept that, compared with beasts and birds, humans feel the flames of desire less urgently, surely it is reasonable to admit that the connection between men and women is not limited to physical relations and that there is ample room to allow the existence of emotional relations. In other words, this is an important way in which humans differ from birds and beasts, and it is therefore not by chance that they have been called "of all creatures . . . the most highly endowed."[10]

As proof of the above, we have the saying that in ancient times the Chinese Imperial courts included as many as "three thousand" court women; in Japan, too, in the feudal ages, many of the upper-ranking daimyo kept women. Yet even if a lord was accompanied by tens or hundreds of handmaidens and ladies in waiting, a large number of them must have been superfluous to the satisfaction of his physical desires. In today's society, too, it happens that young men hire female entertainers for their enjoyment, or that young girls develop feelings for actors and male entertainers, but apart from rare exceptions, they are not necessarily prompted directly by physical desire. We can therefore state clearly that the reason why ancient rulers and nobles in Japan and China kept superfluous numbers of women was because of the natural tendency for mutual attraction between the sexes. This is also why young men today can approach women, and young women can have feelings for men, entirely without the existence of physical desire. In other words, all these phenomena are the outward expression of emotional relations.

Even the sight of blossoms in the trees and fields is enough to give us pleasure in this life of ours. What then must be the emotions that visit men and women at the sight of each other? Since people are like flowers, but are also able to talk and laugh, it is not surprising that men and women fall in love. "A flower with the gift of speech" is a phrase that men use to describe a beautiful woman;[11] if men do not appear as "flowers with the gift of speech" in women's eyes, perhaps they could be described as pine or oak trees that "feel emotion." Therefore, the joyful emotions felt by a man and a woman who are attracted to each other are several levels above the joy we feel on catching sight of scarlet flowers with fresh green leaves, but although the former joy is deeper and more intense than the latter, the essence is the same. In other words, while both the subtle nature of emotional relations and their lack of connection to physical relations are facts that are seldom actually mentioned, just a little reflection will lead us to realize their truth.

Installment Five

As was demonstrated in the previous installments, emotional relations between men and women are distinct from physical relations and develop independently. This is indisputable in theory as well as in fact. However, ever since the ancients established the teachings regarding chastity and related matters, the scholars of subsequent ages have just clung to their words, guarding them stubbornly, without any awareness that they could be changed in accordance with advances in society, or any efforts to adapt them to circumstances. They claimed that since the only alternative to chastity was lewdness, anyone who was not chaste must be lewd; further, they declared that such and such must be done to prevent lewdness, and would not permit even the slightest flexibility. Connections between men and women were made increasingly rigid by introducing limits on their areas of activity that prevented them from either approaching, addressing, touching or looking at each other. For hundreds and thousands of years it has been the custom to organize all human affairs, from the significant to the trivial, according to these principles. In particular, during the two hundred and fifty years' peace of the Tokugawa period, people gradually became dispirited and in all things aimed to be cautious and on the defensive. They were even timid regarding relations between men and women, being inclined to fall back to safety rather than volunteering to take the dangerous path. As a result, women were excluded from the sphere of social relations and treated as if they did not exist. It must be acknowledged that this state of affairs had most tragic consequences for Japan.

In other words, once this custom permeated the minds of the people, it took over and oppressed the whole of society so that even the most powerful could not resist it. A situation like this is known as "**social oppression**."[12] A law issued by the government may seem strict but even if it is oppressive, as long as people rarely experience its direct effects, it can be tolerated. But social oppression violates our physical and mental freedom relentlessly from morn till night and exerts an influence beyond that of any law. In this case, the great principle of the ancient teachings, that men and women should not approach each other and that the former should work outside while the latter stay inside, has become a custom. Social oppression guards this principle so strictly that no quarter is allowed.

The actual consequences have been that in Japan since ancient times relations considered to involve close friendship have been confined to men alone, so that women possess no close friends. Without friends, there can be no social relations. Therefore, the only people with whom women can associate are their relatives, and even this is confined to exchanging letters. Even when a woman is taken to a gathering of non-relatives by her husband or the head of the household, she will merely be present in a physical sense since she will neither chat nor laugh, eat nor drink, but merely watch the men as they enjoy themselves, a hanger-on seated at the back of the proceedings. Yet we should not find this strange, since it is happening to someone who has gone outside even though social oppression dictates that she should be inside. What happens when a woman is inside, however, is that since she has no close friends, no one comes to visit. Even if close friends of the husband, the father or the elder brother call, they do not meet the lady or ladies of the house because they do not know of their existence. Even if they did happen to know that there were ladies in residence, the ladies would say that it was not proper for them to entertain guests in the absence of their menfolk, and the guests, too, sharing this opinion, would not go so far as to suggest a meeting. Therefore, even when we say that women are the managers of their households, what we mean by household is the part at the back only, since their authority does not reach the part at the front.

This being the situation, that women's lot is unpleasant must be clear to all.

Moreover, while they have been more or less trapped in slavery for several thousands of years, alive physically but not emotionally, it is not as if the pleasure of the other half of the population has increased as a result of women's state of deprivation. In fact, not only has the unpleasantness experienced by women failed to contribute to the pleasure experienced by men; men for their part are to be pitied because they have been unable to experience the pleasure of being with women. As was said before, the emotions that lead men and women to be attracted to each other and to feel mutual affection have natural origins, and it is an indisputable fact that they are the key to the greatest and most important pleasures of human life. Yet social oppression prevents this fundamental emotion from flourishing, and the inability of men and women to meet freely and exchange affectionate conversation and laughter is a source of suffering felt no more by one than by the other. If it were possible for a man and woman to meet freely, their hearts would be so joyful that they would be transported to a paradise where hundreds of birds were singing among flowers waving in spring breezes perfumed with plum and peach blossoms. But social oppression acts like a harsh storm of jealousy, ruining the flowers and frightening the birds, transforming the pleasant warmth of spring into the extreme discomfort of midsummer or midwinter. Melancholy suffering swells up inside people like rice in a steamer, producing clouds of discontent that swirl around outside them like snow in a winter storm, transforming society into a cruel and featureless landscape. Surely this produces no benefits or happiness for our country.

We are all familiar with the fact that disputes often occur because of differing opinions related to both trivial and important affairs concerning politics, business, or even scholarship and religion, and that in extreme cases these disputes can even lead to unpleasant scenes of open hostility in which people cause each other actual harm. And yet we are also aware that when such disputes or hostilities are observed from another angle in an attempt to discover the truth, it often turns out that they arose from misunderstandings caused by the failure of the parties involved to exchange accurate information. Therefore, if someone intervenes at the right moment, it is often possible to find a peaceful solution. It is obvious beyond a doubt, that at such a critical moment, the outcome will be completely different depending on whether or not it is possible to take advantage of the emotional relations between men and women. In the civilized countries of the West, social relations are primarily the responsibility of women; even if a woman chooses not to be involved in matters related to society, she will indirectly have a harmonizing effect on men's thoughts and thereby help to smooth the situation. In fact, it cannot be disputed that in those countries there are fewer instances of misunderstandings having a harmful result. In other words, since the responsibility for matters affecting a nation must be borne by the people of that nation, in civilized countries the responsibility is shared by both men and women. On the other hand, because in Japan it is only carried by men, who account for just half the population, even if the wisdom and virtue of people in Japan exactly equals that of civilized countries, the power sustaining the former is clearly half that of the power sustaining the latter.[13]

Installment Six

The words of the ancients turned into the teachings of public morality; the teachings of public morality turned into custom; and custom turned into social oppression. In previous sections we explained how this occurred, and how it caused obstacles to relations between Japanese men and women and has thereby put our society at a great disadvantage. At this point, we will leave the public realm in order to examine the terrible harm that social oppression has wrought upon the private sphere of the family.

Since the connection between a husband and wife lasts throughout their lives, it is only natural that both should be able to exercise choice when the arrangements are made, and that the match should not go against their wishes. However, the strict rule of social oppression that prevents men and women from approaching one another cannot be opposed. The closer growing boys and girls are to marriageable age, the further they must stay apart; they are so worried about what those around them will say that they do not feel free to converse, and even find it difficult to catch a glimpse of each other. Ultimately they grow so far apart that they might as well be living in separate worlds, and when it comes to actual proposals of marriage, they have no way of getting to know each other. We will ignore as exceptional the practice of samurai and others in the feudal past to regard marriage as a way of preserving the family line. This could lead to the most curious matches, since no regard was paid to the looks, age or relative intelligence of the actual partners. Parents who possess common sense would never force marriage on their children; even if the initial choice is made by the parents, the practice in a good family is not to make a final decision until the child has been given ample opportunity to make his or her feelings known. But since the two most directly involved do not know anyone who belongs to the other sex, there is no way in which they can have a preference. Even if it is someone whom they secretly do know, they are very reluctant to express their preference. Since social oppression prohibits men and women from knowing each other, this situation would only occur as a result of their knowing what should not be known. In these circumstances, marriages frequently fail to turn out as they were intended. There can be no greater misfortune in one's life.

On the other hand, this does not necessarily mean that those whose marriages actually do turn out as they were intended experience the delights of true happiness. The Ancient Sage taught that there should be "distinction between husband and wife."[14] While I am unable to fathom the deep meaning intended by the sage, the interpretation of later scholars has imprinted itself deeply on people's minds. Taking "distinction" to mean "behave like strangers," they believe that because couples tend to become excessively affectionate, morality dictates that they should put as much distance between each other as possible. When the negative Oriental custom of respecting men and despising women is added to this, it has the unfortunate effect of leading husbands to reject their wives, turning their backs on them in contempt.

There is a curious story from China. Apparently, a long time ago, Xi Que[15] of the province of Ji had taken up agriculture because he was in straitened circumstances. Even so, when his wife brought his lunch to the fields, she treated him with great respect and ceremony, as if he were an honored guest, and he responded in an appropriate way, without showing unnecessary familiarity towards her. This has become famous as a poignant story, and the imagination of a later artist has made it into a picture of a man sitting on a mat with a haughty air, eating by himself, while beside him his wife kneels reverentially on the ground in order to serve him. This picture never fails to puzzle me. If a poor student turned to agricultural work as a result of his poverty, human feeling would surely lead him to share both poverty and comforts with his wife, so that he would affectionately divide even his lunch with her. But on the contrary, this picture implies that even in his penury, the man preserved an air of being separate from his wife, so that the story seems merely to teach the rather ridiculous and pitiful moral that even in difficult circumstances one should not forget that men should be respected and women despised. Yet married couples since then have understood such affected behavior to be the key to selfless virtue and gradually increased the gap between them. As a result, even if it does not reveal the whole picture, a quick and superficial glimpse of the atmosphere of a household will detect no sign that a couple is surrounded by love. Rather than being close and affectionate friends, they will seem to be joined by the more distant ties of lord and vassal, since the humble wife trembles as she serves her lord and master from morning till night, and when she is in his presence he does not even offer her a kind word.

An extreme example is when a friend has heard that someone's wife is ill and therefore inquires after her condition. Consciously adopting an air of indifference, the husband gives no details of her state, or remarks that she has been causing no end of trouble for several days with her complaints of aches and pains. His voice is so cold and void of emotion that he might be a stranger from Qin observing the conditions of the people of Yue.[16] Out of all the most sincere emotions, who, apart from a worthless wild animal of a man, would not feel affection for his wife? Particularly when she is ill, he must be so worried that he cannot concentrate and his brain is tied up in knots. There can be no doubt that this is the case but why, then, does he outwardly distance himself and act as if he is without emotion? It is only the urging of social oppression that makes him unable to show the true nature of his feelings.

There is a *senryū*[17] that goes:

> After two, three hundred meters
> They form a couple:
> Man and wife.

Although as far as the emotions of a husband and wife are concerned, it is only natural for them to leave the house together when they go for a walk, this is not the present practice. For the first two or three hundred meters, they will purposely walk out of step, one in front and one behind, only forming a couple when they get to an agreed spot. The only reason that marriage partners will give for such behavior is that it is just not done for them to walk as a couple near their house, where people who know them are likely to pass by. In other words, the explanation for this behavior is that the moment after the first two or three hundred meters, when a husband and wife actually form a couple, represents their true feelings; the period before that, when they appear not to be a couple, is the result of social oppression.

Having looked at these examples, we should now turn to the situation within the household. Whatever the class or rank, in every type of family structure, husbands and wives tend to maintain a distance, and the cooler the relations are between them, the more the household is held in esteem. Not only is there somehow a tendency for neighbors, friends and even relatives to praise such a situation, on the grounds that a strict lord and master means a faithful wife; those right on the spot, such as the parents-in-law who live in the same house, will pay great attention to the relationship, joyful if the newly weds are happy together, but at the same time praying that they will maintain a distance. If they seem to hold feelings of tenderness for each other, the parents-in-law will be far from joyful: there are even curious tales of parents-in-law being displeased and finding it unseemly, for example when a bride is reluctant to part when her husband leaves on a journey, or a groom gently nurses his wife when she is ill. In extreme cases, when the parents-in-law are particularly obdurate and hard-hearted, they devote every effort to creating difficulties, devising the most trying obstacles both openly and behind the couple's back in their attempts to suppress the possibility of an affectionate relationship. In my judgment, this must be termed **inhumanity** on their part.

Additionally, from ancient times until the present day, Japan has seen many examples of lovers' deaths. Of course there are many different ways in which this can happen, and in any country one will often come across sad cases such as the individual who pined away as a result of unrequited love, or the bereaved lover who followed the loved one to the grave. But the peculiarly Japanese version of lovers' deaths is what is colloquially known as *shinjū* [double suicide]. This occurs when a couple who have fallen in love, and are strongly attached, are unable to realize their feelings because of a myriad of obstacles, such as the opposition of parents or relatives, or interference caused by public gossip. At this point, they consult with each other and foolishly decide that it is better to die together than live on in empty suffering. Such cases of lovers' death are said to be rare both in Western countries and in Korea and China too. Why is it that a phenomenon that is so rare in other countries is so widespread in Japan alone? This is not necessarily because of a relative lack of discernment in our men and women, but it may be regarded as evidence of the serious degree of social oppression with regard to the connections between them that is a special characteristic of our country. While I in no way support the foolish idea of lovers' deaths, and in fact view it with extreme loathing, if I rethink the issue in terms of spontaneous human feeling, I cannot help wondering whether a reduction in the degree of social oppression might not give a few of the many lovers who die every year the chance to survive and become respectable married partners. This thought awakes some feelings of sympathy within me despite my loathing. Further, it leads me to say that social oppression has finally crossed the border into inhumanity.

Installment Seven
Our examination of the process that led to the social oppression of the present day has shown, as was mentioned before, that the words of the ancients turned into teachings about public morality, and permeated so deeply into people's minds that they turned into customs, and finally developed such authority that they could not be altered. The original intention of the ancients was to promote sincere, pure and unsullied behavior. Yet I must reluctantly draw the conclusion that whether we look at some time in the past or at the situation today, instead of fulfilling this aim the result has been the reverse.

As I have repeated at every turn, the connection between men and women is of such a nature that they attract each other and try to draw close; therefore, whatever teachings are bestowed, and whatever laws are established, Heaven will not allow human agency to introduce any changes. Even so, as cultures slowly advance, it is possible to see a gradual increase in the refinement of these connections. In the past, since barbarians were controlled wholly by physical desires, they understood relations between men and women only in physical terms. But as society advanced there were an increasing number of activities and an equivalent increase in relations between men and women, so that they came to understand each other's feelings, and were therefore able to be affectionate without being led astray or to grow close without becoming defiled, reaching a level of indescribable bliss. This infinitely subtle process is called the development of emotional relations. Yet even though it is the rule that this should happen in all societies as they develop, in Japan, unfortunately, the customs instilled by the teachings of public morality have contradicted this rule. As a result, even now that we are on the threshold of modern civilization, we still cannot visualize any connection between men and women beyond physical relations, and all our efforts are spent on preventing relations of this nature from running out of control.

Our policy of limiting people's relations in this way is no different from an attempt to subject fully grown adults to diet restrictions that have been devised for small children. Since small children have no interest in anything but their appetite for food, when looking after them it is natural to prohibit over-eating, but adults are fully developed both in mind and body, so that their appetites are not centered on food alone. With their five senses functioning in a variety of ways, food represents only one object of their appetites. If an outsider were to intervene in spite of this, and deprive them of the freedom to indulge their appetite for food and drink by setting up a restrictive law just in order to prevent them from over-eating, it would be like treating adults as if they were little children, in other words, absolutely intolerable. The customs instilled by the teachings of public morality function in exactly this way today. Our efforts to prevent physical relations between men and women from running out of control end up as social oppression; the intervention in all links between men and women eventually destroys the charm of emotional relations and robs society of refinement. Therefore, actions that treat advanced people as barbarians should be called the insults of social oppression, a slight to all advanced men and women.

This has been the state of affairs for a long time, and while there are some who are able to endure this social oppression without any problems, the ill effects of what is, after all, something that goes against human nature, are bound to break out at some point. To give one or two examples, in eight or nine out of every ten households today, the relationships between the parents-in-law and the bride and groom are strained. While there are some couples who are praised as filial for serving their in-laws faithfully, in many cases they are just putting on a good face while being at their wit's end. Anyone with the opportunity to overhear the private conversations of such a couple will discover that my reporting is completely without artifice. In fact, if we take one hundred households in which a number of young and old couples are living under the same roof and sharing the same everyday life, in only one of these will everyone exist in pleasant harmony without any disruptions. It would be no exaggeration to say that the other ninety-nine look like paradise on the outside, but are actually living hells, the haunts of fake ladies and gentlemen. The inhabitants were not unpleasant by nature, and may have been educated to a respectable degree, thereby developing a refined way of thinking, but as they manipulate their feelings in order to hide the truth, they unconsciously come to stand in the way of each other's freedom, so that they suffer themselves and yet make others suffer, and just waste their days in misery. Although this situation truly defies logic, as long as people are controlled by social oppression, they cannot take strong action by themselves.

There being few pleasures at home, the natural step is to look for human relations outside it, but since social oppression prevents women from leaving the house, the only people with whom men associate when they go out are other men. The lack of refinement in their relations is like an encounter between rocks and trees that results in a drab and colorless landscape decorated with splinters and pebbles. Unless they find the greatest pleasure in calm and rational discussion, they will just gorge themselves on food and alcohol until they turn into giggling, weeping, or snarling drunks. If they chance upon a lady, they follow rules that are meant to govern relations between men, and their lack of restraint may well lead them to say something that will upset her. This is said to be masculine nonchalance. On the other hand, men who are considerate enough to restrain themselves can only stand straight, silent and emotionless, like withered trees, while the woman, too, having no way of drawing close to a man, stands with her head down, rendered speechless and at a loss; all she can do is pray that no one will look askance at the scene. And this is considered to be the correct etiquette for relations between men and women.

Installment Eight

As was described above, since there is boredom within the home and no enjoyment outside either, it looks as if the ties that lead to emotional relations between men and women have been virtually severed beyond hope of repair. But people are not truly as unfeeling as wood or stone, so they have to find some way of throwing off their gloom. As a result, there are men of wealth and position who take their pleasures by keeping concubines either in their own house or elsewhere, or get female entertainers to call on them. Lower down in the social scale, there are men who take themselves off on visits to the pleasure quarters, where they grow drunk in the heady atmosphere and commit shameful acts that are beyond the human imagination.

Judged according to normal standards, such loose conduct should be likened to the sensual cravings of superficial and shameless men, but if I take the circumstances into consideration, I must concede that we should be a little forgiving. That is, in the present heartless atmosphere of Japanese society, only someone with exceptional spiritual and physical vitality can behave with elegant decorum and yet find enjoyment. Being without enjoyment, men choose the path of pleasure seeking, their only recourse being to keep concubines or invite female entertainers. Their shameless behavior truly lacks shame, but their purpose is not simply to find comfort in physical desire; rather, be it a special room, the house of their concubine, the pleasure quarters or a brothel, they seek a world free of the customs instilled by the teachings of public morality, a realm of enjoyment where they can avoid social oppression. While their methods are base, if their object is to satisfy their capacity for emotional relations, they should be pitied rather than wholly despised. We can compare this to what would happen if a person who has been unwillingly told to give up drink were to unexpectedly have the chance to visit a restaurant. It is obvious that he would be completely intoxicated in no time. We might dislike his intoxication at the same time as feeling sympathy for his circumstances. Therefore, it is true that the shameless behavior of men today contains many shocking aspects. However, since they are completely deprived of the refinement that comes from the emotional side of relations with women, and are forever tied to superficial connections that lack feeling and interest, it is natural for any escape from these bonds to trigger a switch from the extremes of strict restraint to the extremes of uncontrolled spontaneity. Their behavior is like someone flinging off a ceremonial costume and immediately exposing a state of raw nakedness, even though in reality there are many stages of dress in between the two, including unlimited varieties of beautiful garments. In other words, if there were relations between men and women, this would encourage infinite levels of emotional contact, but social oppression will not allow this, and therefore every single day of the year, whether inside or outside, people are always forced to wear ceremonial dress. Since this is beyond human endurance, eventually their only escape is to fling the clothes off and take refuge in raw nakedness.

For their part, the women of Japan greatly enjoy the theater. Some fall in love with the actors and other stage performers and even if they do not associate with them directly, they consider their skills in private, and this becomes a topic for women to discuss. There are people who are moved to anger on the grounds that such behavior is highly unseemly. Of course, it is not desirable for women to get so enthusiastic about the theater that they forget themselves. There is nothing admirable about men becoming so absorbed in sumo wrestling that they lose touch with reality; similarly for women to associate with actors and other stage performers is no better than for men to associate with geisha and other female entertainers. On the other hand since, just like men, women are clearly not made of wood or stone, even if talk of physical desires is banished to another realm, the question remains of what means society will allow them for satisfying their emotions. Men who suffer from the lack of such a means can already seek refuge in shameless acts in the pleasure quarters, and women should naturally be able to seek an outlet too, but here again, the practice of respecting men and despising women acts as a form of pressure. In shameless acts, women are still far behind men since all they can do is go to the theater and enjoy the same air as men from a distance, or perhaps go a step further and spend a short time in light conversation with actors or other stage performers. I find nothing in this state of affairs that should lead to either anger or blame. In fact, when I reflect that these women, deprived of any way to satisfy their natural emotions because of social oppression, have finally sought refuge in actors and the theater, I feel only pity.

With regard to what we have discussed up till now about relations between men and women, we must not recklessly criticize the sayings of the ancients since they were no doubt beneficial at the time. However, scholars of later times, unaware that the Way must adapt to changes in society, clung to every word, gradually establishing restrictive rules and refusing to allow any moves towards the development of emotional relations. As a result, even though we possessed teachings, they were not sufficient to correct social conduct; moreover, because the rules were so restrictive, they had the reverse effect of providing a catalyst that encouraged destruction of the dam holding back the sea of emotions. As a result, the conduct of both men and women came to exhibit the extremes of strict restraint on the surface, but the extremes of uncontrolled indulgence underneath. In other words, rather than being of benefit to society, the teachings of public morality have robbed people of happiness. This state of affairs is upsetting to an unbearable degree.

It is true that nowadays there are many men who behave shamelessly, and at times even women who invite censure for amusing themselves with actors and other stage performers. Yet, among people of average or above average sensibilities, there are none who cannot distinguish between shameless and refined conduct, and no one can really feel happy to be the object of social censure. The present situation upsets me so much that I cannot stop thinking of what would happen if only the degree of social oppression could be reduced a little, allowing some freedom in relations between men and women. Then, we could allow those who are naturally attracted to each other to be attracted, and those who are drawn near to each other to draw near, so that they can combine together just like **positive** and **negative** and thus find satisfaction. The whole expanse of society would be covered with auspicious clouds of spring-like refinement and elegance, lifting the emotional relations of men and women to a higher level so that no one would need to seek refuge in shameless actions and we would all be able to find enjoyment at our ease, in higher pleasures on a higher plane. In other words, to draw on the simile that was used in a previous paragraph, this situation could be described as neither focusing on outward appearances by wearing ceremonial dress, nor attracting people's disgust by exposing one's raw nakedness, but as finding a happy medium and sometimes dressing formally, while at other times just wearing everyday clothes. These are surely the appropriate circumstances for relations between civilized men and women, since even in a polite atmosphere one can relax and find various ways of making one's feelings known. This is the only change that I hope for in Japanese society from the point of view of morality.

Therefore, the only way to allow the men and women of our country to shake off their unrefined and gloomy lives and escape the perils of shameful behavior and bad conduct, is to uproot the social oppression that is the cause of this ancient evil. Then they will be able to enjoy the happiness that heaven intended, and sample the pleasures of the fresh winds of civilization and enlightenment, because they will have gained the freedom to enter into relations with each other. These relations will not necessarily have the logical purpose of seeking a meritorious companion with whom to discuss literature and the arts, but must allow everyone to interact freely and provide them with opportunities to approach and observe each other while engaged in amusing activities or conversation. Meetings can be big or small, formal or informal, with or without a clear object. Examples would be enjoying the beauties of nature, chatting over tea, making music or having buffet-style parties.[18] When men and women get to know each other in this way, they will naturally come to understand each other's feelings; without their realizing it, the women will learn from the men, and the men will be taught by the women. In tangible ways, they will increase their experience of the world, while in intangible ways they will advance in virtue. Moreover, it is beyond all doubt that they will gain many great benefits that we cannot foresee, both within the home and in society as a whole.

The above is a long-held opinion that I strongly wish to advocate to all men and women, but the scholars of Ancient Learning are so full of anxiety that they are likely to think that this is fraught with danger. Of course, they are right in that I cannot guarantee complete safety. There is an old saying that goes "At the sight of fire, imagine a conflagration; at the sight of a person, imagine a thief," and there are occasions when this may be true, but this does not mean that we can afford not to use fire, or avoid all contacts with other people. In this world it is just not possible, however much one might fear either conflagrations or thieves. The same applies to relations between men and women. There may be risks at times, but hesitating will lead one nowhere. To take no action regarding a deep-rooted evil of many centuries and thereby ruin the happiness of millions, all for fear of one or two risks, is no different from panicking about the dangers of swimming in the summer because one or two people have drowned, and therefore prohibiting it completely. Such a policy would not impress me.

Now, suppose I were to concede that relations between men and women are full of danger after all, and that they might lead to highly unpleasant results. Does that mean that we should preserve the customs instilled by the ancient teachings of public morality, leaving things as they are today? What sort of results has this produced since ancient times? In my opinion, these customs have caused needless emotional harm, bringing such unbearable pain and misery to all men and women that small men lose control and openly commit shameful acts, while gentlemen covertly devise private ways of comforting themselves. Such people are frequently to be found, even among the gentlemanly circles of scholars of Ancient Learning. In other words, it is not enough to rely on the teachings of public morality. Therefore, since my humble purpose in advocating relations between men and women, especially the development of emotional relations, is to elevate their conduct to a higher level, I cannot bend my argument in order to follow the theories of Ancient Learning. The days of social oppression are over. Together with the men and women of the whole nation, I refuse to submit to its commands.

One Husband, One Wife, Together Even in the Grave

EDITOR'S INTRODUCTION

This is the twentieth of one hundred essays that were serialized in *Jiji shinpō* from February 1896 to July of the following year, when they were published in book form. By 1909, the book had gone through forty-six printings and a pocket edition was produced. As the explanation in the General Introduction indicates, this is not the only essay in the collection that deals with women and the family. However, Fukuzawa must have given it particular importance because the original manuscript was reprinted in the opening pages of the first edition of his autobiography, before Ishikawa Michiaki's preface.[1]

It has been selected for translation here because of Fukuzawa's introduction of the idea of free love. He immediately says that it is not appropriate now since the stability of society depends on stable married couples and the idea of free love violates accepted standards of behavior. However, Fukuzawa's mention of the idea suggests that he found it to be worthy of attention, perhaps because it indicated that far from being static, moral values changed in order to reflect changes in social structure.

One Husband, One Wife, Together Even in the Grave[1]

It is said that "A man and woman living together is the most important of human relationships."[2] This is a rule of nature that clearly makes sense. Since men and women are born in almost equal numbers, it follows that the most natural way of putting this rule into practice is for there to be one husband to one wife. The next part, "together even in the grave," implies that once married, a couple should never separate. However, there is a theory that men and women should only marry if there is love between them, and that if their feelings dry up they should separate. It is inevitable that as time passes each partner in a relationship will change both physically and mentally; accordingly it follows that their feelings for each other will change as well. Further, to expect two people whose feelings have already changed to live together flies in the face of what is natural. This theory therefore proposes that if a couple love each other, they should join together as husband and wife; however, when their feelings dry up, they should separate of their own will and seek a likely partner elsewhere. It is known as the principle of **free love**. This idea seems worthy of attention. However, the principle that marriage should last until the grave is an important moral value that has existed since ancient times and has become a deeply rooted custom. Since it is also the basic element in the organization of society, it cannot be easily changed.

Generally speaking, discussions about morality in human society tend to rely on customs that have existed since ancient times. If something is considered to be beautiful, all eyes will see it as beautiful; if it is considered to be unsightly, all eyes will see it as unsightly. The same is true of our ideas of clean and unclean. From a scientific point of view, there is nothing in the material world that can be labeled as "unclean." Things that are regarded as "unclean" are not in fact "unclean," but are just viewed in this way for emotional reasons. However, if almost everyone in the world regards something as unclean, this perception cannot be denied. No amount of scientific argument could change it. Therefore, even if free love is the will of Heaven and does not go against reason, if society as present views it as unsightly and immoral, arguments based on reason cannot be aired. In fact, for the foreseeable future, it is clear that marriage laws as constituted at present will represent beauty in the sense of being the essence of social stability. Ideas such as free love can be thought but not expressed; even if there are people bold enough to express such ideas, they should definitely not dare to carry them out. Marriage as an exclusive lifelong commitment is the highest point of morality to which mankind has progressed so far. Anyone who goes against it must be ostracized as less than human.

A Critique of *The Great Learning for Women*; A New Great Learning for Women

EDITOR'S INTRODUCTION

These linked works are Fukuzawa's final piece of substantial writing on any subject. He wrote them during the period August to mid-September 1898, but publication was delayed because he suffered a severe stroke soon afterwards. They were serialized in *Jiji shinpō* after he had recovered enough to be able to correct the drafts, *A Critique of* The Great Learning for Women in eighteen installments from 1 April to 28 May 1899, and *A New Great Learning for Women* in sixteen installments from 1 June to 23 July of the same year. Fukuzawa's longer articles were normally printed in consecutive installments of the newspaper, but this time they appeared only two to three times per week. They were heavily advertised in advance, and were interspersed with pieces on similar or related themes[1] and enthusiastic letters of response from readers, which may or may not have been genuine. In November the two works were published together in one-volume deluxe and normal editions. The former was probably designed as a present for newly married women, and their husbands, as a substitute for *The Great Learning for Women* itself. As was stated in the General Introduction, there were criticisms of Fukuzawa's decision to devote so much attention to attacks on a work published over 150 years before. On the other hand, as *Jiji shinpō* proudly reported, it was considered sufficiently controversial for Kawahara Ichirō, principal of the Kyoto First Higher Girl's School, to regard it as unsuitable reading material for his pupils.[2] Moreover, the published volume sold well, with forty-eight printings recorded up to 1922.

Although Fukuzawa had not completely stopped writing about women, he had not written anything substantive since the serializations of 1885 to 1886. However, as the two prefaces make clear, Fukuzawa had wanted to write an exposé of *The Great Learning for Women* for many years. He viewed it as a symbol and crystallization of traditional attitudes to women, and had already criticized it many times, in a letter to the former daimyo of Sanda in March 1870 (Letter No. 2, pp. 312–313), in *An Encouragement of Learning* and, of course, in his writings on women. In 1898, he was probably also motivated by the possibilities for women opened up by the new Civil Code of that July, which gave married women some property and divorce rights, and by anxiety over the fact that treaty revision the next year would make it easier for foreigners to observe Japanese behavior by removing restrictions on residence and travel.

In *A Critique of* The Great Learning for Women, Fukuzawa quotes each section of *The Great Learning* and follows it with his own evaluation, which is in most cases highly critical. He exposes the underlying prejudice that ensures that men and women are automatically measured according to different standards of behavior and morality. He accepts that many of the injunctions are quite reasonable in themselves, but points out that it is unreasonable to direct them only at women, particularly since men who are adopted into families as the husband of a daughter are in exactly the same position as a female bride. Returning to the "On Japanese Women" concept of the link between pains and pleasures in life, he emphasizes women's rights and responsibilities within marriage, and the importance of their contribution to successful family life through management of the household and its finances. Fukuzawa ends by conceding that the author was sincere in his beliefs, but that his ideas are no longer relevant to Japan. He himself will therefore write a new version.

This new version is, of course, *A New Great Learning for Women*, according to which wives should be treated as equal partners with their husbands. Fukuzawa's advice is based on the present state of Japanese society, but he is optimistic that in the future women will have better opportunities for self-fulfillment. Again, he emphasizes their rights (vis-à-vis parents and husbands) and their responsibilities rather than their duties to parents, husbands, and parents-in-law. The rights include refusing to be sold into prostitution and protesting about a husband's unfaithfulness; the responsibilities include their role in child-rearing, which is ignored in *The Great Learning for Women*. It ends rather abruptly by calling on parents with disposable wealth to give their daughters an endowment when they marry, so that they never have to feel totally dependent on their husbands.

A Critique of *The Great Learning for Women*; A New Great Learning for Women

Preface [1][1]

The twenty parts of *A Critique of* The Great Learning for Women and the twenty-three sections of *A New Great Learning for Women* are not the product of my father's instant inspiration. Their origin lies deep in the past, in the spirit of my late grandfather, Hyakusuke, my father's father, a spirit which permeates my family. In other words, the idea of writing about women's education and their path in life has occupied my father's mind for several decades; he has only postponed the project until today because he was waiting for the right time to make his views public.

However, foreigners will soon be free to travel and reside anywhere in Japan.[2] We cannot afford to hesitate. If we do not use this opportunity to take decisive action and stamp out the evil custom of respecting men and despising women, we will only have ourselves to blame for leaving a permanent blot on our country's glory. It is not chance that has led my father to make his views public now.

In any case, these two works are not being published out of concern for the state of our family. The Fukuzawa family code has been woven from two threads: the spirit that has developed over the generations and the words and actions of my father himself. As a result, when we were relaxing with our parents, we did not even dream of mentioning words such as "mistress" or "prostitute," let alone the sort of topics that are raised here; our parents never introduced them as common-sense matters that we should understand, nor did we intentionally ask questions about them. This should make it clear that the only reason for publishing these works is to improve social customs.

There is another matter that I should like to mention here. Since it is related to private affairs, there is a sense in which it is inappropriate to refer to it, but in fact it is not entirely irrelevant. On 26 September 1898 my father had a stroke; from that day the whole family, my mother, my brothers, my sisters and myself, were in a state of indescribable anxiety. We could do nothing for him but take turns at his bedside, day and night, attending to his needs as best we could. Even now, it frightens me to remember times like the evening of 5 October, when the medical verdict was that there was no longer any hope that he would recover. But that day proved to be a turning point, since he gradually began to improve and is now able to move around without difficulty and even put on shoes and walk outside with the use of a stick. Moreover, this recovery was not only physical; as Mr. Ishikawa [chief editor of the *Jiji shinpō*] says, "... recently, we arranged for someone to read the text of the works to him, whereupon he pointed out and corrected quite a number of mistakes." In other words, while some effects of the illness, such as weakened sight and speech difficulties, have not yet completely disappeared, his mental abilities and willpower are virtually at their normal level of acuity. As my father himself puts it, unfortunately for us he intends to continue his pursuit of those who display low conduct as long as he is on this earth. Since we did not dare hope to see such a recovery of his mental abilities and willpower, we are filled with irrepressible joy and happiness.

When my father had passed the turning point in his illness but was still only semi-conscious, he could often be heard talking to himself. Although he was articulating so indistinctly that it was impossible to follow what he was saying accurately, when we tried piecing together the fragments that could from time to time be heard, he seemed to be arguing about women's path in life. He had completed the manuscripts of these works six or seven days before he fell ill, but the ideas had probably become part of his very being. Thus, in addition to the care he has taken over every word and phrase, his concern over the moral behavior of men and women with each other is present in every section. I therefore hope that the general reader will give his message serious consideration.

Ichitarō (on behalf of his father)
February 1899

Preface [2]

Fukuzawa-sensei[3] commenced writing the twenty parts of *A Critique of The Great Learning for Women* and the twenty-three sections of *A New Great Learning for Women* in the middle of August 1898. Composing one, two or three installments a day, he completed the manuscripts six or seven days before September 26, when he had a stroke. Therefore it took him only about thirty days. It might seem almost as if this was a task chosen to fill in the time between talking to visitors during the hot summer weather, or the result of instant inspiration. However, his decision to write about these issues did not arise by chance, since they have occupied his thoughts for many years, or rather he was ingrained with this attitude of mind. Sensei's father, Hyakusuke, was a samurai in the service of Nakatsu *han* and learned in Confucian studies. While scholars of Confucianism and Chinese studies spend their time discussing morality and ethics, in dealings related to their private lives they are normally uninterested in minor details, adopting a relaxed and carefree attitude. In the midst of this laissez-faire atmosphere, Hyakusuke was held in universal reverence for his refined dignity, the high level of his self-restraint, and the nature of his family spirit, being seen as a gentleman whose actions truly matched his words. Since Sensei lost his father at the age of three [eighteen months by Western reckoning], he has no memories of his voice or appearance, and obviously no direct knowledge of his words or actions. But his mother brought him up in a warm family atmosphere along with his elder brother and three elder sisters. Without their needing to ask, she gradually told the children about their father's words and actions, so that they unconsciously developed a tendency to think and behave with refinement and restraint. As Sensei himself once said, no one ever gave him instruction regarding moral conduct, nor did he ever consciously strive to achieve it. In his personal behavior he simply followed his natural inclinations; the fact that he has not once done anything of which he need feel ashamed can surely be ascribed to this inherited family spirit. Therefore, his ideas about the education of women and their path in life emerged from his natural thought processes. They were automatically applied directly to his public life and in the running of his household, even though he had not yet had the opportunity to present them to society.

At the age of nineteen, he left home to study in Nagasaki, and then in Osaka, at the private academy of Ogata Kōan [1810–1863].[4] During this time, he was concentrating so hard on his studies, in the face of various difficulties, that he had no leisure for other matters. At twenty-three, he went to Edo and for the first time set up house by himself. He was so busy with running his private academy, with writing and translating, and with foreign travel, that he had not even the smallest amount of time to himself. Even so, as part of his normal routine, he would often take out *The Great Learning for Women* by Kaibara Ekiken,[5] and add simple comments for future reference. Sometimes he would misplace the book and buy a new copy, so that apparently he ended up with several copies that contained notes he had written. This proves that these issues have occupied his mind for a considerable time.

Last summer, when Sensei had dictated his autobiography and completed his checking of the manuscript, he found some spare time and therefore began to dictate an overall review of *The Great Learning for Women*, but since this method did not meet with his complete satisfaction he also took up the pen himself. In the twenty parts of *A Critique of* The Great Learning for Women, he reveals the irrationality and injustice that have governed women's education in our nation up till now. Then, in the twenty-three sections of *The New Great Learning for Women*, he goes on to unveil a path in life for the women of the new Japan that is appropriate for society today. Readers who know nothing of Sensei's normal life may feel surprised, but every word and phrase is drawn from his everyday behavior rather than merely being arguments that he has constructed. In other words, since he has just transferred his daily words and actions to the printed page, they should be seen as nothing less than a partial record of his life.

These works were finished before Sensei's illness, but recently we arranged for someone to read the texts to him, whereupon he pointed out and corrected quite a number of mistakes. At this time, when they are being presented to the public, some words of explanation are required. However, since his doctors are still warning him against writing at this stage in his recovery, he has been unable to make any comments himself. As I have been closely involved with Sensei for the past twenty years, I have been a frequent visitor to his home and have a deep knowledge of his words and actions. Therefore, I have written down the results of my close observations in order to show readers that these works are not the product of a passing idea.

Ishikawa Kanmei [1859–1943, editor, *Jiji shinpō*]
February 1899

A Critique of *The Great Learning for Women*

1. Seeing that it is a girl's destiny, on reaching womanhood, to go to a new home, and live in submission to her father- and mother-in-law, it is even more incumbent upon her than it is on a boy to receive with all reverence her parents' instructions. Should her parents, through excess of tenderness, allow her to grow up self-willed, she will infallibly show herself capricious in her husband's house, and thus alienate his affection, while if her father-in-law be a man of correct principles, the girl will find the yoke of these principles intolerable. She will hate and decry her father-in-law, and the end of these domestic dissensions will be her dismissal from her husband's house, and the covering of herself with ignominy. Her parents, forgetting the faulty education they gave her, may indeed lay all the blame on the father-in-law. But they will be in error; for the whole disaster should rightly be attributed to the faulty education the girl received from her parents.[6]

It is not only girls who "go to a new home" on reaching adulthood.[7] There are also cases where boys who have been born after the family heir, as second or third sons, also go to other homes, as adopted sons. In fact, since human societies have equal numbers of men and women, one would expect that the number of men and women who go to new homes will be the same. Some may say that boys differ from girls since they can form a branch family and become the master of that. However, it frequently happens that families with many daughters and no sons arrange for one daughter to remain at home and become heir to the main family by taking an adopted son as her husband, while the other daughters also marry adopted sons and form branch families.

Even so, the precept that a child should "receive with all reverence her parents' instructions" is most apt and follows common sense. Yet it is difficult to understand why this is "incumbent" only on girls, rather than on boys as well. Would it not be equally unwise to allow a boy "through excess of tenderness," "to grow up self-willed"? Would it not be disgraceful if a young man is "capricious" in his adopted house, leads a dissolute life and thus "alienates his [wife's] affection," or for no good reason hates and decries his father-in-law, causing such family turmoil that it ends in his "dismissal"? This is so unreasonable that it cannot be countenanced. Anything that causes "ignominy" to women must cause equal "ignominy" to men.

Therefore, it is very good if parents train their children. This is a task that parents cannot escape as part of their duties, but there is a basic flaw in the idea that weight should only be placed on the training of girls. There are those who hold that the training given by parents to their children is like a good medicine: as long as the purpose of their instruction is beneficial, there is no need to question why more weight should be placed on girls than boys. However, this idea contains a great flaw. To raise children with a sufficient amount of instruction is like giving the correct dose of medicine to someone when sick. If there is a mistake in the dose, even good medicines can have a harmful effect. Therefore, even in the case of instruction that has a beneficial purpose, for parents to treat one child more strictly just because she is a girl is equivalent to giving her a larger dose of medicine when sick even though she has the same symptoms as her brother. If girls are given the correct amount, boys will suffer because they have not had enough; if boys are given the correct amount, girls are bound to feel faint as a result of the overdose.

If it is more "incumbent on [a girl]" than on a boy to receive with all reverence her parents' instructions," and to restrain any tendency to be "capricious," this implies that her parents must take particular care in controlling her words and actions, so that she is led to display gentleness, benevolence, respectfulness and modesty.[8] Of course, these are all human virtues, but if only girls are meant to receive their training "with all reverence," this implies that their instruction should be more thoroughgoing. Put in terms of medication, this means that girls alone are to be given enormous doses. However, as far as this section [of *The Great Learning*] goes, it is extremely doubtful whether girls will have the strength to withstand such enormous doses of training without feeling faint. Suppose that they are already in such a state of gentleness, benevolence, respectfulness and modesty that instructions to withstand all adversity without complaint make them feel faint. They will become passive in all situations and completely unable to take the initiative. Unable to say what should be said, to do what should be done, to hear what should be heard, or to know what should be known, they will be unable to escape the unhappy fate of turning into the despised playthings of men. Therefore, while the meaning of this passage may seem to have a supreme beauty, since it distinguishes between girls and boys in order to emphasize the demands on the former, we can say that it is evidence of a long-held grudge against them.

> 2. More precious in a woman than a beautiful face is a virtuous heart. The vicious woman's heart is ever excited; she glares wildly around her; she vents her anger on others; her words are harsh and her accent vulgar. When she speaks, it is to set herself above others, to upbraid others, to envy others, to be puffed up with individual pride, to jeer at others, to outdo others — all things at variance with the Way that women should take in life. The only qualities that befit a woman are gentle obedience, chastity, mercy and quietness.

This section starts by saying: "More precious in a woman than a beautiful face is a virtuous heart." Since women naturally value their appearance, to state that "a virtuous heart" is "more precious" than the face on which they place such value is a skillful way of giving the passage strength. However, it should not be seen as any more than evidence of the writer's skill. The list of female vices that follows certainly lines up a string of unpleasant traits. Since it is unseemly for any person of the upper classes to be "ever excited" or to glare "wildly around" and so on, it goes without saying that such behavior is not only "at variance with the Way that women should take in life," but also disregards the Way allotted to men. To have irritable moods; to stare menacingly; to be easily roused to vent one's anger on others; to scold others using crude language; to "upbraid" or "envy" others in an attempt to make oneself superior to them; to be "puffed up" with pride over oneself while belittling others; and to be full of self-satisfaction, unaware that one is a general laughing stock — these are absolutely contemptible forms of behavior and unforgivable vices whether displayed by men or by women. All human beings worthy of the name should be quiet, chaste, warm-hearted, and even-tempered. Since there is nothing objectionable about these instructions, it is difficult to understand why everything in this section, whether a warning or a suggestion, is targeted at women alone, as something that either does or does not "befit" "the path that women should take in life." For example, since pregnancy is part of women's natural lot, it seems extremely sensible to dispense instructions about health care during pregnancy to women alone. But surely it is ridiculous to draw up lists of bad and good behavior that are of equal relevance to men, yet admonish women alone.

Any dog that bites people but will not guard the house at night is a vicious and useless animal. Therefore it would be mistaken to associate vicious and useless behavior purely with female dogs, and only speak out against female dogs that bite people but will not guard the house at night. Surely even a male dog would cause problems if it was vicious and useless. Such reasoning is clearly one-sided.

The [supposed] author of *The Great Learning for Women* was a well-known scholar of repute, but because he based his reasoning entirely on Confucianism, he was unable to escape the tendency to value men over women. Examination of the real-life situation shows that it is men who are more likely to exhibit bad behavior, leaving the house unguarded so that they can go out at night, or even shouting at people unreasonably and being cruel to them. The fact that the writer indulgently overlooked men's misdeeds and chose to censure the vices of women alone is evidence of the extreme partiality of Confucianism.

> 3. From her earliest youth, a girl should observe the line of demarcation separating women from men, and never, even for an instant, should she be allowed to see or hear the least impropriety. The customs of antiquity did not allow men and women to sit in the same apartment, to keep their wearing apparel in the same place, to bathe in the same place, or to transmit anything directly from hand to hand. A woman going abroad at night must in all cases carry a lighted lantern, and (not to speak of strangers) she must observe a certain distance in her relations even with her husband and with her brothers. In our days the women of the lower classes, ignoring all rules of this nature, show no restraint in their behavior; they contaminate their reputations, bring down reproach on the heads of their parents and brothers, and spend their whole lives in an unprofitable manner. Is not this truly lamentable? It is written likewise in the *Elementary Learning*[9] that a woman must form no friendship and no intimacy, except when ordered to do so by her parents or middlemen. Even at the peril of her life, must she harden her heart like rock or iron, and observe the rules of propriety.

This section states that from early childhood "a girl should observe the line of demarcation separating women from men, and never, even for an instant, should she be allowed to see or hear the least impropriety." In other words, the idea must be that nothing obscene or impure should come within the range of a girl's sight or hearing. This is an admirable injunction; however, it all depends on the spirit of the family. If the head of the household, the father of the young child, ignores the rules of moral conduct, keeping concubines at home or frequenting the pleasure quarters, all attempts to teach such injunctions, however lengthy, will disappear like foam, because in the home itself, well within her sight and hearing, is an actual model of all that is obscene and impure.

Further, it is all very well to draw attention to the "customs of antiquity" such as the one that men and women should not "sit in the same apartment." But we need to consider the desirability of observing such ancient customs in view of the complexity of human affairs in the civilized society of today. A superficial injunction may attract some attention if delivered with this degree of force, in the manner of a verbal instruction or a high asking price before bargaining begins, but no harm will be done. On the other hand, if the intention is actually to impose observance of these customs, they are likely to be treated as mere outward rituals while behavior that is more inappropriate than it might have been goes on out of sight.

Whether relations between men and women are pure or impure depends on the quality of the people involved. For instance, from a Sinocentric viewpoint, Western ladies and gentlemen must be called barbarians with no sense of propriety, since they do not observe the proper distinctions between men and women. They talk and laugh together; though they do not go so far as to bathe together, they sit and eat side by side; they pass things to each other directly from hand to hand, and to shake hands is actually a form of greeting. Yet, the truth of the matter is that these barbarians are far from being uncultivated. Why is it that many of them display a determination as strong as rock or iron in the maintenance of their high standards of behavior? We can only conclude that the reason lies in their degree of refinement, which is of such a high level that it transcends sexual desire.

Once there was a high-ranking resident of Tokyo who was very enthusiastic about Western culture and acted as if he supported reform and progress in all things. Yet he was really a follower of Confucianism at heart, and his enthusiasm for the West was only skin deep. With regard to morality in particular, he tended to quote Confucius and the Duke of Zhou,[10] advocated the principles of the *Elementary Learning* and *The Great Learning for Women* as sources of injunctions for his children, and maintained such strict family decorum that when the parents were with their children they behaved like hosts receiving guests. His behavior was so smooth that at first glance it seemed to have no flaws. However, the unfortunate truth is that the hero of this tale had no discipline in his relations with women and therefore indulged himself in lewd behavior, keeping concubines inside the home, and amusing himself with prostitutes outside; moreover, while he came from outside the Tokyo area and had left his lawful wife behind when he came here, he had since married a second time. To have both a wife and a concubine is one thing, to have two wives and several concubines is another. As a result, his children submitted themselves obediently to their strict father in all things only because he issued his commands with such a severe air; in fact they had no respect for him at all. As time passed, the children who had studied the *Elementary Learning* turned out to be unfilial; the daughters who had recited *The Great Learning for Women* from memory turned out to be lewd. Is it not ludicrous for a family reared according to Confucian values to have produced nothing more than beasts?

Therefore, it is clear that in relations between men and women, genuine refinement is more important than external ritual. If parents wish to produce daughters who are of such a high level of refinement that they will never bring the family name into disrepute, their one priority above all others must be to discipline themselves so as to demonstrate a good example to their children every day of their lives.

The section also states that a woman should not agree to a marriage "except when ordered to do so by her parents or middlemen." This is also very sensible. In Article 771 of the kindred section of the Civil Code, it states as follows:

> For the marriage of a child the consent of the parents in the family must be obtained. But this rule does not apply to men and women who have attained the full ages of thirty and twenty-five respectively.[11]

Since marriage is a great event in people's lives, it is unthinkable for it to occur without the consent, in other words the permission, of the parents; yet to force a child into marriage according to the will of the parents is even more unthinkable. We often hear of troubles caused because parents have for some reason tried to force a daughter into marriage. This being the case, there is no point in parents' ordering unwilling offspring to marry even when a son is less than thirty or a daughter less than twenty-five. Yet even after sons and daughters have passed thirty or twenty-five, it is in the interests of family harmony for them to inform their parents and obtain their advice and approval, if they are still alive. Laws are established to deal with exceptional cases only. It is important to realize that the emotional links between parents and children should never be weakened.

The teaching that, once married, a woman "must harden her heart like rock or iron" and avoid all impropriety "even at the peril of her life" is very good. While this should be observed equally by men and women, however, observation of Japanese customs from ancient times shows that the evil practice of one man having many wives has been widespread and that examples of one woman having many husbands have been rare. In other words, it is men who particularly need hearts "like rock or iron." As a result, this carefully worded teaching should be valued, but in so far as it ignores men and aims its admonitions at women alone, we can only remark that it is being pointed in the wrong direction.

> 4. In China, marriage is called *returning*, for the reason that a woman must consider her husband's home as her own, and that, when she marries, she is therefore returning to her own home. However low and needy may be her husband's position, she must find no fault with him, but consider the poverty of the household which it has pleased Heaven to give her as the ordering of an unpropitious fate. The sage of old taught that, once married, she must never leave her husband's house. Should she forsake the Way of women and be divorced, shame shall cover her till her last hour. With regard to this point, there are seven faults, which are termed the 'Seven Reasons for Divorce': (i) A woman shall be divorced for disobedience to her father- or mother-in-law. (ii) A woman shall be divorced if she fail to bear children, the reason for this rule being that women are sought in marriage for the purpose of giving men posterity. A barren woman should, however, be retained if her heart is virtuous and her conduct correct and free from jealousy, in which case a child of the same blood must be adopted; neither is there any just cause for a man to divorce a barren wife, if he have children by a concubine. (iii) Lewdness is a reason for divorce. (iv) Jealousy is a reason for divorce. (v) Leprosy, or any like foul disease, is a reason for divorce. (vi) A woman shall be divorced, who, by talking overmuch and prattling disrespectfully, disturbs the harmony of kinsmen and brings trouble on her household. (vii) A woman shall be divorced who is addicted to stealing. All the 'Seven Reasons for Divorce' were taught by the Sage. A woman, once married, and then

divorced has wandered from the Way and is covered with the greatest shame, even if she should enter into a second union with a man of wealth and position.

There is no difference between a man's becoming an adopted son and a woman becoming a bride. The adopted son will make his wife's household his home and the bride will make her husband's household her home. This is only what is to be expected; moreover, all investigations regarding the relative wealth and status of the households, the abilities and morality of the bride and groom, their stamina, and their looks should have been carefully completed before the agreement to marry. If the marriage has taken place with the agreement of both sides, after exhaustive investigations and reinvestigations into every possible aspect of these matters, no excuse such as the poverty of the household can justify divorce. This should apply not only to the "Way of women," but also to that of men.

In recent years, there have often been men who have disregarded this Way. Brought up from childhood in the adoptive household, fed, clothed and even sent to school, their every need has been met by the family of their future bride. However, as they approach the age of marriage and the adoptive parents are about to congratulate themselves on the successful match, they overturn these expectations. Once they reach adulthood and begin to make a mark on society, they chafe at the constraints of belonging to an adoptive family. They apply to revoke the adoption agreement and return to membership of their birth family; worse still, they marry only to abandon their bride and return to the original family, or set up their own household and take a wife of their choice. They show no sign of shame or embarrassment, but appear to be satisfied with the state of affairs.

This is inhuman behavior that shows no sense of duty, human feeling, or indebtedness. Yet for some strange reason, in our society this kind of man is seldom criticized. If we look far enough, we will find many evil women whose actions are truly repugnant, but any comparison of women with men is bound to show that the latter are more inhumane. For that reason, I feel that what we need is a *Great Learning* for men rather than for women.

The writer gives the Seven Reasons for Divorce, the first being "disobedience" to the father- or mother-in-law. If the wife is rude, ill natured and impolite or unfeeling in her behavior towards her husband's parents, divorce is justifiable.

The second item is a "woman shall be divorced if she fail to bear children." This is an excuse that has no evidence to support it. When a couple are unable to have children, even modern medicine as yet has no way of determining precisely whether the cause lies with the husband or the wife. This is because the answer lies in biological, anatomical, psychological, and pathological issues. Sometimes a woman who has lived with her first husband for many years without bearing any children chances to marry a second time and brings forth a child. Then there are cases of very amorous men who keep a number of concubines and yet never have any children. If someone determines that a woman is incapable of having a child without taking these factors into account, this is nothing but an ignorant conjecture.

In any case, if barrenness is a reason for divorce, an adopted son-in-law who does not beget a child with the daughter of the house should also be driven out, on the grounds that a man "shall be divorced if [he] fail to bear children." In fact, it is likely that the writer of the text himself realized that this way of divorce was unreasonable since he softened his stance and added a line to say that a barren woman should not be divorced "if her heart is virtuous."

The statement that "neither is there any just cause for a man to divorce a barren wife if he has children by a concubine" is completely unnecessary; it is hard to understand why it was added. When I think about this, I cannot help suspecting that by declaring at the beginning that a "woman shall be divorced if she fail to bear children" but denying at the end that there was "any just cause for a man to divorce a barren wife if he has children by a concubine," the real intention of the writer was to give men a way of keeping concubines. Between the lines he was surely encouraging women not to complain about the evils of this practice but to recommend it to their husbands, in order to make their own positions secure. In actual fact, since ancient times, daimyo who have acquired a concubine have gone through the pretext of getting their wives to offer her to them. Yet it is surely the depths of hypocrisy for men to expect their wives to share the blame for their disgraceful conduct. Here we can see the influence that has flowed from the poisoned words of *The Great Learning for Women*.

Third: "Lewdness is a reason for divorce." In Japan, from ancient times up until today, is it the men or the women who have been most guilty of lewd behavior? Leaving aside the depth of the lewd desires involved, if someone were to ask whether it is men or women who have more frequently acted out such desires, the answer would be so obvious that no thought would be required. If this rule were to be applied to men and women equally, many more of the former would receive declarations of divorce than the latter. But in this text, the looseness of women is singled out as a reason for divorce. This again is an injunction that has been pointed in the wrong direction.

Fourth: "Jealousy is a reason for divorce." This is also hard to understand. For a man to be unfaithful to the wife with whom he shares a home is to treat her with cruelty. Since the wife has contracted to live with him until the end of her life, it is an act of legitimate self-defense to dispute his behavior. Of course, it is possible that a wife may make a mistake and dispute a husband's behavior when there is no need to do so. Should this be called jealousy? This is not yet sufficient cause for immediate divorce.

Fifth: "Leprosy, or any like foul disease, is a reason for divorce." There is absolutely no reason for this. Since leprosy is a contagious disease, there is a chance that it might attack any normal person, and there is no question that anyone infected should incur blame. What grounds could there be for divorcing a wife who has the misfortune to succumb to such a disease? Surely the path taken by any husband with some degree of human feeling would be to put aside the idea of divorce, nurse her kindly and pray for a lessening of her symptoms even if complete recovery could not be hoped for. Suppose that instead of misfortune visiting the wife, the husband were to succumb to leprosy. Should the wife abandon him and just walk straight out of the house? I myself would certainly oppose such behavior, and the venerable writer would be likely to do so as well. Stories like those known as "tales of dutiful women"[12] often praise the unrivalled virtue of a wife named such-and-such who spent many years caring without complaint for a husband stricken with a foul disease. Our venerable writer would certainly not doubt that such praise was due. Does this mean that he would divorce a wife stricken with a foul disease without a thought, but order a wife in the reverse situation to nurse her husband? This would make his teachings even harder to understand, and I would certainly like to ask him to explain his reasoning.

Sixth: "A woman shall be divorced, who, by talking overmuch and prattling disrespectfully, . . ." This section is vague and incoherent. The idea seems to be that a talkative wife should be divorced because she will not get on well with the relatives and therefore disrupt the household. However, it is difficult to define what is too much, or too little, in the way of talking. The person whom A criticizes for talking too much may seem too quiet to B. Even if a woman really does talk too much, it is hard to accept that this one fault should be an adequate reason for divorce.

Seventh: "A woman shall be divorced who is addicted to stealing." Even where something like stealing is concerned, there are differences in degree; the word itself should not be considered a reason for divorce. The decision should be taken after consulting sources such as the kindred section of the Civil Code.

The wording of all seven of the above is different, but it is clear that in every case the purpose is to give men the opportunity to divorce at will while reducing women's power and denying them freedom of action. And yet, *The Great Learning for Women* has been revered among women as a time-honored treasure and used during their general education to warn them against bad behavior. Moreover, in many cases men themselves have advocated its principles. However, this has been for their own convenience, because the enervating effect that the text has on women allows men to indulge freely in their own selfish desires. There is a bizarre tale of a lascivious man in the provinces who was continually unfaithful to his wife. No longer able to bear her complaining, he schemed to have her join a Christian church in the hope that this would pacify her jealous nature so that he himself could enjoy his animal instincts to the full. But his plot was a failure, for her complaining did not cease. Women must always be alert, for most men who expound on the ideas behind *The Great Learning for Women* are trying to further their own selfish ends, just like this lascivious character.

Now, the rules for divorce given in *The Great Learning for Women* are the seven cited above. However, in the 812th article of the kindred section of the Civil Code, it states that divorce suits presented by one partner in a marriage are permitted only in the cases listed below:

> i. If the consort contracts another marriage.
>
> ii. If the wife commits adultery.
>
> iii. If the husband receives a criminal sentence for an offence against morality.
>
> iv. If the consort receives a criminal sentence such as is prescribed for offences not less than delicts for an offence connected with forgery, bribery, sexual immorality, theft, robbery, defrauding of property, embezzlement of goods deposited, receiving stolen property, or for the offences named in Article 175 and Article 260 of the Criminal Code, or is sentenced for any other offence to major imprisonment for a term of three years or more.

v. If such cruel treatment, or grave insult, is received from the consort as to render living together unbearable.

vi. Desertion with evil intention.

vii. If cruel treatment, or gross insult, is received from a lineal ascendant of the consort.

viii. If the consort treats his, or her, own lineal ascendant with cruelty or gross insult.

ix. If for a period of three years or more, it is uncertain whether the consort is alive or dead.

x. If, in cases of *muko-yōshi* adoption [that is, adoption of a man on the understanding that he will marry the daughter of the family], a dissolution of adoption takes place, or if, in cases where the adopted person has married a woman of the adoptive family, a dissolution, or an annulment, of adoption takes place.[13]

Therefore, according to the laws that bind the Japanese people today, the only cases in which divorce is allowed are the ten given above; there are no other circumstances in which divorce is possible outside the understanding and agreement of both parties. The three and a half lines of the *mikudarihan* divorce statement[14] belong to the past, and we must take note that today we live in an entirely different world. It is true that the first of the seven rules for divorce in *The Great Learning for Women*, the one concerning disobedience to one's parents-in-law, may still apply if it can be interpreted as meaning "cruelty, or gross insult," to older relatives, but there seems to be no other rule that has any relevance at all to the present law.

There is, in fact, a danger that publicizing rules for divorce that have no legal relevance may give people mistaken ideas. To take a similar example, private revenge is illegal. But imagine the creation of a book that encourages people to capture thieves and ruffians and then punish them at will with their fists or with swords; that teaches children to regard enemies of their parents as adversaries who cannot be allowed to live; that claims there is no need to trouble servants of the law with such matters since it is the duty of filial offspring to kill such people; that lists the eternal fame of the Soga brothers Gorō and Jūrō[15] as an example for generations to come! If such a book were published, sales would certainly be banned, because its ideas would run counter to present-day laws. Of course, as a novel or light fiction it would not present any problem, but there would certainly be controversy if it were an educational book for family use or a school text. Now *The Great Learning for Women* is neither a novel nor light fiction; in some parts of the country it is still revered as a treasure of women's education. And yet, many of its pronouncements are clearly against present-day laws. If they sink into the popular mind, unintended crimes may occur as a result. Educators and, of course, government officials, should take careful note.

> 5. It is the chief duty of a girl living in the parental house to practice filial piety toward her father and mother. But after marriage, her chief duty is to honor her father- and mother-in-law — to honor them beyond her father and mother — to love and reverence them with all ardor, and to tend them with every practice of filial piety. While thou honorest thine own parents, think not lightly of thy father-in-law. Never should a woman fail, night and morning, to pay her respects to her father- and mother-in-law. Never should she be remiss in performing any tasks they may require of her. With all reverence must she carry out, and never rebel against, her father-in-law's commands. On every point must she inquire of her father- and mother-in-law, and accommodate herself to their direction. Even if thy father-in-law and mother-in-law be pleased to hate and vilify thee, be not angry with them, and murmur not. If thou carry piety towards them to its utmost limits, and minister to them in all sincerity, it cannot be but that they will end by becoming friendly to thee.

This precept tells women that they should "tend" their own parents "with every practice of filial piety" while they are being raised by them, but that when they marry into another family, they must act with affection, respect, and filial piety toward their husband's parents rather than to their own. While they must honor their own parents, they must never "think . . . lightly of" their parents-in-law. They must obey their every word in all things.

Written out simply in this way, it seems a very straightforward teaching, but we must consider deeply whether it is in people's nature for them to be able to do this, and whether such behavior is in accordance with everyday common sense and feelings. If we urge people to do something that they cannot do, or force them to behave as they cannot behave, we are imposing demands that are inherently unreasonable, and therefore likely to drive people to eventual deceit. Even if a married woman is told to love her parents-in-law more than her own parents, this does not change the fact that they are her husband's parents and not her own. Surely it is going beyond human nature to tell a woman to treat those who are not her parents as if they were, and even to express deep affection towards them rather than towards her own parents. For instance, when a young woman is having a baby, who would give her greater peace of mind as the person in charge of her bedside care, her mother or her mother-in-law? A mother-in-law would not necessarily be cold-hearted; her prayers for an easy delivery might be no different from those of the mother, but because of something subtle that is inherent in blood relations, no one but the real mother can give comfort to an expecting daughter. Similarly, when old people are suffering from a long illness, who would they prefer to have to nurse them, their own daughter or a daughter-in-law? There is no question that it would be the daughter of their own blood.

In other words, the true nature of the relationship between parents and children is revealed in the fact that there is no constraint or reserve between them. This is because of the depth of the love that joins them, a silent love that is found wherever there are parents and children. The rules of nature ensure that human children feel affection and deep attachment for their parents and that parents feel love and affection for their children. This love is not confined to times of childbirth or the illnesses of old age. Accordingly, it would be demanding the impossible to order any woman to act with affection, respect, and filial piety only toward her parents-in-law, thus giving them priority over her own mother and father. Of course, it would be natural for a wife to obey instructions to respect her parents-in-law since they are of prior birth and therefore senior. However, when it comes to love and affection, it would contradict the natural sentiments of a daughter to place her in-laws above her own parents. As proof, we can offer the fact that from the ancient past up until the present day, there has nowhere been any example of such a case; and if a rare exception were ever to appear, it would have to be accompanied by an equally rare cause.

No educator should give instructions that are difficult to carry out because they go against normal emotions. Basically, respect is something external, while affection is internal. Even when there are no natural feelings of love within, it is easy to show respect outwardly in a bow. Therefore, if wives were instructed to be sure to greet their parents-in-law every morning and evening, this would be easy to perform. If they were told to perform their duties faithfully, this would not be difficult either. If we understand this to be the role of the wife, this is what wives must strive to do. But the stricter the precepts, the greater the stress incurred in observing them; the greater the stress, the worse the effect on any genuine feelings of affection. As a result, even if there appears to be warmth on the outside, the inside is likely to be frozen and relations to be naturally distant. In short, we can only conclude that since wives and their in-laws are not truly children and parents, any attempt to make them behave as if they were is bound to end in failure. In fact, there are very many examples of this.

From this point of view, *The Great Learning for Women* might well be regarded as a text that turns people to deceit by demanding the impossible from them, destroying the authenticity of the happy family circle through surface politeness. My personal wish is for people to follow the spontaneous truth in family relations, without erecting any false barriers of artificiality. As far as a wife is concerned, her parents-in-law are her husband's mother and father, not her own; therefore, everyone should accept the situation as it is and regard it as natural for her to serve the former as befits their age and seniority in the family, but not hold them in the same affection as she holds her own parents. In other words, a happy family atmosphere arises if relationships are allowed to develop smoothly along natural lines from the beginning, without unwarranted expectations on any side.

There are some families in which the newly married couple live apart from the parents. This should be seen as a practice that results from great knowledge of human nature. I totally approve with putting the parents at a distance as a way of not growing apart from them; however, there may be situations in which financial or other reasons make this solution unfeasible. Therefore, even if they live under the same roof, the older and the younger couples should refrain from interfering in each other's affairs, leaving everything to happen as it may, just as nature dictates. To cooperate in avoiding all possible difficulties is the ultimate technique for a happy household.

> 6. A woman has no particular lord; she must look to her husband as her lord, and must serve him with all worship and reverence, not despising or thinking lightly of him. Obedience is the Way of women. In a wife's dealings with her husband, both the expression of her countenance and the style of her address should be courteous, humble, and conciliatory, never peevish and intractable, never rude and arrogant; that should be a woman's first and chiefest care. When the husband issues his instructions, the wife must never disobey them. In doubtful cases, she should inquire of her husband, and obediently follow his commands. If ever her husband should enquire of her, she should answer to the point: to answer in a careless fashion were a mark of rudeness. Should

her husband be roused at any time to anger, she must obey him with fear and trembling, and not set herself against him in anger and forwardness. A woman should look on her husband as if he were Heaven itself, and never weary of thinking how she may yield to him and thus escape celestial castigation.

Here it is declared that a woman has no lord [but her husband]. What is meant by this word "lord"? The writer was a man of the feudal ages and his whole argument is based upon the social conditions of his time. Presumably this thoughtless remark was linked to the fact that a samurai was subordinate to the lord of his *han*. While men of the samurai class had official duties in the *han*, their wives had no lord in the sense that they just stayed within the house. In that case, since there were no *han* duties for men who were farmers or townspeople, neither they nor their wives would have had a lord. But that is misleading, for since both farmers and townspeople paid tax this means that they were serving the ruler of the country or *han* in some way, and therefore should be counted as having lords. Consequently, since these taxes were produced from the labor of both men and women in the fields and the towns, it is clearly misleading to claim that women who had such public duties were neither vassals nor servants of the *han*. In short, all we need to say is that there is no basis for the declaration that women have no lords, even in terms of feudal society.

Leaving this issue aside as unworthy of further notice, it is certainly reasonable to expect that women should not despise or think lightly of their husbands. However, if our aim is to examine relations between men and women as they stand at present and correct the worst abuses, I would rather wish us to turn this teaching around and use it to admonish the husbands. In other words, it is surely desirable that *men* should be "courteous" and "conciliatory" in their facial expressions and language. Since women are by nature sensitive and much more likely than men to take things emotionally, a husband's coarse behavior or vulgar and abusive language are very liable to upset his wife and disturb the peace of the household. A husband's first duty should be to be very careful in this regard.

The writer continues: "When the husband issues his instructions, the wife must never disobey" his orders. "In doubtful cases, she should inquire of her husband, and obediently follow his commands. . . . Should her husband be roused at any time to anger, she must obey him with fear and trembling, and not set herself against him in . . . forwardness." If a husband is of perfect intellect and virtue, a wife should certainly obey his instructions and ask questions when in doubt. But this naturally depends on the quality of the man himself. A wife's path in life does not require blind obedience to nonsensical or unreasonable demands just because they come from the husband, particularly if he becomes angry or loses his temper and begins to act violently. Of course, it is not a good idea for the wife to grow angry as well and oppose him; she must regard his temper as a passing fit, soothe him for a while, and admonish him severely afterwards. But I am not impressed by the teaching that a wife should obey her husband "with fear" regardless of the reason behind his anger, as if she was no more than his slave. Further, I am left speechless by the instructions at the end of this section that "A woman should look on her husband as if he were Heaven itself. . . ." If women are required to look on their husbands as if they were Heaven itself, men should look on their wives as if they were deities. Moreover, if women who oppose their husbands are meant to incur "celestial castigation," I wish to declare that men who ill-treat their wives deserve divine castigation.

> 7. As brothers- and sisters-in-law are the brothers and sisters of a woman's husband, they deserve all respect. Should she lay herself open to ridicule and dislike of her husband's kindred, she would offend her parents-in-law, and do harm even to herself; whereas, if she lives on good terms with them, she will likewise make happy the hearts of her parents-in-law. Again, she should cherish, and be intimate with, her husband's elder brother and his wife, esteeming them as she does her own elder brother and sister.

The above is correct to a certain extent. We have a duty to associate with family members, and this involves paying proper respect to brothers-in-law and sisters-in-law in order to please the parents-in-law. We should also cherish brothers-in-law and their wives. However, since they are not blood relations, it is difficult to accept the command to give a brother-in-law and his wife the same amount of esteem as one's own elder brother and sister. It is sufficient to get on well enough to live on good terms and without any unpleasantness. However, I would strongly urge everyone to consider whether it is possible genuinely to have the same affection for one's husband's relations as for one's own. I firmly believe that the very nature of human beings makes this impossible.

> 8. Let her never even dream of jealousy. If her husband be dissolute, she must

expostulate with him, but never either nurse or vent her anger. If her jealousy be extreme, it will render her countenance frightful and her talk repulsive and can only result in completely alienating her husband from her and making her intolerable in his eyes. Should her husband act ill and unreasonably, she must compose her countenance and soften her voice to remonstrate with him; and if he be angry and listen not to the remonstrance, she must wait over a season and then expostulate with him again when his heart is softened. Never set thyself up against thy husband with harsh features and a fractious voice.

Because the purpose of this section is purely to admonish against jealousy, I will begin by giving a clear definition of the word. Jealousy is when we envy the actions of another person even though this has nothing to do with our own situation. We feel resentful and hostile, and might even reach such a state of unreasonable fury that we pray for others to be unlucky or wish to harm them. For an extreme example, imagine that you are poor and have been plagued by a series of mishaps, while your next-door neighbor experiences increasing prosperity and becomes exceedingly wealthy. As a result, you are consumed by envy and malice. Then the old man next door builds a storehouse at a particular angle, with a gargoyle-type ornament on the roof. He must want to put the evil eye on you. Writhing in mental torment, you begin to think the unthinkable: "What fun it would be if the storehouse caught fire!"; or even, "I'll set fire to it for him, while no one is watching!" We should "never even dream" of succumbing to this degree of jealousy.

However, while I would certainly admonish against jealousy of this type, we need to consider carefully whether the state of mind described in the text really falls into that category. The text states, "If her husband be dissolute, she must expostulate with him." In other words, there is clear evidence of his dissolute and immoral behavior. This being so, can we really claim that this state of affairs has nothing to do with his wife and is therefore comparable to the case of the rich old neighbor who has become so prosperous that he has to build a storehouse? The wealth of one's neighbor has nothing to do with one's own situation, but a husband's dissolute and immoral behavior infringes directly upon the wife's rights. Consequently, the two cannot be discussed together.

Of course, since marriage contracts a husband and wife to spend their whole lives together, it is cruel and insulting treatment for one party to ignore this contract and do something equivalent to rejecting the other by going so far as to indulge in dissolute and immoral acts. Such behavior amounts to breach of contract, a serious crime. Therefore, if the wife, being the injured party, clearly makes the case for the husband's guilt, this is a way of relinquishing her contractual rights, and not the action of someone in the passionate throes of jealousy. Even so, it would suit the customs of upper-class society if the wife made her case with a softened voice and composed countenance. Such behavior is natural for a woman, and I myself dislike anything rough and vulgar. Yet in reality, there is no need for even the smallest sign of forgiveness or tolerance for the sin of immorality. Even if a man grows angry as a result, this should not be a cause for fear. To fight with rock-like conviction is the duty of a woman. Would the writer of *The Great Learning for Women* regard such a logical attitude as jealousy? In my opinion, it is self-defense on the woman's part, and my advice is that she should stand firm.

In a previous section on the seven reasons for divorcing a woman the writer declared: "Lewdness is a reason for divorce." He thus called for the immediate expulsion of any woman who behaved immorally, but here he does an about-turn and advises a woman not to "nurse or vent her anger" if her husband commits exactly the same crime. Rather, he instructs her to soften her speech and countenance so that she will not make herself "intolerable" in the eyes of the guilty party. We can do no more than gasp at this unwarranted partiality. In other words, the writer was ignorant of the gravity of the marriage contract, and therefore of the rights of women. He thought of them merely as playthings in men's hands. His sole focus was to ensure their subservience, and he wanted them to carry this attitude to the extent of overlooking even lewd and inhuman behavior as if it was of no importance. If any woman tried to insist on her rights, he would attempt to threaten her into silence by an immediate accusation of jealousy.

A woman in this situation can be likened to someone who has been robbed in broad daylight. Although there is sufficient evidence, when the captured thief is questioned, he immediately begins to accuse the victim of greed and lectures as follows: "Never even dream of being greedy. If a person steals something, you should stop him with soft words, and never either nurse or vent your anger. Moreover, if the thief is angry and will not return what has been stolen, you must stop for a season and then try again." This is nothing but disgraceful neglect of women's rights and contempt for them as individuals.

If a woman suspects her husband for no reason and takes offense without due cause, foolishly causing problems where there were none, this is surely jealousy. But in male circles today, there are so many shameful acts being committed that it is not a matter of taking great pains to detect small signs; on the contrary, rather than needing to expose what are open secrets, it is more a question of exposing what is already fully exposed to open view. Men who have inherited wealth, or who have established themselves through good fortune, government officials, company executives, scholars, doctors, even priests of temples, if you were to ask any of them what they desire beyond fulfillment of their basic needs, they would say that beyond all else they wish to indulge their feelings of lust to the full. Some go about this in private, others in the open, some in subtle ways, others in direct ways. The playboys fall under the spell of the pleasure quarters and amuse themselves among the female entertainers with no attempt to hide. They commit countless shameful acts, behaving like beasts that have assumed human form, yet remain unconcerned, as if they know no shame. Those who carry out their shameful deeds with a little more care for privacy keep concubines in their own homes, calling them maidservants or mistresses and thoughtlessly forcing their wives to live under the same roof. Alternatively, they keep the concubines in separate houses and pride themselves for being the husband of so many.

In fact, since this behavior can only be described as beastlike, it is like an enactment of the situation expressed in the old Chinese saying about "five hens and two sows."[16] Chickens and pigs are genuine birds and beasts; if there are five hens or two sows, they do not try to make distinctions about which of them are the wives and which are the concubines; neither are there any signs of jealousy or arguments over rights. But as "of all creatures . . . the most highly endowed,"[17] human beings should behave differently. Since marriage is the basis of human morality, once a marriage contract has been established, a wife cannot watch her husband breach the contract through some preposterous action without feeling discontent, even if this is what she tries to do. She has the right to induce the contract breaker to reform his ways by making her feelings of discontent plain. Such behavior has been cleverly explained away by overuse of the word "jealousy," and there have been repeated attempts to mislead society by hackneyed claims about women's tendency to develop this feeling. Despite these attempts, human rights must never be disregarded.

Yet the custom of respecting men and despising women has lasted so long that it has become second nature to women as well as men. Many women today are only too willing to forget their rights and therefore willingly accept humiliation; they are only too willing to endure humiliation and therefore willingly end up suffering. Such an attitude is simply to be pitied.

What is the cause that makes them so? The answer is as follows: From early days they are instructed in the code of their family and oppressed by the general customs of society. This has a gradual withering effect upon their vitality. As a result, they come to believe that to reproach a man for immoral behavior is an act of jealousy, that jealousy is a vice that women should avoid, and that to give voice to jealousy or show it in one's countenance will only bring disgrace. Therefore, they tolerate additional preposterous actions and thus cause them to multiply. In short, one can say that women suffer as a result of the weight of custom, which causes them to completely disregard their marriage contracts, willingly abandon their rights, and willingly sink into depression. This is not only bad for women themselves. Men's licentious behavior directly or indirectly leads to unhappiness for their descendants and can even be the root cause behind the downfall of the family itself. Consequently, for their own sake, and for the sake of their families, those who bear the responsibility that comes with being the wife of a household must bring a halt to the reckless and disorderly behavior of their husbands by firmly insisting on their rights. This is what we advise.

There may be people who will have doubts about the argument above. They will say, "This is all very logical, but we cannot immediately agree to the extension of women's rights since, from another point of view, to do so now would disrupt the social order." However, it is normally impossible to rectify the evils of any particular society without some degree of upheaval. Anyone worried about such upheavals must be prepared to accept evil customs without complaint. To take the example of the Imperial Restoration just thirty years ago, hatred of the feudal oppression of the Tokugawa regime had grown to such an extent that great upheavals occurred throughout the land as people attempted to correct the abuses. The happy result was the new Japan that we see around us today. Suppose people had hesitated at that time because of doubts about disturbing the social order. We Japanese citizens would still be suffering under the yoke of feudalism today. Therefore, to encourage women to assert their legitimate rights so that we can build a social order in which they are equal with men in Japan today is similar to the abolition of the old feudal structure and the establishment of the constitutional system of the Meiji government.

People overcame great obstacles in order to achieve important aims in political affairs. I have difficulty in understanding why the same should not be possible in the case of human affairs. After all, as far as human affairs are concerned, the social order in relation to marriage and other aspects of male-female relationships has already been clearly defined in the kindred part of the Civil Code. All that remains to return us to the correct path are the concerted efforts of female society, supported by those educated in the ways of civilization. There is no need for new ideas or new methods. Success is truly just around the corner.

> 9. A woman should be circumspect and sparing in her use of words; and never, even for a passing moment, slander others or be guilty of untruthfulness. Should she ever hear calumny, she should keep it to herself and repeat it to none, for it is the retailing of calumny that disturbs the harmony of kinsmen and ruins the peace of families.

By declaring that "A woman should be circumspect and sparing in her use of words," the writer is presumably telling women to be reticent. There is a proverb that goes, "A plethora of words, a paucity of ideas," and in the West they say, "An empty barrel rings loud." If a talkative fool is truly irritating, it goes without saying that in women, quiet elegance is to be desired. I have nothing but contempt for the tomboy, but if the only teaching that women are given is to be reticent, this will also have negative consequences.

In fact, it is not unusual for women who have already reached the age of marriage to be unable to voice stock phrases about the weather clearly, let alone talk about business affairs. Their mumbled whispers cause all listeners perplexity. Apparently, particular difficulties can occur when a woman is unwell, since she does not know how to describe her condition to the doctor. She seems to be so shy or so frightened when answering his questions that she muddles the order in which the symptoms of the illness appeared, and cannot give clear statements about how hot or cold she feels, or the extent of the itching and pain. As a result, the time that the doctor spends examining her is spent to no purpose; he can make no firm conclusions, and has no idea of how to treat her. In this way, to instruct people to "be circumspect" in their use of words and to be reticent can lead to practical inconveniences if the practice of reticence becomes habitual and dries up the power of speech that is so necessary to human life. I do not particularly like talkativeness, but sealing women's lips will not solve anything.

It is well known that in the past, the women who served in the private quarters of the daimyo had an excellent letter-writing style, spoke fluently, and were also far from ill mannered in their deportment. This fact is worthy of consideration. In other words, while the training received by the palace ladies is obviously no longer relevant for today's women as such, the following preparation is essential if they are to avoid ridicule: From their early days, they should, of course, practice writing the *kana* syllabary and receive instruction in composition and letter-writing. Apart from this, since the way in which they are educated should faithfully follow in the steps of our daily progress in civilization, they should learn the basic principles of the sciences, geography, history, and such subjects. If family circumstances allow it, some foreign languages may be added. They should acquire a general familiarity with domestic and foreign events, enabling them to understand educated converse. When they converse themselves, they should be able to communicate effectively even if they do not have anything profound to say. It is regrettable that throughout *The Great Learning for Women* there is not even one reference to the need to train women's intellects.

Finally, this section declares that a woman should "never . . . slander others or be guilty of untruthfulness," or repeat calumnies to other people. This is common sense, but we will not discuss this part since the warning should be directed to men as well, rather than to women alone.

> 10. A woman must ever be on the alert, and keep a strict watch over her own conduct. In the morning she must rise early, and at night go late to rest. Instead of sleeping in the middle of the day, she must be intent on the duties of her household; she must not weary of weaving, sewing, and spinning. Of tea and wine she must not drink over-much, nor must she feed her eyes and ears on the licentiousness of Kabuki performances, *joruri* songs and *ko-uta* ballads. To Shinto shrines or Buddhist temples and other like places where there is a great concourse of people, she should go but sparingly till she has reached the age of forty.[18]

To instruct women to take charge of household affairs, to "be intent on" work about the house, and "not weary of weaving, sewing, and spinning" is highly appropriate, for these are clearly duties for which women are suited. In the West, there tend to be many women who do not know how to sew clothing. The customs of Japanese women in this regard are to be valued; therefore, however advanced society may become, however wealthy a family may grow, women must not tire of anything to do with needle and thread, for sewing is a craft that is not only noble, but also essential for them. Women are also told that they "must not drink over-much" tea and wine. Since even tea can be harmful to one's health when taken in excess, wine must be even worse, so both men and women should drink it only in moderation. Up to this point, I therefore agree with the text, but when it comes to prohibiting performances of plays, songs and ballads, and even limiting visits to temples and shrines, I cannot suppress my doubts.

Since human life is normally composed half of pleasure and half of pain, where there is hardship, enjoyment soon follows. Our writer is therefore likely to accept the logic that throughout our lives we should work hard and play hard, so that we can experience pleasure and pain in equal measure. On marrying, the man and wife contract to share both pleasure and pain as long as they are together. Of course, when a family is poor they will have difficulty in providing for their daily needs, and will have to struggle hard just to earn a living. Kabuki and forms of musical entertainment will therefore be beyond their reach. However, once they have accumulated some savings as a result of their efforts, there is no reason why both parents and children should not go on excursions together, forgetting all their daily cares and just enjoying themselves. This is just what is meant by "Work hard, play hard."

On a close examination of the text, however, it seems that the references to theatrical performances etc. mean that women are strictly prohibited from going out to plays or listening to music, regardless of whether the household is rich or poor. Moreover, they are expected to make only infrequent visits to temples and shrines until they reach the age of forty. On the other hand, the implication is that men are under no such restrictions. In that case, does it mean that since human life is composed half of pleasure and half of pain, the enjoyment should be the exclusive property of men while the burden of lifelong hardship should all be allotted to women? Surely nothing could be more unreasonable and outrageous!

Even if we ignore the above, while society expects women to take charge of household affairs and men to work hard outside the home, there are many men who abuse this division of the male and female circles of activity. Their rushing about is not only because of business affairs or socializing activities. When they claim to be occupied with such matters, they are often drinking and amusing themselves in the pleasure quarters. When nonentities from both government and non-government spheres who fancy themselves to be renowned and high-ranking figures congregate for what they claim are meetings or banquets, are these truly necessary for actual discussions or genuine socializing? Eight or nine times out of ten, they are not really meeting in order to discuss something, but only claiming that they need to do so as an excuse for gathering together. They are not really drinking in order to socialize, but socializing in order to drink. The time that men spend eating, drinking and amusing themselves is time that is spent outside the home. In other words, it is time that they spend in increasing bliss, secure in the knowledge that while they are indulging in obnoxious behavior and all types of entertainment, going to Kabuki with geisha or listening to ditties and ballads, getting drunk and then losing themselves in loose and frivolous activities such as gambling, their wives are back at home quietly looking after the house all by themselves, eternally imprisoned within the confines of *The Great Learning for Women*. Thus, when our writer admonished women rather than men and instructed them not to feed their eyes and ears on licentious spectacles, his teachings actually resulted in giving men the freedom to indulge in looseness and frivolity. By shutting one up inside, he has allowed the other free range outside; instead of preventing families from suffering any harm, he has actually invited it to occur.

This is not all. Cunning and immoral husbands wishing to indulge their animal passions but understandably fearing their wives' complaints, scheme to win their favor by ingratiating themselves. They allow their wives to obtain all the clothes that they desire, and to fulfill all their wishes with regard to viewing plays, traveling to hot springs, and going on seasonal excursions to enjoy the gentle breezes in spring or to view the moon in autumn. Thereupon, their naïve wives are so overjoyed by this indulgence that they spend their time outside the home, losing themselves in excessive social activity, ignoring not only their household duties but even the education of their children. Meanwhile, some of them also ignore their husbands' adulterous and immoral behavior, seemingly unconcerned. This situation clearly works out in the interests of any lascivious man, and there are strange tales of the most extreme cases, where the wife and the concubines share the same house and the wife feels affection for the concubines, with both the wife and the concubines bearing babies and living together extremely happily, even if only for the sake of outward appearances. This is as bizarre as anything that could happen in the animal world.

A certain American lady who arrived on a visit to Japan in the spring of this year heard stories about wives and concubines living together and so on during her observation of the customs of our society. Initially she was very skeptical, but finally obtained knowledge of the true state of affairs. With tears in her eyes, and at times gritting her teeth in indignation, she declared:

> I myself saw the evidence, but when I tell women friends upon my return home, it will be difficult to get any of them to believe me. They will probably think me untrustworthy and consequently cease to take my reports on other matters seriously. The life of a woman in Japan is just not worth living. I feel only sorrow and pity for them. We Americans would not tolerate such a situation for even a moment, but would fight it even at the risk of our lives. Japan and America are separate countries, but as women we are united in mutual sisterhood. For the sake of our Japanese sisters, we must find a way to drive out this evil custom.

When I heard the above story, I could not retain my calm. The exposure of this grave blot on the face of the new Japan filled me with such shame that I felt as though I had undergone a public whipping.

In just a few months from now, revision of the unequal treaties will be realized and foreigners will be able to reside freely alongside the Japanese. I am stunned at the brazenness that allows us to imagine that it will be possible to retain our national honor without doing anything about the situation above. Even though people are people in both East and West, the nature of relations between men and women is so different that in extreme cases in Japan, where a man has both a wife and several concubines, the wife and concubines may become so used to sharing the same house that they live together cordially, with no feelings of embarrassment. Ultimately, even if this friendship is not genuine, the reason why women in Japan have reached such heights of docility and acceptance despite the almost inconceivable animal passions of men must be the legacy of the rough valor of earlier ages, in particular the teachings of *The Great Learning for Women*. In other words, we must admit that women are unaware of the rights that are theirs in a civilized society. Over generations, they have willingly forgotten the rights promised to them in the marriage contract and have come to believe that to oppose a husband's wishes even slightly is to be willful, while to reproach him for his immoral behavior is to be jealous. Not only do they bear everything in silence, in fact they think that a truly virtuous woman will defend the guilty party, although he should really be the target of her ire.

It is the natural duty of a husband to provide for his wife if they are living together. This being the case, it is a truly ridiculous state of affairs if some wives are willing to discard the basic rights that are of such importance to them in return for no more than some beautiful clothes and delicious food. Husbands and wives must never forget that they should share the pleasures and pains of life; a husband or wife who tries to hide either the pleasures or the pains instead of sharing them is a husband or wife in name alone. A married couple should argue and discuss things exhaustively; they should never hold back, even if this means that at times they shock the neighbors.

> 11. She must not let herself be led astray by male or female shamans, become shamefully familiar with the gods and buddhas, or obsessed with praying. If only she satisfactorily perform her duties as a human being, she may let prayer alone without ceasing to enjoy divine protection.

I agree that women should not be "led astray by male or female shamans, become shamefully familiar with the gods and buddhas, or obsessed with praying." In general, it is ignorance and an inability to understand the reason behind things that cause people to be led astray in this way. If a comparison of men and women today shows that women really are more susceptible to superstition, it will therefore be because they have received less education. For this reason, rather than simply censuring women for being superstitious, we should promote opportunities for them to receive education in the ways of civilization and thus remove the fundamental causes of the problem.

> 12. In her capacity as wife, she must keep her husband's household in proper order. If the wife be evil and profligate, the house is ruined. In everything she must avoid extravagance, and with regard to both food and raiment must act according to her station in life, and never give way to luxury and pride.

The text says that a wife should keep the house "in proper order" and "in everything...avoid extravagance," while "with regard to both food and raiment, [she] must act according to her station in life, and never give way to luxury and pride." This is very good advice for maintaining a household. I greatly approve, but would like to go one step further and press for women to be taught the principles and techniques of economics and accounting.

In some cases, a wife leaves the economics of the household to her husband, allowing him to do as he pleases and remaining in complete ignorance. She simply accepts the money that he gives her and uses it to purchase the everyday supplies, while being completely oblivious as to whether the money belongs to them or has been borrowed. Moreover, if it has been borrowed, she does not know how it was borrowed, from whom it was borrowed, or how it is to be returned. While living with a husband and therefore being a housewife in control of half of the household, she does not even know whether they are rich or poor. This is an unacceptable situation.

There are many reasons for the powerlessness of Japanese women, but responsibility for their lack of attention to the economics of their households lies with the inadequacy of the education they receive from their parents before marriage. They are provided with classes in calligraphy and various artistic accomplishments, but their parents bring them up without any training or guidance regarding economic issues; in fact, they strive to keep them in ignorance of such matters. This upbringing has condemned them to the misfortunes that arise from such lifelong oblivion. In other words, since human affairs today have grown so complex, any woman who wants to keep her household safe must have a general idea of business methods and of how to earn a living. This will enable her to lay down clear rules for the household budget even if she is not going to be directly responsible for running a family business. It should be clear that such knowledge is necessary for all women, regardless of their wealth or social position. To this end, in addition to instruction in reading, writing and the use of the abacus, from girlhood they must learn the outlines of economics, and reach a level in knowledge of subjects such as law that will allow them more or less to follow conversations about them. It is a great mistake to think that artistic or literary accomplishments such as *waka* poetry are the only subjects that women need to be educated in.

I once said[19] that [to be successful in business] a man should have the refined spirit of a samurai of the Genroku era [1688–1704],[20] and the practical attainments of a minor official. Similarly, in versatility and in the elegance of her deportment a woman should be like a lady-in-waiting; in the innocent playfulness of her conversation and amusements, she should be like a child. She should never neglect scientific thinking or forget the principles of economics and law, but should store them deep in her mind so that she can put them into practice whenever necessary. Finally, in every move she makes and every word she utters, she should aim to be lively and yet refined. Only if she can achieve all this, will she be a proper lady.

Although I earlier referred to economics and law as subjects that women should understand I am not expecting them to achieve the expertise of bankers or lawyers. They should master them purely as a means of self-defense, in the same way as samurai women used to carry daggers on their persons.

> 13. While young, she must avoid the intimacy and familiarity of her husband's kinsmen, comrades, and retainers, ever strictly adhering to the rule of separation between the sexes; and on no account whatsoever should she enter into correspondence with a young man.

"While young, she must avoid the intimacy and familiarity of her husband's kinsmen, comrades" and so on; "on no account whatsoever should she enter into correspondence with a young man." The writer's intention must be to ensure that women avoid suspicions of misconduct, but there is no need for women of noble spirit to fear suspicions that are based on outward appearances. I hope to guide women's thinking to a higher level, so that there is no need for them to pretend to be unsophisticated. Instead, I want them to relax and amuse themselves in mixed company, although they must not arouse suspicions by behaving without restraint. It is clear that education is needed in this regard. There is no need to admire anyone who puts birds in cages and rejoices because they cannot fly high into the sky. I prefer to let them range freely so that I can take pleasure in their happiness.

We often hear actual cases of women who bring shame upon themselves through their loose behavior, but this is not necessarily because their parents or husbands have failed to keep them confined deep within the walls of the house. The way in which people behave is influenced by their inborn nature, the situation at the time, and the way in which they have been educated, but it cannot be denied that the factor that is most likely to lead people astray is the family spirit.

A child may grow up in a disorderly and abnormal household where the father is strict, but only in the sense that he scolds other people, while he himself indulges in all sorts of indecent acts. In extreme cases, children with the same father but different mothers may all live together, observing the words and actions of the single father and the multiple mothers all day long. In such circumstances, the behavior of the parents does not seem particularly indecent to the children. When a girl with such a background marries a husband who exhibits violent and loose behavior, it will be like leaving one indecent situation only to enter another one. Unless she has an unusually strong character, we need not be surprised if something goes wrong. In most cases, women who are dubbed unfaithful have usually spent most of their lives in indecent environments and been hardened by other indecent influences. Their behavior should be condemned, but the cause behind it is clearly the family spirit. On the other hand, immoral behavior is virtually unknown in women who have been born into pure and upright homes, brought up by pure and upright parents, and married to extremely pure and upright husbands. Therefore, any household head who wishes to encourage his wife to maintain high moral standards must first create a wholesome family spirit by behaving correctly himself.

Thus, the "bird in a cage" approach, while probably the most obvious, does not gain my approval. Additionally, there is absolutely no justification for instructions such as the one against writing letters to young men. How can women function in civilized society with its complex human affairs if they are forbidden to write letters? If the husband is otherwise occupied, the wife may have to deal with the correspondence in his stead. In particular, if he is ill, it will be her duty to write to the doctor to report his condition, request a house call, or ask for medicine. I can see no point in instructing women not to correspond with men regardless of the situation. I can only laugh it off as ridiculous talk.

> 14. Her personal adornments and the color and pattern of her garments should be unobtrusive. It suffices for her to be neat and clean in her person and in her wearing apparel. It is wrong in her, by an excess of care, to obtrude herself on the notice of others. Only that which is suitable should be adopted.

The text says that a woman's "personal adornments and the color and pattern of her garments should be unobtrusive.... Only that which is suitable should be adopted." This presumably means that women should take account of the family income and make a principle of simplicity. This I can agree with. However, since women place such importance on their garments, it would be wrong to give sweeping instructions for simplicity. Men do not know women's hearts, and older people cannot understand what makes young women happy. Therefore, we should lay down general guidelines about simplicity, but leave the actual choices of color and pattern to those concerned.

Unfortunately, it often happens that women from the provinces have money to spend on garments but do not know how to match colors and patterns. They make city people laugh because their expensive clothes do not suit them. Since this is all a question of artistic taste, even if women are told to observe simplicity in all things, I would like to add that it is important for them to learn about art regardless of their income, so that even in the midst of simplicity they can come up with ideas for their adornment.

> 15. She must not selfishly think first of her own parents, and only secondly of her husband's relations. At New Year, on the Five Festivals and on other like occasions, she should first pay her respects to those of her husband's house, and then to her own parents. Without her husband's permission, she must go nowhere, neither should she make any gifts on her own responsibility.

The text says that a woman "must not selfishly think first of her own parents, and only secondly of her husband's relations" and continues "At New Year, on the Five Festivals and on other like occasions" etc., but as I remarked before, even if this should be the case with surface formalities, it has nothing to do with the true nature of human feelings. Besides, what about the part where it says "Without her husband's permission, she must go nowhere"? It might be natural for women to consult with their husbands in case there are household affairs that might stand in the way of their going out, but this does not mean that they should not go out if they have a reason for doing so. If a wife cannot go out without permission from her husband even in such circumstances, she is a prisoner in her own house. Then again, the text says that a woman should not "make any gifts on her own responsibility." A woman in charge of household affairs has the authority to use the household assets for her own ends. To say that the lady of the house cannot buy anything on her own initiative is equivalent to treating her like a maidservant. I am opposed to everything in this section.

> 16. Because a woman does not continue her parents' line but follows on after her father- and mother-in-law, she must value the latter even more than the former, and tend them with all filial piety. Her visits, also, to her parents' home should be few after her marriage. Much more then, with regard to other friends, should it generally suffice for her to send a message to enquire after their health. Again, she must not be filled with pride at the recollection of the splendor of her parental house or sing its praises.

The text says that "a woman does not continue her parents' line but follows on after her father- and mother-in-law. . . ." But, as I mentioned before, in a family that has adopted a son-in-law, the daughter *does* "continue her parents' line." Presumably the writer overlooked the fact that while some women marry into other families and therefore follow on after their parents-in-law, others remain part of the family they were born into and follow on after their own parents. Be that as it may, the injunction to value one's parents-in-law even more than one's own parents, "and tend them with all filial piety" is beyond what anyone could perform with a sincere heart. Demanding the impossible in this way will lead to deceit. An educator should take more care about such matters.

The text continues: "Her visits, also, to her parents' home should be few after her marriage. Much more then, with regard to other friends, should it generally suffice for her to send a message to enquire after their health." First of all, this seems to be useless advice. A woman after marriage is so busy with household affairs that she naturally loses her enthusiasm for going out, especially after she has borne children. But to love one's parents is a natural human sentiment that cannot be criticized in any way. Therefore, if at all possible and as long as her household duties permit, she should be able to make frequent visits to her parents' home and ask after their health, or spend some happy hours talking and eating with them, so that they remain fresh in her memory. In her contacts with other people as well, the same way should be followed: as long as she takes proper care of the household, in any spare time she should be free to call on them or exchange messages as she pleases. Marrying into another family does not make the bride into a prisoner, so she should not be made to feel trapped. Finally, to say that a woman "must not be filled with pride at the recollection of the splendor of her parental house or sing its praises" is sensible advice. Idle bragging about the superiority of one's own family is something that all of us, not only women, should take care to avoid.

17. However many servants she may have in her employ, it is a woman's duty not to shirk attending to everything herself. She must sew her father- and mother-in-law's garments, and make ready their food. In the course of serving her husband, she must fold his clothes and dust his rug, raise his children, wash what is dirty, be constantly in the midst of her household, and never go abroad except when necessary.

The text says that a woman must do everything herself even if she has many male and female servants in her employ. "She must sew her father- and mother-in-law's garments and make ready their food. In the course of serving her husband, she must fold his clothes and dust his rug, raise his children, wash what is dirty, be constantly in the midst of her household, and never go abroad except when necessary." What a busy life she must lead! Leaving aside the question of whether or not all these tasks can be accomplished by only one person, I would approve of any woman who took care of her household in this frame of mind.

However, while it is a good idea to work hard to the limit of one's physical capability, I am irritated by the use of the verb "to serve" in the part that goes "In the course of serving her husband." "To serve" is basically used when a person of a low rank has dealings with a person of a high rank, particularly in the case of hierarchical relationships such as those of a lord and his vassal or a master and his servants. Therefore, to say that wives "serve" their husbands means that the relations between husbands and wives are similar to those between lords and vassals or masters and servants; in other words it is a clear admission of the fact that a wife is regarded as no more than a servant by another name. This sort of attitude should definitely not be permitted.

It is the custom in Japan today for men to be responsible for the running of all matters outside the house, such as government service or business affairs, while it falls to wives to manage all duties within the house. Taking care of the clothing and food, keeping things clean, and bringing up the children are vital aspects of domestic life and no different in importance and difficulty from men's outside affairs. Therefore, if the wife's management of duties within the house constitutes her way of "serving" her husband, one must describe the husband's efforts outside as his way of "serving" her. If a man and a woman marry, live together in the same house, divide their duties so that one looks after work inside the home and the other work outside the home, and take equal shares of both mental and physical labor so that they experience both pleasure and pain together, what reason can there possibly be to treat them as lord and vassal or master and servant?

It may be argued that compared to domestic duties, outside affairs are more stressful and their results more significant. But what about the anxieties and hardships of a wife looking after a husband who has fallen ill — can we say that these are not great? Or what about the stress of bringing up a child: giving birth after nine months of troublesome pregnancy and on top of that the lack of time to eat or sleep during the summer days and winter nights? In addition, how important are the results of the wife's efforts? After making sure that her children are properly clothed for the weather when they are small, and that the food that they eat is not harmful, teaching them to speak, training them in manners, and keeping them from harm, finally she turns them into adults. In other words, the facts show beyond dispute that those who live together as man and wife make contributions of equal merit in size and value. To give a comparison from the world of politics, in managing domestic affairs within the house, the wife is similar to the Minister of the Interior, while in dealing with the running of matters outside the house, the husband is like the Minister of Foreign Affairs. Both ministers are responsible for managing the national affairs of their country; their official titles might differ, but their ranks are exactly the same. Consequently, where *The Great Learning for Women* talks about the wife "serving her husband" this is no different from expecting the Minister of the Interior to serve the Minister of Foreign Affairs, a truly ridiculous idea. It should be clear that what is infeasible in a national government is equally infeasible in a family situation.

18. Her treatment of her maidservants will require circumspection. These low and aggravating girls have had no proper education; they are stupid, obstinate, and vulgar in their speech. When anything in the conduct of their mistress's husband or parents-in-law crosses their wishes, they will fill her ears with their invectives, thinking thereby to render her a service. But any woman who should listen to this gossip must beware of the heart-burnings it will be sure to breed. Easy is it by reproaches and disobedience to lose the love of those, who, like a woman's marriage connections, were all originally strangers; and it were surely folly, by believing the prattle of a servant-girl, to diminish the affection of a precious father- and mother-in-law. If a servant-girl be altogether too loquacious and bad, she should speedily be dismissed; for it is by the gossip of such persons that the harmony of kinsmen is troubled and the household put into disorder. Again, in her dealings with these low people, a woman will find many things to disapprove of. But if she be forever reproving and scolding, spending her time in bustle and anger, her household will be in a continual state of disturbance. When there is real wrongdoing, she should occasionally notice it and point out the path of amendment, while lesser faults should be quietly endured without anger. While in her heart she feels compassion for her subordinates' weakness, she must outwardly admonish them with all strictness to walk in the paths of propriety and never allow

them to fall into idleness. If any is to be succored, let her not be grudging of her money, but she must not foolishly shower down gifts on such as merely please her individual caprice while performing no useful service.

This section gives instructions about the treatment of servant girls. First, it says that women must not be quick to believe the words of servants since this leads them to "diminish the affection" of their parents-in-law; servants who talk too much should be dismissed without delay, because they will surely cause trouble among the family members and relatives; moreover, in "dealings with these low people" there will be much that is displeasing; however, a mistress must point such matters out "without anger." Finally, "If any is to be succored, let her not be grudging of her money, but she must not foolishly shower down gifts" on those whom she favors.

There is nothing that needs to be criticized here. I am particularly impressed with the part that says "While in her heart she feels compassion for her subordinates' weakness, she must outwardly admonish them with all strictness to walk in the path of propriety."

19. The five worst maladies that afflict the female mind are: discord, discontent, slander, jealousy, and silliness. Without any doubt, these five maladies infest seven or eight out of every ten women, and it is from these that arises the inferiority of women to men. A woman should cure them by self-inspection and self-reproach. The worst of them all, and the parent of the other five, is silliness.[21] Woman's nature is passive (yin). Yin, being of the nature of night, is dark. Hence, as viewed from the standard of man's nature, the foolishness of woman prevents her from understanding the duties that lie before her very eyes, from perceiving the actions that will bring down blame upon her own head, and from comprehending even the things that will bring down calamities on the heads of her husband and children. Nor when she blames and accuses and curses innocent persons nor when, in her jealousy of others, she thinks to set up herself alone, does she see that she is her own enemy, estranging others and incurring their hatred. Lamentable errors! Again, in the education of her children, her blind affection induces an erroneous system. Such is the stupidity of her character that it is incumbent on her, in every particular, to distrust herself and to obey her husband.

We are told that it was the custom of the ancients, on the birth of a baby girl, to let her lie on the floor for the space of three days.[22] Even in this may be seen the likening of the man to Heaven and the woman to Earth; and the custom should teach a woman how necessary it is for her in everything to yield to her husband the first, and to be herself content with the second place; to avoid pride even if there be in her actions aught to deserve praise; and, on the other hand, if she transgress in aught, incurring blame, to wend her way through the difficulty and amend the fault, and so conduct herself as not again to lay herself open to censure; to endure without anger and indignation the jeers of others, suffering such things with patience and humility. If a woman act thus, her conjugal relations cannot but be harmonious and enduring, and her household a scene of peace and concord.

This is the last section of *The Great Learning for Women* and its attack on women is so severe that it would not be an exaggeration to call it vicious and foulmouthed abuse. The text declares: "The five worst maladies that afflict the female mind are: discord, discontent, slander, jealousy, and silliness. Without any doubt, these five maladies infest seven or eight out of every ten women, and it is from these that arises the inferiority of women to men." However, it is not possible to accept the truth of this declaration without careful consideration. In fact, most people would agree that women's nature leads them to be gentle and mild in their speech and actions. Even in situations where men would become extremely angry, women will often remain calm and diffuse the tension with warm words and humor. It is not rare at all to see men quarrelling or arguing with each other, but it is very rare to see the same men arguing with women. This is not because the men have the power to remain calm on their own, but because there is something about the gentle and mild nature of women that makes it impossible to threaten them. This is not the case only when men and women are involved; even when men are arguing with other men, we are all surely accustomed to seeing women intervening to calm the storm. Even though these examples draw on the female virtue of cordiality, the writer denies these facts and claims, completely without evidence, that discord is one of women's maladies.

Is it possible, however, that the writer has some insight into a mysterious part of the female heart? When he lists every conceivable evil, not only discord but anger, resentment, slander and jealousy, and states that they are vices peculiar to women, does he have some insight into grievances that lurk hidden deep below the surface, but occasionally leak into women's words and actions? If such is the case, I will not deny his insight but I wish to say that he has impressive powers of perception.

Naturally, if Japanese women are forced to watch as their marriage contracts are ignored and their equal marital rights snatched away, if they are constantly crushed by oppression and despised by men, it is only human nature for them to harbor grievances. But if, on some rare occasion, they allow their grievances to appear in a facial expression or in something they say, there are calls of slander or jealousy. This is comparable to putting people in close confinement, making them handle fire or swallow boiling water, and then criticizing them for lacking the virtue of endurance if they make any complaint about the heat. Women's sense of grievance does not lead them to slander or jealousy but, whether they know it or not, to the fervent desire for the rights that belong to them.

It is beyond reason and totally unacceptable to just assume, without any attempt to understand the true nature of their feelings, that women's behavior results from their vices. Tied down by uncouth traditions for many hundreds of years, they have somehow been able to preserve a thin veneer of calm, but barbaric customs cannot be allowed to exist forever. I wish to clarify the causes of the "vices" that we ascribe to women and call them to the attention of civilized men and women.

At the beginning of the section, it says that women's fifth malady is their silliness, but a little later we are told that "The worst of them all, and the parent of the other five, is silliness." This is equivalent to saying that silliness is the root of silliness, which does not make sense. Leaving aside such trivial points about the writer's choice of words, however, I would like to inquire into the standards being used to determine the "silliness" of women.

While in every household men and women have different responsibilities, I am of the strong opinion that the same amount of intelligence is required to manage either domestic matters or outside affairs. However successful a man is at managing his outside affairs, if the woman responsible for domestic matters is ignorant and foolish, the household will always be in such disarray that it will not feel like a household. Even if the head of the house is luckily able to keep things together for a time and therefore avoid total disaster, if he dies prematurely or meets some other misfortune, the children will get out of control, the assets will be badly handled, and even a great household will fall in an instant. By contrast, however, if the woman in charge of domestic matters is wise, the household head will be able to rely on her even if he himself is stupid, and her unseen efforts will ensure that his reputation outside the house is maintained. In addition, both now and in the past, it has often happened that after a husband's death, the wife has proved to be a wise mother, bringing up and instructing the children, and maintaining the household in every aspect entirely through her own efforts. In fact, it is likely that many of the able gentlemen and wise ladies who have risen to prominence in our society were brought up solely by their mothers.[23] Under women who are wise, households prosper; under women who are foolish, they fail. In other words, the role played by women in the rise and fall of households is no less than that of men. Yet although women's role in this regard clearly depends on their wisdom and virtue, we thoughtlessly rate them as ignorant. This thoughtless rating is so lacking in thought that it is beyond serious consideration.

Some may argue that women are ignorant because they know so little about the management of the many different aspects of affairs outside the household. But the reason why they know so little is not to be ascribed to innate foolishness; rather, since they have had nothing to do with such matters, they are unfamiliar with them. There are very few women who understand and discuss the politics and economics of the country. In that regard they do seem foolish. But if we change direction and carefully examine the realm of everyday household matters of which women take sole charge, it is clear that when taken together, the household expenses and other domestic matters which seem so trivial are in fact nothing of the sort. They range from food, clothing, the treatment of servants, the management of correspondence, the entertainment of guests, and arrangements for outings at different times of the year, to the bringing up of children and the care of invalids. To deal with such matters, it is obvious that women need wisdom, wisdom requiring a degree of subtlety and attention to detail that is innate to women but that cannot be conveyed either by word or in writing, and which is beyond the power of any man to imagine or imitate. In regard to these matters, we must declare *men* to be foolish and silly.

That is to say, the wisdom of men and women differs only in its nature, according to situation and place, with the former being related to external affairs and the latter to domestic matters. Therefore, if they have the chance to gain training and experience, men can take on women's duties and women can carry out men's tasks, at least to the extent of their innate capabilities. The evidence for this is beyond dispute. Even if we set aside the fantastic tales from ancient times onwards of women who accomplished brave deeds, Japanese history has many examples of women with outstanding abilities in literature. In the West, special stress is placed on women's education and a number of women have made names for themselves in fields such as science, literature, and economics. And because one characteristic of women is said to be their precision, they are employed in accounting positions in government offices. Some scholars also stress the need to train more female doctors on the grounds that women are more suited to the study and practice of medicine than men; in fact, it is predicted that the number of women doctors will increase. Viewed from any perspective, the idea that women are by nature foolish, and can therefore be tossed aside, is clearly nothing more than the personal opinion of the writer of *The Great Learning for Women*.

Further, the text begins to explain that "Woman's nature is passive (yin)" and that "Yin, being of the nature of night, is dark" so that women are foolish by comparison with men. How ridiculous to line up all the faults one can think of and attribute them to yin, in other words, to produce the yin-yang theory as the basis of one's reasoning! This is absurd rambling, with nothing to commend it; it must be what is meant by the tale of an idiot.

First of all, what does yin-yang mean? According to the school of Chinese learning, since the south is yang, the north is yin; since the winter is yin, the summer is yang; heaven is yang while earth is yin; the sun is yang while the moon is yin, and so on. In the dark ages of ancient times, the ignorant and unlettered barbarians divided everything that they could see or sense into two, even though they had no reason for doing so, and gave them the puzzling labels of yin and yang. In the case of humans, it just happened that male and female were also lumped in along with everything else, so that men ended up as yang and women as yin. Like the classification of nouns as masculine, feminine, and neuter in Western grammar books, it is a relic of the illiterate past, and has never had any deep meaning.

The pretext may be that since men are active with a large and strong physique, they belong to the yang half, while since women are quiet, small, and weak they are yin. However, it would be possible to create another explanation and claim that in their beauty and charm women are like spring blossoms, while men's lack of both grace and adornment make them resemble the clear streams of autumn or trees that have shed their leaves. Since spring is yang and autumn is yin, this would make women yang and men yin. It would be difficult to present serious objections to this interpretation. By putting ourselves in the position of the ancients and creating a new explanation at will, thus counteracting existing theories of yin and yang, we can easily upset the old explanation and turn yin and yang upside down. This is because there is no basis for either explanation. The writer did not hesitate to use this baseless theorizing as grounds for his assertion that women are foolish, on the grounds that women are yin and yin is night and therefore dark. While I feel sorry for him and realize that I am being less than polite, I feel drawn to say that in his support for the yin-yang system, the writer is giving voice to absurd superstitions.

If an argument is wrong at its very basis, it will naturally be worthless in all its details. The text says that women are so foolish that they do not understand what is in their interest even when it lies before their very eyes; that they do "not recognize the actions that will bring blame upon" their heads; do "not comprehend even those things that will bring calamity to" their family members; thoughtlessly blame and accuse those who are without sin, without realizing that this actually works to their disadvantage; and worst of all do not even know how to raise their own children. In fact, the writer's conclusion is that because of their utter stupidity and incompetence women must obey their husbands! It is hard to imagine any insults worse than these. I will leave the writer's words as they are for the time being, but I would just like to inquire into the character of Japanese husbands.

Does the writer mean to say that because all men are yang and yang means the brightness of daylight, men are familiar with all things and suited to both domestic affairs and external matters; that they are particularly enlightened as regards the ways of morality, correct in their behavior and extremely tender and affectionate towards their wives? If this were actually the case, wives should of course be content to obey their husbands and consult with them. But the present mood of society suggests that men's behavior cannot be reliably guaranteed. I advise women, in their own interest, not to be misled by the statements in *The Great Learning for Women*, but to cultivate self-respect and self-esteem, and to quietly protect their rights through their own efforts.

Further, the text says that "it was the custom of the ancients, on the birth of a baby girl, to let her lie on the floor for the space of three days. Even in this may be seen the likening of the man to Heaven and the woman to Earth." This argument is as empty as the one above, and is therefore not worthy of consideration. Why should men be high as heaven and women as low as the earth? Men and women have different natures, but there is no distinction between them in nobility or value. If we are to insist on a distinction, it must first be proved with factual evidence. To give no evidence and treat "the custom of the ancients" as the basis of one's argument can only result in nonsense. To place blind trust in old customs and sayings as if they were eternal ways to salvation and thereby fail to recognize both the principles of creation and ever-changing historical trends is definitely the common failing of scholars of the school of ancient learning. But progress in human intellect leaves no space for such blind trust. In the ancient past, people may have let baby girls lie on the floor as a symbol of the contrast between men as heaven and women as earth, but since this practice was something that they had invented, it should not be regarded as justification for any everlasting custom. Whether they belong to the past or to the present, people are members of society and both the present and the past are influenced by their own particular historical trends. I am not so infatuated by one example from the illiterate past that I wish to apply it to society today.

In short, the writer of *The Great Learning for Women* wished to justify the doctrine of respecting men and despising women, but in all likelihood the lack of evidence put him in such a difficult position that he had to take drastic measures. After managing to dig up a "custom of the ancients," he wielded empty theories about heaven and earth to give power to his reasoning, and was able to overpower women and force them to hide in the darkness. Once it is accepted that men should be placed above women, it is easy to issue orders to a wife. She can be told "how necessary it is for her in everything to yield to her husband the first, and to be herself content with the second place; to avoid pride even if there be in her actions aught to deserve praise; and, on the other hand, if she transgress in aught, incurring blame, to wend her way through the difficulty and amend the fault," thereafter showing greater care; "to endure without anger and indignation the jeers of others, suffering such things with ... humility." Such attitudes of patient endurance may be seen as highly virtuous, but in my opinion, there should be no differences in rank among married couples: if a husband issues orders to his wife, the wife should also be able to issue orders to her husband. In other words, we should give the same instructions to both partners in a marriage, directing the teachings in the quotations above to husbands as well, as follows:

How necessary it is for a husband in everything to yield to his wife the first, and to be himself content with the second place. He should avoid pride even if has performed great deeds; and, on the other hand, if he commits a blunder, he should accept his wife's reproaches, amend the fault, and thereafter show greater care. He should endure without anger and indignation jeers from his wife, suffering such things with humility and restraint.

If both partners become aware of this ideal, I am prepared to guarantee beyond doubt that their relationship will become more peaceful and that they will be able to spend the rest of their lives together in a household with a pleasant atmosphere.

How might the author of *The Greater Learning for Women* have responded to the above? I would really like to know if he would have accepted this theory of mutuality. To reject it, and persist in admonishing women, while leaving men uncorrected, free, as it were, to run loose and do as they please, would be equivalent to reducing the virtue of peaceful endurance to a recipe for slavery. If the relations between husband and wife should not resemble those between lord and vassal or master and servant, how could it possibly be acceptable to treat one of the parties as a slave? I stand firmly against any such thing.

Parents! Teach the foregoing maxims to your daughters from their tenderest years. Copy them out from time to time, that they may read and never forget them. Better than the garments and diverse vessels that the fathers of the present day so lavishly bestow upon their daughters when giving them away in marriage, would it be to teach them with care these precepts, which will prove to be a precious jewel to guard them throughout their lives. How true is that ancient saying: 'A man knoweth how to spend a million pieces of money in marrying off his daughter but knoweth not how to spend an hundred thousand in bringing up his child!' Such as have daughters must lay this well to heart.
The end.

Finally the text says "Parents! Teach the foregoing maxims to your daughters from their tenderest years. . . . Better than the garments and diverse vessels that the fathers of the present day so lavishly bestow upon their daughters when giving them away in marriage, would it be to teach them . . . these precepts. . . . How true is that ancient saying: 'A man knoweth how to spend a million pieces of money in marrying off his daughter but knoweth not how to spend a hundred thousand in bringing up his child!' Such as have daughters must lay this well to heart." This is the conclusion to the nineteen sections in which the writer has thoroughly expounded his deeply-held opinions. In fact, it has never been my intention to throw doubt on his sincerity. However, in the more than two hundred years that have passed since the composition of *The Great Learning for Women*, we can observe advances in human knowledge and changes in the trends of the times. Therefore, if we are to seek happiness in the future by referring to the truths of the past, it is clear that we definitely cannot follow the theories of the ancients but must rather attempt to achieve the opposite.

In the feudal ages of the past, society was structured so that every aspect of human life including government was subject to oppression. Relations between men and women naturally followed this general trend as well, with a clear distinction in rank so that men acted like lords and women like vassals. Regardless of their actual social status, all these men acted arrogantly towards their wives as if they were copying the behavior of feudal rulers, either by just treating them coldly and ignoring their existence or, at the worst, by giving themselves up to acts of lewdness. In the society of the day, there were none to censure this cruel and insulting conduct towards their marriage partners; on the contrary, women were called wise and faithful for submitting to this treatment. The spreading trend won over both high and low; the teaching that jealousy was a female vice was picked up by the lower classes, who mocked any woman who showed signs of it. As a result, women willingly revoked the rights attached to their marriage contracts, and willingly sank into the depths of despair. This in itself defies belief, but they also paid no attention to the suffering that might be passed down to their descendants through their husbands' irregular behavior; or rather, they were willingly oblivious.

The above may appear to be little more than disquieting, but when social oppression occurs over a long period, it forms a custom accepted by the whole nation and thus becomes second nature. The message of *The Great Learning for Women* was written for a particular time, as if to encourage people to adapt to the order of feudal society, or to produce indirect support for it. Since the writer's teachings were directed towards only one of the two parties involved, the situation was equivalent to the proverb about government that goes "Even if the lord ceases to act as a lord, the vassals must continue to act as vassals." In other words, women's path in life consisted of patience, endurance, and blind obedience, as if the proverb went "Even if husbands cease to act as husbands, wives must continue to act as wives." Therefore, although the writer's arguments defy belief from our present-day viewpoint, there was nothing incredible about them at the time.

Today the bow and arrow or sword and spear are quite useless as weapons, having been reduced to mere playthings, but there was a time when one spear was able to decide the fate of a whole army. The essential tool of the past becomes a plaything to the people of the present. Such differences between the past and the present should be called progress in human knowledge and changes in the times. People of education should pay attention to this. Consequently, I regard *The Great Learning for Women* as the equivalent of the bow and arrow or the sword and spear among guidelines for female behavior, and therefore as something of no relevance today. Yet leaving aside its content, I can only confess admiration for the writer's fervor in advocating the need to actually give instruction to women. Therefore my plan is to write down the general outline of my own ideas about women's education, give it the title of "The New Great Learning for Women" and seek the reaction of our writer from his grave. Since he must have seen the changes that have occurred in the past two hundred years, it is highly likely that he will agree with me.

A New Great Learning for Women

1. Since women are born equal to men and are normally reared by their fathers and mothers, it is clear that the parents bear a heavy responsibility until their daughters reach adulthood. If a mother has many children or is unwell, it may be necessary to hire a wet nurse on health grounds, but whenever possible she should use her own breast milk. This is why the everyday health of a mother is so important. Some say that infants should be fed cow's milk, and in wealthy families they sometimes hire wet nurses just for convenience. Even though the mother has milk she does not breastfeed her child but merely stands by as a witness to its growth. Such behavior is beyond the bounds of reason and contrary to the principles of nature.

2. The hardships of pregnancy and birth are obvious, but even after that there are a host of less obvious demands on a mother, such as breastfeeding the infant, dressing it, and keeping watch in all weathers and all hours of the day and night. Her body may even waste away. The father should therefore take a share of the hardships; even if he has duties outside the house, as far as possible he must find time to assist in rearing the infant, so that he can give his wife some respite, however brief. Some husbands deliberately pay no attention to their wives because they are worried about society and their reputation; others are actually paying attention but put on a surface pretence of not doing so. This is spineless behavior. If a husband blithely ignores his wife's suffering this is a shameful sin against human morality; if this is just a surface pretense, he is a cowardly fool.

3. When a girl has grown a little, she should be allowed to devote herself to physical exercise just like a boy; she should also be given permission to take part in rough games as long as she does not injure herself. There is a harmful tendency to dress up a daughter even when she is at home, just because she is a girl; to worry that she will tear or soil her clothing because it is so fine; and, as

a natural consequence, to limit her chances to exercise and therefore hinder her physical development. This is beyond the bounds of reason. While she is of playing age, she should be given plain and simple clothing that may be torn or soiled without getting her into trouble. Her parents' only concern should be to allow her to exercise in a lively manner.

Moreover, while parents must obviously take care to ensure that the food that their children eat is both nourishing and free from harm, it would be beyond the bounds of reason to depend on food alone. However good the food may be, unless there is a proportionate amount of physical activity to go with it, the food will actually harm children's growth. The children of ordinary families in the countryside are allowed to eat simple foods in great quantities, without any attempt to control their diet, and yet they are generally healthy. In fact, they say that when a wealthy family in the Kyoto and Osaka areas has a sickly child, they will sometimes entrust the child to a farmer's home in nearby Yase or Ōhara. This is because while food eaten in the countryside is certainly plain, the physical benefits of eating and playing energetically like a country child can be greater than those to be gained from the delicacies available in a city. Therefore, any family wishing to raise a healthy child, even a family of great wealth, should adopt the Yase-Ōhara style and combine this with the advice of experts in physiology.

4. When a girl has grown a little more, she must first be taught her letters and how to hold a needle. Next should be the phrases used in letter writing, basic skills in the use of the abacus, how to make everyday clothes, and how to record and reckon the household accounts. There is nothing easy about this process of education, but parents should show patience. In addition, every female should obviously be familiar with all household matters related to the kitchen. Even a girl of high enough status to have many male and female servants at her disposal should obtain detailed mastery of not only how to cook rice, but also how to plan menus and prepare simple dishes. It is clearly important for a female to become familiar with these matters from an early age; even if she does not have to perform any of these tasks herself, she must be able to run her household without falling into a panic.

5. The items mentioned in the section above should not be thought of as constituting "learning," since they are the basic elements of education required

by any female, regardless of her station in society. As for learning itself, no distinction should be made between the education of girls and boys. They should both make physical science the foundation of their studies and proceed from there to study particular fields. In other words, just as the Japanese diet is based on rice and the Western diet on bread, with other dishes playing only a secondary role, so we should acknowledge that physical science is the basis of all learning. After they have achieved an overall understanding of this basic subject, they should study what particularly interests them as individuals.

If we take this argument to the logical extreme, it must follow that the only subject that is of no use to women is military science. However, we should take great care in deciding how much they should study. First, since women have to handle the affairs of their households, they do not have time to spare for scholarly studies. From a financial point of view, if a woman has enough money, she can leave the household duties to someone else and devote herself to studying. However, her physical condition is different from that of a man. Once every month she experiences restricted control of her body and mind; moreover the tasks of breastfeeding and childcare that follow pregnancy and childbirth are a full-time responsibility. So much of their time is spent in this way that it would be easy to argue that nature prevents women from studying at the same pace as men.

In the specific case of Japan, the neglect of women's education goes back to ancient times and has become a custom of society. To change the situation now, without warning, and immediately permit women to enter higher areas of education is a wish that we should entertain, but that we cannot actually realize. I therefore do not expect much to change in the coming ten or twenty years. I will leave the completion of this future goal to the people of the future, and concentrate rather on the urgent need of the present, which is, after all, to allow women to obtain the basic everyday knowledge of today's civilization. It is obviously important to learn the elementary laws of physical science, physiology, and hygiene, and the outlines of geography, history and so on; the study of nature and other such pursuits might also be of interest to women. However, there are two fields of knowledge related to society that I particularly wish Japanese women to explore: economic and legal thought. It may seem that women have little to do with economics and law, but their ignorance of such thought is the single biggest cause of their powerlessness. Therefore, once they have attained the normal amount of learning, they must next acquire the main points of these two fields. Figuratively speaking, such knowledge will play the role of a concealed dagger[1] for women who live in civilized times.

6. Because women are valued especially for their elegance, they must not copy male students and behave as if they are lacking in sophistication, reserve, or manners just because they have achieved some learning; nor should they become over-talkative or start to answer back. There are rules that govern human relations. When a problem calls for serious discussion, one should participate without reserve. But women should pay particular attention to the fact that there is a difference between a passionate argument and a calm discussion.

The art of spoken discussion is similar to the art of writing. Even in two pieces of writing with the same aim, it is possible for one piece to have an elegant and lofty style while the other is vulgar and over-emotional. It can sometimes be effective to address an issue directly and with passion, but skilled writers are able to exert a considerable influence on their readers by taking a more roundabout path and gradually, as it were, ratcheting up the pressure. This is already the case in the writing styles adopted by men, and is even more important when women engage in discussions. They should never be over-emotional or aggressive. They should maintain a modest countenance and a soft tone of voice; their object should simply be to explain their reasoning with clarity and politeness over and over again. This will enable them to preserve the dignity of womanhood, while even the most confident of men will be unable to stand against them. Those who are publicly known as "female students" only attract ridicule when they open their mouths and push themselves forward, forgetting their shallow knowledge and limited experience. I do not recommend such behavior.

7. We have already mentioned how elegance is valued in women. Accordingly, artistic pursuits such as music, of course, but also the tea ceremony, flower arranging, various types of poetry, calligraphy, and painting are their special preserve. As long as the household finances make this possible, their training in these fields should not be neglected. However, they should not confine themselves to the study of ancient Japanese texts and recitation of poetry that are normally considered to be learning suitable for women in today's society. Ancient texts and poems are, of course, lofty and refined; yet they are no more

than pleasurable pastimes that can be of no direct use in the practical realm of everyday life. The subtleties of music, the tea ceremony, or flower arranging have no place in the kitchen.

Moreover, the traditions of ancient texts and poems often tend to be attractive on the surface but prove to be lacking in logical ideas. The language may be elegant, but in substance they frequently stray into lewdness. For instance, the familiar lines of the *Hyakunin isshu* card game cause no harm to young girls as they call them out or listen for them while playing.[2] But when each poem is examined and carefully rendered into modern Japanese, it becomes clear that some are obscene and dirty, as unfit for the ears of a young girl as a vulgar *dodoitsu* love song. The only difference is that *dodoitsu* are sung to the shamisen and accompanied by rhythmic shouts in time with the beats of the plectrum that make the crudity only too evident. If those poems were sung to the shamisen against a similar rhythmic refrain, they would sound equally crude. Thus, classical poetry is not necessarily worthy of esteem, and this is also the case with *dodoitsu* and other styles of singing such as *nagauta* and *kiyomoto*. When we listen to all of these, just as when we listen to priests reciting sutras, our attention is on the sound of the words rather than their meaning. After all, it is absolutely clear that there is nothing to be gained from examining the latter. This can be confirmed by the existence of a number of female scholars who consider themselves skilled in discourse about Japanese literature and poetry but are correspondingly uninformed about important subjects close to home. They do not know how to treat themselves when they are ill, and make mistakes when nursing both old and young. At the worst, they go to embarrassing lengths with palmistry, geomancy, astrology and other forms of divination in their prayers concerning good and bad fortune. The cause lies clearly with ignorance and superstition. Thus, while the time-honored practice of studying Japanese-style writing [rather than the Chinese classics] as a purely artistic endeavor certainly has elegance, I do not favor the idea that this should be the only subject that women ever study.

8. Many books exist for the moral education of women and there are also the tales told by parents and older people. However, more accessible and effective than anything one might read or hear is the conduct of one's parents. As I have frequently stated, moral instruction should involve the eyes not the ears, and this fact should not be ignored. If parents behave correctly and have lofty ideas, the

spirit of the family will naturally be without blemish and so will the morals of the children, even if they receive no instruction. Therefore, it is clear that for parents to control their behavior and manage their households is not only in their own interest, but is also an essential duty that they should carry out for their descendants.

9. Among the many factors that produce a family spirit that has no blemish, the most important is a happy atmosphere in which nothing is kept hidden. What the children tell their mother, they also tell their father; what the father announces to his children, the mother also knows; whatever the mother says is also known to the father. Except in very special cases, there are no secrets, as if nothing were closed off anywhere in the house. Only then can family relationships run smoothly.

"This is what I want to do, but do not tell father"; "Such-and-such is my own decision and must be kept secret from mother." Such remarks are commonplace, but regardless of the moral aspects of such situations, machinations among family members have a negative effect on the development of the children.

10. When a girl has reached maturity and completed her education at home and at school, it is time for her to marry. This marriage is a great event in her life. Apparently, the method in Western countries is for the man and the woman themselves to get to know each other by spending time together and make a choice based on mutual affection. When they have finally made the decision, they tell their parents and having obtained their consent, hold the wedding ceremony.

However, in Japan the process is different. It is the responsibility of the parents to seek a spouse for their son or daughter. When the boy or girl reaches marriageable age, the parents begin the arduous search; they discuss the strong and weak points from various angles and finally settle on someone that satisfies the two of them. At this point, they consult their son or daughter and the matter is only decided if the children agree with the parents' selection. Therefore, on the surface it will appear as if marriages are arranged by the parents and the children themselves only wait for their decision, but this is not true. The role of the parents is to suggest, not to decide. They tell the children and ask their opinion; even if the children do not agree, there is no question of coercing them. In such a case, the custom is to abandon the first proposal immediately and search for a new candidate. Accordingly, although foreign observers have deduced that marriages in Japan are arranged by the parents, this is the worthless conclusion of people who are ignorant of the actual state of affairs. A similar situation can be found in the feudal period, when it was said that samurai had the right to cut down farmers or townspeople at will, although no one ever did this. The practice existed in name, but custom did not allow it.

However, the world is large, and since there truly are parents who sell their daughters for money, there may be parents who use their authority to coerce their daughters into marriage. Like the foolish samurai of a bygone day who cut down a passing commoner in a drunken fit, they should be rejected for their inhuman lack of compassion. Therefore, aside from such extreme cases, women today in general should not have any great complaints about the actual working of the laws of marriage.

11. For parents to seek a husband for their daughter is a very beneficial practice that seems not to interfere with the daughter's freedom. But my wish has always been for a more advanced society, where the boundaries of relations between men and women in society have acquired greater breadth and become refined and elegant. This would allow relations between them to be free and unrestricted in a way that is harmonious rather than unwholesome. Once such a state has been achieved, it will be easy for a woman to make up her mind about a match that her parents have suggested since she will have such a lot of experience. Or, if she is able to find a man who is to her liking, she may very quietly talk to her parents or privately ask someone to communicate her wishes. This will be very beneficial for all those concerned.

Although this is something I look forward to, it must, however regrettably, remain a hope; it would not work at present. I greatly fear that if this practice was to be pushed through now, the benefits would not be enough to compensate for the harm that would be caused. As long as relations between men and women are not fully developed, they are only aware of physical ties, and have no idea of emotional relations. For instance, when the worldly men of today amuse themselves with geisha, they refer to this as relations between men and women, but it is extremely vulgar, ugly, and uncultivated, far outside the boundaries of emotional relations of a refined nature. Even if a man keeps himself from direct contamination, he will still be half floating half drowning in a raging sea of physical relations.

Therefore, to improve the refinement of both men and women today and broaden the scope of their relations so that their marriage agreements become free and unrestricted, all we can do is wait for society to improve. No, rather than wait in idleness, all honorable and right-minded men and women should bring about this improvement through their own actions. This is what I both wish and advise.

12. Marriage for a woman is similar to marriage for a man. Some marry into other families; others remain in their original family and the husband is adopted; sometimes the newly weds both leave their original families to create a new one. Whatever the situation, once they are married, they must never go back on their agreement, but stay together through both pleasure and pain until they die. Since it is possible that women who never marry lead more carefree lives, it might seem that to marry out of a sense of duty is to go out of one's way to ask for trouble. But the laws of nature call for men and women to live together; the pleasure that comes from married life more than compensates for the pain. It therefore follows that being married doubles the pleasures and pains of being single; the pleasures are many, but the pains are many also.

A husband and wife should be like one person, sharing the same body. If the wife is ill, the husband will suffer; if the husband is disgraced, the wife will grieve. There should be no distinction whatsoever in what they feel. Perhaps from ignorance of this simple rule, some couples expect marriage to bring only pleasure and forget that pain is also involved. Then we find strange cases such as a man abandoning his ageing wife and keeping a concubine, or a wife so disenchanted with the poverty of the household that she walks out on her husband. This is nothing other than inhuman action by those who fail to value their marriage agreements. Care must be taken to avoid such behavior.

13. From ancient times, strong opinions have been expressed about how women should serve their parents-in-law after marriage, particularly if they have married into the husband's family. Moreover, it is a fact that conflict between mothers-in law and daughters-in-law is not unusual. Even if there is no open conflict, it is likely that in almost every family in Japan there are unspoken grudges that prevent a warm relationship. This is not because all mothers-in-law, or all daughters-in-law, are wicked. The fact that they are unable to get on well

together regardless of their personalities shows that the fault does not lie with them, but with the circumstances in which they are placed. Further examination shows that the cause must lie with public morality and customs. Public morality dictates that a wife should serve her parents-in-law just as she does her actual parents, and show them even greater warmth, affection and respect; at the same time parents-in-law are told to love a daughter-in-law just as much as a real daughter. This behavior would be very fine if it could be put into practice, but our natural feelings cannot be changed in this way. It is impossible to treat those who are not one's parents as if they were one's parents, and equally impossible to treat someone who is not one's daughter as if she were. In such situations, relations between the parties involved cannot be based on sincere emotions, and may often become stuck at the level of superficial ceremony.

Even if one side truly wishes to be affectionate and develop a warm relationship, it will be difficult to make advances anyway, either because the other party bears a grudge, or because this is imagined to be the case. As a result they have no choice but to follow the intent of the adage "Let sleeping dogs lie," observing the general rules of polite behavior and keeping their true nature to themselves. In other words, they each have something lodged in their hearts. Even if there is nothing evil about it, even if it is made up of pure kindness and sincerity, as long as they are hiding this something from each other, they cannot feel at ease together.

There is no comparison between this and the relations between blood relatives, who can express their true feelings without reserve. Children and parents may disagree or misunderstand each other; parents may scold their children; children may find fault with their parents. Yet the whole affair will be dismissed with a laugh without any harm to their original affection for each other. In other words, regardless of character or family spirit, when it comes down to human affairs, there is only the rare chance of one in a thousand or even ten thousand of fulfilling the hope that a wife will be able to form ties with her parents-in-law that are similar to her relationship with her real parents. The problem originates with the traditional method of educating girls, which gradually led to a custom at all levels of society that has become a source of hardship for both daughters and their parents-in-law. Rather than setting up impossible hopes that are bound to fail, we should accept that what is impossible cannot be achieved and look for more feasible methods. I hope that by returning to true human feelings we will be able to work out how to produce fully contented families.

14. In-laws, as the word itself indicates, are related by law, not by blood. Therefore, genuine human feelings dictate that we devise ways to develop harmonious relationships among them that accord with the true nature of this link. This is an issue that is of particular concern to me. A husband and wife obviously attract each other when close together, yet if they are separated, their mutual attraction grows all the more. Parents-in-law and daughters-in-law repel each other when close together, yet if they are separated they actually begin to feel mutual attraction.

Therefore, once a girl has got married, the most suitable solution is for the new couple to be provided with a new home of their own apart from the parents. However, not all marriages are the same, and depending on the financial situation or the occupation of the family members, it may be difficult for marriage to be accompanied by separate housing. Even so, I would strongly urge that at the every least the young couple should have a separate kitchen. For instance, on the marriage of the male heir, or if an adopted son marries a daughter of the house in order to become the heir, the old and new couples should not live together. They should set up completely separate households, whether this means that one of the couples lives nearby, or in a separate house on the same plot of land, or even under the same roof because the family budget does not allow anything more. In short, it is essential for the old and new couples to have as few points of contact as possible.

From the bride's point of view, it is not just that the parents-in-law are not her own parents; they are separated in age, and naturally their ideas and preferences concerning clothing, food, drink, and every minor detail are different. When these differences come into mutual contact, it only stands to reason that they should repel each other and every time this happens it will lead to ill feelings. On the other hand, if they live at a distance, neither in contact nor out of contact, without interfering in each other's domestic secrets, both couples will be free to manage their household budgets like independent units. Moreover, their separation itself will lead to mutual attraction, for distance conceals anything that might appear unpleasant. Before they realize it, parents-in-law and daughter-in-law will have come together in harmony, and will even be able to look forward to the happiness that comes from a warm family circle. This method will allow the mutual attraction felt by the new couple to increase even further; meanwhile, the old and new couples can be prevented from repelling each other and allowed to develop a mutual attraction as a result of separation.

There are many elderly parents who find a bride for their son or adopt someone as a husband for their daughter, expect the young couple to live with them, and then complain after some disagreement that they have stayed close at hand and shown so much kindness to the young couple, and yet detect signs of dissatisfaction. This is something that we frequently hear. Yet strange as it might seem, the very behavior of the parents-in-law in staying close at hand and showing so much kindness has actually been a cause of pain. This, after all, is no one's fault, but the result of custom. Although both are unwilling, the old and new couples have to live in close contact and suffer accordingly. This is surely a very poor way of managing household affairs.

15. Assuming that newly married couples will have a separate household, as far as the family circumstances permit, how should a new bride behave towards her parents-in-law? Her husband should be as dear to her as her own parents are. Since her parents-in-law are none other than the elderly parents of her dearest husband, who loves and respects them, her sincere feelings for her husband should ensure that she will behave warmly towards them even though they are not directly related to her. A wife's love for her husband leads her to value all that he treasures down to his dog, horse or even the things that he uses every day. All the greater, then, should be the esteem that she pays to his elderly parents, those most worthy beings who brought him into the world. She should look after them and show them kindness, taking pains to ensure that nothing displeases them. Above all, because older people have experienced so much, whenever something occurs she should tell them as much as she can or ask their advice, without hiding anything. She may fear that this will be a burden to them, but since by asking their advice she shows that she does not regard them as a nuisance, they will in fact be put at ease.

There was a scholar of Western learning who took a wife. The wife also understood a little English and the couple were happy together. Although the husband's elderly mother was there, they never asked her advice, let alone shared any of their news with her. Since they made all their decisions by themselves, the mother might just as well not have existed. One day, the mother noticed that various things belonging to the house were being packed and carried out.

She asked her daughter-in-law what was going on, only to be informed that they were moving to another house that very day. The consternation of the old woman was beyond words. She was not yet very old, being sound in mind and body and fully able to manage her affairs, but the young couple must have found her a nuisance. Because their habit was to arrange all their daily affairs by talking to each other in English, the old lady did not hear anything about the move until the very morning that it occurred. Before she had recovered from the shock, she was transported to the new house just like the rest of their belongings. This was obviously disrespectful, unreasonable and appalling behavior on the part of the son; the outrageous attitude of the daughter-in-law also deserves severe criticism. Among uneducated people from the lowest depths of society such conduct might be understandable, but it is utterly shocking to hear of such bizarre happenings among ladies and gentlemen of the so-called upper classes. As this English-speaking husband and wife discussed the matter they had probably concluded that it would be pointless to tell the old lady about the move, since it was not a decision that should be left to her anyway. Yet this is a clear example of being able to satisfy the physical needs of an elderly person but not the emotional needs. Rather than disrespectful or outrageous, they should be called idiots lacking in common sense, beasts unable to understand human morality. Women should pay attention and mark this deep in their hearts.

16. Because the bringing up of children is the special domain of women, even those in wealthy or noble positions should follow the rules of nature and offer their own breast milk. Even if a mother hires a wet nurse because she is ill, or for other health reasons, she must not for one moment neglect the care that her child requires. Even after a child no longer drinks breast milk, the mother must still be sure to satisfy its daily food and clothing needs, and never overlook even the most trivial of concerns. This is the vocation to which women have been called; accordingly it is not something that can be performed by a substitute.

Since food and clothing are material objects, it may seem that it does not matter who provides them. However, we must realize how much the non-material influence of motherly virtue will shape the thoughts and behavior of the child as its mother performs these services. The effect will be a hundred or a thousand times stronger than that of the services themselves. They say that even the growth of silkworms suffers if they are left to hired hands rather than being cared for by the owner's family. Imagine, then, what must happen in the case of the child to whom one has given birth. It should be absolutely clear that the care of one's children must not be entrusted to other people.

Some women, perhaps because they are unaware of their allotted role, have many children but complain that mending their clothes is bothersome, and that seeing to their meals is worse. Accordingly, they delegate such tasks to maidservants while themselves leading idle lives dedicated to seeing their friends and going on outings. This is highly regrettable. Admittedly, there is no reason why women should be criticized just for enjoying themselves. To get rid of stress and maintain one's health, it is certainly a good idea to visit hot springs or see the cherry blossoms. Meetings and dinner parties are also of benefit. But it seems that if the children are left behind when the parents are out, they are entrusted to the servants, and the newly born are forced to drink cow's milk. This makes them like the silkworms whose care is given to hired hands. It is easy to imagine what the results will be. In the past, many of the children of daimyo and high-ranking families were weak in intellect and lacked physical vitality, the reason being that the ladies of the nobility knew how to bring forth children but not how to raise them. This is a matter that calls for deep reflection. Therefore, I have no intention of preventing women from going out; rather, I encourage them to do so. I want them to be active, but I am not prepared to tolerate the behavior of any woman who neglects her duty to bring up her children in order to follow frivolous pursuits. On this point, there are many Western-style social customs of which I cannot approve.

Further, because a woman's circumstances in life keep her at home to manage the affairs of the household, it is essential that she have some knowledge of diseases and the functions of the body. When someone in the family falls ill, there should be no question of her attempting to treat them by herself; that must be strictly prohibited. But in the case of a sudden illness or an injury, she should have some idea of how to cope until the doctor arrives. Panicking serves no purpose, and can often actually aggravate the situation. She must always have her wits about her. For instance, when a child complains of a stomachache, a mother must not administer wonder medicines such as black-roasted plants, animal organs, or other "cures" of unknown pharmaceutical value. If the situation is acute, external remedies can be cautiously applied while waiting for the doctor to arrive. The child can be placed in warm water up to its waist or a medicinal compress can be used; if there is severe constipation, an enema can be given. But internal medicine should be strictly avoided until the doctor has examined the patient. On the other hand, if a child falls from a height and loses consciousness, sips of alcohol may be given. Equally, disinfected cotton may be placed over cuts before they are bound up tightly. Any treatment beyond this should not be attempted. There was a person who stopped a razor cut from bleeding according to the time-tried method of using the fluff that had gathered in the corner of his kimono sleeve. This worked, but the cut became infected because of germs in the fluff, making him seriously ill. This was nothing other than a punishment resulting from his lack of education, and it is therefore a case that we should all consider very carefully. Information about such matters is available both in books in Western languages and in translations. It does not involve too much effort to read this material, and it should actually be of interest to women.

17. Employing either male or female servants requires much effort. Those who are employed exert themselves physically; those on the employing side exert themselves mentally. In actual fact, it is the employer who has to endure the most. Servants have all sorts of personalities, and while some are extremely loyal, they are the exception. In general, since servants become servants because they have no wealth or education, an employer must instruct and train them, whatever their personalities may be, and with all kindness assign them to their posts. At the same time, the employer must accept that no servant will turn out entirely as wanted, and not expect too much. There is no point in listing each careless mistake of the maidservant, or every oversight of the manservant, or in fretting and losing one's temper to no effect. Those who are dissatisfied with their present male and female servants should think back over the past few years and list those servants who were most suited to their needs over that period. It is likely that all of them had weak as well as strong points, and that few were perfect. If this was the case in the past, it is likely to be the same now, and in the future as well, so we should show forbearance. When an employer scolds a servant for some mistake or error, it is the employer rather than the servant that attracts unfavorable attention. Employers of servants should bear this in mind.

18. Women manage the household and look after the domestic finances, which is more or less to say that they deal only with what goes out and know nothing about what comes in. But this makes them very insecure. Husbands are not

immortal, and if we take their relative ages into account the husband is likely to die before the wife. In some unfortunate cases, this happens early and the wife is left with the sole responsibility for everything to do with the management of the household, including her many children. If she does not know the details of what her husband was doing before his death — what his business dealings were outside the home, what personal contacts he had (and with how many people), the status of any debts or loans, and the terms for each —, or if she cannot understand the accounts, all sorts of misunderstandings are bound to arise and in some cases this may even lead to legal action. The problem lies with the fact that she has ignored the other side of the household budget. Therefore, even though business dealings outside the home are the husband's responsibility, it is important for the wife to be acquainted with the general outline and to pay attention to the occasional changes and fluctuations. When I say that women require a knowledge of financial matters, this is what I have in mind.

19. However highly educated, well read, knowledgeable or talented a girl might be, if she is lacking in refinement, if she shows the slightest signs of vulgarity or low behavior, one can say that she has already lost everything that is ladylike. "Signs of vulgarity or low behavior" here does not necessarily mean condemnation of actual acts of licentiousness alone. It also covers vulgarity in everyday speech and conduct, any disregard for the taboos of polite society, and all low behavior that should be despised as immoral, such as the tendency to let slip words that should not be allowed even on informal occasions — something that embarrasses the listener rather than the speaker herself. For instance, when despicable females such as geisha dress up, and become so familiar with their drunken clients that they go around singing and dancing, the fact that they show no restraint, but say whatever occurs to them, gives them an air of vitality and innocence, and some of them may really be innocent and without blame. But in view of this behavior, we can only see them as prostitutes at a party. Since geisha are outside respectable society I will leave them aside as a separate topic, but even among the upper class mistakes are sometimes made out of ignorance.

The spread of education in recent years has been accompanied by an increase in the number of words in use, and many terms of Chinese origin that were previously only employed in learned circles are now found in the daily conversations of ordinary people. One that I find irritating is *shikyū* [for womb]. In former days, women's illnesses were referred to simply by the vague term "feminine matters;" the details were talked about only by the physicians, and neither spoken of or heard by ordinary people. Yet nowadays people openly use the word *shikyū* without restraint in everyday social converse, and it can even be spotted in billboards advertising patent medicines. Worse still, there are also shocking claims that the word drops from the lips of women.

The direct equivalent of this word in Western languages is "**uterus**," and in Western countries its use is confined strictly to medical circles. It is only uttered in front of a patient or her family when necessary during examinations or treatment and even then, in circumstances of extreme privacy. Otherwise, it would never be heard from any Western man, let alone from the lips of a woman. She would not utter the word even at the risk of her life. Yet Japanese people apparently speak it without hesitation. Even if they do so in ignorance, how shameful this is! Moreover, there are other habits that are equally unpleasant to either see or hear. Even so, we cannot put the blame wholly on women. We should realize that the cause lies with the superficial nature of scholars and educators, who are the leaders of society, and the ignorance and inattention of those in government circles.

20. With progress in education, women have begun to chatter about things most improper to their station in life; in the worst cases they use the most outrageous words without hesitation. Since the blame lies with superficiality of which they themselves are unconscious, they can only be pitied. There are various causes for this, but chief among them is the mistaken path that their education has followed since childhood. The virtue of self-respect was not valued, and the practice of scientific reasoning was neglected; as a result they were led astray by frivolity and amused themselves with trivial literature.

For instance, once schoolgirls have reached a certain level of reading ability and are able to understand books in Western languages, they put all their energy into poetry and Japanese literature, or have no interest in anything but novels and popular fiction. Those who wish to acquire cultivation will certainly benefit from Japanese literature and novels, but there are many other directions that the young should apply themselves to. In actual fact, there are many ladies of distinction who are skilled writers of poetry but have never considered the issue of their individual identity, even in their dreams, who have read thousands of novels, but who have never set eyes on a book about the workings of the body. What is more, novels and popular fiction often awaken such an emotional response that they can actually have an undesirable effect on the carnal instincts of young women. If they are to read because of the educational importance of reading, great care must be taken in choosing the genre.

21. Since it is increasingly important for women to maintain an air of refinement, they must learn not to harm other people in order to preserve their personal feelings of self-respect. Society has always been less than pure, with geisha and women who act as concubines, and even cases where those who began as either geisha or concubines have risen to become proper wives in charge of their own households.[3] They are none of them fit to be treated as human beings, nor should they be ranked among women of the nobility. Yet even though they can only be viewed with the utmost contempt, it would be unseemly to make open show of such feelings. To humiliate them by making it clear that you are pure while they are soiled, that you have honor while they have only shame, would only serve to harm one's own reputation. It is therefore pointless behavior that should by all means be avoided. If by any chance you find yourself having to associate with such a woman, charity dictates that while you may privately pity her lack of any education or sense of shame, you should not forget your manners, but behave kindly and without showing any feelings of superiority. In other words, all you should try to do is avoid becoming closely involved by staying aloof and, as much as circumstances will allow, preserving your distance.

22. When a married couple share the same roof, it goes without saying that the wife should keep faith with her husband. They have made a contract to unite as one in body and soul, sharing both pleasures and pains, and promised to guard this contract at the cost of their lives. While there is a difference in that one looks after internal, household, affairs, and the other external, business, affairs, where their relative status is concerned, there should be no difference in the level of respect they afford each other. They should be on an equal footing in all matters, so that neither yields and neither makes the other yield either. This is because of the rights held by each party to the marriage as a result of the contract they have entered into.

It is said that women value gentleness. Gentleness certainly constitutes the true nature of women, a quality in which they differ greatly from men, and rightly so. It is a quality that I praise and encourage in them as the basis of womanly virtues and their best point. However, by "gentleness," I mean that they should be gentle in their words and conduct, not that they should be servile or submissive. When fundamental principles are at stake, it is correct to defy one's parents' orders, or to oppose one's husband's dealings. For example, when parents sell a daughter into the world of shame to solve problems with the household accounts, or force her to marry a man who is not of her choice because of the material benefits, they are trying to use her as a source of profit. The daughter is absolutely right to refuse the demands, even though they come from her parents.

Since this is the case with parents and their daughters, it is also the case with husbands and their wives. If a husband fails in his external business affairs and sinks into poverty, the couple must bear the misfortune together without any complaining. But although a wife should share the bad times as well as the good times, if a husband is of such loose morals that he keeps a concubine or amuses himself in the pleasure quarters, there is no reason for her to tolerate it. By indulging his animal instincts and neglecting his wife he is guilty of behaving with contempt and cruelty towards a partner who is supposed to be his equal. She should fight him with all her might. On seeing this, some may ascribe it to jealousy, but such cheap comments should be ignored. If he is allowed to indulge his animal instincts in this way, the repercussions will go beyond him, leading to disharmony in the family and estrangement between brothers and sisters; after his death, his descendants will be left with sickly constitutions that will weaken their bodies and his immoral ways will also be passed on. There will be no chance of achieving the happiness of a harmonious family. In extreme cases, disputes among family members may even lead to ridiculous upheavals on the scale of *o-ie sōdō*,[4] with secret plotting among relatives and numerous heated discussions about who is to succeed as the family head and how the property should be shared. At the center of these riotous disturbances will be the widow, who is at present the wife. Since it is as clear as day that the root of all the trouble is the infidelity of the master of the house, the inability of the mistress of the house to control him will leave her with no defense against the charge that she has abandoned her rights and rendered meaningless her heavenly duty. A woman who draws back for fear of developing a reputation for jealousy may lay herself open to a lifetime of shame.

23. Married couples pledge to grow old together and share the same grave, but unfortunately, only Heaven can choose how long or short our lives may be. It

is not always possible for a couple to grow old together, and sometimes a husband will die early. When such a tragedy occurs, the wife who has been left behind should remain in the family as a widow if she is over forty or fifty and has many children. But if she is still not yet forty, that is, still in her twenties or thirties, she should certainly not remain in this position. I have always advised remarriage in such cases, but the trend of Japanese society is very against such ideas. Even among scholars, there are few who discuss the notion. To my regret, they are more likely to see the acceptance of widowhood as a beautiful virtue, and place obstacles in the way of remarriage by endlessly repeating the empty justification that a virtuous woman does not have two husbands.[5] The old saying about never taking two husbands surely refers to women with husbands who take up with other men; in other words, it is a warning against deliberate misconduct resembling that of men with wives who amuse themselves in the pleasure quarters. By contrast, the question of life or death is decided by Heaven, and none of us have the power to do anything about it. However much we loved someone yesterday, they may be as nothing today. Those who have returned to nothing must be seen as nothing, while the living must make plans for the living. Our feelings as humans make us want to treat the dead exactly as we treat those who are alive, but human affairs should not be governed by the emotions. For example, when the living hold ceremonies for the dead they make offerings to them as an expression of their feelings, yet however strong those feelings may be, they cannot cause the dead to eat or drink those offerings. The living will mourn the dead from the bottom of their hearts; regret for what has passed will outlive heaven and earth, and never disappear. But since the realm of the dead is different from ours, our feelings for what is gone should not stand in the way of the affairs of the present. The dictates of self-realization call on us to make a fresh start and forget all extraneous concerns, to abandon the past and embrace the new. This is why I will always advocate remarriage, particularly since it is accepted that men and women should remarry in every country except Japan, where men can act freely but women are caged. Since this inevitably affects their relative equality, this is something that I can by no means ignore.

Every one of the above twenty-three parts is quite contrary to ideas that have been accepted in Japan since ancient times. Moreover, I have previously refuted every part of *The Great Learning for Women* severely, and am here advancing new principles in my *New Great Learning for Women*. As the old and the new fit together like a round peg in a square hole, there will certainly be some objections to my views.

The old ideas attempt to control ties between males and females through the use of formulas, while I aim for the full development of emotional relations in accordance with the natural inclinations of human beings. Elderly people of a Confucian persuasion are so deeply engrained with the customary formulas of hundreds or thousands of years that they have, as it were, produced a second sex. Since they accordingly have no problem with the evil teachings about respecting men and despising women, it stands to reason that they will not realize the truth. There is nothing surprising about their failure to accept the new ideas of civilization. However, the new Japan of today has led to the appearance of a new type of person. Since I have allied myself with those who belong to this new type and intend to work in tandem with them, I have nothing to fear from the opposition of older men.

However, the problem does not lie only with older men with their white hair, but even with able adult members of the elite who have publicly declared that they will support the principles of civilization in all things, both material and spiritual, and are actually putting this into practice. How ridiculous that they make an exception when it comes to the ties between men and women and draw on the evil customs of the old Confucian ways in an attempt to avoid the sins of licentiousness and infidelity! These civilized scholars and gentlemen are actually deceiving civilized society by hiding under the sleeves of worthless Confucianists and protecting themselves with Confucian ideas. We can only pity their predicament. If those who seek the protection of those worthless ideas feel so threatened that they try to create new theories in their defense, so much the better. I shall take up my old writing brush and pursue them mercilessly, even if the whole world turns against me.

Every word of my criticisms of the old *Great Learning for Women*, every word of my fresh arguments in this *New Great Learning for Women*, has been written from a humble desire to save the women of Japan from centuries of submission and gloom, to equip them with the self-respect and confidence that they need to stand on an equal basis with the rest of society. This will benefit not only women but also men, not only a family, but also its descendants; it will bring great profit and happiness and cause not the slightest harm. Therefore, we should explain the general message of these books to our daughters from their infancy. When they can read, we should give them copies so that they can read the originals themselves; when they have questions, we should explain carefully so that there are no misunderstandings.

Since ancient times, the sentiments of parents have been the same. Be a child male or female, the eldest or the youngest, the love felt by the parents has been identical down to the last inch. Therefore, they consider the future of their precious sons and daughters, and anxiously calculate the chances of their being happy or unhappy. What terrible agony would they feel on finding that one was destined for unhappiness! They would be unable to forget even for a second their anguish over a single bruise or missing tooth, let alone any weakness of the mind or body or a disability affecting either arms, legs, hearing or sight.

Popular sayings such as "The foolish child is best loved." and "Disability just brings more affection." accurately reflect the true feelings of a parent. In other words, parents pray with equal sincerity for the happiness of every child. To love one's children to the same extent, without any favoritism whatsoever, girls as well as boys, younger as well as older, is the essential nature of both the father and the mother, the absolutely genuine feeling of a parent. Yet if one were to ask if parents felt any particular concern over the future of their daughters, the answer would definitely be "Yes, very much." When a daughter is joined to another family as a bride, the parents worry about the response of the parents-in-law; relations with the brothers- and sisters-in-law and other relatives are also a cause for concern. With luck, these relationships may go smoothly, but it is nevertheless the husband himself who is the source of the greatest anxiety. If the bride is truly fortunate, he will treat her considerately and be upright in his moral behavior. But what can be done if this is not so and he falls prey to animal-like passions, as so often happens? He may ignore his wife, give himself up to frivolous and immoral pursuits and finally abandon himself to crazed lust, openly keeping mistresses and setting up a Chinese-style household by bringing them home and making his wife live alongside them.

Up until now, custom has dictated that a woman in this situation has no choice other than to submit silently to this crazed lust or leave and allow herself to be divorced. For a daughter, therefore, to marry is like the purchase of a lottery ticket. Whether good or bad, the result lies with Heaven, or rather with the husband's nature: paradise or hellfire, pleasure or pain, joy or sadness, the bride is merely a plaything in the hands of her husband. Since daughters are in such an insecure position, it is only natural for their parents to feel concern over their future and discuss ways of bringing them security. This is exactly the reason why it is so important for women to learn about the ways of civilization. If their parents love them, it is their duty to ensure that even if their daughters do not become scholars with extensive knowledge, they are familiar enough with the general outline of human affairs to be aware of the following: first, they must know themselves and be able to weigh their relative importance with regard to men, so that they can acknowledge the equality of men and women and the rule that says that neither is above or below the other; and they must have a deep sense of their rights, so that they will never suffer from uncertainty about their self-worth or self-respect.

At the end of *The Great Learning for Women*, there is a line that goes something like "It is better to spend a hundred thousand pieces of money bringing up a daughter than to spend a million pieces of money in marrying her off." I greatly admire this sentiment, but I would like to go one step further and encourage parents to add a sizeable share of the family estate to the clothes and other items that they give her when she marries. Leaving aside parents who have difficulty earning a livelihood, the natural desire of those who have means must be to give a daughter lifelong security by granting her a marriage endowment big enough to enable her to support herself, so that she is free from the need to be a burden to others if something untoward occurs. According to the old-style teachings, a woman must obey three types of people: her parents as a child, her husband on marriage, and her children when old. This may not seem unreasonable from a strictly moral point of view, but as we try to cross the seas of emotion in this uncertain world it is not always possible to stay afloat. There are many cases where obedience to a husband or child changes into subjection and unconditional submission, and the woman can do nothing to improve an impossible situation.

When a husband thinks only of himself and is so full of greed and bereft of feelings that he shouts that even the ashes under the stove are his, the most obedient of wives will be driven to her wits' end. At such times, a wife who has some means of her own will feel strengthened and find it easier to make plans for the future. Even when things do not go to such extremes, if a wife is able and ready to support herself, she will have fewer conflicts with her husband because she wants something, and no dissatisfaction because she has been unable to get what she wants. In other words, although this may seem vulgar and verging on the cynical, if a wife is not dependent on her husband, clashes are less likely to occur between them. An old saying has it that civility does not flourish until there is enough food to eat and clothing to wear. A woman without means is like someone who lacks food and clothing. By giving their beloved daughter a share of the family estate parents can ensure that she will have ample food and clothing, and thus be sure that she will develop a civil relationship with her husband. However, if a wife does not know how to manage what they have given her, even millions will be of no worth. Once a wife owns something she must devise ways of keeping it safe, guess what is happening and listen to what people say, but neither suspect nor trust them without good reason. In short, since the responsibility will be hers and hers alone, the management will not be a simple business. It is said that in Western countries, there are many women of good families who are very sharp with regard to such matters. This is a state of affairs that we should not take lightly.

*
* *

[Appendix to the published version of *A Critique of* The Great Learning for Women and *The New Great Learning for Women*]

The article below appeared in *Jiji shinpō* on 14 April, during the serialization of *A Critique of* The Great Learning for Women and *The New Great Learning for Women*, to give Fukuzawa-sensei's informal explanation of the circumstances behind their publication. It has been appended here in order to explain the reasons for the publication of this book.

A reporter for *Jiji shinpō*
September 1899

The Circumstances behind the Publication of Fukuzawa-sensei's Views on *The Great Learning for Women*

The serialization of Fukuzawa-sensei's "A Critique of *The Great Learning for Women*" has already reached its fifth part. As was stated in the prefaces, it was not the product of instant inspiration, but emerged, as it were, from his natural thought processes. Even so, it is not immediately clear why he suddenly decided to take up his pen and make his views public last year. According to his own explanation of the circumstances, this issue has been of great concern to him for a long time. Since first coming to Edo at the age of twenty-three, he has often turned the pages of Master Kaibara's *Great Learning for Women* and has many copies containing his brief comments. Thus, he prepared a draft in his head many years ago, but the general state of public opinion seemed so unsettled, even possessed, that it was highly unclear whether anyone would pay any attention to the matter or consider it calmly. Therefore, rather than publishing it prematurely, he stored it up and waited for the right moment. Since then, the progress of events has gradually calmed the popular mood and public perceptions and discussions have gradually become more sophisticated. As this has been occurring, the new Civil Code has presented Japanese society with the opportunity for an unprecedented transformation. In particular, the section on kindred should be seen as having a revolutionary effect on morality and public feelings, since it presents a radical change that destroys the principles of Japan's traditional family morality at the very roots, replacing them with new ideas in a form that allows them to be directly applied to public life and the running of households. The draft of the code spread around long before the actual promulgation and became widely known. However, there were no disagreements about its provisions; it was actually passed by the twelfth special session of the Diet [19 May to 10 June, 1898] and has been in operation since that July.

Fukuzawa-sensei was pleased by the thought that this situation provided powerful backing for his ideas. Yet on the other hand, the date for the implementation of the new treaties [with the Western powers] had been set at July 1899, which meant that in only a year's time foreigners would be able to live anywhere in the country and interact as neighbors with Japanese people. If they were confronted with the sight of men and women behaving towards each other in the traditional way, and this despicable situation became the subject of comment throughout the world, it would be a stain on Japan's honor that the people would be unable to bear. Every day that we spent without correcting this situation would amount to one more day of shame. However unworthy, he must take the initiative and give absolute priority to cleansing the country's reputation through urging reform on its people. He therefore concluded that at last the moment had come to publish his long-held ideas. These were the circumstances that led him to start writing in mid-August last year, at a speed that enabled him to produce the manuscript in as little as thirty days. In other words, although these two volumes are the product of thoughts that naturally formed in his mind many years ago, there was no opportunity to make them public until now. However, whether it was the progressive spirit of the times, the changing popular mood on the one side or the new Civil Code on the other, he now felt that he had gained powerful support for his views; moreover, concern about the fast approach of mixed residence convinced him of the need to publish, and so he decided to make his store of ideas public for the first time. Since the fifth installment of "A Critique of *The Great Learning for Women*" refers to the new Civil Code, he thought that it would help readers to know something about his reasons.

PART II

Private Writings

Daily Lessons

EDITOR'S INTRODUCTION

Fukuzawa wrote these lessons for his two eldest sons in 1871, when Ichitarō was eight and Sutejirō six. They were first published in 1906, with the basic details from Ichitarō that are translated below. It looks as though the lessons took place from mid November 1871 to mid January 1872, every day at first, and then more irregularly.

Fukuzawa was clearly interested in writing for children around this time. During the period 1868 to 1877 he produced seven textbooks. This was because he was unable to find any existing Japanese-language works that met the criteria of being both interesting and easy to understand.[1] Two of the entries in "Daily Lessons" are clearly influenced by an English-language work that he used as the source of one of these textbooks. This was *The Moral Class-Book*, edited by William and Robert Chambers (first published in 1839). Since the Japanese version was published in 1872 (as *Dōmō oshiegusa*), he may have been studying it at the same time as he was giving his sons these "Daily Lessons."

Writing much later about his reasons for writing *Dōmō oshiegusa*, Fukuzawa linked it to his discovery of Western ethical ideas in Francis Wayland's *Moral Science*.[2] This discovery may also have influenced the tone of "Daily Lessons." Certainly, there are clear traces of Christian morality, such as the similarity between the rules at the beginning of part two and the Ten Commandments.[3] These traces, and the other moral elements, are surprising since Fukuzawa was generally opposed to Christianity and also thought that morality should be taught by example. References to "God," and to the punishment of the wicked in part two, are also contradicted by later advice not to give children obviously false and unscientific explanations.[4]

The "Daily Lessons" may not have been as interesting as Fukuzawa hoped. In the passage below, Ichitarō claims that he enjoyed them. Yet Sutejirō apparently "recalled in later years that he thought the lessons very boring, but he sat through them patiently because his father would reward him with a piece of cake after each lesson."[5]

On the Occasion of the Publication of "Daily Lessons"[6]
These "Daily Lessons" date all the way back to thirty-five years ago, when my younger brother and I were still messing about in the mud and chasing after cicadas. I don't

remember now whether it was a present or something, but my father gave us both a considerable supply of large fine-quality sheets of pure white paper. They were smooth and well-suited for writing with ink, but for some reason they were folded so that every other sheet was the wrong side up. Well, we were both overjoyed to have been given such unusually good paper and got ready to draw pictures of shaggy giants etc. But our clever father, who did not like to make us listen to anything against our will, had been looking for a way to make the difficult and often boring subject of morality interesting. He took several of the sheets and made two notebooks by folding the paper into four.

He wrote "Daily Lessons, Part One" down the middle of the top page, with "Meiji 4" [1871] on the right and "10th month" [13 November–12 December] on the left. He added Fukuzawa Ichitarō to one, and Fukuzawa Sutejirō to the other. Every morning he wrote something in these notebooks — it might be a moral topic, or information about some familiar thing. We would get up, have breakfast, and then sit side by side in front of father's desk in his study, waiting excitedly for him to finish so that we could see what he had written for us that day. Most of that time has faded away into dreams, but even now I cannot forget my excitement. Anyone who picks up "Daily Lessons," whatever their standing, even a man old enough to be able to preach to his own children, will feel like a child again.

Daily Lessons[1]

PART ONE

10th month   1871
Fukuzawa Ichitarō/Fukuzawa Sutejirō

Rules to Follow
1. You must not lie.
2. You must not take things that are not yours.
3. You must not accept presents without asking mother or father first.
4. You must not insist on having your own way.
5. Quarreling between brothers is not allowed.
6. Talking about others behind their backs is not allowed.
7. You must not want what belongs to someone else.

14th day, 10th month [26 November]
To read a book and forget the beginning is like trying to fill a bucket that has no bottom. However hard you work to collect water, the bucket will not fill. Therefore, Ichi, and Sute, be sure to go over what you have read so that you do not forget the beginning. If not, however hard you work on your reading, your brains will not fill with learning.

15th day, 10th month [27 November]
If you wish to be a proper human being, you must not do anything cruel such as killing insects or hurting animals. If you show no mercy to insects and animals, one day you will find yourself behaving in the same way to your fellow human beings. Be sure to control your actions.[2]

16th day, 10th month [28 November]

You may be children now, but you will not be children forever. Bit by bit, you will grow to become proper men. Therefore, even though you are small now, you should do your best not to depend on others. Gargling, washing your face, dressing, putting on your socks, anything you can do without help, you should do by yourself. In the Western language, they call this "**independence**," and in Japanese "*dokuritsu*." "*Dokuritsu*" means to stand [*ritsu*] alone [*doku*] and not rely on help from others.[3]

17th day, 10th month [29 November]

People differ inside[4] just as they do on the outside. No one shares the same feelings as anyone else. There are people with round faces and people with long ones. And from the time of our birth, we are all different inside as well: some of us are quick to lose our tempers, others are slow to do so; some are quiet, others noisy. So even if someone acts in a way that hurts your feelings, you must not lose your temper or show that you are angry. You should live and let live as far as you can. This is the way to get along with other people.

18th day, 10th month [30 November]

We call those who are blind or deaf "handicapped." Ichi and Sute, you are both fortunate not to have been born with any handicaps. But handicaps can affect people inside as well as harming their eyes or ears. Anyone who refuses to hear the voice of reason is in a worse state than someone who is deaf. It is better to be blind than to be able to see but not read. Therefore, there is nothing shameful about being "handicapped" in the sense of being blind or deaf. On the other hand, children who handicap themselves inside should be ashamed of themselves.

19th day, 10th month [1 December]

There is no need to be ashamed of wearing plain clothes such as cotton kimono and over-garments in simple stripes. But you should feel ashamed if your clothes are grubby and if your face, hands or feet are dirty. Good children must always be sure to wash their hands and feet, and keep their clothes clean.

21st day, 10th month [3 December]

People must have courage. Courage means to be strong, to have a nature that fears nothing. Whenever you decide to do something, you must keep at it until you finish without allowing any difficulties to put you off. For instance, if you do not master a book at the first reading, this does not mean that you should throw it away. You should summon your courage, reading it over and over, ten times or twenty times, until you have mastered it. Be strong and persevering.

27th day, 10th month [9 December]
Throughout the world, there is no one better than your father and mother, nor anyone kinder than them. All children hope that their fathers and mothers will stay healthy and live long, but those who live today may die tomorrow. It is up to **God** whether your parents will live or die.[5] **God** made your father and mother and brought them to life, but **God** may also let them die. Of all the things in heaven and earth, there is nothing that was not created by **God**. People should feel thanks toward **God** from their childhood, and show obedience to **God**'s wishes.

※

We spend every day of our life in the same way: eating breakfast, lunch and dinner, going to bed at night and getting up in the morning. This life lasts only fifty years, so before we know it we have grown old. Yesterday turns into today, and the old man with white hair has turned to dust in a temple grave.

However, even pigs and horses eat, sleep and get up in the morning. Is it enough for those with the status of human beings to do no more than pigs and horses? This would clearly be shameful behavior. Since you have been born into this world as a human being, you must carry out feats that are beyond the capabilities of birds and beasts to show your superiority. People are superior because they can understand reason, and are not lead astray by their emotions when things that they desire are placed in front of them; they can read and write, find out about the wide world that they live in, understand the world of the past and the world of the present and how things change; they can live on warm terms with other people and act so that they need feel no shame in their hearts. Only through behaving like this can people show that they are "of all creatures . . . the most highly endowed."[6]

※

The old tale tells us how Momotarō went to Demon Island to take away the treasure. Wasn't that a terrible thing to do? The treasure belonged to the demons.

It was so precious to them that they had put it carefully away. Taking away someone else's treasure for no reason makes Momotarō into a wicked thief.

If they had been wicked demons who were causing trouble in the world, Momotarō's action in bravely going to punish them would have been good beyond compare. But the story tells us that he brought back the treasure to give to the old man and the old woman [who had raised him]. This shows us that he was simply acting out of greed. His behavior was beneath contempt.[7]

*

If you hurt your hand or foot, look after it carefully by binding it with a piece of paper or applying some ointment, and the wound will soon heal. If it is a small hurt, it will not even leave a scar. Now, if you wish to be a proper human being, you should not tell lies, neither should you steal. To lie or steal even once, will hurt you on the inside. A hurt on the inside is more serious than any hurt to the hands or feet. Since neither medicine nor ointment can bring healing, the harm will remain for the rest of your life. This being so, you boys should look after your insides more carefully than your hands and feet.

*

Children must know their numbers. For instance, people have five fingers on each of their hands and five toes on each of their feet. All together, they have twenty fingers and toes. Now, if someone asks you how many fingers and toes there are on the hands and feet of all five of the Fukuzawa brothers and sisters, what will be your answer?

*

We divide the time from sunrise in the morning to sunrise the next morning into twelve, and call each part one hour.[8] We call the time when the sun rises in the morning the sixth hour, then come the fifth, fourth, and ninth hours. The ninth hour comes at the middle of the day, which is time to eat the noon meal. The ninth hour is followed by the eighth, seventh, and sixth. The sixth hour is when the sun sets. And so, there are six daytime hours between the sixth hour in the morning and the sixth hour in the evening. Nighttime hours are counted in the same way, so there are six hours from the sixth hour in the evening until the sixth hour in the morning, when the sun rises again.

Children should be gentle and behave so that people treat them with affection. When they go out and meet people they should, of course, have good manners, but at home, too, when giving orders to male and female servants, they should not behave with arrogance. For instance, when you want to have a drink of water, if you say, "Will you please bring me some water to drink?" the maid is more likely bring it quickly and with a pleasant air than if you say, "Bring me water!" Take this attitude at all times, and as far as possible try to avoid any haughtiness.

※

Those who do difficult work in our world are given high status; those who do easy work are given low status. To be of use to society by reading and considering matters is difficult work; to mix earth to make walls or to pull rickshaws along is easy, because no mental strain is involved. Therefore, whether someone is of high or low status is decided simply according to whether their work is difficult or easy. In society today there are a great many people who call themselves lords, courtiers, and samurai, and ride about on horses with a pair of long and short swords at their waists. They look splendid, but inside they ring as hollow as empty barrels. Since they can neither read nor follow difficult reasoning, they idle their days away. There is clearly no reason to regard them as having high status or noble rank. They are only able to live in this splendor because of the rice and money that have been handed down from their ancestors; their true status is no higher than that of a rickshaw puller.

※

There is a saying that warns people not to make remarks about the appearance of other people until they have made sure that their own appearance is acceptable. Not once in your lives have you gone in want of food or clothing. But suppose you lost your gentle manner and developed a low nature, stopped reading books, and became ignorant. However splendid the clothes you wore, however large the house you lived in, people would despise you and point to you with scorn. You would feel more shame than a beggar.

PART TWO

11th month   1871
Fukuzawa Ichitarō / Fukuzawa Sutejirō

Hear ye, hear ye! Part Two of "Daily Lessons" is about to begin.

The rules given here are in six parts. Listen carefully with pointed ears; learn by heart and never forget.

1. Fear the Sun (*Tentōsama*), revere it, and follow its wishes. But by "Sun" I do not mean the globe that shines in the sky but the being called "**God**" in the Western language and "The Creator of All Things" (*Zōbutsushu*) in Japanese translation.
2. Revere your father and mother, love them, and obey their wishes.
3. Do not kill your fellow human beings. Avoid cruelty to animals and do not kill even a worm to no purpose.
4. Do not steal. Do not take what someone has dropped.
5. Never conceal the truth. Do not cause trouble by lying.
6. Do not be greedy. Do not fill yourself with empty desires and covet what others have.

※

From the present day, right back into the distant past, there has been no flaw in the rules of the Sun. Those who sow wheat will harvest wheat; those who sow beans will harvest beans. A boat made of wood will float; a boat made of mud will sink. Since these things happen without fail, people do not stop to wonder at them. In just the same way, if you do something good, your deeds will be repaid with good; if you do something evil, your deeds will be repaid with evil. These too are the rules of the Sun, and there has been no flaw in them since ancient times. But fools who know nothing of the rules of the Sun are sometimes led astray by desire for the things in front of them. Since they have no fear of the rules of Heaven, they seek happiness through evil deeds. This is no different from trying to sail across the ocean in a boat made of mud. Will the Sun be deceived by such actions? Those who sow evil will harvest evil. There are ears in the wall and eyes in the doors! Do not imagine that you can do evil and escape without sin.

The period from sunrise this morning to sunrise tomorrow morning is called one day. Thirty days make one month. A long month is thirty days and a short month is twenty-nine days. But if we count all the months as thirty days, one year will last 360 days because a year is made up of twelve months. Ten years will be 3,600 days; fifty years will be 18,000 days. If you two go to bed 360 times counting from tonight, you will be one year older. The New Year will be here, bringing all sorts of delights. But if you go to bed many, many, more times, up to 18,000 times more, you will be old men of 56 or 57 and you will no longer find much to take delight in. Waste not a day now but be diligent in learning your lessons.

In Japan, we divide the day and night into 12 and say that it lasts 12 hours, but in Western countries, they divide it into 24 and say that one day and one night last 24 hours. This means that one hour by their reckoning is similar to one-half hour of Japanese time:

Japanese Time	6	6½	5	5½	4	4½	9	9½	8	8½	7	7½
Western Time	6	7	8	9	10	11	12	1	2	3	4	5

We count in this manner and then go back to six and start again, following the same order.

One Western hour is divided into 60. This unit of time is called 1 *funji*, or 1 **minute** in the Western language. One *funji* is divided into 60 again and this unit is called 1 **second**. One **second** is just about the interval between each beat of your pulse.

By the Western way of counting, one day is 12 hours, or 720 **minutes** when counted in **minutes**, and 43,200 **seconds** when counted in **seconds**.

The length of a *tatami* mat is 6 *shaku*[9] and the height of an upper door frame (*kamoi*) is 5 *shaku*, 7 *sun*. One *shaku* divided by 10 is 1 *sun*, 1 *sun* divided by 10 is 1 *bu*, and 1 *bu* divided by 10 is 1 *rin*. Therefore, 1 *shaku* is 1,000 *rin*, or 100 *bu*, or 10 *sun*.

Six *shaku* make 1 *ken*, 60 *ken* make 1 *chō* and 36 *chō* 1 *ri*. Therefore, 1 *chō* is 360 *shaku*, and 1 *ri* is 12,960 *shaku* or 2,160 *ken*.

If the length of a person's step is 2 *shaku*, 1 *ri* will take 6,480 steps. Therefore, a person who walks 10 *ri* in a day has taken 64,800 steps.

The above are all based on the unit of measurement known as *kanejaku*. This is used to measure the length of things when building houses, making boxes, and so on. For measuring lengths of cloth, there is another unit, called *kujirajaku*.[10] It is used by drapers and tailors. The *kujirajaku* is longer than the *kanejaku*. Eight *sun* according to the *kujirajaku* equal 1 *shaku* according to the *kanejaku*.

⁂

One *tsubo*[11] is an area 1 *ken*[12] long and 1 *ken* wide, which is the same as 2 *tatami* placed side by side. When farmers measure the size of paddy fields, they call 1 *tsubo* 1 *bu*. Thirty *bu* make 1 *se*, 10 *se* make 1 *tan*, and 10 *tan* make 1 *chō*. Therefore, 1 *chō* equals 3,000 *tsubo*, 1 *tan* equals 300 *tsubo*, 1 *se* 30 *tsubo*, and 1 *bu* 1 *tsubo*.

For instance, when someone says, "This field is 4 *tan*, 7 *se*, and 15 *bu*," they mean that the field is 1,425 *tsubo*. A room with 1,000 *tatami* is 500 *tsubo*; if we describe it in the measurements used for paddy fields, it will be 1 *tan*, 3 [in fact 6] *se*, and 20 *bu*.[13]

⁂

Snow is white; charcoal is black. Everyone who has eyes knows this. Things that are right are good; things that are wrong are bad. Everyone who has a heart [*kokoro*] knows this. Our world contains people without eyes, but there is no one without a heart. Anyone who has a heart should immediately know what is right and what is wrong. To do something bad and try to hide it, or to tell a lie and try to deceive someone is similar to showing snow to someone who has eyes and saying it is charcoal, or showing charcoal to another and saying it is snow. No one is likely to be taken in by such actions.

⁂

If you wish to be a proper human being, you must be of use to society. Everyone has a particular role. For example, the farmer grows rice, the carpenter builds houses, the townsman sells things, the doctor cures illnesses. The scholar increases people's knowledge and refines social customs by teaching the Way, and the official ensures that society runs smoothly and improves the circumstances of everyday life. All these roles are essential. People who are of use to society in this way find their own reward, and are able to make a fine living. On the other hand, those who do not share this way of thinking assume that any deed that will bring them money is good. They do not seek to be of use or benefit to society and only wish to quench their own desires. As a result, they tend to behave in a low way without feeling any shame: they try to win money by gambling, talk others into buying useless goods, or fill their pockets by deceiving women and children. Greedy to profit themselves at the expense of other people, they harm society rather than being of any use. They cause ruin throughout the country and therefore end up by harming themselves. This is what is known as the "sagacity" of a monkey.[14]

*
* *

If you lie about what is white and what is black, you can deceive a blind person. If you lie about the sound of a drum and the sound of a bell, you can deceive a deaf person. But it is impossible to deceive or lie about good and bad since this is a matter of reason. The reason behind things can never be distorted: it is clear even to the eyes of the blind or the ears of the deaf. The hearts of human beings throughout the world are the same: there is not one who is unable to tell good from bad. If one of these human beings does something wrong and tries to deceive the rest, who will forgive him? He will be hated by all, abandoned by Heaven, and will end up worse off even than the beggar under the bridge, with no place to lay himself to rest. Worse still, he may be arrested, put in prison, and even condemned to death.

Reasons for Sharing Some Old Coins with My Children

EDITOR'S INTRODUCTION

In January 1878, Nakamura Ritsuen (1806–1881), a Confucian scholar and close friend of Fukuzawa's father, wrote to him out of concern that the new education system was giving more attention to practical subjects than to the teaching of filial piety. He wanted Fukuzawa to do something to correct the balance, and suggested that this would allow him to fulfill the duty of filial piety to his father that had been left unpaid because Hyakusuke had died when Fukuzawa was only eighteen months old.[1] In his first reply to this letter, Fukuzawa remarked that he had now reached the same age as his father on his death.[2] As Hirota Masaki suggests,[3] this realization probably set off various trains of thought. One of them led to this letter to his children, which was written in early February 1878, and published in *Jiji shinpō* in 1896. In it, he tells the children about their paternal grandfather, and hopes that they will prove themselves worthy of the high moral standards that he exemplified.

The letter shows a belief that families exist over more than one generation, and that the living have an obligation to ensure that the family values that they have inherited from previous generations are understood and treasured by their offspring, so that they will be transmitted to future generations. His pride in the Fukuzawa family line is also expressed in Letter No. 29, to Ichitarō.[4] This attitude, which is clearly influenced by the hereditary family system of the Tokugawa samurai class, contradicts the preference for one-generation families that he expresses elsewhere, a point that is taken up in the General Introduction.[5]

Reasons for Sharing Some Old Coins with My Children[1]

5 February 1878

To Ichitarō and my other children,

Your grandfather, Fukuzawa Hyakusuke [1792–1836], was a samurai of the former Nakatsu *han*. He was placed on official duty at the *han* residence in Dōjima, Osaka from the age of 24, and all of us children, two boys and three girls, were born there. And that was where he passed away, at the age of 45.

Your grandfather was fond of learning. He studied under Nomoto Setsugan [1761–1835] of Nakatsu and Hoashi Banri [1778–1852][2] of Bungo, and gained a reputation as an outstanding student. He did not have a reputation only in literary circles; they say that he was generally held in esteem for his naturally mild disposition, his tolerance in all things, his broad-minded thinking, and the moral purity of his private life. Unfortunately, since he died more than forty years ago I do not remember anything about him, not even his appearance, but your grandmother knew all the details of his words and actions.

While grandfather was in Osaka, he took pleasure in collecting old coins. In those days the coins in use in Osaka were called *ichimon*. They were *aosen*, like our copper coins today, with holes in the center. The custom was to put a piece of string through 96 coins and call them 100 *mon*. The strings of coins were used as they were, and people would not necessarily count each coin, but accept a string simply by glancing at its length. No one cared if there were one or two coins too many or too few, and it was highly unusual for anyone to connive to reduce the number of coins in order to trick other people out of their money.

One day, grandfather found several interesting specimens on two or three strings of coins. He slipped the coins off the strings, retied them, and went out leaving them behind, but forgetting to explain what he had done. When he returned home in the evening and asked what had happened to them, he found to his horror that since no one knew that they were some coins short, the

REASONS FOR SHARING SOME OLD COINS WITH MY CHILDREN

strings had already been used to pay for some fish.

Taken aback, grandfather asked for the name of the fishmonger, but unfortunately, it was not the usual fellow and no one, including the servants, knew his name. Grandfather grew extremely worried. He called together all the members of the household who had been in close contact with the man and made careful inquiries about his age and overall appearance, his clothing, the baskets for his fish, and even the yoke with which he carried the baskets.

All these he noted down in detail, and then he quietly called in a harbor worker who handled rice for the *han* and hired him to search for the fishmonger in Ajikawa and Zakoba because he reasoned that the fishmongers who came to sell in Dōjima were likely to be from either of those two places. After two or three days the man was found. Grandfather called him to the house, explained what had happened, and paid him the 5 or 10 *mon* which were missing from the strings of coins. He also paid him for his trouble and apologized for his carelessness.

At the time, no one either inside or outside the *han* residence knew of this incident. We children were so small that even if we had seen what was happening, we would not have understood. The only person who knew the details was your grandmother. Considering his temperament, I imagine that grandfather wanted to avoid suspicion that he was seeking praise. However, the incident belongs to the past now; moreover, more than forty years have gone by since he left this world. I cannot bear to let the facts of what happened disappear into oblivion, for it should prove an inspiration to the morality of the whole of society, and not only to the Fukuzawa family line itself.

When you children reach adulthood, I want you to share this story openly with others to exalt the virtue of your ancestor. And as you do so, reflect upon your own behavior. What kind of grandchild is worthy of such a grandfather? You are descended from an honorable family. Only through your wholehearted efforts can you ensure that you will not pour shame on your ancestor.

On the other hand, your grandfather was not a small-minded person whose reputation depended solely on his honesty. As a young man, he was sent to Osaka as the official in charge of Nakatsu's accounts and found himself keeping company with the richest of the large merchants of the day. Managing the *han* finances involved many activities, such as selling the rice produced by the *han*, raising loans, and negotiating the interest rates or deadlines for debt repayments. At times, he had to curry favor with loan merchants by providing them with drink and entertainment. After more than twenty years of exposure to this rough and vulgar atmosphere, one might expect all traces of his former refinement to have been worn away. But he was able to retain a refuge away from his busy life in the form of his deep devotion to learning.

He delighted in the study of the Chinese classics according to the Kyoto school of Itō Jinsai [1627–1705] and his son, Tōgai [1670–1736][3]. He was also interested in writing both prose and poetry. Men like [the Confucian scholar and prose stylist] Noda Tekiho [1799–1859] were among his close friends. Therefore, grandfather had the status of a lowly official, but he was also a classical scholar and a writer of both prose and poetry. His interests were many; his thoughts were wide ranging and never confined to a single direction.

The incident involving the fishmonger that was related above was simply a chance happening that revealed his inborn nature. Even so, this small anecdote does not tell us everything about his normal life. Moreover, as far as my own ideas are concerned, I am not so single-mindedly obsessed by honesty that I regard it as the only worthwhile virtue, or the be-all and end-all of a lifetime. Yet even though this is just a small anecdote, if I desire anything of you as your father, it is that you will bear witness to this spark of virtue that is evident among the records of his words and actions.

Very fortunately, I have here today 87 old *mon* which grandfather collected over his lifetime. Among them must be the coins from the strings that were handed to the fishmonger. I have always kept them about my person. Even when I left home to study in my youth, these were the only possessions that I always treated with care. But because you are all growing up and will soon be ready to join adult society, I intend to divide [most of] the coins among the six of you to serve as reminders of the importance of moral conduct, while keeping a few to myself as I always have, to treasure for the rest of my life.

The Fukuzawa family began as impoverished samurai on a small stipend, and never had money to spare. When I inherited the household, all we possessed were several hundred volumes of Chinese books, a few scrolls of paintings and calligraphy, and some swords. They had to be sold off to defray my expenses while I was studying, so that today practically no heirlooms remain to be handed down to you. However, there is no need for regret, since even if some had survived they would have been the sort of thing that can be easily purchased today.

The old coins alone are treasures, providing a radiant glimpse of your ancestor that could not be purchased even at the cost of a thousand gold pieces. They are splendid heirlooms that allow us all to enjoy this glimpse of the past together. Take care not to misplace them. Take care not to forget the spirit of this treasure. If you have children, pass this heirloom on. If you have grandchildren, ensure that this heirloom is passed on to them as well. Generation after generation, children and grandchildren of the line of Fukuzawa will doubtless run their households with wisdom, applying themselves earnestly, and needing no help from others. Yet if, by some ill fortune, their affairs fall into the unhappy state of poverty, they must never forget the great principles of civilization and independence or sink into spiritual deprivation by sacrificing their standards.

Yukichi

[Note in *Jiji shinpō,* March 11, 1896: In 1878 Fukuzawa did indeed have six children, two sons and four daughters, as the article states. But since one daughter and two sons were born later, at present there are four sons and five daughters.]

Selected Letters from Fukuzawa

EDITOR'S INTRODUCTION

Fukuzawa was a prolific letter writer. One of his children remembered that on family trips to hot springs, once they had arrived at the hotel Fukuzawa would soon sit down, and taking up brush and inkstone, write letter after letter.[1] There are 2584 letters in the nine hardback volumes of *Fukuzawa Yukichi shokanshū* (The Collected Letters of Fukuzawa Yukichi), and more have been discovered since then. The letters, and extracts from letters, that are translated here have been selected in order to give the private context to Fukuzawa's public writings about women and the family. They have been arranged chronologically, but they can also be divided into the following categories:

A. Letters Nos. 1 and 2
These show Fukuzawa adjusting to the new situation after the Meiji Restoration and help to provide some background to "A Message of Farewell to Nakatsu." The first letter reveals his desire to gather all his family members together in Tokyo, and the difficulty of getting his mother and sisters to realize the magnitude of the changes that were taking place. In the second, he is already criticizing the unequal position of women in Japan and contrasting it with the situation in the West.

B. Letters Nos. 3–21, 23–33, 35, 36
These are mainly translations of 29 of the 116 letters that Fukuzawa is known to have written to his two eldest sons, Ichitarō and Sutejirō, during the five years (mid 1883–mid 1888) that they were studying in the United States. The first letter from Fukuzawa's wife, Kin, that is translated in the appendix, was also sent during this period.

Taken as a whole, these letters illustrate the point made in the General Introduction about the struggle that Fukuzawa experienced in reconciling his publicly expressed convictions about independence with his private anxieties as a parent. It is clear from the letters that he regarded this period of study abroad as an opportunity for his sons to become truly independent beings, both in the sense of achieving psychological self-reliance, and in the sense of acquiring the ability to earn a living by themselves. Yet although he frequently tells his sons that they should make their own decisions, he cannot refrain from giving them advice, about the subjects they should study, the need to care for their health and take regular exercise, and even the importance of being discreet in what they say about events at home to Japanese acquaintances.

Thirty-four of the 116 letters are addressed to both sons, and eighteen to Sutejirō. But over one half, at least of those that have survived, were for Ichitarō, the eldest son, who is clearly Fukuzawa's main target of concern. In the very first letter, which is really a list of instructions addressed to both sons, Fukuzawa strongly advises Ichitarō to give up alcohol while abroad, because he cannot hold his drink. (It becomes clear in the course of the letters that Ichitarō does not follow this advice.) Some remarks were made about Ichitarō in the General Introduction. We do not have Ichitarō's letters, but Fukuzawa's replies suggest that Ichitarō lacks confidence, and is easily discouraged. His handling of Ichitarō clearly illustrates the struggle mentioned above between what he regards as the rational duty of a father to cultivate independence in his sons, and his emotional inability to give Ichitaro the freedom to learn by his mistakes. Thus on the one hand, Fukuzawa urges Ichitarō to act as an adult and to use his time in the United States to prepare to pursue an independent livelihood on his return to Japan since it is not the job of his parents to look after him indefinitely; on the other hand, he does not hesitate to state what he thinks Ichitarō should do, and to assure him that as a result of his father's achievements, the family's financial position is secure so that Ichitarō need not have any worries about money.

At first Ichitarō is destined to study agriculture, mainly, it would seem, because it does not involve mathematics. Even so, he has difficulty in reaching the standard of mathematics required for entrance to Cornell, his chosen university. Fukuzawa encourages him, and is delighted when he succeeds. However, Ichitarō decides to leave Cornell before completing his degree in order to enter a school of commerce. Fukuzawa has his doubts about Ichitarō's idea, although he accepts that business studies may be of use in the future. But again, Ichitarō is unable to carry his plans out to the end. He gives up the business course and decides to specialize in literary studies. Fukuzawa expresses pleasure that Ichitaro has at last found what he wants to do and begins to plan for Ichitaro either to join the staff of *Jiji shinpō*, or to teach at Keio. There is some talk of Ichitarō's entering the Literature Department at Cornell, but this never materializes; instead he studies under at least one private tutor, with whom he quarrels. In the end, while Sutejirō was able to graduate with a degree in civil engineering from the Massachusetts Institute of Technology, Ichitarō returned with no tangible results from his five-year stay.

Fukuzawa is admirably sympathetic and patient in the face of Ichitarō's inability to stick to one path and his frequent need for encouragement, though Ichitarō may have been irritated by the extent of his father's concern. There is only one letter (at least of those that survive) in which Fukuzawa appears to lose his patience. Ichitarō seems to have sent an emotional letter in which he accuses his father of asking his private tutor to send reports about Ichitarō and to issue instructions about his behavior. His mother is so concerned at the effect of this letter on her husband that she writes to rebuke Ichitarō for causing his father anxiety, and reminds him of a promise to write about his worries to her rather than directly to his father. (See the appendix to this section.) On his part, Fukuzawa appears to have more or less ignored this letter until the lack of any follow up moves him to write in strong terms (Letter No. 29). He even threatens to travel to America in order to bring Ichitarō back.

Another issue that clearly caused Fukuzawa worry was the short-lived possibility that Ichitarō might marry an American woman. Ichitarō appears to have mentioned this in strictest confidence after a chance reference by Fukuzawa to the practical differences that were likely to follow such a marriage. Fukuzawa strongly explained his negative view but followed this, inevitably, by telling Ichitarō that he was an adult, and that the decision was therefore up to him. (See Letters Nos. 21, 23–25.)

In addition to his love and expectations for his sons, the letters also reveal Fukuzawa's awareness that their behavior and achievements will affect his reputation. When the conscription law is changed so that Keio students will also be eligible, he is glad that the change occurred after their departure for the United States, since otherwise it might have looked as if he had sent them to study abroad in order to escape conscription (Letter No. 11). When he asked both of his sons to be careful of what they said about events at home to Japanese acquaintances (Letter No. 9), this was at least partly because he feared that any criticisms they attracted for indiscreet talk would affect how people viewed him as well. Similar concerns appeared when he was (fruitlessly) urging Ichitarō to obtain some sort of certificate to prove that he had spent his time abroad studying (Letter No. 31). He did not wish Ichitarō to be compared to sons of the new Meiji peers who had wasted their time abroad in idle pursuits.

C. Letters Nos. 4–6, 10, 22, 28, 34, 37–39, 44, 46–53

These letters show glimpses of family life, mainly happy, and the close relationships between Fukuzawa and his wife, and Fukuzawa and his elder sisters. These glimpses are presumably closely related to the vision of the ideal family described in works such as *A New Great Learning for Women*, where the wife and husband are joined in mutual affection and respect and there are no secrets between them, or between any other family members. The letters also give more evidence of the difficulty Fukuzawa had in allowing his children to live independent lives, after marriage in the case of his daughters, and after finishing their education in the case of his sons.[2]

D. Letters Nos. 36, 37, 40–46

These are all letters related to Ichitarō's ill-fated first marriage, to Minoda O-Katsu, which ended six months later when she suddenly left for her parents' house and refused to return. Unfortunately, at present no material is available to give O-Katsu's side of the story. However, it is significant that at first Fukuzawa assumes that she has left because Ichitarō has behaved badly in some way. He only begins to turn against her and her family, and the fact that they are merchants, when they refuse to discuss the issue and then try to secure the return of O-Katsu's trousseau before any decision about the marriage has been made. The situation is made worse by Fukuzawa's anxiety over his eldest daughter O-Sato, who had fallen seriously ill two or three weeks before O-Katsu left, and the strain of helping to care for her. According to Fukuzawa, Ichitarō was initially determined to remain faithful to O-Katsu even if the marriage was terminated (Letter No. 40) but, as Letter No. 46 shows, he married again within about six weeks of the divorce.

Letter No. 28 (22 June 1887) shows that Fukuzawa and his wife were already thinking about suitable brides for Ichitarō while he was in the United States. In his speech at the wedding reception,[3] Fukuzawa explained that the parents had performed the arduous task of finding possible candidates, but the ultimate choice had been left entirely to Ichitarō (and O-Katsu). He also revealed that on both sides of the Fukuzawa family, there had been no cases of divorce or remarriage for four generations, and that they wished to pass this tradition on. Since this speech had been printed in *Jiji shinpō* (27 April 1889), he must have been particularly embarrassed when the divorce occurred.

This section ends with an appendix containing two letters from Fukuzawa's wife, Kin. One belongs in category B, and the other in category D.

SELECTED LETTERS FROM FUKUZAWA

NOTES ABOUT THE TRANSLATIONS

1. The letters are numbered in chronological order. The notes give the name of the recipient in Japanese and the letter number, volume and pagination of the originals as printed in the *Fukuzawa Yukichi shokanshū* (9 vols, Tokyo: Iwanami shoten, 2001–2003). The only exceptions are the instructions to Ichitarō and Sutejirō dated 10 June 1883 and the letters in the appendix from Kin, Fukuzawa's wife. In this case, the reference is to *Fukuzawa Yukichi zenshū* (2nd ed., 21 vols, Tokyo: Iwanami shoten, 1969–1971).

2. Most of the information in square brackets in the text and in the footnotes has been obtained from the annotations in the *Fukuzawa Yukichi shokanshū*.

Selected Letters from Fukuzawa

No. 1
Letter to Yana Kihei [a samurai who has remained in Nakatsu][1]

27 July 1869

Dear Sir,

I apologize for my infrequent correspondence, but I must confess that the reason for this letter is to ask for your good offices, since I am at my wit's end. This April, my mother suddenly changed her mind and decided that she was willing to move to the capital, but just when everything was ready, one of my three older sisters expressed her opposition, and the whole plan was put on hold. Inquiries revealed that this sister's sole pretext was anxiety about the journey. At the beginning of June, I sent people to Nakatsu to fetch my mother, and asked Hattori Matashiro [the husband of Kane, the youngest sister] for his help while they were traveling. Moreover, since some of the Keio boarders have families living along the Tōkaidō [the coastal route from Kyoto to Tokyo], I made plans to ask them for their assistance in the event of problems such as illness. I was therefore confident that there was no more reason for prevarication, so that they would be able to set off without further difficulties. We threw ourselves into getting rooms ready and preparing bedding for them, but on 4th July, just when both the rooms and the bedding were ready, we suddenly received news. There was nothing from my mother or sisters, but in a letter to my wife, my mother-in-law mentioned that they were still so anxious about the journey that they were unlikely to set out. Desolation!

The original reason for bringing my mother to Tokyo was not just because I wanted to meet her. The times are gradually changing. We can no longer rely on hereditary stipends and posts; the Tokugawa family has already lost its power;

the title of daimyo has been changed [to *chihanji*][2]. This change in title signifies that the meaning of the position has also been lost. Moreover, foreigners realize that Japan contains citizens, but do not realize that these citizens have a government. All they want is to trade freely with us. Now is the time for us to play the part that is expected of us as human beings: being in Japan, we should not make a living in empty pursuits, nor should we accept any sign of contempt from a foreigner; we should use our fleeting lives to establish freedom and independence. To achieve this it goes without saying that we should not seek to avoid any hardship whether physical or mental, but in addition, we must work to support our households and preserve the principle of avoiding waste. However, my family duties are divided between the east [Tokyo] and west [Nakatsu], and in addition to the pointless expense, to be separated in these times naturally leaves one open to the possibility of disasters that cannot be calculated in monetary terms. The sole responsibility lies with me. My plan is, therefore, quickly to gather everyone in one place where I can keep an eye on them. Then I will be able to return to my studies and my wife to her household affairs, while my mother looks after the children. We will all be able to live together happily, and without waste. Once this is accomplished, we can, to quote the proverb, put our trust in "the benevolence of Heaven" that we will accumulate a modest amount of capital, our household expenses will be reasonable, and my mother will be able to relax. My only concern is that if I die, my children will not have to enter any lowly form of service, but will be able to engage in a learned profession and become accepted members of society.

Of course, from a woman's point of view, service in a samurai house might seem pleasantly undemanding. Moreover, it is true that in the past such service was thought to be prestigious and made one the envy of all. However, have a look at the situation now. Is there any trace of even the Tokugawa? Viewed as master and lords by the samurai and daimyo, they have all of a sudden dwindled away to nothing. In the eyes of his vassals, a daimyo was honored as "My lord" or "Master," but what has become of them now? They are just ordinary officials with the title of *chihanji*. In the eyes of townspeople and farmers, samurai were held in awe as "Sir samurai," but with the disappearance of the daimyo they have all of a sudden turned into worthless vagrants.

At this point in time, it is foreigners who should be viewed as our rivals. In dealings with foreigners, anyone who is without property or learning will be viewed with great contempt. Surely there is no one who would be pleased to be viewed with contempt by foreigners, complete strangers, in his native country. This is the reason why I have devoted myself entirely to my studies in the capital, without seeking any master, or going to Nakatsu. In the opinion of my sisters, if I were to return to Nakatsu, live with my mother and enter the service of the lord or become a teacher, it would be of benefit to both parties, and this may be so. However, a man of learning and virtue chooses for himself where to live, and who to have dealings with. Since there are few people I know in Nakatsu who have anything to teach me, my studies would be unlikely to progress. Yet in life, there is no substitute for learning. Even if rivers flowed inland and the sun rose in the West, I would never reside in the provinces and seek a master.

Even if I explain this situation to my female relatives, it will be beyond their comprehension, and might even lead to misunderstandings and therefore make things even more difficult. Therefore, I would be in your eternal debt if you could persuade my mother for me. I ask for your good offices in the hope that she will soon set out with Matashiro.[3]

Respectfully yours,

Fukuzawa Yukichi

※

No. 2
To Kuki Takayoshi [governor, and former daimyo, of Sanda] (Extract)[4]

16 March 1870

My Lord,

...Recently, I presented a small book on **morals** [Francis Wayland, *The Elements of Moral Science*, possibly the abridged version] to Mr. Kawamoto [Kōmin, 1810–1871, a leading scholar of Dutch learning who had opened a school of Western learning in Sanda]. I gather that you have seen it, and hope that you will have the opportunity to hear him lecture about it.

There is only one way to seek the true path and lead a life of virtue. First one must establish the basis of human morality. This is the relationship between husband and wife. There is a well-known book called *The Great Learning for Women*. It sees only women as guilty, and censors them severely, but this strikes me as extremely unfair. I have a strong desire to write a book titled *The Great Learning for Men* in order to censor them too. In all the countries of the East it is customary to despise women, which is one reason why we attract the scorn of Westerners. In this respect, our moral teachings [that is, Confucianism] are a great obstacle. Even if they have two parents, the children of Japan are to be pitied as if they had in reality only one.

Leaving aside the issue of husbands and wives, I would humbly advise you to concentrate on behaving with discretion. To aim to lead without behaving virtuously oneself, to try to inspire others while unable to achieve self-control, will only cause people to act in a similar way. In other words, everyone in the land will try to inspire others, and there will be no one to be inspired. What hope can we have for the civilization of the country then?

The ideas above are taken from the book I mentioned. I hope that you will take them into consideration …

***

No. 3[5]
To Ichitarō[6] and Sutejirō[7]

10 June 1883

Instructions for your studies

1. While you are studying abroad, you should not return to Japan under any circumstances until told to do so by your parents. Even if you hear that one of us is ill, you should not return home in a panic.
2. Since Ichitarō has chosen to study agriculture, this is what his studies should focus on. He should concentrate on practical matters rather than agricultural theories, so that he can apply what he has learnt as soon as he returns to Japan.
3. Sutejirō has selected physics as his subject. I would like to suggest something like electrical engineering, but I will leave the final decision up to him.
4. You should both take care not to damage your health, and give only second priority to your academic progress. Therefore, you should not worry if you need to extend the length of your studies — even, for example, if what should

take three years requires five. There are natural differences in the stamina of people from the East and West. You must take great care.

5. Ichitarō is not a heavy drinker, but he easily becomes drunk. He lacks the willpower to control his alcoholic intake by himself, but luckily he has not yet developed an ingrained habit of drinking. Since it should be easy to give up alcohol at this stage, he should definitely do so. Once he has reached around the age of thirty, his temperament will have settled down and he may do as he pleases. But if he gets drunk during his studies, other people will despise him, and it will cause him unhappiness. Moreover, it will break the hearts of his parents. Both of you should behave with discretion. This item is not a demand of your parents, but rather an entreaty. You must definitely show your consent.

I have recorded these items before our parting.

Yukichi

*
* *

No.4[8]

19 June 1883

Dear Ichitarō and Sutejirō,

After parting from you at the boat in Yokohama at 9:00 on the 12th of this month, we went to the second floor of the Mitsubishi office to have a short rest. After 10:00, we watched the ship as it set off into the distance, and went back to Tokyo on the 11:00 train.

The weather has been good here since you left, with no rain at all, even though it is the rainy season. How has the weather been at sea? I am trying to convince myself that you are having good weather as well.

After you had left I was pleased to hear that a large group of Japanese entertainers were on board with you. You will find that the company of other Japanese people, whoever they might be, will cheer you up during the long and boring sea voyage.

We are all well, but the sudden disappearance of the two of you has left a gap. Hide [Imaizumi Hidetarō, Fukuzawa's nephew] is loath to eat alone without you at the table, so he is spending most of his time in his mother's quarters,[9] while O-Sato, O-Fusa and O-Shun[10] have all come back here and are sharing meals with us.

We have cleared away both the desks and all your books, burnt boxes and other things which seem no longer necessary, tidied up everything else and put it where it will not be disturbed, so put your minds at rest.

Gentarō [Sakamoto Gentarō, Fukuzawa's gatekeeper] is looking after the doves, so they are safe. We have also been making a sparrow hut so that we can keep some sparrows for Sanpachi[11] and O-Mitsu[12] to enjoy. The hut was ready this morning, but it is difficult to get the sparrows to come near.

I am busy working on the newspaper [*Jiji shinpō*] as usual. I naturally neglected it around the time of your departure, but have been writing again from around two or three days ago. I expect that my labors will continue until you return. Life cannot always be full of amusement.

As I have already made clear, once you have arrived in America you should ask Messrs. Terashima [Munenori, 1832–1893, then Minister to the United States] and Sameshima [Takenosuke, 1855–1931, then Secretary to the Japanese Legation in Washington][13] for advice concerning education. I have asked the Morimura Company[14] to take care of financial matters so you should have no difficulties in that regard, but since mistakes involving money matters often occur you should keep me informed of the date when you obtain any money, the exact amount, accurate to the smallest unit, the name of the Morimura employee who handed you the money, and what the money is for. In addition, as I have already made clear, no matter what the circumstances might be, you should not borrow money from any source apart from the Morimura Company; neither should you lend any. This prohibition does not apply only to the lending of money itself. You must not allow anyone to use the name of Ichitarō or Sutejirō. To lend your name, stand surety, or even arrive at some private understanding because of a particular situation, is no different from actually handing money over to someone. Please take the utmost care in this regard.

There is absolutely no need for haste in learning. To make swift progress at the expense of your health would be pointless. Do not forget how it was health concerns that led to Sutejirō's leaving the preparatory school for the University of Tokyo before. In Ichitarō's case as well, my intention is not to turn you into an expert in the theory of agriculture. Gain a basic theoretical knowledge and then focus on **practice**. Above all, take care to behave well. Make every endeavor to avoid being criticized for **shyness** by forming a wide circle of close and active friendships. I have no serious demands of you beyond this.

It will gradually grow hotter. If you have difficulty in adapting to American customs, for example as regards taking baths, your first year will cause you some problems. However, just as [the great Chinese general] Kongming [Zhuge Liang (181–234)] crossed the land of Yunnan in June [at the height of summer], men should not allow matters such as the heat or the cold to prevent them from accomplishing their goals. If they use their brains, they will be able to find ways of enduring hardships. The thought that even now people from Europe and America are making a living by travelling vast distances should act as a spur in your efforts.

In haste, just wishing to assure you that all has been well since you left.

Yukichi

P.S.

I have arranged for you each to receive a copy of *Jiji shinpō*. Of course, until your lodgings are decided I will address them to the Morimura Company, but once I know your address, I will immediately get it changed.

You will probably have to rely particularly on the kindness of Mr. Murai [Yasukata, a Morimura employee]. I will write to thank him, but please give him my regards. The same goes for Mr. Morimura Yutaka.

⁂

No. 5[15]
(Extract)

27 August 1883

Dear Ichitarō and Sutejirō,

... As I have frequently remarked, Ichitarō should aim to study agriculture, but I think that skill in the **practical** is much more important than **high science**. Even if your level of scholarship is low, it does not matter. What Japan needs now is people who are fluent in English, and can read and write it. Note this, and work hard. In addition, Ichitarō is not good at mixing with people, and has a tendency to hold himself aloof. He should make an effort to copy the temperament of American people. If he consciously learns from them how to behave in an **amiable** manner on all occasions, it will become second nature. This is the first secret to deepening the roots of **happiness** in one's life. . . .

We all gazed at the photograph [that you sent]. It is such a good likeness that when we showed it to Sanpachi, he pointed to you happily, saying "Itchan," "Teichan." We were all amazed that he still remembered your appearance so well.

***

No. 6[16]
(Extract)

4 November 1883

Dear Ichitarō and Sutejirō,

. . . The essay on the **analytic synthetic** [distinction] sent by Ichitarō is so well done that there is hardly anything that needs correcting. But I would like you to write more neatly, and make sure that there are no mistakes in your use of characters.

Sutejirō's passage in English is also splendid. I am sure that you will continue to improve. After reading them both, I explained everything to your mother, while weeping tears of joy. To tell the truth, since being parted from you both, she has been so anxious that at times she goes off by herself to think about you and becomes very gloomy. She has kept silent about this in the face of my positive attitude, but when your pieces arrived and I told her of your progress, she felt vitalized enough to accept your long absence. While I join her in welcoming your progress, my single worry is still your physical health. Please take every precaution.

Yesterday was the Emperor's birthday and a party was held at the Ministry for Foreign Affairs. I was among the 100 Japanese and overseas guests. As I observed the proceedings, the feeble and diminutive appearance of the Japanese men and women there made me feel deeply ashamed. I also considered how much I hope that you will pay special attention to building up your physical stamina while you are away.

⁂

No. 7[17]
(Extracts)

22 December 1883

Dear Ichitarō and Sutejirō,

We have received your letters of 13 and 14 November, and are relieved to hear that your studies are proceeding well. It must be very cold by now, and I expect that your first winter in the United States is difficult to bear. In fact, that is the only thing that concerns me at present. I want you to be extremely careful. Take every measure to preserve your health, however much money this may require. Sutejirō reports that he is taking exercise at a fixed time every day, but what about Ichitarō? I pray that he will not be neglectful in this respect.

All is well here. The children are all full of life. On the 18th we pounded rice to make [the seasonal] rice cakes and invited 188 Keio students (including the elementary school children and their headmaster Mr. Wada [Yoshirō (1840–1892)]) to the house to eat rice cakes with sweet bean paste. It was a very festive occasion.

...With regard to the direction of your studies, as I said at the time of your departure, my suggestion is that Ichitarō should specialize in agriculture and Sutejirō in a scientific subject, possibly **electricity**. But these are just my **speculations**. My intention was not to limit your options; I merely assumed that it would be sensible for you to pursue your strengths. I have no problem with you making your own choices. I only suggested agriculture for Ichitarō because I know that mathematics is his weakness. It was not my intention to order him to limit himself to agriculture. If there is some aspect of **literature** that interests him, he should just go ahead and make his own decision.

Recently in Japan there has been real public interest in favor of the railway question, with no hint of any opposition. Since it is highly likely that the future will see a great increase in railway construction, it may be of great help to Sutejirō's future prospects if he learns about steam railways.

No. 8[18]
(Extracts)

4 January 1884

Dear Ichitarō and Sutejirō,

Your letter(s) of 20 November arrived a few days ago. On opening the envelope I was above all relieved to find that you were both well. Things here are unchanged. It is the fourth day of January 1884 and the New Year is proving very busy, with everyone bustling around. For both of you this is the first spring in a strange land. You must be feeling lonely. And yet, looked at from another point of view, how enjoyable it must be to spend the New Year in each other's company, as brothers, travelers in a distant land, with no other Japanese in sight! You must feel as if you are truly independent young men. This thought is the only source of comfort to both your mother and myself.

[...]

At the New Year we had our customary gathering of youngsters, who had a lively time playing new year games, but you were not here and with O-Sato being married and therefore also away, everything seemed somehow out of balance, strangely quiet and a little sad.

No. 9[19]
(Extract)

22 February 1884

Dear Ichitarō and Sutejirō,

... I gather from your letter(s) of 14 January that after arriving at Poughkeepsie you consulted Dr. [Duane B.] Simmons[20] [1835?–1889], that you have more or less chosen where you intend to study next, and are now making **preparations**: Ichitarō for Cornell [University], and Sutejirō for Troy [Rensselaer Polytechnic

Institute] or Massachusetts [MIT]. The rest is up to you. But as I said in my last letter, there is no need for you to limit your choice of subjects to agriculture or electrical engineering. It is probably a good idea for Ichitarō to study agriculture. Alongside that, he can study literature and language. If he becomes able to speak English fluently and also write it well, he will have developed a skill that could very well prove to be the basis of his **life** in the future. He must not rely on hopes of inheriting property from his parents. In other words, he must be prepared to support a family through his own abilities. In the case of Sutejirō as well, I chanced on the idea of electrical engineering, but this was not in order to restrict your range of choices. The job of a **civil engineer** is very important too. This is particularly because civil engineering works are bound to increase in Japan. In any case, people who are studying something that they are not good at make slow progress. Think about what is in your best interests and do not worry about my preferences.

Sutejirō says that he is thinking of going to Britain after finishing his studies in the United States. This is very sensible. Any scholar worth his salt must visit Britain once. Moreover, once you have a sufficient knowledge of English, you should also learn French and German. This will keep you busy! But in making all these remarks about your studies, I am not forgetting the issue of your health. Your physical state is much more important than your scholarship. Above all, please make sure to take care of yourselves. I was very happy to hear that when Dr. Simmons examined you the other day he pronounced that you were both in good health.

You report that you have started skating as a form of exercise and spent 20 dollars on boots and skating blades. I am very pleased to hear this. I hope you will wear them out through constant practice and outshine those **Yankee boys** with your skating prowess!

I absolutely agree with you that Western-style clothing is best for an active life. With this in mind, my view is that you no longer need the Japanese-style clothes that you left behind with us, and I do not intend to store them. I assume that on your return to Japan you will change completely to Western dress and am planning to prepare a Western-style house for you both on the assumption that you will want Western-style rooms. I am already enjoying myself by wondering whether to buy an old house in the Ginza area, or build a new one in Sankōzaka [in the present day Shirokane area of Tokyo].

You expected the winter weather to be cold, but how is it in reality? We are worried that it might be difficult for you to bear.

There is a warning that I wish to repeat to you both. If you can sense the situation in Japan from abroad, you will realize how impossible it is. There are many ridiculous affairs going on in both politics, education, and commerce. However, there is no need to discuss what is happening. Moreover, since no good will come of such discussions, you should not go on and on about what is happening in our country, even at the end of letters you write to friends in Japan. Not everyone in our society is a stubborn fool. There are many **liberal** thinkers both in the government and outside it. Even among government officials, there are people who are not narrow-minded. Young students should devote themselves single-mindedly to their studies. In addition, since you are now in New England, you are bound to have associations with many other Japanese who are living abroad. On such occasions, do not make all sorts of comments about Japan when there is no need to do so. You must realize that if you assume that you are free to say what you please since you are in a foreign country, and make many inappropriate remarks, people will criticize you and say that Fukuzawa's sons do not know how to behave properly. In other words, my reputation will be damaged as well. Please be discreet. . . . Of course, I believe that you are unlikely to behave so carelessly, but when people are abroad, they develop a tendency to be outspoken, and it is sometimes difficult to avoid mistakes. I remember behaving like this when I myself was young.[21]

***

No. 10[22]

(Extracts)

8 April 1884

Dear Ichitarō and Sutejirō,

. . . I have asked Morimura to send 1 box of *yōkan* [bar of sweet jellied bean paste], 2 boxes large and small of *chamame* [soy beans], and the same of *nikkeimame* [cinnamon-flavor beans]. Ichitarō likes *yōkan*, doesn't he, and I know that Sutejirō is very fond of *chamame* and *nikkeimame*. . . .

Sanpachi is rather timid, and was afraid of going in a rickshaw. Since he weighs over 15 kilos, he is too heavy for a long piggyback, but if we let him walk, he dawdles along at a snail's pace, so it has been impossible to take him on any long journeys. At the beginning of this month, he and I had several negotiations, and finally arrived at the unanimous conclusion that he would finally get into a rickshaw. On the morning of the 6th, we all set out for Asakusa, whereupon he discovered that there was actually no reason to be frightened of the vehicle. He chattered away confidently as we crossed the bridges of Ryōgoku and Azuma, ate lunch at Asakusa, and returned home in the evening. Since then he has not ceased to talk happily about his first trip to Asakusa, particularly his surprise at the length of the bridges, the size of the sea (by which he means river), and the great number of pigeons, and how a parrot talked to O-Take [a maidservant] using human speech....

∗∗∗

No. 11[23]

(Extracts)

24 April 1884

Dear Ichitarō,

I have read your letter of 18 March. First of all, I am relieved that you are well. There are no changes here. Everyone is in good health.[24] You write that Dr. Simmons is of the opinion that you should enter the regular course at Cornell, but that the preparations are giving you a lot of work, and that you are having some difficulties with the mathematics. I am not unaware of this. Therefore, I have frequently written to both Messrs. Terashima and Sameshima, and similarly to Dr. Simmons, saying that it is not necessary for you to enter the regular course. My desire has always been for you to acquire some knowledge of American agricultural methods and also to gain fluency in spoken and written English. However, it is only natural human behavior for someone who is entrusted with responsibility for someone else's offspring to want him to do as well as possible. I have just recently received a letter [from Dr. Simmons?] to the effect that Ichitarō is no mathematician, but that on the other hand, his ability is definitely not below average. He thinks that if you do some preparatory work now and over the summer, you should be able to enter the regular course without any difficulty. Therefore, it seems to me that I cannot really tell you how you should proceed. If you were to say that a degree is worth no more than the piece of paper that it is written on, that would be that; however, from the point of view of gaining a position in society after your return to Japan, a degree would certainly be worth more than a piece of paper, so Dr. Simmons' view is very reasonable. On the other hand, if the work you must do in preparation, particularly in mathematics, is so hard that it causes you mental stress and there is a possibility that you will fall ill, I would certainly think that to continue would be out of the question. Only you can decide which is the better course. In any case, for the time being, whatever you decide about the preparations for entering Cornell, you should continue with your English-language classes, since in academic terms this will certainly be to your advantage. When the autumn comes, either you will enter the regular course at Cornell, or you will do practical work. If you can enter Cornell, you should do so; if you are unsuccessful, you will focus on the practical. However, it is not my intention to order you to do anything that is against your will.

... recently there has been a tremendous rise in the number of students going to the United States from Japan. ... there seems to be no end to the number of Keio students bound for that country. One reason for this is that the Japanese have realized how important it is to understand the circumstances of foreign countries, and even older people have become more willing to spend money on this. Another is the reform of the conscription law, which has encouraged the idea that study abroad is preferable to being called up.[25] Whatever the case, it seems likely that as far as the near future is concerned, there will be a great number of young men bound for the United States. I am sure that very soon you will both cease to make any comments about feelings of loneliness. Since you are exactly twenty this year, you would be eligible for conscription were you in Japan. Therefore, even though you have suffered some inconveniences, it is extremely fortunate that you left Japan last year. In particular, if you had left this year, we would have had no defense against the charge that the Fukuzawa boys had set off in order to avoid conscription. But we have no need to worry: since the decision to leave had already been taken last June, there is obviously no link with this law.

Because of the situation I explained above, even if you enter Cornell and are therefore separated from Sutejirō, since there is a stream of Japanese, especially Keio students, going to the States, you are likely to feel very much at home although you are in reality so far away. Remember that it is important to interact with others. Talk lightheartedly or have discussions with every type of person, in a pleasant manner. It is essential to spend some time relaxing even when you are studying hard.

⁂

No. 12[26]
(Extracts)

20 July 1884

Dear Ichitarō,

...Regardless of whether you enter the standard course at Ithaca [Cornell] or not, I want you to achieve excellence in some field or other, so that you can live an independent life once you return to Japan. Whether you work for the government or join the private sector does not matter. What is important is for you to become a person of value who can support his own family.... Parents do not act as parents forever. Once you are fully grown, you should no longer need to rely on us.

⁂

No. 13[27]
(Extract)

29 July 1884

Dear Ichitarō,

Your letter of 23 June has arrived. I gather that you left Poughkeepsie on the 12th, spent one night with Sutejirō in New York, and then left for Ithaca, where you visited Dr. Roberts and met Mr. Tsumaki [Yorinaka, a former Keio student and future architect]. I also understand that you have had a difficult time.

You tell me that since Mr. Tsumaki has since graduated and moved elsewhere, and the person called Arakawa has already left Ithaca, you are the only Japanese person there for the moment. This is a lonely situation to be in but seeing that life is full of great hardships, we should always be prepared for relatively small problems like this. Moreover, it will surely be good for your English **practice** to have no Japanese people nearby. On the other hand, recently more and more people are going to the United States from Japan, and some of them are bound to come to Ithaca.

Speaking of Ithaca, you say that the customs are not very refined. I can understand why this troubles you, but ultimately it is the individual's power of will that determines his level of behavior. Even if other people are drinking heavily, all you need to do is retain your self-control. Since you have never been able to hold your drink, you must take particular care when it comes to alcohol. Stay sober until you come back to Japan and you can drink in your father's company again.

You also wrote that the university entrance examinations began on July 15, and that you did well in the first part but failed the rest. You should put that in the past, and study during the summer so that you can do the retake. I have also had a letter about this from Dr. Simmons. His very sensible advice is that you should prepare with the help of a **private tutor**. Let us do as the good doctor says; if you fail again in September, you can enter the **special course**. I do not think badly of you in any way. I shall be satisfied as long as you return to Japan healthy, and with some skill that will enable you to support yourself and a household. Life is not easy. It is becoming more difficult to make a living every day. This is only to be expected as Japan develops. You should not forget to bear this in mind.

*
* *

No. 14[28]
(Extracts)

4 November 1884

Dear Ichitarō,

...You write that you successfully passed the entrance examination on 17 September. Congratulations! You also write that the successful result surprised you. My long experience has taught me that this often happens. People differ in the level of their **self-estimation**, and those who have a poor opinion of themselves are often surprised when they achieve something. As a young man,

I led a sheltered life and had such difficulty even making the stock greetings to those I did not know, that I convinced myself that I could not interact with ordinary people. This feeling remained both when I went to study at Nagasaki and when I was at Ogata [Kōan]'s academy in Osaka, but on my way to Edo at the age of 25 [by Japanese reckoning], I stayed at inns on the Tōkaidō and found that I could make teasing remarks to the men who were employed as casual labor along the way. Once I arrived and gradually got used to getting along with other people, I discovered that I was not as unsociable as I had feared, but was in fact quite good at making conversation. In fact now, I find it hard to believe how awkward I used to feel. My only weak point is that I am still not good at using my chopsticks to pick up bits of food to serve to drinking companions. This is probably a still-remaining trace of my sheltered upbringing. Your success in the entrance examination is a similar case. A young man who greatly **underestimated** his ability at mathematics surprised himself when he actually passed. . . . We should avoid arrogance and self-satisfaction, but it is a great help to be self-reliant and full of self-confidence . . .

To change the subject, I thought deeply about your question regarding your future direction, and also consulted your mother. On reflection, even if there may not actually be any great difference between the regular and special courses, recently in Japan, as a result of the increase in the number of people with academic qualifications, it has become harder to evaluate individual graduates when deciding whether to employ them, both in government and private positions. People now assume that anyone who has studied abroad and obtained a **diploma** can be trusted, and they do not ask for anything else. Inevitably this has led to a tendency for people to study just in order to get a **diploma**. What status will you have in the future? In order to obtain work, either in a government office or in a private post, it is important to be known and valued. Therefore, if you can, I would like you to complete the four-year regular course and come back to Japan bearing a graduation certificate. If this way of thinking is correct, your idea of attending a school of commerce should be postponed until your graduation in four years' time.

[...]

Your mother and I are counting out the time until you return in 1888, having persevered until your graduation. But, as I have said before, you do not have to find a job and set up your own home immediately; since I have been managing the household finances during your absence so that we should have money to spare, . . . there will be no need for you to rush around in order to earn your living as soon as you return, like a miserable dog belonging to a once-splendid family that has met its ruin. . . .

Another concern is the fact that since there are no other Japanese in Ithaca, you are virtually alone. . . . I will talk to former Keio students who are planning to go to the United States and try to find people who might enter Cornell, so please send a **catalogue** about the university by the next post. . . .

P.S.

. . . eventually, my intention is to hand everything over to [both of] you, with a fixed sum going to your mother and I so that we can settle down in retirement. She and I are really looking forward to this and often talk together about how enjoyable it will be. But even though the Fukuzawa household finances are not in a bad state at the moment, there are lots of you children. Looking after the younger ones will be a hard task for the two older brothers, but I am relying on you. I have already made an agreement with a life insurance company for Sanpachi and Daishirō[29] to receive 3,000 yen each when they reach the age of 18. This is being paid in yearly installments. . . .

※

No. 15[30]

2 October, 1885

Dear Ichitarō

Sutejirō's letter of 4 August arrived yesterday, but we have no tidings from you. Even so, it is clear from what Sute says that you are doing well.

I was very impressed by the article that you sent to Mr. Takahashi called "Thoughts about 'On Japanese Women,'"[31] and intend to use it as an editorial.[32] The published version of "On Japanese Women" [Part Two] has had a great impact in Japan. It seems to be encouraging the adoption of Western-type hairstyles and clothing, and even influencing wedding ceremonies. However, it is not unusual for a trend that attracts great popularity at the beginning to have no ultimate effect. I have **expected** this from the beginning and will not be particularly disappointed if it turns out to be the case.

I gather that you recently met Sutejirō and consulted with him about the direction of your studies. It might be possible to grow tobacco [in Japan], but even if it is, cultivating something is not the same as turning it into a product, although the two are very closely linked. Having the answer to one is not good enough if you lack the answer to the other. In my opinion, you should consider the matter carefully. In any case, in all matters related to your future work, even if you have an idea unrelated to tobacco, you need to have thorough consultations with Dr. Simmons and with Sutejirō. Since Japan is increasingly part of the world of English and English prose, at the very least, you must make every effort not to neglect your studies in that direction.

Until now, young men have single-mindedly aimed to enter government service, as if this was the only way to gain status, but already there is no **room** left, and now they have no choice but to turn in the direction of commerce or manufacturing. In any case, the trend to equate money with power in all things is very strong. Even among my acquaintances, there has been a great change, leading to a rising clamor of voices talking about money. Of course, this is the influence of the American way, but even though it will lead to various abuses, there is nothing that we can do. Be sure to bear this in mind, and to give thought to how you will make a living in the future. This was the reason why I once advised you to enter a school of commerce. If they have courses that last six months, you should register and get a qualification.

Recently, people with a specialist training do not have a good reputation in Japan. The reason is that if you make someone a judge, for example, on the grounds that he has graduated with a specialty in law, he is of no use at all. In the worst cases, someone may be completely unsuited to the work, hardly able to write down a guilty verdict since his sentences are ungrammatical and his writing is as twisted as a badly hammered nail. The only skill such people have is in arguing: they chatter away, but to no effect at all. People give them trial employment for a year, on the grounds that actual experience is needed, and put up with them for three years, but they show no sign of improvement. This being the case, many complaints are directed at specialists who have degrees, to the effect that scholars are useless and that up till now society has been tricked into overvaluing learning. In other words, scholars know a lot about scholarly matters but little about the real world, and they have fallen into the sin of self-satisfaction. I hope that you will take this situation into account as well and consider it carefully. Learning is not the only factor in our society; everyday friendships and skills can be of greater importance in achieving success.

I have to spend so much time with visitors every day that I have been at my wits' end. I have therefore made some alterations to the Kōjunsha[33] building so that I can set aside a day and meet people there. I have been thinking of getting a Western-style house at some point, but in any case, when you both return from the United States, if you decide to live in the Western manner and build houses in that style, I might occasionally ask you to lend me the use of a room where I could entertain visitors. Therefore, I will not take any action towards building a house of my own while you are away. Since it will just be your mother and I from now on, we will have no difficulties living in a small place. Since you members of the second generation will each build your own separate houses according to your means, your aged parents will sometimes come to stay as your guests. This will be one of the enjoyments of our declining years.

That being said, the household finances at present are in an extremely good state. The losses from Maruya have been made up from another source.[34] Since we are far from poor, you will not find yourself pressed for money immediately after you return to Japan. This means that there will be no need for either of you to take up an occupation that you regard as less than ideal and worry about the picture you present to the world on that account. I want you to set your minds at rest on this point, since this is something that makes your parents feel somewhat self-satisfied. (Big smile.)

In any case, everything is going well.

Yukichi

P.S.

Since I gather that you are living in different places at the moment, I will write separately to Sutejirō.

※

No. 16[35]
(Extracts)

Evening, 22 October 1885
Under the lonely light of one lamp

Dear Ichitarō,

According to the letter I received from Dr. Simmons in the last mail, you intend to enter a school of commerce in Poughkeepsie and expect to graduate in six months. You are therefore thinking of spending about one more year from now (that is, September 1885) in the United States and then perhaps returning to Japan. However, my view is somewhat different, since even if you return home having graduated from a school of commerce, this "souvenir" will not be enough to enable you to start your own enterprise. For example, this may be the school that Morimura Yutaka and Iwata Shigeho[36] graduated from, but that is not the only reason why they have a valued position in Japanese society. Of course, it is important to graduate, but this is only one accomplishment; for people to be able to contribute to society they also need to have their own personal convictions.

As far as this applies to you at the moment, if you were to return to Japan now, it would be extremely difficult for you to find work in the immediate future, whether in farming or in business, and equally hard to make a living as a writer. In fact, if your natural talent is for writing, there are many things that you still have to master. I will only mention one or two here:

> You need to work hard at improving your handwriting skills, both in English and Japanese. Some people say that it is only necessary not to make any errors in one's handwriting, but this is a great **mistake**. It is similar to the difference between speaking eloquently and being inarticulate. Among humans too, some have beautiful faces while others are ugly. Those who claim that calligraphy is not important any more might as well be saying that neither speaking skills nor facial appearance are important either. These ideas would not receive mass agreement. Therefore, you should listen carefully to your father's advice, and work hard on your handwriting. I have been making this point frequently since last year, and I am very disappointed that you have not been practicing; at any rate, there is no sign of any improvement in the letters or other samples of writing that you send.
>
> Your style is your strong point. Yet while it is distinctive and not without signs of excellence, it is not yet sufficiently developed. Supposing you were a complete stranger employed by *Jiji shinpō*, we would not be able to let you work unsupervised in the editorial office. It would probably not be possible to pay a salary to someone who could not work without supervision. In other

words, you are not yet in a position to earn your own living.

In view of the two points explained above, once you have graduated from the school of commerce, you should apply yourself single-mindedly until your calligraphy and style have reached a level that will not cause you embarrassment in front of other people. At the same time, it is also vital for you to improve your level of general knowledge. I know that you read history books, and that you have a good memory, so it should not be difficult for you to study historical records of people's words and actions. This is what I meant in my last letter about entering a college literature department or employing a private tutor after you graduate from your school of commerce.

If you study for one or two more years in this way, people will say that Fukuzawa's eldest son, Ichitarō, is a literary gentleman who is a) skilled at both Japanese and English calligraphy; b) a fluent writer whose prose is polished, whose style is both distinctive and sincere, but who can completely adapt himself to other people's needs; and moreover, c) has such a wide general knowledge that he is the one whom everyone turns to when historical research is needed. If, in addition to these three points, you become used to interacting with other people while you are in the United States and therefore gain a wide reputation for refined behavior, for being able to chat pleasantly with people without showing either flattery or disrespect, for being helpful and polite and always looking cheerful, you will easily find a position. In other words, graduating from the school of commerce will serve a practical purpose. If you use this to add to your reputation you will gain a source of happiness for life and therefore be secure. The hopes of your mother and father will be fulfilled. In any case, make sure that you read this letter carefully and take my words to heart. My intention is to create an opening for you here [at Keio] during your absence, if this is what you would like. Please, therefore, study conscientiously.

10 November 1885

[in red ink]

I wrote the above on October 22, but before I could send it, on 6 November your letter dated 9 October arrived. The passage with the title "My future goals" gave me a good idea of your intentions. Since they coincide with mine, I am very pleased. It is a good idea to go back to Cornell and enter the **literature** section after graduating from Eastman [Business College]. I will not give you any detailed guidance, but leave most of the planning to you. . . .

P.S.

In fact, it is the chance resemblance between your plans regarding literature and my own views that pleases me most. It is much more agreeable if the child says what he thinks first and his ideas coincide with his father's wishes rather than for the father to write first and the child to form his opinion in accordance with the father's intentions. This is why I am sending you what I wrote on the evening of the 22nd without changing any of it, regardless of your present plans. Parts of it may sound rather harsh, but that evening I wrote exactly what I was thinking.

*
**

No. 17[37]
(Extract)

Evening, 1 December 1885

Dear Ichitarō,

. . . Literary studies should begin with calligraphy. You write English neatly, but the same cannot be said for your Japanese. For example, when mail from America arrives and visitors call hoping for news, there are occasions when, if at all possible, I would like to show them a letter you have sent me. However, I often find myself hiding them instead, for fear that they will be shocked by handwriting that is terrible for a man of over twenty years of age. You should feel ashamed. Your letter of 18 October was particularly bad in this respect, and I was far too embarrassed to let anyone see it. I have therefore returned it to you so that you can look at it with your own eyes and realize how shocking it is. Of course, there is no lack of people with bad handwriting. Your father should be included in their number. But if you take a little care, you should improve enough to avoid being laughed at. Moreover, you are still young. There should be nothing that you cannot accomplish if you try. It all depends on how much attention you pay to this in the normal course of things. . . .

No. 18[38]
(Extract)

9 April 1886

Dear Ichitarō,

... On my return [from a trip to Hakone], there were two letters from you waiting for me. The contents suggest that you are full of worries, which has made me very worried as well. First, you mention the expenses caused by your foreign studies, but as I have mentioned to you before now, this is something for which I have been preparing since you were born, so there is absolutely no need for concern. You also seem to be upset by your slow rate of academic progress, but you must realize that everyone has different preferences, and learn to view your interests as strengths. Your strength lies in writing, and your weakness in numbers. At the moment, you are pursuing something that involves numbers, your weakness, so you should not be discouraged even if it is not enjoyable. I have also received a letter from Dr. Simmons in which he develops various ideas about your future study program, and suggests the employment of a **private teacher**. I leave this up to you. In his letter, Dr. Simmons also has high praise for your mental capabilities, news that overjoyed your loving father. I have enclosed it so that you can read it in confidence. In any case, I hope that when you return you will be a master of English prose, particularly since nothing can stem the growing influence of English and English literature in Japan today. This accomplishment will allow you to make a good living for yourself.

While I am gradually growing older, I am still in good health. In fact, I was the strongest member of the party that went on the trip from which I have just returned. I crossed the Hakone mountains on foot, leaving my companions far behind. I look forward to sharing many good experiences with you on your return, so whatever else, please do not feel discouraged! Please also reflect on the fact that although scholars are generally poor, this is not the case with Fukuzawa. There will never be any need for me to kneel in front of anyone to obtain money. As my son, you should realize that you are unlikely to ever need to do this either. Therefore, do not have any worries about your studies. . . .

I am overjoyed to see that the English passages that you include in your letters are showing such steady improvement. Although we do not say anything publicly, your mother and I share our satisfaction in private. We also marvel together about our courage in letting you go away to the United States.

*
**

No. 19[39]
(Extract)

2 May 1886

Dear Ichitarō,

[...]

Yesterday, we had about 50 ladies as guests. Instead of providing [a traditional Japanese meal with] separate dining trays (*zen*) for each guest, we organized a buffet-style meal, with both Japanese and Western food laid out on **tables**, so that each guest could take what she wanted. Although it was a new experience for them, all the ladies seem to have enjoyed this. The hosts were our daughters and eight or nine Keio **bachelors** and it was a truly elegant and lively occasion. I am congratulating myself because this suggests that it will not be difficult for women to gradually become used to social occasions.[40]

*
**

No. 20[41]
(Extract)

31 July 1886

Dear Ichitarō,

. . . I gather that with Dr. Simmons' agreement you have decided to leave Eastman College and turn completely to the study of literature. As I have remarked before, I cannot give detailed instructions about your studies; you must follow your own preferences. Literature is a very good choice, but there are two types: the practical and the abstract. I prefer practical approaches. In other words, I favor proceeding upwards from the lowest point; for example, in studying English literature, you should first aim to master the spoken form, until you can speak it as fluently as you speak Japanese. Are you already able to do so? If not, I would like you to pay attention to this. Next, you must study the calligraphy of English and Japanese. You should study the prose of both languages. I do not have any appreciation for arguments involving highbrow **speculation**. Whether you study literature, physics, or mathematics, there is nothing that cannot play a part in worldly success. I am in no way upset by your decision to study literature, but I pray that you will take care to focus on the practical, so that you can put it to actual use in meeting the needs of the everyday world.

It seems that you intend to become a Christian. Of course, I will not forbid this; you must do as you think right. It is very important for people to show restraint in their behavior concerning both drinking and women. If religion helps you to follow your conscience and actually improves your behavior, this will be a very good thing.

From this September, we are introducing large-scale reforms at Keio. I intend to employ many foreigners and promote the study of English. If you study and become so skilled at speaking and writing English that you can actually take the place of a foreign teacher, it will be very good news for Keio as well. There will be no need for you to worry about your future employment. It will just depend on how hard you study.

∗∗∗

No. 21[42]
(Extract)

6 January 1887

Dear Ichitarō,

[...]

I received a letter from Kimura Jūtarō [a former Keio student, by 1887 owner of a Yokohama trading company] in San Francisco. In it he mentions news concerning Takashima Kokinji [a former Keio student (1861–1922), by 1887 working as a businessman] and his landlady. Whether true or false, it is highly interesting. I do not find it ridiculous at all for a Japanese to marry a foreign lady; in fact, I highly approve. But the standards of living in Japan and the United States are so different that grave difficulties are bound to occur as soon as the wedding is over and they begin a life of poverty on a diet of *miso* soup and pickles. If this problem did not exist, everything should go well, but what does this Takashima intend to do? I have written a letter to Kai [Orie (1850–1922), an ex-samurai from Nakatsu, by 1887 a successful San Francisco businessman] in San Francisco, asking him privately, and in a roundabout way, to see if he knows anything. I would be grateful if you too could find out if Takashima himself has any capital, or if the lady herself is wealthy.[43]

***

No. 22[44]
To Hattori Kane [Fukuzawa's third elder sister, whose husband has just died]

25 January 1887

Dear O-Kane,

You must be feeling lonely as a result of your sad loss. I have sent a bill of exchange for 20 yen to you via Odabe [the husband of their eldest sister, Rei]. Please tell me if there is anything that you need as I will do everything that is in my power in order to help you. I do not want you to face any problems such as worries about your livelihood as you grow older. Please consult with Rei over whether it would be better for you to live with O-Ichi [the daughter of their elder brother, whom Kane had helped to bring up after the brother's death] or to move near to the Odabe's. You need only focus on remaining healthy, since as long as I am alive there will be no reason for you to worry about anything. There are plays and other entertainments available in Nakatsu, so I hope that you will arrange with Rei to go out and enjoy yourselves, whatever else happens. Life is not just a matter of having clothes to wear and food to eat. The older one gets, the more one needs to have some enjoyment. Please talk with Rei and make some plans. Let me at the very least send you funds to ensure that you can both keep in good health in this way. This is all I have to say now, until my next letter.

Affectionately yours,

Yukichi

No. 23[45]
(Extract)

1 February 1887

Dear Ichitarō,

... With regard to the matter that you have raised in confidence, neither your mother nor I wish to do anything to prevent this. We are just extremely worried that it will lead you into financial difficulties. There is no lack of examples of men who have made rash promises that they could not actually sustain financially in everyday life. Their promises ended in disaster, leaving them with nothing but hardship and ridicule. Since you are no longer a child, you should understand what I mean. I urge you to think over this matter extremely carefully, and to refrain from action until you are sure that you have found a way of assuring your future prospects. In any case, please keep me privately informed of your thoughts on this matter.

No. 24[46]
(Extracts)

9 February 1887

Dear Ichitarō,

Life back in Japan continues as normal, but O-Fusa, O-Shun and O-Taki have started at a school in Yokohama,[47] and O-Sato is now living with Sadakichi [her husband] since he has returned from abroad. That leaves only O-Mitsu, Sanpachi and Daishirō. It is much quieter, which is all very well, but we feel lonely in the evenings.

[...]

P.S.

[...]

How are things with you? I have not heard much from you since your confidential news. I do not wish to force you to do anything against your will, and I realize that it is hard to make such important decisions. Perhaps you should make a visit to Japan before you finally decide. I would like us to be able to consult properly. I am just waiting for your next letter.

*
* *

No. 25[48]
(Extracts)

16 March 1887

Dear Ichitarō,

I have read your letter of 4 February....

You have asked me once more for my true opinion regarding the confidential matter that you raised previously. As I wrote before, my only concern is your future ability to earn a living. In my view, it will definitely not be easy. I realize that children grow and become independent, and that parents should not interfere in every aspect of their behavior. However, it is highly disagreeable to watch as a child's way of living unravels. This American lady may appear to be intelligent, but she does not know anything about the real nature of Japan. I am deeply concerned that if she comes to Japan and actually has responsibility for running a Japanese-style household, she will inevitably be unhappy and there will be a high likelihood that the match will not last long. For example, let us consider the situation of those who graduated from Keio after you and stayed in Japan. Whether they have found employment in government or in the private sector, they are earning 100 yen per month at the most, in most cases around 40 to 50, and in some, even less. Even if you are lucky enough to earn 70 or 80 yen per month, this will not ensure you a high standard of living. What will you do if this American lady cannot bear such conditions? You will be in an impossible situation. If you want my frank opinion, your plan is all very well, but since it will probably not work out in practice but end in failure, the only really safe course is to give it up. However, you are no longer a child, so you should consider the matter very carefully yourself. Please tell me your decision as soon as you make it.

Alternatively, are you ready to earn a living independently in the United States? This would also be one possibility. But while it may be easy to earn money there, it is also easy to spend it, so it would be even harder for you financially than in Japan. In fact, I find it hard to believe that you would be able to earn an independent living there. I am extremely worried that whether you set up here or in the United States, you will find yourself in financial straits. In your letter you said that you had some ideas about what to do. If this is so, please tell me the details.

※※

No. 26[49]
(Extract)

13 April 1887

Dear Ichitarō,

[...]

P.S.

I very much agree with the plans that you outlined for after your return to Japan in your last letter. After you come back and begin to teach at Keio, I intend to make great efforts to collect the funds to develop it into a university. For you to become a teacher at the university, or even the **director**, would give me great satisfaction. To tell the truth, the ideas you expressed in those plans, and the way in which you expressed them in English, left me with no complaints. Anyway, redouble your efforts at studying until you come home. I pray that you will find that the trials you have experienced in the United States have not been in vain. Please believe this yourself as well. . . .

※※

No. 27[50]
(Extracts)

21 May 1887

Dear Sutejirō,

In your last letter you wrote that you were looking into the best field to take up in order to put your studies to practical use when you return to Japan after graduating next year. This is a very important issue, and I have also been making inquiries. At the moment, railways are being established in various parts of Japan, and it looks as if this will be a good means of employment now. But the real present need is for bridges and tunnels, and Japan lacks specialists in both these areas. Therefore I would like you to study the construction of railways in general, with a particular focus on bridges and tunnels.

While Japan does not have enough people who have studied railway construction, they are not entirely absent. However, when it comes to the **management** of the railway business overall, there is no one, probably because no one has yet realized its importance. For this reason, anyone who has knowledge of administering railways as well as building them will be unbeatable....

Therefore, for the present as well as your major at university, you should read books, newspapers and so on in order to learn about building bridges and boring tunnels. If you have time after investigating these thoroughly, there is railway **management**:

    Issuing shares

    Buying and selling them

    The level of wages

    The selling of tickets

    The regions where railways run at a profit and where they run at a loss

    The salaries of company officials

There are a host of other important issues, but I would like you to do your investigations with the above points in mind.

*
* *

No. 28[51]

(Extracts)

29 June 1887

Dear Ichitarō,

I have read your letter of 20 May extremely carefully.[52] Most of it makes very good sense, but you are mistaken in thinking that Dr. Yunghans [Ichitarō's private tutor, an American doctor who had worked in Japan for a time] has written to me about you. After Dr. Simmons left the United States, I did ask Dr. Yunghans to keep an eye on your health and educational progress, but I definitely did not request him to direct your actions as if he were your father. Therefore, do not worry about what he might say. You should tread your own path. . . .

. . . as I write, I am imagining the happy future of the Fukuzawa family. Such matters are not anything that other people should interfere with since they are for your mother and father alone to discuss with you. Overall, the Fukuzawa family has nothing to be ashamed of: parents and children are close to each other, and our standards of behavior are pure. Fortunately, nothing up till now has led to any betrayal of these principles. . . .

When you were born, you did not get enough milk and this slowed down your development a little; for example, you did not begin to speak until you were five.[53] As a result, your mother and I were extremely worried about how you would develop. But fortunately you have made steady progress and grown into a healthy young man of intellectual ability, able to develop your natural talents without any help from us by studying literature in the United States. Therefore, we are incredibly proud at the thought that you will come back as an independent young man without anything to be ashamed of, ready to be a teacher at Keio or take up some other field, with no need to take a post which just involves obeying someone's orders. Once you have completed your studies, our one wish will be for you to have a family.

This is just between ourselves, but what shall we do about finding you a bride? Although parents should not order a child to marry, they have a duty to advise their children and either give or withhold their approval. This is probably completely illogical behavior, but because we want to secure the best bride for you in Japan, recently whenever your foolish parents go out, they find themselves looking intently at all the young ladies of marriageable age. We laugh together at this strange tendency. . . .

No. 29[54]

18 July 1887

Dear Ichitarō,

Since the arrival of your letter dated 20 May, there have been three mails from the United States and letters from Sutejirō and Momosuke,[55] but nothing from you. What is your news? I would like you to send something assuring us of your wellbeing every mail, even if it is not a long letter.

I have just read your letter of the 20th again. Despite its length, the only point that you make is your dislike of the restraints that Dr. Yunghans places on your actions. I have certainly not asked him to behave in this way.[56] All I have done is make the simple request that in addition to tutoring you, he should also pay attention to your health. I fail to understand both why you are so angry, and why you state that you do not care if you die.

After all, the reason for your trip to the United States is to follow your studies. Your only duty is to devote yourself to this and develop a reputation that will enable you to set up an independent household. All I want to know is whether you are achieving this. Whatever your relationship might be with the doctor, this is only a temporary misunderstanding that will be solved in due course. Your idea of turning it into a noisy argument does not strike me as calm behavior.

As I have frequently told you, although I have taken great pains over the education of you both, I do not expect that you will look after me in my old age in return. Therefore, there is also no reason for you to expect much from your parents once your education is finished. All I ask for in the way of filial conduct is that you refrain from causing your parents unnecessary worry. While it is hard for me to understand the intention behind your letter of 20 May, it did not make for pleasant reading, and far from giving us joy, made us extremely worried. Please make sure that this does not happen again.

You have already spent a full four years in the United States, and seem to have made great progress in your literary studies. If you spend one more year there and come back with Sutejirō, you should have a variety of different opportunities for work, and I am already considering what you might take up. Since you have been receiving assistance from your parents during your studies, you have been able to spend time as you wish. However, the duties of parents are not meant to continue indefinitely. I am not getting any younger, and I cannot continue to support a young man in the prime of life at the expense of my own health. In other words, each day that you spend in study now lays down the capital to support another day of your life in the future. It is not time that you can afford to waste. What should you have to focus on apart from studying? Please consider my words.

It might be that you are thinking of coming back to Japan now instead of staying longer in the United States. However, since you left with Sutejirō, I think you should return with him as well, and I therefore encourage you to spend one more year. If a time comes when you can no longer bear your situation and I feel that there is something wrong, I am perfectly ready to go to the United States to bring you back with me. The trip would not be hard, despite my age. However, since you are already more than an adult, I doubt that you want to cause your father such trouble. I trust that things will not reach this point.

In short, you should therefore spend one more year abroad focusing on your studies, and return with Sutejirō. During this time, you should keep your mind on your duties and work hard like any other foreign student. Students have no need for alcohol: heavy drinking is forbidden. I gather that you tend to exercise a little, and then grow lazy. Regardless of how I have obtained this information, this is unacceptable behavior. Why do you neglect your health in this way? From now on, make sure that you pay attention to this matter. If there are any other difficulties or problems unrelated to the wishes that I have stated above, I am resolved to carry out my paternal duties towards you by coming to the United States and bringing you home with me. The Fukuzawa family is as clear as water; as perfect as a sphere. Whatever the circumstances, I will not allow you to put a blemish on this perfection. I still have enough strength to protect our honor.

If you have anything to say, please feel free to do so. I will answer you conscientiously. You must know that my love for you will not change as long as I live. When you have a strong affection for someone, it sometimes leads one to say more than is necessary. This seems to have happened in the case of this letter. It should be read carefully with this in mind. I will write more in my next letter.

In haste,

Yukichi

⁂

No. 30[57]
(Extract)

1 September 1887

Dear Ichitarō,

Your letter of 3 August has arrived. I was very relieved to read that you left Poughkeepsie on 26 July in the company of Iwasaki Seikichi [a former Keio student, later a businessman] and are now living with Sutejirō in Salem. As I have said many times, everything is fine here; our only prayer is for you to pursue your studies without experiencing any problems. I hope that you will settle down and focus on your literary training. The tone of your letter suggests that since leaving Poughkeepsie you have become more relaxed. I am overjoyed. As I wrote in my last letter, you should study harder than ever for one more year. After that, you can either return with Sutejirō for a short time to rest on your laurels before visiting Europe for a while, or it might be interesting to travel back via Europe and the Indian Ocean, working in some sightseeing on your way. I wish to write more about these possibilities later.

⁂

No. 31[58]

16 January 1888

Dear Ichitarō,

In the last mail there were two boxes of books sent by the Morimura Company that seem to belong to you. I expect that a letter explaining the situation will arrive soon.

With regard to your return to Japan this year, [it concerns me that] you will have no graduation certificate. Of course, this is a childish matter, and it is of no matter to me if you do not have one, but I fear that this is not the way in which the world at large thinks. I have discussed the matter with Dr. Simmons and asked him to consider whether you can obtain a certificate from the **private teacher** that you had in Poughkeepsie or get one just for literary studies from a college, or whether there is some other method. Please think about this too, and endeavor to find a way of procuring one if at all possible. You should be prepared to do this even if means enduring some unpleasantness.

Dr. Simmons may contact Dr. Yunghans about this. Since you previously had a disagreement with Dr. Yunghans, you will probably not wish to ask a favor of him now, but this is the sort of occasion in life when one must endure. I hope you will be prepared to behave politely to him for the sake of a certificate. There are scions of the aristocracy[59] who have spent five or even seven years abroad, and come back with no skills apart from the ability to play billiards or go fishing. It would be completely unfair if your achievements were regarded in the same light. We can safely say that you have achieved a high standard in your literary studies. I should be most unhappy if you were seen in the same light as those scions of the aristocracy just because you do not have a certificate. Please give this matter careful thought and obtain a certificate, even if it means swallowing your pride. If Dr. Simmons' negotiations by mail [with Dr. Yunghans] are ineffective, please consult with Sutejirō about what efforts can be made.

I have no time to write more.

In haste,

Yukichi

I will write something about your plans to come back via Europe in a separate letter addressed to both of you.

***

No. 32[60]

16 June [? probably January] 1888

Dear Ichitarō and Sutejirō,

When Sutejirō graduates this June, you plan to travel home together via Europe and the Indian Ocean. Please read my thoughts about this.

1. Finish your preparations for departure before June and cross over to Britain as soon as Sutejirō graduates. You should visit each country in Europe; in particular, be sure not to miss Russia out. You should definitely pass through St. Petersburg on your way to Moscow. (This is the first time you will need a visa.)

2. You should tour cities such as Paris and Berlin, but it does not matter if you only gain a general idea of them. It would be a good idea to go as far as Turkey, via Italy, and see Constantinople.

3. You may find the cultural products of Europe to be similar to those of the United States, but there are differences between the Old World and the New. Focus on getting a general grasp of the region, since this will be of help on any further visits.

4. Once you have crossed the Mediterranean, you should have a quick look at Alexandria. Then enter the Indian Ocean, stop at Ceylon and be sure to visit Bombay and Calcutta. In China, Kwantung is more important than Hong Kong.

5. If you leave the United States in June and follow the above course, it should take you five months to get to Japan. Your parents and also your brothers and sisters are waiting impatiently for your return, but the chance to observe the customs and human nature of the various countries of the world, however superficially, is something that will serve you well in the future and also enhance your reputation in Japan.

6. You should obtain the money to pay for your expenses from the United States to London from Morimura. In London, I will arrange for you to obtain money from the local branch of the [Yokohama] Specie Bank. This should be enough for your needs.

7. Since we want you to return home as soon as possible, please arrange to set out the day after Sutejirō obtains his graduation certificate. You should not need to do any further sightseeing in the United States.

8. It is essential for you to visit India and China. If you begin to read about them now, it will be of great help once you have actually arrived.

9. It may seem foolish to spend only five months in this way, just staying at

hotels and travelling by train, but this is not so. Actually seeing all these places will be more useful than it may seem.

10. You should collect even trivial things as souvenirs wherever you go. They will become precious **memories** for life.

11. There is no reason for you to post any letters while you are touring Europe, India and China. It should be possible to send messages assuring us of your safety wherever there is a Japanese consular office. Please be sure to do this whenever you can. For example, there are consular offices in Hong Kong, Tenshin and Shanghai. The present consul at Tenshin is Hatano Shōgorō [1858–1929, a Keio graduate].

12. I would like you to write about your travels so that I can publish your articles in the newspaper, so please send occasional reports, either in Japanese or English.

13. Dr. Simmons thinks that your travels will last until next March. But since both boat and rail transport are so convenient nowadays, I think that they should be over by November or December, or even earlier.

14. These are my thoughts. Of course, I understand that you may have your own ideas about the itinerary. I have just focused on pointing out places that are so far unfamiliar to Japanese people.

In haste,

Yukichi

***

No. 33[61]
(Extract)

23 March 1888

Dear Sutejirō,

[…]

Do not worry about Ichitarō's lack of a graduation certificate. In fact, we need someone who is fluent at reading and writing English at *Jiji shinpō*. Ichitarō has just the right qualifications, and if we were to employ an outsider, it would cost 60 to 70 yen. Even if it is proving difficult to obtain a certificate, there is therefore no need to worry. Father and son will manage splendidly through independent cooperation....

***

No. 34
To Odabe Rei and Hattori Kane [his first and third elder sisters] (Extract)[62]

14 May 1888

My dear sisters,

Spring is upon us and it is gradually getting warmer. I am so glad that you are both in such good health. I was also pleased that you were able to travel to Kobe and spend a relaxing time with En [the middle elder sister]. I feel a bit jealous since I was unable to get away from work in order to accompany you. The older we become, the more important it is for us to be able to enjoy ourselves. I hope you will let me help you to cover the expenses of a similar trip next year.

I have written to Mr. Shimazu [Manjirō, a Keio graduate living in Nakatsu] asking him to give Kane 3 yen every month from January, which will amount to 36 yen by December. Please accept this as a gift.

This is all I have to say until I next write.

Yours affectionately,

Yukichi

P.S.

Thank you for the photograph. I do not have any photographs of myself at the moment, but when my boys return from America this year they are going to bring some photographical equipment with them. Since they know how to use it I am purposely waiting to have any pictures taken until they come back....

***

No. 35
To Nakamigawa Hikojirō [son of Fukuzawa's middle sister, En][63]

26 January 1889

Dear Hikojirō,

I need your advice once again concerning Sutejirō, this time with regard to the reform in the rules about conscription.[64] According to the old rules he was part of the second reserve so there was no cause for concern, but with the new rules it seems that this will no longer be the case. We cannot afford to ignore the situation. My first thought was the Tokyo Municipal Public Works Department, so I immediately asked for the help of Mr. Yamana [Jirō, Keio graduate and businessman] in applying to Mr. Takasaki [Goroku, Governor of Tokyo]. If that does not work, I hope to ask Hyōgo Prefecture to give him a post as a civil engineer or a translator and interpreter and arrange for him to be transferred after that to the San'yō Railway.[65] I would be grateful if you could prepare the ground for my request. Of course, if Tokyo will accept him, there will be no problem, but my information so far is that Hyōgo can make no promises. If my efforts fail, I will immediately send you a telegram, so that you can take what steps are necessary as quickly as possible. According to the new rules, an application must be made between the 1st and 15th of March. There is no knowing whether we can get Sute[jirō] into one of these positions or not, but it is a very troublesome affair and I want to make all the preparations that I can.

Thanking you in advance,

Yukichi

※

No. 36[66]
(Extracts)

30 January 1889

Dear Hikojirō,

Thank you for the telegram. I gather that you could arrange a post for Sutejirō in the prefectural headquarters, but that there is no benefit in becoming an official. I see now that this is the correct interpretation of the new rules. On reflection, another possibility is for Sutejirō to answer the summons without any attempt at evasion. This year, there will be an unusually large number of recruits, and on average the uptake should be one in forty. Even if he has no alternative but to appear, even the smallest defect should ensure rejection. His one weakness is his teeth, of which four or five are decayed. Since decayed teeth are regarded very seriously, if he can manage to be examined by a doctor who takes this view, there will be less cause for worry. Accordingly, we will try this first.[67]

If his teeth are sufficient cause for rejection, I have an idea of an occupation for him. Of course, at the moment work related to the railways would be very suitable for him; on the other hand, we are extremely busy here, and in great need of fresh help. . . . I think it would be useful to have Sute work at least part time at Keio and expound high-flown arguments. I think that Ichitarō should work at the newspaper (*Jiji shinpō*) rather than at Keio. He is more suited to this because his natural taciturnity will make it difficult for him to hold his own against the outspoken lads at the academy. So I am thinking of dividing the time of both Sute and Ichi, with Ichi working mainly at the newspaper and sometimes going to Keio, and Sute working mainly at Keio and learning about the office and accounting side of the newspaper. It may look as if they are good-for-nothings if they just stay with their parents like this without attempting to go out into the world, but as I grow older, I grow more attached to both Keio and the newspaper. To put them completely into the hands of outsiders and stand silently by while they mess things up in front of my eyes would be unbearable. For example, I might have to watch as the person in charge at Keio made all sorts of plans to spend money before it actually materialized and employed teachers who were not even necessary. Even now, we have three or four staff too many, but no one is willing to take the decision to get rid of them quickly by giving them compensation money. . . .

I think it would be a good idea for Ichitarō to marry and have been working on this for some time. The road has been long, with many turnings, but it is virtually decided that we will obtain [*morau*] the eldest daughter (aged 18) of a

Yokohama merchant named Minoda Chōjirō. I will tell you the details when the time comes. The go-between is Dr. Kondō Ryōkun[68] who has treated the family for illness and knows a lot about them. I intend to proceed as long as Ichitarō does not disagree. . . .

※

No. 37[69]
(Extract)

24 April 1889

Dear Hikojirō

. . . Ichitarō's wedding ceremony occurred without a hitch on the 18th, so I am very relieved. As I wrote to you before, the bride is the eldest daughter of Mr. Minoda. Her name is O-Katsu, and she is 18 years old. The betrothal was entirely due to the efforts of Dr. Kondō Ryōkun. He has acted as physician to the Minodas for many years and has detailed knowledge both of their physical health and the various family doings. His private knowledge was of great help in deciding the matter. Ichitarō and his wife will live separately from us, in the plot where Dr. Simmons' house used to be. The marriage has made me extremely busy, and even involved a trip back to Nakatsu. The wedding reception will be held here tomorrow, with about 200 guests and a buffet meal. Once that is over, we will have completed the marriage of two children; but we still have seven to go. The growth of one's children is a source of both joy and trouble.

※

No. 38[70]

7 September, 1889

Dear Sutejirō,[71]

The day before yesterday, I arranged for a shipping company to take the bedding that you asked for. It should arrive on the 11th.

We should start our joint family trip to the Kyoto area in four to five days;

at the moment we are in the midst of preparations. There has been much discussion about the itinerary, and it looks as if it will be difficult to get to our destination in two days, let alone make it directly in only one. Therefore, I thought that we would leave Tokyo in the morning, spend one night in Shizuoka in order to visit the shrine at Mt Kuno etc., set out from Shizuoka the next morning, and then spend a night at Nagoya so that we can see the golden dolphins on the roof of the castle and pay a visit to Atsuta Shrine. I thought that we could leave immediately for Kobe the next day, but it looks as if this will be difficult too. Instead, my guess is that we will go to Kyoto and stay about two or three nights while we see all the sights there and also go to Ōtsu for the Eight Views of Ōmi; then we will leave Kyoto for Nara, see all the famous places, including the Kasuga Shrine, the giant Buddha statue etc. and spend the night; then on to Osaka, where we will spend two or three nights visiting Sumiyoshi [Shrine] and Sakai; after that Kobe for about two nights, seeing [the famous beaches of] Suma and Maiko as well as [the site of the battle of] Ichi no tani on the way back from Himeji [Castle]; then after leaving Kobe, we will get off the train at Kusatsu, take the old Tōkaidō road from Yokkaichi to Tsu, worship at the great shrine [of Ise], go back to Yokkaichi and take a boat there back to Tokyo. However, our plans may well change as we go. Our party will consist of sixteen people, including four young ones, headed by O-Mitsu.

This is a family trip to visit famous and historic sites. Moreover, because I have had my fill of visitors and meetings, my intention is to snatch 15 to 20 days of vacation at hotels that no one knows about. While we are on holiday I intend to refuse visitors and to call on no one apart from our relatives, the Nakamigawas, so I would like you to keep this trip to yourself; I have not yet even told anyone here about it. I am going to play truant! Please be sure that you do not let the secret out.

I will send you a telegram just before we set off. If you can, come to Kyoto so that we can spend one or two days together as a family. Please propose this to the Nakamigawas too.

Ichitarō was originally going to stay behind to look after things in Tokyo, but since it would be disappointing if all of the children except one joined in, we have changed our plans and he will be coming too; this means that if we can add you, the full set of nine will be there.

Originally we intended to go to Kobe first, then Osaka, Nara, Kyoto, Ōtsu, Kusatsu and Ise, but we reversed the order since we were afraid that the young ones would have difficulty with the long journey between Nagoya and Kobe.

I will contact you again as soon as we are certain about the schedule and the number of people.[72]

In haste,

Yukichi

*
**

No. 39[73]
(Extracts)

25 October 1889

Dear Sutejirō,

Your telegram inquiring after O-Sato's illness arrived last night and I replied this morning "Looking better," but it is now the ninth day since her illness began and she is running a very high fever. It was 40.6 degrees yesterday afternoon and today, around the same time, has risen to 40.8. She is in pain and unaware of what is going on around her, and we are fighting to prevent her condition from deteriorating over the next 48 hours. We have consulted with Drs. Matsuyama [Tōan, 1839–1920][74] and Intō [Gentoku, 1850–1895].[75] Since the symptoms are very clear they agree on the diagnosis, and visit the patient from time to time.

[...]

Her body has not completely lost its vitality, but she has no appetite, and we are forcing her to drink wine, **milk** and **soup** in order to sustain her. We are employing two nurses, who look after her very conscientiously. She seems lonely, and frequently calls out for her parents, brothers and sisters, so we go to her bedside to show her our faces as long as it does not interfere with the nurses.

The doctors say that the illness is severe, but there is only a slight possibility that it will become life threatening. I am not saying this to console you, but because it is true. But since she is so closely related to us all, we are suffering from terrible anxiety. We have no thought of eating or sleeping, but feel restless and distracted. I will keep you informed of her condition.

In haste,

Yukichi

* *
*

No. 40
To Dr. Kondō Ryōkun (Extract)[76]

7 November 1889

Dear Dr. Kondō,

With regard to our private conversation yesterday evening, I talked to the person concerned [Ichitarō] this morning. Since my object was to uncover everything that had gone on, not just his wife's return to her family in Yokohama, we talked for about three hours and came to the same opinion. Ichitarō possesses no wish to separate from his bride and is astounded by her unexpected departure. The betrothal was not forced on him by his parents; in fact he was extremely satisfied with the match and had absolutely no unpleasant feelings about the arrangement. Moreover, if they do separate because of some misunderstanding, he has no intention of marrying again. According to the Japanese way, one can marry any number of times, but from the day of the wedding he had vowed to himself to remain faithful to his bride for the whole of his life. It was clear beyond doubt that he is absolutely determined to remain pure and to refrain from remarrying even if there is a separation.

I therefore questioned him further, to see if he had any idea why this crisis had manifested itself. He said that he had, and that he was prepared to accept the responsibility. There seemed little point in talking about it now, but from the start of their marriage, they had not developed deep emotional feelings towards each other. (During trips together, and when taking photographs and so on, he had behaved in a Western manner, which may have shocked a young lady used to Japanese ways. If we put this matter to trial, both the one who persuaded and the one who was persuaded would surely be found not guilty.) In any case, she treated him like a guest and while everything seemed fine on the surface, whenever it looked as if things might become more relaxed between them, and they might be able to act together without the constraints of politeness, she would withdraw into formality. He found this hard to bear, and although he realized that he should approach this topic indirectly and with sensitivity, at times he grew too impatient and hurt her feelings even more. Far from feeling wronged, he seems full of remorse: He had promised himself that this, the only marriage of his life, would be pure and without blemish, but through the words and actions of a moment he had injured her feelings. (This seems to be a misunderstanding caused by one side valuing manners and being very polite, and the other being insensitive, thinking that manners change according to the situation, and assuming that they are not needed in the home.)

When I asked him what his intentions were now, he was unable to give an immediate reply. He asked me for advice, and I told him that reason and emotion run counter to each other in human affairs, and that the relationship between man and wife has no room for reason. For example, to talk about unnecessary things is unnecessary from a logical point of view, but in the room of a married couple, it was a mistake to talk only when necessary and otherwise remain silent. That would be like a marriage between a tree and a rock. Therefore, when Ichitarō comes home, he should talk about the various things he has heard that day, while his wife tells him about the strange and amusing things that happened at home during his absence. As they chat together pleasantly, they should start to feel deep emotions arise. Another way of enjoying themselves in the evening would be to practice cooking a meal and invite her brothers and sisters from Yokohama and the Fukuzawa children. "Watch over your words!" goes the old adage, but I would counter this with "Many words bring about affection." In any case, the gentleman values what is elegant and open hearted, and it is commonly said that everyday talk is a source of pleasure. I advised him that if he took care in this way, all should be well. He seemed to realize where the problem lay and sincerely said that he would give the matter his full attention.

In addition, I mentioned everything that I could think of, including financial and other matters, ways of studying, and the importance of tact in relations with friends. In the course of doing so, we came to the issue of alcohol, and whether he could really give it up at last. His mother and I have long worried that drinking might destroy him. Since I do not like to scold my children for no reason, I was determined to speak kindly and eventually he made a strong promise to stop drinking. Thereupon I made sure to tell his mother, and we once again checked that his mind was made up.

The above is a record of our conversation, but a written account leaves something to be desired. I will tell you the rest when we meet.

Meanwhile, in what direction does the other party wish to take this? Is she certain that there is no point in talking, in other words, that Ichitarō is not the person that she wishes to entrust with the rest of her life? Does she consider that even if he improves his behavior, after a short period of time he will lapse back into his old ways? If that is the case, there is nothing to be done. However, Ichitarō is neither a bad person, nor someone who refuses to listen to other people. A husband and wife are the basis of morality, and to break this tie is something that requires careful consideration, even if the situation is desperate. Moreover, although my wife and I are no longer young, we have a good ten years of life left. Whatever storms might occur, it should be easy for us to deal with them. In other words, she should not despair at the possibility of a second attempt, since as long as we are alive, they should be able to develop their skills at running a happy marital household. As I have said from the beginning, I still intend that the bride should have full power over the new household, make her own decisions with regard to everything and do the housework as she pleases. But I hope that she will develop a close relationship with us, and tell us about any problems so that we can help to build the foundations of the new family. I beg you to tell her all of this and to ask for her true opinion.

※

No. 41[77]

11 November 1889

Dear Dr. Kondō,

My sincere thanks for your visit yesterday evening. After you left, the patient sweated profusely. I am extremely pleased since this seems to be a good sign.

I was very busy this morning, but with regard to the matter that we spoke about in snatches, if the other party are determined to say no, I suppose that we must accept that there is absolutely nothing that can be done. However, since there is normally a connection between the beginning and the end in human affairs, we need to determine the cause of what has occurred. In particular, what happened was completely unexpected, since before the bride left, saying that she was just going back to Yokohama for a little, she did not say anything about the origins of this grave matter, nor show any outward sign that something was wrong. When we later heard what was actually going on, we were so taken aback that we thought there must have been some mistake. In particular, what makes us most puzzled is that ever since the marriage we have been absolutely open with her, and have regarded her as one of our daughters. We have only held back because we assumed that to be around at all times would be an intrusion on the newly weds. She must certainly have been aware of the depth of our feelings towards her. Since she must have understood our feelings, she would surely have told us of any problems that were troubling her. This would have been common sense from the point of view of human affairs, and not in any way unusual. We do not understand why she had to leave without warning just when a family member was suffering from a life-threatening illness and everything was in such confusion that we could not tell night from day. Since she left no explanation, we did not realize the significance of her departure until we sent to enquire. When we asked for an explanation, the answer was that her husband sometimes drank and became rough in his words and actions, that he spoke little in the mornings and evenings, and seemed not to be very affectionate. So sometimes he drinks, and sometimes he behaves a little roughly and is not a gentleman. It must also be awkward for a lady to share quarters with a man of little refinement and few words. She may have other grounds for discontent, but this is the more or less the gist. Is this enough for her to make a decision that will decide her whole future? As I remarked today, this is similar to feeling a pain somewhere, and deciding by oneself, without asking for any expert help, that death is inevitable. Moreover, in this case, expert help was available in the form of the parents, who would have produced many ideas for treatment if only they had been told of the suffering. But they were not told that anything was wrong. There are many other matters to be considered, such as the fact that the husband will be deprived forever of his wish for someone who will be the mother of his children. They cannot be quickly dealt with. When we look at this young lady who has been married for just six months, it is hard to believe that she is willing to bring things to an end so rapidly. On the one hand, she had her parents to consult, on the other, she had her parents-in-law to talk to. Private discussions between the parents and parents-in-law would also have been possible. Nothing should be decided in such a case until all the possibilities have been exhausted, yet despite this she just went back to her previous home one morning, without a word to either her parents-in-law or the go-between. To make a final decision after talking only to her parents is definitely not the normal method of procedure in human affairs.

This is what I have to say with regard to the relations between our two families. However, if a similar case in which I was not directly involved was to attract public attention and I was therefore consulted, I would respond with frankness and calm that the bride's behavior was rash and against her interests for the following reasons:

1. Those who understand the importance of morality will neither marry nor divorce lightly. There is even the colloquial saying that those who have married once are damaged goods. If this is what is said by ordinary people, how much more must it be the case among those of education and refinement! It is a state of affairs that should be avoided. Therefore, if the marriage ends in divorce, who will be blamed? There can be no more disadvantageous position for a woman. To get married in the morning and divorce in the evening is the behavior of the lower levels of society. In that sense, it cannot be tolerated.

2. Divorce has a deep significance. Everyone will assume that there was a good reason, and even if no public statement is made, your closest friends and associates will all come to believe this, either openly or in private. Will it really be in the interests of a young woman and her reputation if, after only six months of experience, she makes a firm decision to divorce with the support of her parents?

The above is the advice I would give if I were not directly involved. Please give it your consideration as if it were nothing to do with me. Both we ourselves, and Ichitarō, understand completely the importance of morality in this matter, and are in complete agreement. Since hearing your words the other day, our amazement has not ceased to grow. How is it possible to make such destructive pronouncements without serious thought? We have begun to suspect that they began the betrothal arrangements with a similar lack of thought. Please give this your consideration. I have no further proposals at this point. My only object is to convey our thoughts. Please proceed slowly and carefully.

Respectfully yours,

Fukuzawa Yukichi

∗∗∗

No. 42[78]

12 November 1889

Dear Dr. Kondō,

A maid named Fuku was sent from Yokohama in order to examine the clothes needed by the bride, as I discussed with you recently. We collected all the clothes that seemed to be for daily use and sent them back with the maid. In fact, as you suggested in your recent note, I agree that it is only natural to give her what she needs. However, there is a slight catch. She is still meant to be a Fukuzawa wife, who is just staying in Yokohama for a while. Therefore, she surely has no need for finery. For example, there is unlikely to be any need for her to attend an occasion that requires the wearing of a long-sleeved kimono. It may be the practice in the lower levels of society for families to immediately enter discussions about taking back the bride's clothes, but at our level of status such talk is unbearably embarrassing. We are hardly likely to lose or damage a few articles of clothing; they are worth less than nothing in our eyes. To turn one's attention to the return of the bride's clothing, and to checking that all is in order even before matters have been decided, is nothing other than a custom of the lower levels of society. Even if one party behaves in an unrefined way and places only second priority on the outcome of the matter, in order to preserve her honor I first wish to come to a quiet settlement. It is most regrettable that we are faced with such questionable behavior from people whom we are trying to treat as our equals. With regard to possessions, there is no call for back-street suspicions of whether or not they will be handed over; the whole idea is distasteful. If we can solve the problem, there will be no need for concern anyway, but even if our attempts fail, we can still be trusted. I would be most grateful if you can ensure that we can deal with the issue in a gentlemanly way.

As I wrote to you yesterday, even if our attempts fail, there may be no need to make a public announcement, but it will still be necessary to inform friends and relations privately about the following: the cause that led to the divorce, how the problem started, how it progressed, the normal behavior of the couple, the attitude taken by the parents on both sides, all the details, both large and small, and how everything was settled. Our sincere intention from the beginning has been to treat the bride as our own daughter. Even if one's daughter does something wrong, the only course open to a parent is to guide her with patience. Even if someone behaves in a way that would cause one to lose patience in a normal situation, marriage is a basic principle of human morality and must be maintained even if it means enduring the unendurable. I feel that the dividing line between the lower and upper levels of society lies at exactly this point. With regard to the matter at hand, even if the worst happens and the other party actually breaks the marriage tie, my intention is to make them accept the responsibility. The plaintiffs in this destruction of human morality will be the other party, while it will be us who have the misfortune to be the defendants. In this regard too, I wish to maintain our reputation as members of the upper levels of society. I earnestly entreat you to act as a go-between concerning this situation.

Yukichi

***

No. 43[79]
(Extracts)

15 November 1889

Dear Dr. Kondō,

[...]

I am most grateful for your great efforts with regard to the other matter. We have no alternative but to leave the outcome to the decision of the other party. We ourselves cannot just offer endless apologies and wait in silence hoping for reconciliation. Yet there will be no escaping the charge that both the marriage and the divorce were decided without due consideration. Even in disputes concerning a simple employee, reasons are necessary and procedures have to be followed. If the household involved is in a state of emergency, it is regarded as common sense to simplify everything as far as possible and carry out discussions at a gradual pace. But in this case, the bride left suddenly, without any explanation, at a time when a serious case of illness was turning everything upside down, and has refused to reconsider. It is obvious that she will be harshly dealt with in the court of public opinion, and that we will also have to take a small share of the opprobrium. It is an intolerable nuisance. While news of divorce is not unusual, the lack of attention to the proper arrangements in this case makes it out of the ordinary. I am still in a state of shock, and have yet to feel any anger.

[...]

P.S.   15 November 1889

There is one thing that I have just remembered. The reason why I am convinced that the bride's decision to leave was taken on the spur of the moment is her behavior on our recent trip to the Kyoto-Osaka region. Each day was passed in pleasant conversation and laughter, and she seemed to be very happy as well. If she had been brooding about something, she would surely have refused to join us on the trip. Therefore it is clear that she did not decide to go until after our return on 5 October. During the trip, she even asked, "Papa, I would like you to teach me some book-learning." My reply was, "That would be fun. I will do so whenever I have a spare moment." If she had been resolved not to settle down with us, she would never have suggested this. I therefore surmise that she left that morning on the spur of the moment, and that she only made up her mind once she had returned home and discussed the matter with her parents. This is just something that I thought would help your considerations.

Yukichi

***

No. 44[80]
(Extracts)

25 November 1889

Dear Sutejirō,

[...]

The unfortunate matter of O-Katsu is so preposterous that we find it hard to believe. As the go-between, Dr. Kondō has been doing all that he can, but they are as stubborn and inflexible as ever. My honest belief is that it is the parents rather than the bride herself who want the divorce. The whole thing is ridiculous, as if they had been making fools of us from the outset, so even if the divorce actually occurs my intention is to make the other party bear complete responsibility. However, it is difficult to find room for agreement; we just go round and round.

[...]

P.S.

One more matter: The time for O-Fusa to get married is fast approaching.... I intend to make proper arrangements before the end of this month. ...

Matsuki Naoki [a native of Nakatsu who became a teacher and then a businessman] has suggested Kinzaburō [?Kinjirō], the second son of Kawasaki Hachizaemon, as a husband for O-Shun. You probably got to know him while you were in the United States, and the same should be true of Ichitarō and Momosuke. I would like to know your opinion as soon as possible. In fact, I am thinking of adopting Ono Yūjirō [as a bridegroom for O-Shun], but your Mama's opinion is also important. I am not allowed to arrange these things all by myself. If you can suggest someone suitable for adoption [as a bridegroom], I would be most grateful.

※

No. 45[81]
(Extract)

25 February 1890

Dear Dr. Kondō,

... Some time ago I wrote to you about the Minoda's request for divorce, but what has happened since then? Neither Ichitarō nor my wife and I have any wish to cause the other party difficulties by making unreasonable demands. But the fact is that while we cannot stop them from behaving in the way that they have chosen, it is only one party to the marriage that is seeking divorce. The reason why we would like them to state this in writing is not in order to make the matter public, but only so that my wife and I can prove to our country relatives that we did not send the bride away ourselves. As I mentioned to you before, the idea of leaving Ichitarō in his present situation for as long as five or six years is highly unpleasant. I sincerely feel that to leave the matter up in the air without a clear settlement will cause him great unhappiness in the future, and I would therefore like to bring everything to a finish as soon as possible. I entreat you to negotiate with them about this. Mr. Minoda began by taking the initiative, and wanting us to hand over the bride's belongings before anything was settled. This shocked us greatly. But now, it looks as if he is vacillating. I absolutely fail to understand his intentions. . . .[82]

※

No. 46[83]
To Odabe Rei (Extract)

9 May 1890

Dear elder sister,

[...]

P.S.

The children grow every day, and the house is full of activity. Ichitarō's wife has been fetched back by her family in Yokohama. They were together for around six months but something went wrong, and finally they were divorced. The root of the problem lay in marrying someone from the merchant class. The family customs are completely different, and they know no shame.

As a result, Ichitarō parted from his first wife and has now obtained a new one, the second daughter of a Dr. Ōzawa. She is the younger sister of the wife of Utsunomiya Saburō [1834–1902],[84] who has long been a close friend of mine. Since she grew up in the family of a scholar, she is likely to be of good character, so the match should go well.

Next I should mention O-Fusa, who married our adopted son Momosuke last winter. They are to live in Sapporo, Hokkaido. They started out on the 4th, and a telegram arrived yesterday to say that they had arrived safely. They have gone to Hokkaido so that Momosuke can take up his post as an executive at the headquarters of the Hokkaido Rail and Mining Company.

O-Shun is also betrothed. Her fiancé, Kiyooka Kuninosuke, comes from Tosa and became a student at Keio when he was still young. He has a mother living in Tosa, but no brothers or sisters. He is a fine young man, whom I would have been ready to adopt. In fact, I intend to treat him as if I were adopting him. Therefore, as soon as the betrothal arrangements are complete I intend to send him to study in England for two years as preparation for a career. They will marry once he returns. This means that four out of the nine are settled, but Sutejirō still has no one. So many children means that there is much to be done, but also much to enjoy. Luckily I am still in good health. On most days I pound the rice [to remove the husks], just as I used to do when we all lived in Nakatsu. I hope that memory brings a smile to your face.

※

No. 47
To Fukuzawa Momosuke and Fusa (Extract)[85]

19 May 1890

Dear Momosuke and O-Fusa,

[...]

P.S.

You write that O-Fusa seems to be in a delicate condition. Although it is too soon to be certain, supposing that she actually is pregnant, where do you plan for her to give birth? We are already worried at the thought of the difficult time you will have getting used to life in such a cold region, but now it looks as though O-Fusa will be giving birth during the very coldest period, in a place where proper care may not be available. We would really like her to return to Tokyo around September, and go back to Hokkaido after she has given birth; otherwise we expect that you will face many hardships. We would like to go to Hokkaido ourselves in order to look after her during the birth, but it would be extremely difficult for us to leave home and spend the whole winter with you. Your mother and I have been talking about what we should do since last night. In any case, please tell us how O-Fusa has been since your last letter. One's first experience of morning sickness is very wearing. One loses appetite, and sometimes even develops a fever. Of course, it is not a real illness, but a natural occurrence that is not in the least to be feared; even so, it can come as quite a shock. Please understand that there is no cause for alarm. We await more detailed news in your next letter.

No. 48
To Masuda Eiji [Head Administrator at Keio][86]

31 May 1890

Dear Mr. Masuda,

As I mentioned to you previously, the pet dogs[87] of Miss von Fallot, the schoolteacher, are extremely dangerous. Although I have been worried by their aggression towards the children, up till now I have not taken any action. But today, as usual, they began to bark at my fifth daughter, Mitsu [aged around 11], and she hurt herself when she fell while running away.

I expect that the dogs give Miss von Fallot much happiness; however injuries to children cannot be ignored. Therefore, I would like you to take care of the matter as soon as possible. Miss von Fallot may offer to tie the dogs up or something, but that is not enough. Please talk to her and explain that the rules governing this property state that the dogs must by all means be got rid of.

I am reluctant to make you deal with such a troublesome matter, but I must ask you to tie them up at once before any more dangerous incidents occur, and to remove them from the premises as soon as this can be arranged.

In haste,

Yukichi

No. 49[88]
(Extract)

19 June 1890

Dear Sutejirō,

... The other day, there was a short sword blade, a Hirosuke,[89] so finely crafted that it was likely to be extremely sharp, and at first glance could have been mistaken for a Muramasa.[90] Since it was only 2 yen, I indulged myself and bought it. I kept it by me for two or three days, but when I picked it up in order to compare it with a real Muramasa, the mouth of the wooden scabbard was a little loose, with the result that the blade slipped out and I cut my little finger. ⟤▭▭⟥ The cut [the vertical line on the far left in Fukuzawa's drawing] was about 15 mm long and about 3 mm deep, but I did not lose any blood as I immediately pressed down on it. I summoned a pupil of Dr. Matsuyama, washed the cut, disinfected it with **iodine** and wrapped the finger in a piece of cloth. I waited with some trepidation, but injuries caused by sharp blades are quick to mend; there was no infection, I did not develop a fever, and the cut has healed itself, without itching or aching. So before anything else, set your mind at rest. However, this one mishap has delivered a great blow to Papa's reputation throughout the family, and my swords have been hidden away in a box so that I cannot "play" with them any more. This is a truly embarrassing situation since whatever they say to me about it, I cannot give an excuse. All I can hope for is that talk of my injury will only continue for a week. I am negotiating with the children to the effect that they can make fun of me as much as they like during that time, but after that I want them to stop. The rest of my life will be very awkward if at any moment they can start teasing me about "that sword cut."

In haste,

Yukichi

*
**

No. 50[91]
(Extract)

24 October 1890

Dear Sutejirō,

[...]

Yesterday evening, we just could not get the cork out of a bottle of beer, so I decided to pull the **corkscrew** with O-Taki and Momosuke pulling the bottle at the same time. We all pulled as hard as we could at the agreed sign, but only the **screw** came out and with such force that I fell on my backside. This landed on a wooden part of the floor, and I lost my balance completely. It was the fleshy part of my backside that I landed on so no bones were affected. But even though I was not seriously injured, I felt a little pain when I woke up this morning. I just add this for your amusement.

⁂

No. 51[92]
(Extracts)

14 January 1891

Dear Sutejirō,

... Railways are so dangerous that it is frightening. Regardless of the effect on the company as a whole, I am just delighted that you were not hurt. It was only last year that Mr. Sekiguchi [Takayoshi (1836–1889)], the Governor of Shizuoka Prefecture, was severely injured in exactly the same sort of rail truck accident and died in great pain ten or so days later. Since last night I have continued to savor my relief as I thought about what your parents, brothers and sisters would do if anything like that were to happen to you. In fact, my joy was so great that I sent a telegram of congratulations this morning, along with 70 yen. I intend to present you with another 30 yen as an expression of my joy, so please get ready to accept a total of 100 yen. I beg you to use this dangerous experience to good effect by taking special care from now on to ensure that nothing like this ever happens again.

With regard to the aftereffects of my attack of influenza, as I told you in my last letter, my fever passed away on New Year's Day, but I am still not up to my usual strength. Because I am not able to go out yet, I am just staying indoors. Your mother's fever has also subsided, but she complains about the buzzing sound in her ears. O-Fusa should be giving birth soon, but she also has a clear case of influenza. While there is no real cause for anxiety, she has lost her appetite and is not putting on enough weight. However, her condition has been improving over the last few days. O-Shun is also improving. Probably because of her usual robust health, O-Taki only had a high fever for about two days and recovered immediately. Ichitarō's fever lasted longer, but he is now fully recovered and made his first trip outside today. It is hard to describe the state to which this vast city has been reduced by the epidemic. Yesterday Dr. Indō paid a visit to his patients here and said doctors were having no time to sleep or even eat properly. . . .

P.S.

The 30 yen that I mention in this letter are for you to use as you please. I will not instruct you how to spend them, but you could buy a drink for the people who were with you on the rail truck that had the **accident**, or to an engineer who acted particularly quickly. It is impossible to put into words the joy that the whole household has been feeling since yesterday. Do not feel uncomfortable about the 70 yen either, and if you need more, do not hesitate to say. In some situations, no expense should be spared. All that is required is **presence of mind**.

※

No. 52
To Kiyooka Kuninosuke and Shun[93]

28 April 1895

Dear Kuninosuke and O-Shun,[94]

Although it is only April, the weather is getting hotter. I am glad that you are well.

Regarding the cholera outbreak, I understand from your last letter that the situation at Hiroshima will not allow you to return to Tokyo until the middle of next month. This being the case, you must both resolve to be patient for a little longer, and just focus on protecting yourselves from infection. Just this morning, I saw Dr. Matsuyama and when our conversation came round to the cholera at Hiroshima, he also said that there was nothing to fear about cholera as long as one took the proper precautions. These are:

1. On no account drink fresh water. All the water that you use must first be boiled. This does not apply only to the water you drink. When you wash cups and anything that will go past your mouth, use water that has been boiled. There will even be a risk of infection if the cloths that you use to wipe things

have been washed in water.

2. Since cholera is not transmitted by the air but through the mouth, there is a risk if you put anything that is infected with the germs into your mouth by mistake.

3. Make sure that you prepare everything that you eat by yourselves, so that your food does not come into contact with anyone else's hands. For example, if Kuni-san went to Ujina and ordered a packed lunch, there would be a risk if the pickled vegetables had been washed in ordinary water. So even though this means extra work, O-Shun-san should send a lunch that she has made herself.

Please take all reasonable steps to protect yourselves on the basis of these guidelines.

In haste,

Yukichi

***

No. 53[95]
To Hattori Kane (Extracts)

After 3:00 p.m., 19 June 1897

Dear elder sister,

Your telegram of 7:00 a.m. arrived at 1:00 this afternoon, and your same of 9:40 arrived at 2:47. I have therefore received the news that our sister's condition worsened, and that she has finally left us. Since her illness was said to be serious from the start, I realized that there was probably no hope. I myself consulted various doctors, but none of them could suggest a likely treatment. Yesterday evening, when Dr. Matsuyama Tōan came here and discussed her condition with me, she had been in a coma since the 14th, and he could only say that nothing more could be done. Waiting for your telegrams in a vacant state, I lay down for an afternoon nap today, only to leap up when I heard that a telegram had arrived. It was your 7:00 a.m. telegram saying "Critical." "Is this it?" I thought to myself, unable to relax. Then your second telegram arrived saying

"Departed," and I felt as if all the strength had been taken from my body.

Last year, O-En became ill, and passed away on 22 January, all our worries being of no avail. Now, less than six months later, there has been a further tragic event, making 1897 into a year of unparalleled darkness. However, it is Heaven that decides whether humans live or die, so we are powerless against it. I have no religious belief, but I am resigned to the fact that life is short and do not fear death. All that concerns me is what happens after death. . . .

Both you and I belong to a family of five brothers and sisters who were born in Osaka and grew up as if they had no links with Nakatsu people. We were raised to adulthood by our mother, and not even once did we ever quarrel among each other. Of the five of us, three are now lost, leaving only the two of us facing each other. We feel bereft, but since this is the will of Heaven, all we can do is accept the situation. All I wish is for you to be able to live comfortably from now on. Thanks to the gifts I inherited from our ancestors and to the way our mother raised me, I have been able to work hard and have neither broken any moral rules nor attracted social opprobrium. I am financially well off, and my many children are not a financial burden, so my life is comfortable. Please let me look after you; I am completely at your disposal. Please do not hesitate to tell me what you need in order to live without any cares, since I will endeavor to care for you on behalf of our father and mother. . . .

*
* *

Appendix: Two Letters from Fukuzawa's Wife
Letter No. 1[96]

9 July 1887

Dear Ichitarō,

I am sorry not to write more frequently. First of all, I am glad to hear that you are keeping well. Please be assured that we are all well, too.

In your last letter [of 20 May 1887?], it seemed that you were in a state of high anxiety. I was extremely anxious as well, and we even wondered whether it might turn out to be a good idea for you to come back early, without waiting for your brother's return. This is still a possibility. In the following, my intention is to give you my private opinion regarding your father in confidence:

Your father is extremely busy in many ways. He seems very well, but he is no longer a young man, and it seems to me that any worries have a bad effect on his health. Our many children are not yet able to make a living independently, so that he is not in a position to relax in any way. Therefore I devote my efforts to seeing that even though he is still unable to reduce his actual workload, he will at least experience the minimum of mental stress. I do not ask you to perform any specific act of filial piety, but to try not to cause him any anxiety. Your previous letter was really a great cause of anxiety for your parents. We were shocked for a time, and waited for further news. I have aged a lot recently myself. I make lots of writing mistakes, so I made many attempts at this letter and frequently lost track of what I wanted to say. As a result, I twice lost the chance to send it and felt at my wit's end since what I really wanted was to actually have a face-to-face talk with you. Recently I have been busy every day, either with invitations to go out that cannot be turned down, or with guests to look after, so I had given up the idea of writing to you, and thought that I would just ask your father to send regards to you on my behalf. I have added this part without telling him. As I have mentioned before, you have promised to write to me about anything that is worrying you. Therefore, from now on please put such matters in a separate letter addressed to me, so that I can tell the details to your father myself.

In haste,

Mother

Letter No. 2[97]

November (?) 1889

Dear Sutejirō,

I hope that you are well even though it is gradually getting colder. To our great relief, O-Sato is on the mend, but her illness was so severe that her recovery will be slow. We cannot let our guard down yet, but have every hope that she will be able to start walking a little before the year is out.

O-Katsu is still with her parents, and has been away so long that we can no longer be silent about what is happening. When we spoke about it to someone, they said that her father is famous for his obstinacy and absolutely beyond persuasion. There is no point in trying to talk to him as he always insists on getting his own way. His daughter has been taught how to behave, but does not seem to know anything about the feelings that should underlie such behavior. Her lack of shame is beyond belief. However angry a wife might be, to leave her marital home without a word and return to her parents is the act of a woman with no sense of the virtues required of a wife. She had better remain where she is. Even if she returns to Ichitarō, I will have no peace of mind since she is not to be trusted. It is a good thing that she has gone back to her parents. But it's a disgraceful situation for her, so we have to be forgiving and wait patiently until everything is settled, however difficult this may be. Ichitarō seems to feel worried about the problems he is causing us, so he is not saying very much. Anyway, nothing good will come of this situation. I feel that we have been made utter fools of, and am so angry that I cannot sleep. Dr. and Mrs. Kondō have behaved like incompetent fools.

In haste,

Mother

Appendix
A Chronology of Japanese History, with Special Reference to Fukuzawa Yukichi and his Writings on Women and the Family

*Entries for Fukuzawa's private life are in italics; texts by Fukuzawa are in bold; the names in brackets are of women mentioned in the texts translated in this volume

1160	Heiji Rebellion (Tokiwa Gozen)
1180–1185	Genpei War between the Taira and the Minamoto (Tomoe Gozen, Shizuka Gozen, Akoya)
1193	The Soga brothers finally succeed in revenging their father's death (Tora Gozen, Shōshō)
1336–1573	Ashikaga (Muromachi) period
1467–1568	Civil war (*sengoku*) period, during which Japan has no stable central government
1568–1600	Closing stages of the struggle for complete control of Japan (Asahi-hime)
1568	Oda Nobunaga gains control of the main island
1590	Toyotomi Hideyoshi gains control over all Japan
1600	Victory for Tokugawa Ieyasu brings him complete control of Japan, heralding the start of the Tokugawa period.
1615	Hideyoshi's son is defeated in the siege of Osaka castle, securing the future of Tokugawa rule.
1635	The voluntary system of alternate attendance (whereby the daimyo spend every other year at their *han*, while their families live permanently at Edo) becomes compulsory.
1639	The process by which the Tokugawa regime gradually assumed control of contacts with the outside world is completed, and the period of self-imposed isolation (*sakoku*) begins.
1657	Establishment of Shin Yoshiwara as the licensed brothel area for Edo, because it was then distant from the administrative center of the city
1716	*Onna daigaku (The Great Learning for Women)*
1836	*Fukuzawa's father, Hyakusuke, dies; the family returns to Nakatsu.*
1856	*Fukuzawa's elder brother, Sannosuke, dies, and Fukuzawa becomes the head of the house.* *Fukuzawa begins to lodge with Ogata Kōan's family in Osaka.*

1858	*Fukuzawa opens an academy of Dutch learning on the secondary estate of Nakatsu-han in Edo. This is the beginning of the private educational institution that he names "Keiogijuku" in 1868.*
1859	The first "treaty ports" are opened to foreign trade as a result of the "unequal treaties" with various Western countries, ending Japan's self-imposed isolation. Regular examination of prostitutes for syphilis is gradually introduced, initially as a result of the desire of the Western powers to protect their nationals.
1860	*The first of Fukuzawa's three visits to Western countries*
1861	*Fukuzawa marries Kin.*
1863	*Ichitarō, the first of nine children, is born.*
1865	*Sutejirō, Fukuzawa's second son, is born.*
1868	The Meiji Restoration occurs. *Sato, Fukuzawa's third child and first daughter, is born.* **Seiyo jijō, gaihen (Conditions in the West, Supplementary Volume)**
1869	John Stuart Mill, *The Subjection of Women* The status divisions of Tokugawa Japan are abolished, with court nobles and former daimyo becoming *kazoku*, people of samurai lineage becoming *shizoku*, and farmers, artisans and merchants becoming *heimin*.
1870	*Fusa, the second daughter, is born.* *Fukuzawa returns to Nakatsu to bring his mother to live with his family in Tokyo.*
1871	**"Nakatsu ryūbetsu no sho" ("A Message of Farewell to Nakatsu")** The first Meiji Penal Code gives concubines equal status with wives. **"Hibi no oshie" ("Daily Lessons")**
1872	Introduction throughout Japan of the *koseki* system of registering people as members of a family with one member designated as household head
1872–76	**Gakumon no susume (An Encouragement of Learning)** (Fukuzawa's first public criticism of *The Great Learning* is in Section Thirteen, which appeared in 1874.)
1873	*Shun, the third daughter, is born.* The Meirokusha is formed; from 1874 to 1875 it carries out a famous debate on the position of women.
1875	Fukuzawa acts as a witness to Mori Arinori's wedding by contract. **Bunmeiron no gairyaku (An Outline of a Theory of Civilization)** **"Danjo dōsūron" ("The Equal Numbers of Men and Women")**
1876	A small school for girls is established on the second floor of Fukuzawa's house on the Keio compound, but the arrangement only lasts for sixteen months. *Taki, the fourth daughter, is born.*

1878	"Fukuzawa-shi kosen haibun no ki" ("Reasons for Sharing Some Old Coins with My Children")
1879	*Mitsu, the fifth daughter, is born.* "Joshi kyōiku no koto ni tsuki Bōshi ni kotau" ("An Answer to a Certain Gentleman's Inquiry about Female Education")
1880	The new penal code removes recognition for concubines.
1881	*Sanpachi, the third son, is born.* The government responds to the demands of the People's Rights Movement by promising to establish a National Diet in 1890.
1882	Fukuzawa begins his own newspaper, *Jiji shinpō*. Kishida Toshiko, a beautiful and well-educated young woman, speaks in favor of women's equality at public meetings of the People's Rights Movement, drawing national attention.
1883	*Fukuzawa's two eldest sons leave Japan for a period of study in the U.S. Daishirō, the fourth son and final child, is born.*
1885	"Nihon fujinron" ("On Japanese Women") *Jogaku zasshi* begins. Nihon fujinron kōhen (**On Japanese Women, Part Two**) Hinkōron (**On Moral Behavior**) Ueki Emori, "Haishōron" ("On Banning Licensed Prostitution") Iwamoto Yoshiharu, "Warera no shimai wa shōgi nari" ("Prostitutes Are Our Sisters")
1886	*Fukuzawa holds his first mixed gender social gathering, for female relatives of his acquaintances and bachelor Keio staff.* Danjo kōsairon (**On Relations between Men and Women**) Formation of the Tokyo branch of the Women's Christian Temperance Union
1887	*Three of Fukuzawa's daughters are enrolled in a Christian boarding school for girls, but he withdraws them after two months.* *Momosuke, whom Fukuzawa has just adopted as the future husband of his second eldest daughter, leaves for two years in the U.S.*
1888	Nihon danshiron (**On Japanese Men**) *Ichitarō and Sutejirō return from the U.S. via Europe.*
1889	Promulgation of the Meiji Constitution *Fukuzawa's eldest son marries but six months later the bride goes back to her family, leaving no message.*
1890	*A divorce is agreed, and Fukuzawa's eldest son remarries.* The government moves to restrict political activities by women. Formation of the first National Diet, with limited male suffrage for the Lower House
1896	*One of Fukuzawa's three elder sisters dies.*
1897	*A second elder sister dies.* Fukuō hyakuwa (**One Hundred Reflections by Fukuzawa**)

1898	Introduction of the Meiji Civil Code, after a long process of deliberation and revision ***Fukuō jiden*** (*The Autobiography of Fukuzawa Yukichi*) *In September, Fukuzawa suffers from his first stroke.*
1899	***Onna daigaku hyōron*** (*A Critique of* **The Great Learning for Women**) ***Shin onna daigaku*** (*A New Great Learning for Women*) The revised treaties come into force, bringing an end to extraterritoriality.
1901	*Fukuzawa suffers a second stroke, and dies.*

Further Reading

Anderson, Marnie S. *A Place in Public: Women's Rights in Meiji Japan*. Cambridge, Mass.: Harvard University Asia Center, 2011.

Bernstein, Gail E. et al, eds. *Public Spheres, Private Lives in Modern Japan, 1600–1950*. Cambridge, Mass.: Harvard University Asia Center, 2005.

Bernstein, Gail E. ed. *Recreating Japanese Women, 1600–1945*. Berkeley: University of California Press, 1991.

Blacker, Carmen. *The Japanese Enlightenment: A Study of the Writings of Fukuzawa Yukichi*. Cambridge: Cambridge University Press, 1964.

Copeland, Rebecca L. *Lost Leaves: Women Writers of Meiji Japan*. Honolulu: University of Hawai'i Press, 2000.

Craig, M. Albert. *Civilization and Enlightenment: The Early Thought of Fukuzawa Yukichi*. Cambridge, Mass: Harvard University Press, 2009.

De Becker, J. E. *The Nightless City: or the "History of the Yoshiwara Yūkwaku" by an English Student of Sociology*. Yokohama: Z. P. Maruya & co., 1899.

Fuess, Harald. *Divorce in Japan: Family, Gender, and the State, 1600–2000*. Stanford: Stanford University Press, 2004.

Galan, Christian and Lozerand, Emmanuel, eds. *La Famille Japonaise Moderne (1868–1926): Discours et Débats*. Arles: Éditions Philippe Picquier, 2011.

Ishimoto, Shizue. *Facing Two Ways: The Story of My Life*. With an introduction and afterword by Barbara Molony. Stanford: Stanford University Press, 1984.

Koyama, Shizuko. *Ryōsai kenbo: The Educational Ideal of 'Good Wife, Wise Mother' in Modern Japan*. Translated by Stephen Filler. Leiden: Brill, 2013.

Lublin, Elizabeth Dorn. *Reforming Japan: The Woman's Christian Temperance Union in the Meiji Period*. Honolulu: University of Hawai'i Press, 2010.

Meiroku zasshi: Journal of the Japanese Enlightenment. Translated and with an introduction by William Reynolds Braisted, assisted by Adachi Yasushi and Kikuchi Yūji. Tokyo: University of Tokyo Press, 1976.

Molony, Barbara and Uno, Kathleen, eds. *Gendering Modern Japanese History*. Cambridge, Mass.: Harvard University East Asia Center, 2005.

Patessio, Mara. *Women and Public Life in Early Meiji Japan: The Development of the Feminist Movement*. Ann Arbor: Center for Japanese Studies, University of Michigan, 2011.

Seigle, Cecilia Segawa. *Yoshiwara: The Glittering World of the Japanese Courtesan*. Honolulu: University of Hawai'i, 1993.

Sekiguchi, Sumiko. "Confucian Morals and the Making of a 'Good Wife and Wise Mother': From 'Between Husband and Wife there is Distinction' to 'As Husbands and Wives be Harmonious.'" *Social Science Japan Journal*, 13.1 (2010), pp. 95–113.

———. "Gender in the Meiji Renovation: Confucian 'Lessons for Women' and the Making of Modern Japan." *Social Science Japan Journal*, 11.2 (2008), pp. 201–221.

Sievers, Sharon. *Flowers in Salt: The Beginnings of Feminist Consciousness in Modern Japan*. Stanford: Stanford University Press, 1983.

Stanley, Amy. *Selling Women: Prostitution, Markets, and the Household in Early Modern Japan*. Berkeley: University of California Press, 2012.

Tomida, Hiroko and Daniels, Gordon, eds. *Japanese Women: Emerging from Subservience 1868–1945*. Folkestone: Global Oriental, 2005.

Tonomura, Hitomi et al, eds. *Women and Class in Japanese History*. Ann Arbor: Center for Japanese Studies, The University of Michigan, 1999.

Wakita, Haruko. *Women in Medieval Japan: Motherhood, Household, Management and Sexuality*. Translated by Alison Tokita. Victoria: Monash University Press, 2006.

Watanabe, Hiroshi. *A History of Japanese Political Thought, 1600–1901*. Translated by David Noble. Tokyo: International House of Japan, 2012.

Yamakawa, Kikue. *Women of the Mito Domain: Recollections of Samurai Family Life*. Translated and with an introduction by Kate Wildman Nakai. Tokyo: University of Tokyo Press, 1992.

Notes

General Introduction

1. See *Fukuzawa Yukichi on Japanese Women: Selected Works*, translated and edited by Eiichi Kiyooka, Tokyo: University of Tokyo Press, 1988, and *Fukuzawa Yukichi on Education: Selected Works*, translated and edited by Eiichi Kiyooka, Tokyo: University of Tokyo Press, 1985.

2. Some of them have previously appeared in Helen Ballhatchet, "Fukuzawa Yukichi as a Father: Translations of Letters Written to His Two Eldest Sons While They Were in the United States, 1883–1888," *The Hiyoshi Review of English Studies* 62, March, 2013, pp. 1–49.

3. *Danjo kōsairon* (*On Relations between Men and Women*), 1886, pp. 191–193 in this volume.

4. "Fukuzawa-sensei no jogakuron happyō no shidai" ("The Circumstances behind the Publication of Fukuzawa-sensei's Views on *The Great Learning for Women*"), 14 April 1899, translated on pp. 281–283 in this volume.

5. Letter No. 2, pp. 312–313 in this volume.

6. See *An Encouragement of Leaning*, revised translation by David A. Dilworth, *The Thought of Fukuzawa* 2, Tokyo: Keio University Press, 2012, pp. 62–63.

7. All are translated in this volume.

8. Because of its length compared to other primers, and from inspecting old copybooks (*tenaraichō*), Ishikawa Matsutarō suggests that it was used mainly for reading practice, and that only parts were copied. "Kanshū o oete: kanshū to *Onna daigaku takarabako* no shiteki kōsatsu o chūshin ni," p. 5, in Koizumi Yoshinaga ed., *Onna daigaku shiryō shūsei, bekkan*, Tokyo: Ōzorasha, 2006, pp. 1–9.

9. Kō Mideyon, "Kaibara Ekiken no joseikan" in *ibid.*, pp. 2–29; Koizumi Yoshinaga "*Onna daigaku* no sekai," also in *ibid.*, pp. 165–198.

10. Ishikawa Matsutarō, "Onna daigaku ni tsuite" in *Nihon shisō taikei* 34, *Kaibara Ekiken, Muro Kyūsō*, Tokyo: Iwanami shoten, 1970, pp. 531–545; "Onna daigaku kankei nenpyō" in Koizumi, *op. cit.*, pp. 113–122 (numbered from the back of the book).

11. I must thank Ken Sugiyama for helping me to read this.

12. For example, see Yokota Fuyuhiko, "Imagining Working Women in Early Modern Japan" in Hitomi Tonomura et al, eds., *Women and Class in Japanese History*, Ann Arbor: Center for Japanese Studies, University of Michigan, 1999, pp. 153–167; Martha C.

Tocco, "Norms and Texts for Women's Education in Tokugawa Japan" in Dorothy Ko et al, eds., *Women and Confucian Cultures in Premodern China, Korea, and Japan*, Berkeley: University of California Press, 2003, pp. 193–218.

13. On this, see Yamakawa Kikue, *Women of the Mito Domain: Recollections of Samurai Family Life*, translated and with an introduction by Kate Wildman Nakai, Tokyo: University of Tokyo Press, 1992, p. 106.

14. *Go-isshin to jendā: Ogyū Sorai kara kyōiku chokugo made*, Tokyo: Tokyo Daigaku shuppankai, 2005, pp. 11–190 passim. For a shortened English-language version, see "Gender in the Meiji Renovation: Confucian 'Lessons for Women' and the Making of Modern Japan," *Social Science Japan Journal* 11.2 (2008), pp. 201–221.

15. For an example of the former, see Anne Walthall, *The Weak Body of a Useless Woman: Matsuo Taseko and the Meiji Restoration*, Chicago, Ill: University of Chicago Press, 1998. For an example of the latter, see Joyce Chapman Lebra, "Women in an All-Male Industry: The Case of Sake Brewer Tatsu'uma Kiyo," in Gail Lee Bernstein ed., *Recreating Japanese Women, 1600–1945*, Berkeley: University of California Press, 1991, pp. 131–148.

16. Yamakawa, pp. 15–19, 30–31, 58, 102.

17. *On Japanese Women, Part Two*, pp. 117–120 in this volume.

18. "On Japanese women," pp. 77–78 in this volume.

19. Ōta Motoko, *Edo no oyako: chichioya ga kodomo o sodateta jidai*, Tokyo: Chūō kōronsha, 1984, pp. 164–167; Muta Kazue, *Senryaku to shite no kazoku*, Tokyo: Shin'yōsha, 1996, p. 125; Koyama Shizuko, *Ryōsai Kenbo: The Educational Ideal of "Good Wife, Wise Mother" in Modern Japan*, translated by Stephen Filler, Leiden: Brill, 2012, pp. 12–21.

20. Ōta Motoko, *Kinsei no "ie" to kazoku: kosodate o meguru shakaishi*, Tokyo: Kadokawa Gakuen shuppan, 2011, pp. 57–67.

21. *Ibid.*, pp. 84–120, and *Edo no oyako*, pp. 140–142, 231–232.

22. Yamakawa, *op.cit.*, pp. 24, 27–29, 31–34.

23. *Ibid.*, p. 142.

24. *Ibid.*, pp. 91–93, 104–106, 142–143.

25. *Kokumin dōtoku to jendā: Fukuzawa Yukichi, Inoue Tetsujirō, Watsuji Tetsurō*, Tokyo: Tokyo Daigaku shuppankai, 2007, pp. 10–11.

26. "Fukuzawa-shi kosen haibun no ki" ("Reasons for Sharing Some Old Coins with My Children"), on pp. 299–303 in this volume.

27. For Fukuzawa's memories of this time, see *The Autobiography of Yukichi Fukuzawa*, revised translation by Eiichi Kiyooka, with a foreword by Albert M. Craig, New York: Columbia University Press, 2007, pp. 51–52. In developing this idea, I benefitted from discussions with Sekiguchi Sumiko.

28. Yamakawa, *op.cit.*, pp. 106, 107–109.

29. This is my translation of the Japanese text in *Fukuzawa Yukichi-shū, Shin Nihon kotenbungaku taikei, Meiji-hen 10*, Tokyo: Iwanami shoten, 2011, pp. 346–347 (annotated by Matsuzawa Hiroaki). See also the extended footnote on p. 455. The relevant pages in Kiyooka's revised translation, *op.cit.*, are pp. 305–306.

30. *Op.cit.*, pp. 96–97.

31. Nishizawa Naoko, *Fukuzawa Yukichi to josei*, Tokyo: Keiogijuku Daigaku shuppankai,

2011, p. 51; "Tokubetsu taidan: Fudangi no Yukichi to Eigo kyōiku," p. 11, *Kotoba no uchū* 1.5, Oct. 1966, pp. 5–24 (an interview of Shidachi Taki by Maruyama Masao).

32. Yamakawa, *op.cit.*, p. 109; *On Moral Behavior*, pp. 152–157, 167 in this volume.

33. See Constantine N. Vaporis, *Tour of Duty: Samurai, Military Service in Edo, and the Culture of Early Modern Japan*, Honolulu: University of Hawai'i Press, 2008, esp. pp. 174–175, 197. For English language works on the Yoshiwara and on prostitution in general in Tokugawa Japan, see, for example, Cecilia Segawa Seigle, *Yoshiwara: The Glittering World of the Japanese Courtesan*, Honolulu: University of Hawai'i Press, 1993, and Amy Stanley, *Selling Women: Prostitution, Markets, and the Household in Early Modern Japan*, Berkeley: University of California Press, 2012.

34. For Fukuzawa's memories of these trips, see *The Autobiography*, pp. 104–120, 125–140 and 166–174. For an analysis of his intellectual journey during the 1860s, see Matsuzawa Hiroaki, *Kindai Nihon no keisei to Seiyō keiken*, Tokyo: Iwanami shoten, 1993, pp. 185–228.

35. See Masao Miyoshi, *As We Saw Them: The First Japanese Embassy to the United States (1860)*, Berkeley: University of California Press, 1979, pp. 70–76. Fukuzawa, *op.cit.*, pp. 114, 120.

36. Nishizawa, *op.cit.*, pp. 6–7; Fukuzawa Yukichi, *Seikō techō bessatsu*, deciphered and annotated by Tomita Masafumi and Nagao Masafumi, Tokyo: Fukuzawa Yukichi Kyōkai, 1984, pp. 140–141.

37. For the House of Commons reference to the report, see "Parliamentary Intelligence," *The Times*, 3 May 1862 and "Captain Jackson's Report," *Morning Post*, 3 May 1862. For the letter, from "A Veteran," see "The Soldier in Time of Peace," *Daily News*, 2 May 1862. The visit to Aldershot took place on 23 May and was reported in *The Times*, 26 May 1862, under the headline "The Japanese Mission." The last of these can be found on pp. 190–187 of "Articles on Bun Ken-ō Shisetsu in the *Times* and the *Morning Post*," *Kindai Nihon kenkyū* 1, 1964, pp. 216–163.

38. See *On Moral Behavior*, pp. 152–153, 163 in this volume.

39. In fact, Craig has shown that the whole volume was a translation either from John Burton's *Political Economy, for Use in Schools, and for Private Instruction* (Edinburgh: William and Robert Chambers, 1852) or from other books. See Albert M. Craig, *Civilization and Enlightenment: The Early Thought of Fukuzawa Yukichi*, Cambridge, Mass.: Harvard University Press, 2009, pp. 58–81.

40. Burton, *op.cit.*, pp. 2–3; Fukuzawa, *Seiyō jijō*, *Fukuzawa Yukichi chosakushū* 1, Tokyo: Keiogijuku Daigaku shuppankai, 2002, p. 36. See also the analyses in Nishizawa, *op.cit.*, pp. 7–9; and Sekiguchi, *Kokumin dōtoku*, pp. 7–13.

41. James Vernon examines how rapid population growth, urbanization, and increased mobility led to "the emergence of the modern world" through a case study of Britain in *Distant Strangers: How Britain Became Modern*, Berkeley: University of California Press, 2014. For the effect on family life, see pp. 44–50.

42. *Kindai tennōsei to kokumin kokka*, Tokyo: Aoki shoten, 2005, pp. 66–68.

43. This and the following two tables are based on the table in Nishizawa Naoko, "Fukuzawa Yukichi no joseiron, kazokuron," p. 55, in Komuro Masamichi, ed., *Kindai*

Nihon to Fukuzawa Yukichi, Tokyo: Keiogijuku Daigaku shuppankai, 2013, pp. 47–67. Works included in this volume are in bold type.

44. See pp. 63–68 in this volume.

45. See Francis Wayland's *The Elements of Moral Science*, Boston: Gould and Lincoln, 1865, p. 296. (For the general influence of Wayland on Fukuzawa, see Craig, *op. cit.*, p. 29.) Sekiguchi Sumiko suggests Rutherford Alcock as Fukuzawa's source (*Go-isshin*, pp. 268–269). Alcock refers to this idea in *The Capital of the Tycoon: A Narrative of Three Years' Residence in Japan* 2, London: Longman, Green, Longman, Roberts, & Green, 1863, pp. 251–252. He even suggests that violating this "law of nature" will obstruct a nation's advance towards higher levels of civilization. However, Fukuzawa is known to have drawn widely from Wayland's *Moral Science*, so it is a more likely source.

46. Ōtake Hideo, *"Ie" to josei no rekishi*, Tokyo: Kōbundō, 1977, pp. 247–248. Kanazu Hidemi has suggested that in the 1871 Penal Code, the government used "concubine" to refer not only to the mistresses of the elite, but also to the "common law" spouses of ordinary people, as a step towards the standardization of marriage customs. See "Meiji shonen no 'mekake' rongi no saikentō: 'Kindaiteki ippu ippusei' ron o megutte," pp. 242–246, in Nagahara Kazuko, ed., *Nihon kazokushi ronshū* 5, *Kazoku no shosō*, Tokyo: Yoshikawa kōbunkan, 2002, pp. 236–270; cited in Marion Saucier, "Le débat sur le Couple dans la *Revue de l'an 6 de l'ère Meiji*," p. 359, in Christian Galan and Emmanuel Lozerand, eds., *La Famille Japonaise Moderne (1868–1926): Discours et Débats*, Arles: Éditions Philippe Picquier, 2011, pp. 347–360.

47. See, for example, Fukuzawa Yukichi, *An Outline of a Theory of Civilization*, The Thought of Fukuzawa 1, revised translation by David A. Dilworth and G. Cameron Hurst, III, Tokyo: Keio University Press, 2008, pp. 17–26.

48 *Op.cit.*, pp. 62–66, 96–97, 110.

49. Fukuzawa possessed an 1870 American edition of the work, published by D. Appleton and Co., New York, and had marked important points with pieces of red paper. For an analysis of these parts, see Anzai Toshimitsu, *Fukuzawa Yukichi to jiyūshugi: kojin, jichi, kokutai*, Tokyo: Keiogijuku Daigaku shuppankai, pp. 1–25.

50. "On Wives and Concubines," Parts 1–5, Issues Eight (May 1874); Eleven (June 1874); Fifteen (Aug. 1874); Twenty (Nov. 1874); Twenty-Seven (Feb. 1875), Meiroku zasshi: *Journal of the Japanese Enlightenment*, translated and with an introduction by William Reynolds Braisted, Tokyo: University of Tokyo Press, 1976, pp. 104–106, 143–145, 189–191, 252–253, 331–333.

51. At least two other ex-samurai with experience in the United States also chose this form of marriage at around the same time. See Hayakawa Kiyo "Bunmei kaika no naka no dansei josei, kazoku katei," p. 59 in Abe Tsunehisa et al, ed. *Danseishi* 1, *Otokotachi no kindai*, Tokyo: Nihon keizai hyōronsha, 2006, pp. 47–76. Unfortunately, Mori's marriage to Hirose Tsune ended in a mutually agreed divorce eleven years later. The standard English-language biography for Mori is Ivan Hall, *Mori Arinori*, Cambridge, Mass.: Harvard University Press, 1973.

52. "The Distinction between Husbands and Wives," Issue Twenty-Two (Dec. 1874); "On Destroying Prostitution," Issue Forty-Two (Oct. 1875), Meiroku zasshi, pp. 277–

279, 517–518.

53. "On Concubines," Issue Thirty-Two (March 1875), *op.cit.*, pp. 392–399.

54. "The Equal Numbers of Men and Women," Issue Thirty-One (March 1875), *op.cit.*, pp. 385–386.

55 "Meiji keimōki no mekake rongi to haishō no jitsugen," *Kikan Nihon shisōshi* 26, 1986, pp. 48–68. Also see Hayakawa, *op.cit.*, pp. 42–65. For letters written by women to popular newspapers (*koshinbun*) in the 1870s, see Hirata Yumi, *Josei hyōgen no Meiji shi: Higuchi Ichiyō izen*, Tokyo: Iwanami shoten, 2011.

56. Koyama, *op. cit.*, pp. 59–64.

57. See pp. 225–226, 236 in this volume.

58. See Kaneko Sachiko, *Kindai Nihon joseiron no keifu*, Tokyo: Fuji shuppan, 1999, pp. 23–43.

59. In particular, see Katō Hiroyuki, "Abuses of Equal Rights for Men and Women" Parts One and Two, Issue Thirty One (March 1875) Meiroku zasshi, pp. 376–377, 377–379. For the imprecise nature of "*dōken*," see Marnie S. Anderson, *A Place in Public: Women's Rights in Meiji Japan*, Cambridge, Mass.: Harvard University Asia Center, 2010, pp. 56–99. For the concept of "rights" in general, see Douglas R. Howland, *Translating the West: Language and Political Reason in Nineteenth-Century Japan*, Honolulu: University of Hawai'i Press, 2002, pp. 122–152.

60. "Creating Good Mothers," Issue Thirty-Three (March 1875), *ibid.*, pp. 401–404.

61. Nishizawa Naoko provides evidence that he considered setting up a girls' school at the Keio Mita compound in the late 1880's, but nothing came of it. See *Fukuzawa Yukichi to furī rabu*, Tokyo: Keiogijuku Daigaku shuppankai, 2014, p. 174.

62. There seems to have been widespread anxiety around this time that the government system of education was also failing in this area. Fukaya Masashi, *Zōho Ryōsaikenboshugi no kyōiku*, Nagoya: Reimei shobō, 1981, pp. 78–86.

63. P. 365 in this volume; Nishizawa, *op.cit.*, pp. 171–175.

64. Koizumi ed., *Onna daigaku shiryō shūsei* 5, pp. 3–108.

65. *Ibid.*, vol. 5, pp. 203–300.

66. *Ibid*, vol. 7., pp. 3–134. Doi's versions of *The Great Learning for Women* are widely cited, for example by Koyama, Ryōsai Kenbo, pp. 26–29. For information about him, see Hasegawa Ken'ichi, "Minken undōka to chiiki keimō: Doi Kōka no shisō to kōdō, in Kano Masanao and Takagi Shunsuke, eds., *Ishin henkaku ni okeru zaisonteki shochōryū*, Tokyo: San'ichi shobō, 1972, pp. 382–433.

67. For books, see the catalogue in Meiji bunka kenkyūkai ed., *Meiji bunka zenshū* 16, *Fujin mondai-hen*, 2nd edn, Tokyo: Nihon Hyōronsha, 1968, pp. 405–412. This gives 3 works in 1885, rising to 10 in 1886, and a peak of 15 in 1887. From the next year there were 3 to 8 annually until 1901, when the peak of 15 was reached again. For articles in general-interest magazines, see the analysis in Muta Kazue, *Senryaku to shite no kazoku: Kindai Nihon no kokumin kokka keisei to josei*, Tokyo: Shin'yōsha, 1996, pp. 51–77. With regard to interest in newspapers, see "Hakkō no shushi" p. 4, *Jogaku zasshi* no.1, 20 July 1885, pp. 3–4.

68. On this topic, see, for example, Anderson, *op.cit.*, pp. 100–141.

69. Nishizawa, *Fukuzawa Yukichi to josei*, p. 80.

70. See pp. 135–137 of this volume.

71. For *Jogaku zasshi*, see Nobe Kiyoe, *Josei kaihō shisō no genryū: Iwamoto Yoshiharu to Jogaku zasshi*, Tokyo: Azekura shobō, 1984. For the temperance movement see, in English, Elizabeth Dorn Lublin, *Reforming Japan: The Woman's Christian Temperance Movement in the Meiji Period*, Honolulu: University of Hawai'i Press, 2010.

72. Note to Itō Hirobumi, 14 April 1887, in *Fukuzawa Yukichi shokanshū* 5, Tokyo: Iwanami shoten, 2001, p. 183. This was pointed out to me by Professor Nishizawa Naoko.

73. See "Kokkai nankyoku no yurai," 1892, *Fukuzawa Yukichi zenshū* 6, 2nd edn, Tokyo: Iwanami shoten, 1970, pp. 71–95. For an English-language analysis of the effect of the Rokumeikan activities on the image of women in Japan, see Margaret Mehl, "Dancing at the Rokumeikan: A New Role for Women?," in Hiroko Tomida and Gordon Daniels, eds., *Japanese Women: Emerging from Subservience, 1868–1945*, Folkestone: Global Oriental, 2005, pp. 157–177.

74. All the works from *Jiji shinpō* attributed to Fukuzawa in this volume are definitely by him. It has been suggested that Fukuzawa did not actually write all the *Jiji shinpō* articles that were included in the posthumous second and third versions of his collected works. However, Nishizawa Naoko suggests that even if handwritten manuscripts do not survive, all the leading articles (*shasetsu*) of 1883–1886 are by him, or closely follow his views, because he was directly in charge of the newspaper during this time. See *Fukuzawa Yukichi to josei*, pp. 113–114.

75. Hayakawa, *op.cit.*, pp. 68–70.

76. Nishizawa, *op.cit.*, pp. 83–92; *On Japanese Women, Part Two*, pp. 121–122 in this volume.

77. Fukaya, *op.cit.*, pp. 79–85.

78. On this, see Kaneko, *op.cit.*, p. 78.

79. Nishizawa, *op.cit.*, p. 134.

80. It is perhaps worth noting that "Nihon fujinron" was a popular title around this time. It was used for a leading article in *Kokumin no tomo* and a book by Ueda Sutekichi, both in 1887, and for another book, by Hata Ryōtarō, in 1890.

81. Nishizawa, *op.cit.*, pp. 110–111, 124–128, and *Fukuzawa Yukichi to furī rabu*, pp. 154–159.

82. Nishizawa, *Fukuzawa Yukichi to furī rabu*, p. 91.

83. *Jiji shinpō*, 8 and 18 Oct., 1883, *Fukuzawa Yukichi zenshū* 9, 2nd edn, Tokyo: Iwanami shoten, 1970, pp. 207–223.

84. "Gakkō shikin no uchi ni geishōgi no kifu o uku bekarazaru no ron," *Fukuzawa Yukichi zenshū* 19, 2nd edn, Tokyo: Iwanami shoten, 1971, pp. 588–589 (originally published in *Katei sōdan* no. 18, 4 Nov. 1876). Cited in Sekiguchi Sumiko, *Go-isshin*, p. 272.

85. Sekiguchi calls these texts "two sides of the same coin." See *Go-isshin*, p. 282.

86. Komuro Masamichi with Matsuzaki Kin'ichi, *Bannen no Fukuzawa Yukichi: Fukuzawa Yukichi ni miru Nisshinsengo no sejō to "rōgo no hannō"*, Tokyo: Keiogijuku keizai gakkai, 2005.

87. Koizumi ed., *Onna daigaku shiryō shūsei* 9, pp. 3–166.

88. For the development of women's education in this period, see Fukaya, *op.cit.*, pp. 138–188. On *ryōsai kenbo*, also see Koyama, *Ryōsai Kenbo: The Educational Ideal*.

89. For example, see "Rinri kyōkasho o yomu" *Jiji shinpō*, 18 March, 1890, in *Fukuzawa Yukichi zenshū* 12, 2nd edn, Tokyo: Iwanami shoten, 1970, pp. 397–400.

90. In *Kokumin dōtoku,* pp. 112–120, Sekiguchi Sumiko compares Inoue's commentary with Fukuzawa's views on morality.

91. Inoue Tetsujirō and Takayama Rinjirō, *Shinpen rinri kyōkasho* 2, Tokyo: Kinkōdō, 1897, pp. 5, 8, 27–32.

92. Komuro, *op.cit.*, pp. 20–21. *One Hundred Reflections* is available in *Fukuzawa Yukichi chosakushū* 11. The essays referred to in this paragraph and the next two can be found on pp. 53–80, 90–95, 117–126.

93. See p. 108 in this volume.

94. They have been translated by Kiyooka under the title "Fukuzawa Sensei's Random Talks on Men, Women and Society" in *Fukuzawa Yukichi on Japanese Women: Selected Works*, pp. 138–157.

95. It is not surprising that this view has been criticized, for example by Bill Mihalopolous, *Sex in Japan's Globalization: Prostitutes, Emigration and Nation-Building*, London: Pickering & Chatto, 2011, pp. 83–104. On the other hand, Mihalopolous relies heavily on Kiyooka's translations, and is misled by an unfortunate error in the original version of *On Moral Behavior*. See *ibid.*, p. 90 and pp. 162, 402 (note 21) in this volume.

96. See pp. 222–226 in this volume.

97. See pp. 240, 282 in this volume.

98. This is my translation. The relevant page in Kiyooka's revised translation of *The Autobiography* is 336.

99. See Nishizawa, *Fukuzawa Yukichi to josei*, pp. 32, 212–213.

100. For example, see *ibid.*, pp. 41–55.

101. Less than ten years after his death, a critic of his view of *The Great Learning* was already snidely remarking that even members of his own family were not following his teachings. Two of his daughters had not remarried after being widowed and were looking after their respective mothers-in-law, while another had not divorced despite rumors about her husband's behavior. See Miwada Motomichi in Tōa Kyōkai ed., *Onna daigaku no kenkyū*, Tokyo: Kōdōkan, 1910, pp. 26–27; cited in Nishizawa, *op.cit*, pp. 246–247.

102. *The Autobiography*, pp. 1–6; "Reasons for Sharing Some Old Coins," pp. 299–303 in this volume.

103. *The Autobiography*, pp. 1–15 passim. For Nishizawa's interpretation, see *op.cit.*, pp. 41–44.

104. Letter No. 53, pp. 369–370 in this volume.

105. Letter No. 1 (pp. 310–312) shows that he had difficulty in doing so because at least one sister wanted him to return to Nakatsu instead. The fact that his mother and sisters in Nakatsu were reluctant to obey his wishes suggests that they had little respect

for his position as family head, perhaps because he had always been the youngest.

106. See Letters Nos. 34, 46, 53 in this volume (pp. 348, 363–364, 369–370).

107. Nishizawa, *op.cit.*, pp. 53–55.

108. Kiyooka Eiichi, "Haha no mukashibanashi," pp. 99, 100–101 in Fukuzawa-sensei kenkyūkai, ed., *Chichi Yukichi o kataru*, Tokyo: Keio tsūshin, 1958, pp. 73–140; "Kodomo to mago ga katatta Yukichi," pp. 13, 84, in Nishikawa Shunsaku and Nishizawa Naoko, eds., *Fudangi no Fukuzawa Yukichi*, Tokyo: Keiogijuku Daigaku shuppankai, 1998, pp. 3–89; Nishizawa Naoko, "Kaisetsu: Yukichi, Kin fusai to sono kodomotachi," p. 92, in *ibid.*, pp. 90–97.

109. For example, see *On Japanese Women, Part Two*, pp. 128–129, 130 in this volume.

110. See pp. 370–371.

111. "Kodomo to mago ga katatta Yukichi," *op.cit.*, pp. 12, 33; "Tokubetsu taidan: Fudangi no Yukichi to Eigo Kyōiku," *op.cit.*, pp. 9, 12.

112. Fukuzawa Daishirō, *Chichi, Fukuzawa Yukichi*, Tokyo: Tokyo shobō, 1959, pp. 32–33, 146; Nishizawa Naoko, "Kaisetsu," p. 94; "Kodomo to mago ga katatta Yukichi," p. 35. For Taki's view, see also "Tokubetsu taidan," pp. 17–18.

113. Koizumi Shinzō, "Fukuzawa Yukichi shokan," p. 162, in *Dokusho zakki*, Tokyo: Bungei shunju shinsha, 1948, pp. 141–168.

114. Nakamura Sen'ichirō, *Kikikaki: Fukuzawa Yukichi no omoide, chōjo Sato ga katatta, chichi no ichimen*, Nakamura Fumio, ed., Tokyo: Kindai bungeisha, 2006, pp. 19–21; "Kodomo to mago ga katatta Yukichi," pp. 4–5.

115. See *The Autobiography*, pp. 297–304, and letters such as Nos. 10, 37 and 38 (pp. 321–322, 351–353). However, in *Fukuzawa Yukichi to furī rabu*, Nishizawa points out that in the autobiography Fukuzawa was probably painting a picture of his ideal family for didactic purposes, rather than meaning to give a realistic account. See *op.cit.*, p. 61.

116. For example, see Letters Nos. 4 and 7 (pp. 315, 318). See also "Fukuzawa Yukichi shijo no den," *Fukuzawa Yukichi zenshū bekkan*, Tokyo: Iwanami shoten, 1971, pp. 121–136. This gives details of the early years of his first six children, particularly the two eldest (and the stillbirths). It also contains details of the child-rearing methods that he was trying to practice at the time.

117. For example, see pp. 289, 294 in this volume.

118. "Tokubetsu taidan," p. 6; "Kodomo to mago ga katatta Yukichi," p. 20; "Monkasei ga kataru Fukuzawa Yukichi", p. 106, in *Fudangi no Fukuzawa Yukichi*, 101–209; Kiyooka, "Haha no mukashibanashi," pp. 87–88; *Chichi Fukuzawa Yukichi*, p. 4. See also Letter No. 10, pp. 321–322 of this volume.

119. *The Autobiography*, pp. 299–301; Nakamura, *Kikikaki*, p. 19; *Chichi Fukuzawa Yukichi*, p. 59. For more about Daishirō's adoption, see Marion Saucier, "Lettres d'un père à ses fils," pp. 483–484, in Christian Galan and Emmanuel Lozerand eds., *op.cit.*, pp. 473–485.

120. See Koizumi Shinzō, "Kaidai," in Fukuzawa Yukichi, *Aiji e no tegami*, Iwanami shoten: 1953, pp. 221–222.

121. See, for example, Letters Nos. 4, 7, 8, 12, 14 (pp. 314–316, 318, 319, 324, 325–327).

122. *Fukuzawa Yukichi to josei*, pp. 159–163; see footnote 44, Carmen Blacker, *The*

Japanese Enlightenment: A Study of the Writings of Fukuzawa Yukichi, Cambridge: Cambridge University Press, 1969, pp. 157–158; "Kodomo to mago ga katatta Yukichi," pp. 81–82, 84.

123. "Yaso kyōkai jogakkō no kyōiku o hihan su," July 29, 30, 1887, *Fukuzawa Yukichi zenshū* 11, 2nd edn, Tokyo: Iwanami shoten, 1970, pp. 318–323.

124. "Tokubetsu taidan," pp. 13, 16.

125. "Kodomo to mago ga katatta Yukichi," pp. 81–82, 84; *Fukuzawa Yukichi to josei*, pp. 162–167.

126. "Tokubetsu taidan," pp. 12–13, 16. Taki's analysis of her mother's personality seems to be confirmed by the letter translated on pp. 371–372, in which Kin gives vent to the frustration that she is feeling as a result of Ichitarō's problems with his first wife.

127. Sekiguchi Sumiko uses the evidence from Taki's Maruyama interview to suggest that there was something fundamentally wrong with the family (*Kokumin dōtoku*, p. 149). This is certainly one possible interpretation, but the various reminiscences of the children, both direct and indirect, show that they had many happy memories, even if they were being silent about less happy ones.

128. In his analysis of Fukuzawa's autobiography, Matsuzawa Hiroaki has demonstrated that its centralizing theme was his attaining, and retention of, independence ("Kaisetsu: Jiden no 'shizō': dokuritsu to iu monogatari," in *Fukuzawa Yukichi-shū*, pp. 501–506).

129. See, for example, Letters Nos. 7, 9, 11, 20, 25, 32 (pp. 318, 319–321, 322–324, 334–335, 338–339, 345–347).

130. Letter No. 29, p. 343.

131. Letters Nos. 9 and 11 (pp. 321, 323).

132. For example, see Letters Nos. 3 and 29 (pp. 313–314, 343).

133. *Chichi, Fukuzawa Yukichi*, pp. 16–18, 122, 130; "Kodomo to mago ga katatta Yukichi," p. 10.

134. "Monkasei ga kataru Fukuzawa Yukichi," pp. 115, 119, 127; "Kodomo to mago ga katatta Yukichi," pp. 5–6; *Chichi, Fukuzawa Yukichi*, pp. 110–111.

135. *The Thought of Fukuzawa* 1, pp. 149–154.

136. See pp. 81, 101 in this volume.

137. On this topic see, for example, Maruyama Masao, "Fukuzawa Yukichi no Jukyō hihan" in *Senchū to sengo no aida, 1936–1957*, Tokyo: Misuzu shobō, 1976, pp. 93–115; Komuro Masamichi, "Edo no shisō to Fukuzawa Yukichi," *Fukuzawa Yukichi nenkan* 32 (2005), pp. 131–142; and Watanabe Hiroshi, "Jukyō to Fukuzawa Yukichi," *ibid.* 39 (2012), pp. 91–116.

138. This translation is based on James Legge, *The Chinese Classics* 3.2, London: Trübner & Co., 1865, p. 283, but I have removed the implicit gender bias by substituting "man"/"men" with "humans"/"them."

139. Examples of the use of quotations from the Chinese classics to support a point can be found in *On Japanese Women, Part Two*, p. 128 (*Analects* 13.18), and *On Moral Behavior*, p. 158 (*Mencius* Book V, Part B.1). On this issue, see also Sekiguchi, *Kokumin no dōtoku*, pp. 14–30.

140. See Watanabe Hiroshi, "'Fūfu betsu ari' to 'Fūfu aiwa shi,'" *Chūgoku – shakai to bunka* 15, 2000, pp. 208–253, especially 211–213, referred to in Sekiguchi Sumiko,

"Confucian Morals and the Making of 'a Good Wife and Wise Mother': From 'between Husband and Wife there is distinction' to 'as Husbands and Wives Be Harmonious,'" p. 99, *Social Science Japan Journal* 13.1 (2010), pp. 95–113.

141. See p. 64 in this volume.

142. See Watanabe, *op.cit.*, and also Tsuda Mamichi "The Distinction between Husbands and Wives" Issue Twenty-Two (Dec. 1874), *Meiroku zasshi*, pp. 277–279.

143. See pp. 186–187, 195–197 in this volume.

144. See pp. 148–149 in this volume.

145. *On Japanese Women, Part Two*, pp. 109–110.

146. *Op.cit.*, pp. 65–66.

147. "Joshi to Yasokyō" part 1, *Jogaku zasshi*, no. 36, 25 Sept. 1886, pp. 101–105; part 2, no. 38, 15 Oct., pp. 141–143.

148. "*Jiji shinpō* no shōgiron," *ibid.*, no. 10, 8 Dec. 1885, pp. 183–185.

149. Nishizawa, *op.cit.*, pp. 119–120.

150. "Danjo kōsairon," *Jogaku zasshi*, no. 26, June 15, 1886, pp. 232–233.

151. "Joshi to Yasokyō" part 1, *ibid.*, no. 36, 25 Sept. 1886, pp. 101–105. See also the cautious response of "Matsuya shujin" in *Yomiuri shinbun*: "Danjo no kōsai ni kiritsu o mōku beshi," (8 Feb. 1887) and "Danjo no kōsai to shite heigai nakarashimu beshi," (11 May 1887) and "Danjo kōsairon" part 3, *Jogaku zasshi*, no. 104, 16 June 1888, pp. 75–80. For other examples of disapproval, see Nishizawa, *op.cit.*, p. 234.

152. See "Onna daigaku no ron," *Asahi shinbun*, 9 April, 1899 and the review of press responses in *Jogaku zasshi*: "Jogakuron no arasoi," no. 487, 14 May, 1899, pp. 327–330.

153. "Danjo kōsai," no. 491, 10 July 1899, pp. 447–449; "*Shin onna daigaku* no hyō," no. 494, 25 Aug., 1899, pp. 580–581.

154. "Saigo no kessen," 15 May 1900; "Kyōto-fu jogakkō no *Shin onna daigaku* kinshi," 3 June 1900. See also Sekiguchi, *Kokumin no dōtoku*, p. 145 and Nishizawa, *op.cit.*, pp. 213–229. Nishizawa suggests that the principal was influenced by Inoue Tetsujirō, who thought that Fukuzawa's emphasis on "independence and self respect" (*dokuritsu jison*) was incompatible with the Imperial Rescript on Education and its focus on loyalty to the Emperor.

155. Nishizawa, *op.cit.*, p. 232; also see Sekiguchi, *Kanno Sugako saikō: Fujin Kyōfūkai kara daigyaku jiken made*, Tokyo: Hakutakusha, 2014, pp. 135, 165.

156. Tōa Kyōkai, ed., *op.cit.*, pp. 3–52, 80–126. See also the comments in Nishizawa, *op.cit.*, p. 224, 226–229.

157. *Shinchū onna daigaku*, rev. edn., Kyoto: Jinsei dōjō, 1943, in *Onna daigaku shiryō shūsei* 18, cited in Sugano Noriko, "*Onna daigaku kō*" in Koizumi, *op.cit.*, pp. 78–95. Ten years after that, Nakagawa Zennosuke's *Onna daigaku hihan* drew on Fukuzawa again, but the purpose was to affirm his message in what the author hoped would be the final blow to *The Great Learning*. See *Onna daigaku shiryō shūsei* 20, especially pp. 72–73, 136–137 (originally published 1952).

158. Tokyo: Dōbunkan, 1911, pp. 374–422 *passim*; cited in Nishizawa, *op.cit.*, pp. 121–122.

159. "Ko to mago ga katatta Yukichi," p. 35.

160. See *Fukuzawa Yukichi zenshū* 21, 2nd edn, Tokyo: Iwanami shoten, 1971, pp. 378–379, and *Fukuzawa-sensei aitō-roku*, Tokyo: Misuzu shobō, 1987 (originally printed 1901), pp. 78, 98, 99, 296–297; both cited in Kano Masanao, "Kaisetsu," p. 316, *Fukuzawa Yukichi senshū* 9, Tokyo: Iwanami shoten, 1981, pp. 311–334.

161. Kyōfūko, "Fukuzawa-sensei no shi o itami nozomi o *Fujo shinbun* ni yosu," no. 41, 18 Feb. 1901, in *Fukuzawa-sensei aitō-roku*, p. 296–297. See also the letters of condolence from "A Woman of Mita" and "A Merchant Woman of Utsunomiya" translated in Miyamori Asatarō, *A Life of Mr. Yukichi Fukuzawa*, Tokyo: Z. P. Maruya, 1902, pp. 138–139, cited by Mikiso Hane, "Fukuzawa Yukichi and Women's Rights," p. 112, in Hilary Conroy et al, eds., *Japan in Transition: Thought and Action in the Meiji Era,* London: Associated University Presses, 1984, pp. 94–112.

162. See pp. 107, 327–328 in this volume.

163. *Nihon fujinron* has been reprinted in Meiji bunka kenkyukai, ed., *Meiji bunka zenshū* 16, *Fujin mondai-hen bessatsu*, Tokyo, Nihon hyōronsha, 1968, pp. 21–61. See also, Yoshida, *op.cit.*, pp. 380–381 and Nishizawa, *op.cit.*, pp. 121–122. They have both misread the "*san*" of "*sanron*."

164. *Onna nidai no ki* (originally published 1956), in *Yamakawa Kikue-shū* 9, Tokyo: Iwanami shoten, 1982, pp. 106–107, cited in Nishizawa *op.cit.*, pp. 231–232.

165. See pp. 106–108, 110–111. On p. xii of her introduction, Kate Wildman Nakai speculates about Yamakawa's reasons for quoting Fukuzawa instead of giving her own views.

166. *Facing Two Ways: The Story of My Life*, (originally published 1935), with an introduction and afterword by Barbara Molony, Stanford: Stanford University Press, 1984, pp. 28, 38, 279–281, 361.

167. *Kaihō* (Oct. 1921) reprinted in *Yamakawa Kikue-shū* 3, Tokyo: Iwanami shoten, 1982, pp. 29–40. The quotation is from pp. 36–37. Yasukawa's citations can be found in *Fukuzawa Yukichi no kyōikuron to joseiron*, Tokyo: Kōbunkan, 2013, pp. 145, 159, 164, 188, 197–198, 200.

168. Yasukawa, *op.cit.*, pp. 46–49.

169. On this issue, see Nishizawa, *Fukuzawa Yukichi to furī rabu*, pp. 217–219; Sekiguchi, *Kokumin no dōtoku*, pp. 88–91, 96–101.

170. Some of the English-language works are given in the section on further reading at the end of this volume. Many of them reference Kiyooka's translations.

171. Of course, in this he was no different from women with similar agendas such as Tsuda Umeko, Yosano Akiko, and Hiratsuka Raichō. See Hirota Masaki, "Kindai erīto josei no aidentiti to kokka," in Wakita Haruko, S. B. Hanley eds., *Jendā no Nihonshi 2, Shutai to hyōgen, shigoto to seikatsu*, Tokyo: Tokyo Daigaku shuppankai, 1995, pp. 199–227.

172. See *On Japanese Women, Part Two*, p. 117 in this volume.

173. See, for example, the remarks on p. 3 in the introduction to P. F. Kornicki et al eds., *The Female As Subject: Reading and Writing in Early Modern Japan*, Ann Arbor: The Center for Japanese Studies, The University of Michigan, 2010.

174. "Fukuzawa Yukichi no joseikan," p. 131, *Fukuzawa Yukichi nenkan* 24 (1997), pp. 117–139. For an analysis of the image of women in these two works, see Sugano

Noriko "Nozomareru joseizō: *Yōgaku kōyō, Fujokan* o chūshin ni" *Teikyō shigaku* 26 (2011), pp. 141–169.

175. *Op.cit.*, pp. 196–199.

176. For the influence of Galton, see, for example, *Jiji shogen* (1881), *Fukuzawa Yukichi zenshū* 5, 2nd edn, Tokyo: Iwanami shoten, 1970, pp. 207–231.

177. For the 1870 American edition of Mill that Fukuzawa read, see pp. 87–88. Like Fukuzawa, Mill has been accused of inconsistency because of this, as Marnie Anderson also notes (*op.cit*, pp. 71–72), but see the remarks of Mary Lyndon Shanley in *Feminism, Marriage and the Law in Victorian England*, Princeton: Princeton University Press, 1989, pp. 65–66. Sekiguchi points out the influence of de Toqueville on Fukuzawa's arguments about women in *Kokumin no dōtoku*, pp. 71–74. In Volume 2, Section 3 of *Democracy in America*, "How Americans understand the equality of the sexes," de Tocqueville also supports the separate spheres idea.

178. See pp. 43, 57 of the 1870 American edition that Fukuzawa read.

179. Kiyooka's original translations of "On Japanese Women" and *On Moral Behavior* tend to gloss over Fukuzawa's references to both the sexual frustration of wives and the pleasures to be gained from sexual activities. See *Fukuzawa Yukichi on Japanese Women*, pp. 14, 18, 21–23, 78.

180. *Ueki Emori-shū* IV, Tokyo: Iwanami shoten, 1990, pp. 180–96, originally published in *Doyō shinbun*.

181. "Warera no shimai wa shōgi nari," *Jogaku zasshi*, no. 9, 25 Nov. 1885.

182. "Girō zenpai subeshi," *ibid.*, no. 35, Sept. 15, 1896, pp. 81–85.

183. "Fukuzawa-sensei no ippu ippu o yomu" *Fujin shinpō* 9, 20 Jan. 1899, pp. 1–11, cited in Hayakawa, *op.cit.*, p. 71.

184. *Fukuzawa Yukichi to furī rabu*, pp. 176–187.

185. On this issue, see, for example, Hirota Masaki, "Fukuzawa Yukichi no Fujinron ni furete: Kindai Nihon joseishi no jakkan no mondaiten," pp. 1–10, *Okayama daigaku hōbungakubu gakujutsu kiyō (rekishi-hen)* 39, 1979, pp. 1–17.

186. Writers such as Joanna Liddle and Sachiko Nakajima (*Rising Sons, Rising Daughters: Gender, Class and Power in Japan*, London: Zed Books, 2000, pp. 37–38), Mihalopolous (*op.cit.*, pp. 89–90) and Yasukawa Junosuke (*op.cit.*, passim) would probably disagree, but their focus is narrower.

A Message of Farewell to Nakatsu

♦NOTES TO EDITOR'S INTRODUCTION

1. *Autobiography*, pp. 278–280; 230–234.

2. The translation was by Mori Arinori, then Japan's chargé d'affaires in Washington, and his secretary, Magome Tamesuke. See Tokura Takeyuki, "'Who would not think, as I do, of his native place?': 1872 nen-yaku 'Nakatsu ryūbetsu no sho,'" *Fukuzawa techō* 135 (Dec. 2007), pp. 32/1–26/7.

◆NOTES TO TEXT

1. "Nakatsu ryūbetsu no sho" (中津留別之書), 1870. This revised translation is based on the text in *Fukuzawa Yukichi chosakushū* 10, pp. 1–8.

2. This is a quotation from *Shang Shu* (*The Book of Documents*), one of the Five Classics. The translation is taken from James Legge, *The Chinese Classics* 3.2, London: Trübner & Co., 1865, p. 283. In Legge's translation, the full passage is as follows: "Heaven and Earth is the parent of all creatures; and of all creatures man is the most fully endowed. The sincere, intelligent, and perspicacious among men becomes the great sovereign; and the great sovereign is the parent of the people." Fukuzawa used this extract numerous times in his writings on women, as evidence for their equality with men. (Legge's translation mentions "man/men," probably without any intention of excluding women, but this gender bias is not present at all in the original and I have tried to avoid it myself, by using the third personal plural rather than singular.)

3. In the first part of *Seiyo jijō* (*Conditions in the West*, 1866), Fukuzawa had used an already-existing word, *jiyū*, in his efforts to explain the Western concept of freedom. He referred to other possible equivalents in Part Two, but *jiyū* became the accepted translation and is the word that he uses here. However, since the original meaning of *jiyū* had negative connotations of willfulness, he is careful to prevent misunderstanding. For more details about the translation and explanation of "freedom" and "liberty," see Douglas R. Howland, *Translating the West: Language and Political Reason in Nineteenth-Century Japan*, Honolulu: University of Hawai'i Press, 2002, pp. 97–107.

4. This explanation is almost certainly influenced by the section on "Personal Liberty" in Francis Wayland's *The Elements of Moral Science*, Boston: Gould and Lincoln, 1865, pp. 200–205.

5. These are four of the Five Relationships of Confucianism, as laid out in *Mencius* Book III, Part A.4 (p. 102 in Lau's translation).

6. As Oberman and Tomoatsu point out in a previous translation of the text, this forestalls explanations of freedom in *An Encouragement of Learning*, *The Thought of Fukuzawa* 2, Section 1, p. 5, and Section 8, p. 60. See "An Annotated Translation of Fukuzawa Yukichi's 'A Letter of Farewell to Nakatsu,'" p. 652, *Hokudai hōgaku ronshū* 40 (1990), pp. 662–647.

7. It is not clear whether Fukuzawa used "*kuni/ikkoku*" here to mean "*han*" or "the nation," and "*tenka*" to mean "the nation" or "the world." This would depend on whether Fukuzawa was identifying here with Nakatsu, or with Japan as a whole. In *Fukuzawa Yukichi to furī rabu*, pp. 14–15, Nishizawa decides that Fukuzawa was identifying with Japan as a whole, and later in the text, "*ikkoku*" is certainly used to refer to a nation. However, even if this was Fukuzawa's intention, it is likely that many of the early readers of this text saw themselves as members of individual *han* rather than as citizens of Japan.

8. Presumably this is echoing "A man and woman living together is the most important of human relationships," *Mencius* Book V, Part A.2 (p. 139 in Lau's translation). The Chinese and Japanese are much closer than the English versions suggest.

9. This numerical argument for chastity is given by Wayland in *op.cit*, p. 296. Fukuzawa repeats it in his *Meiroku zasshi* article "Danjo dōsūron" ("The Equal Numbers of Men

and Women"), Issue Thirty-One, March 1875. For an English translation, see Meiroku zasshi: *Journal of the Japanese Enlightenment*, translated and with an introduction by William Reynolds Braisted, assisted by Adachi Yasushi and Kikuchi Yūji, Tokyo: University of Tokyo Press, 1976, pp. 385–386.

10. Fukuzawa is referring to one of the Five Relationships that were laid out during the reign of the Shun Emperor, but has got the source wrong. It appears in *Mencius* Book III, Part A.4 (p. 102 in Lau's translation). Lau translates it as "distinction between husband and wife," and the orthodox Chinese interpretation was that married couples should observe propriety above all else in their relations with each other. In the *Book of Rites* this was expanded to the idea of separate spheres. Although Fukuzawa gives this interpretation in other works (for example "On Japanese Women"), and criticizes it, here he presents a different interpretation that was not unusual in Tokugawa Japan. For more details about this, see the General Introduction, pp. 44–45.

11. This is an important 4th century BCE commentary on the *Chunqui* (*Annals of the Spring and Autumn Period*, c.771–476 BCE). The latter has traditionally been attributed to Confucius.

12. This is the ideal that Confucius upholds in *The Analects* 17.20, pp. 170–171 in Chichung Huang's translation.

13. The text says "over ten years of age," but according to the traditional Sino-Japanese way of counting age, a baby was one year old at the time of birth and increased one year in age every New Year. The other reference to age in this text has been similarly adjusted.

14. Fukuzawa is probably referring to Wayland, *op. cit.* See pp. 322, 327–328.

15. This is a phrase attributed to Han Xin, a famous Chinese general of the 3rd century BCE. He used it when criticizing Xiangu Yu, a Chinese warrior overlord whom he had once served. Han Xin meant that although Xiang showed kindness to sick soldiers, he did not reward successful officers with promotions.

16. Fukuzawa uses the term *kōgaku* (皇学), literally "Imperial [way] learning," but he is referring to the field of scholarship generally referred to as National or Nativist learning. This developed in opposition to Chinese (Confucian) learning in the late eighteenth century and focused on the study of early texts in order to rediscover the ancient "purity" of Japan before it fell under the influence of China. It is associated with figures such as Moto'ori Norinaga (1730–1801) and Hirata Atsutane (1776–1843). National learning inevitably drew attention to Japan's Imperial line, and provided ideological support for the movement to overthrow the Tokugawa.

An Answer to a Certain Gentleman's Inquiry about Female Education

♦NOTES TO EDITOR'S INTRODUCTION

1. After this, an article critical of mission schools was published in Fukuzawa's newspaper, *Jiji shinpō*. As well as criticizing the Eurocentric curriculum, it complained that fee-paying girls shared the same dormitory as lower-class charity pupils, learning bad habits, and that since moral teaching was based on the Bible its practical relevance

was unclear. "Yasokyōkai jogakkō no kyōikuhō," 29–30 July 1887, *Fukuzawa Yukichi zenshū* 11, pp. 318–323. It is likely that there was a link with the experiences of the Fukuzawa daughters.

2. See Nishizawa, "Keiogijuku ni okeru joshi kyōiku" pp. 187–188, *Kindai Nihon kenkyū* 24 (2007), pp. 177–226. For an English-language study of the work of the SPG in Tokyo, including its links with Keio, see Cyril H. Powles, *Victorian Missionaries in Meiji Japan: The Shiba Sect; 1873–1900*, Toronto: University of Toronto-York University Joint Centre on Modern East Asia, 1987.

♦NOTES TO TEXT

1. "Joshi kyōiku no koto ni tsuki Bō-shi ni kotau" (女子教育の事に付某氏に答), 1878. This (new) translation is based on the text in *Fukuzawa Yukichi chosakushū* 10, pp. 343–346.

2. During the Tokugawa period, registration at Buddhist temples was compulsory. All funerals were held at Buddhist temples, and the dead were represented by "ancestral tablets" kept in the Buddhist altars of every household. However, ideological support for the Meiji Restoration came from Nativist scholars who wished to return to Japan's pre-Buddhist "roots." One of the first steps of the new government was a move against the close links that had developed between Buddhism and Shinto. This led to a violent anti-Buddhist movement known as *haibutsu kishaku*.

3. For the possible identity of the schoolmistress, see the introduction to this piece.

4. This is part of a chapter on the division of labor. Fukuzawa points out that the division of labor makes economic sense for enterprises above a certain scale, but not to families. Wives must be able to handle business affairs while the husband is away, and husbands must be competent in the basic running of the household. Schoolboys must also be able to do various tasks alongside their studies. See *Fukuzawa Yukichi chosakushū* 6, Tokyo: Keiogijuku Daigaku shuppankai, 2003, pp. 112–116.

5. Fukuzawa quotes a famous poem from the *Book of Poetry* (*Shi jing*), one of the Chinese Classics. My translation is a paraphrase.

6. Flora Best Harris, the wife of a prominent Methodist missionary to Japan and a great supporter of mission education for women, published a critique and partial translation of this letter in a missionary periodical. She described it as "the product, puerile as its logic is, of one of the finest minds in the 'new Japan'" (p. 105). However, the translation missed Fukuzawa's point that Japanese girls needed to be trained in the skills required by Japanese culture rather than being thoroughly Westernized. See "An Asiatic View of Higher Education," *Heathen Women's Friend* 10.5, November 1878, pp. 105–106. My knowledge of this article comes from the reference in Nishizawa, *Fukuzawa Yukichi to furī rabu*, p. 172.

On Japanese Women

♦NOTES TO EDITOR'S INTRODUCTION

1. See, for example, *An Outline of a Theory of Civilization*, pp. 25, 45–46, 57–58 and *Jiji*

shogen (*Fukuzawa Yukichi zenshū* 5, pp. 95–231, originally published 1881), where he introduces Francis Galton's theory of eugenics in a discussion of the need to "nurture the vitality of the Japanese people" (pp. 207–231). See also Nishizawa Naoko, *Fukuzawa Yukichi to furī rabu*, pp. 86–87 and Ōta Tenrei, *Nihon sanjichōsetsu hyakunenshi*, Tokyo: Shuppan kagaku sōgōkenkyūjo, 1976, pp. 42–46.

◆NOTES TO TEXT

1. "Nihon fujinron" (日本婦人論). The revised translation is based on the text in *Fukuzawa Yukichi chosakushū* 10, pp. 11–53.

2. This was the newspaper begun by Fukuzawa in 1882, in which "On Japanese Women" itself was being serialized. In 1884, Takahashi Yoshio (1861–1937), a Keio graduate and one of the newspaper's editorial staff, had published *Jinshu kairyōron* (*On Racial Improvement*), in which he proposed marriage with Westerners as a way of improving the Japanese race and promoting equality between Japan and Western countries. Fukuzawa must be referring in part to this work, which was later criticized by Katō Hiroyuki. See Nagatsuma Misao, "Shinkaron juyō no shosō: Miyake Setsurei ni okeru "jinshu" to "shintai," pp. 241–243, in Ō'oka Nobuo and Suzuki Sadami eds., *Gijutsu to shintai: Nihon kindaika no shisō*, Kyoto: Minerva shobō, 2006, pp. 240–252 and Nakazawa Tsutomu, "Jinshu kairyō no ronri: Meiji Taishōki ni okeru yūseigaku no tenkai," pp. 254–256, in *ibid.*, pp. 253–266.

3. *The Great Learning for Women* was a moral primer that was widely used in the Tokugawa period to teach girls reading and writing. It assumed that women should be subordinate to men. First published in Japan in 1716, it became a standard text in women's education. See the General Introduction, pp. 10–12, 32, 51–52, for more about the text itself and Fukuzawa's attitude to it.

4. In the Tokugawa period, gender restrictions on succession in farming and merchant families had gradually become less rigid, but in families of samurai rank and above only males had been eligible to act as household heads. Edicts of 1873 had given limited succession rights to women belonging to the nobility and to former samurai families. In 1875 these provisions had been extended to include the rest of the population. See Nishizawa, *Fukuzawa Yukichi to furī rabu*, pp. 108–109.

5. Confucius concludes by saying "Can this alone be considered filial piety?," implying the reverse. In other words he is pointing out that filial piety is not merely a question of how people behave on formal occasions. (See *The Analects* 2.8, p. 54 in Chichung Huang's translation.) Fukuzawa, however, is criticizing the relationship between men and women in Japanese society.

6. Mill makes a similar point in *The Subjection of Women*: "many women of the higher classes ... [are brought up as] a kind of hot-house plants [sic], shielded from the unwholesome vicissitudes of air and temperature, and untrained in any of the occupations and exercises which give stimulus and development to the circulatory and muscular system ..." (See p. 112 of the 1870 American edition that Fukuzawa read.)

7. From *The Analects* 17. 24 (Chichung Huang, p. 172). Confucius continues, "If you stay close to them, they become insolent; if you keep them at a distance, they are resentful."

8. "The five obstacles" is a Buddhist term meaning that however hard they try, women cannot achieve enlightenment. (They must first be reborn as men.) The "three obediences" are of Confucian origin and comprise obedience to the father while in his care, obedience to the husband when married, and obedience to the son after the husband's death. Fukuzawa expands his attack on the three obediences in *A Critique of The Great Learning for Women*. (For example, see pp. 215–217, 255–256.)

9. According to Philip Almond, in Europe this image of Islam had been fostered by the translation of the *Book of the Thousand and One Nights* in the early eighteenth century. See "Western Images of Islam, 1700–1800" 421–423, *Australian Journal of Politics and History* 49/3, 2003, 412–424. Fukuzawa may have been influenced by this Western image. Alternatively he may have come to similar conclusions after reading the first Japanese version of the *Book of the Thousand and One Nights*, a translation from English, which appeared in 1875.

10. During the Tokugawa period, feudal lords had to shift their residence every year, from Edo to their *han*, and then back again to Edo. This system of "alternate residence" (*sankin kōtai*) was one of the mechanisms by which the Tokugawa were able to maintain control of the country for so long.

11. This must be a reference to *Shiji* (*Records of the Grand Historian*) Chapter 82 (or Memoir 22). During the Warring States Period, an envoy from the Yen army tries to force Wang Chu to support his side, but Wang Chu replies: "'A loyal vassal does not serve two lords and a virtuous woman does not take a second husband.... I would surely rather be boiled alive than to live without righteousness.'" He then hangs himself. William H. Nienhauser, ed. *The Grand Scribe's Records* VII, *The Memoirs of Pre-Han China by Ssu-ma Ch'ien*, Bloomington: Indiana Press, 1994, p. 278.

12. One example of the sort of Confucian writings that Fukuzawa is probably referring to is *The Great Learning for Women*, which he has already criticized on p. 76. This includes the injunction that a wife should "never even dream of being jealous." See p. 264 of the revised version of Basil Hall Chamberlain's translation by W. T. de Bary in Wm Theodore de Bary et al, eds, *Sources of Japanese Tradition 2, 1600–2000*, 2nd ed., New York: Columbia University Press, 2005, pp. 262–267. A good example of the sort of play that he is referring to would be Chikamatsu Monzaemon's *Shinjū Ten no Amijima* (*Love Suicides at Amijima*), written for the puppet theater (*bunraku*) in 1720, but adapted for Kabuki too. Jihei, the husband of Osan, is passionately in love with Koharu, a geisha. Rather than reproach Jihei for his behavior, Osan is prepared to help him find the money to buy Koharu's freedom. See Donald Shively, *The Love Suicides at Amijima: A Study of a Japanese Domestic Tragedy by Chikamatsu Monzaemon*, Cambridge, Mass.: Harvard University Press, 1953.

13. There is a reference to "'hysterics'" in John Stuart Mill's *The Subjection of Women* (p. 111 in the 1870 American edition). But his use of *katakana* to write the word as *hisuterī* suggests that his source is the German "*Hysterie*" (or French "*hystérie*") rather than English. According to *Nihongo daijiten*, the first use of *hisuterī* (rendered as "*heisuterī*") was in Ogata Kōan's translation of Christoph Hufeland's *Enchiridicum Medicum* (*The Practice of Medicine*) which was published in 1857, when Fukuzawa was a student at

Ogata's academy of Dutch learning. However, this is not explicit about the link between hysteria and sexual frustration. Dr. Erwin Baelz (1849–1931) was a professor in the Department of Medicine of the Imperial University of Tokyo, and the institute from which the department was formed, from 1876 to 1902. Gynecology was among the subjects he taught, and women suffering from hysteria were among his private patients. (For example, see Toku Baelz ed., *Awakening Japan: The Diary of a German Doctor, Erwin Baelz*, New York: Viking Press, 1932, p. 44.) In an analysis of fox possession that appeared in the Osaka edition of the *Asahi shinbun* in early 1885, he described one case as "a form of hysteria" ("Kitsune-tsuki no byōsetsu" part 4, 4 February, 1885). Baelz therefore seems a likely source of Fukuzawa's knowledge of the term, and possibly of the link with sexual frustration. Western medicine at the time acknowledged that sexual deprivation was a cause of hysteria. For example, see Carol A. B. Werner, "Genital Surgeries and Genital Stimulation in Nineteenth-Century Psychiatry," pp. 175, 182–85 in Marcia Texler Segal et al, *Gender Perspectives on Reproduction and Sexuality*, Amsterdam: Elsevier, 2004, pp. 165–197.

14. Evidence from 8th and 9th century Japanese literature, including the historical myths of the *Kojiki* and the love poems of the *Manyōshū* and *Kokinwakashū*, suggests that women had considerable freedom in initiating and refusing relations with men, even though the legal structure adopted by the state at that time was modeled on China and therefore followed patriarchal norms. See the love poems of women such as Kasa no Iratsume and Ono no Komachi in the *Manyōshū* and *Kokinwakashū* respectively. They are available in translation in both book form and online. See also Hiroko Sekiguchi, "The Patriarchal Family Paradigm in Eighth-Century Japan" in Dorothy Ko et al, eds, *Women and Confucian Cultures in Premodern China, Korea, and Japan*, Berkeley: University of California Press, 2003, pp. 27–46.

15. Fukuzawa may be referring to Confucian scholars such as Yamazaki Ansai (1619–1682), Kaibara Ekiken and Yamaga Sokō (1622–1685) who criticized *Ise monogatari* (*The Tale of Ise*), a collection of mainly love poems loosely linked by prose narratives, along with *Genji monogatari* (*The Tale of Genji*), because of their questionable morality. See James McMullen, *Idealism, Protest, and the* Tale of Genji: *The Confucianism of Kumazawa Banzan (1619–91)*, Oxford: Clarendon Press, 1999, pp. 58–60 and Peter Kornicki, "Unsuitable Books for Women? *Genji monogatari* and *Ise monogatari* in Late Seventeenth-Century Japan," *Monumenta Nipponica* 60.2 (2005), pp. 148–162.

16. The first example refers to people caught up in the Genpei War between the Minamoto and the Taira (1180–1185), Kiso Yoshinaka being a cousin and rival of Minamoto no Yoritomo. The second example refers to the final part of the Civil War Period, during which Oda Nobunaga, Toyotomi Hideyoshi, and finally Tokugawa Ieyasu, emerged as unifying leaders.

17. Tokiwa Gozen was a famed beauty and a wife or concubine of Minamoto no Yoshitomo. In the Heiji Rebellion (1159), Yoshitomo was killed by Taira no Kiyomori, who later captured Tokiwa Gozen and her three young sons, Yoshitomo's heirs. (However, the youngest of these sons, Minamoto no Yoshitsune, was mainly responsible for the final defeat of the Taira in 1185.)

18. The system of registering people by family membership through household registers (*koseki*) had been introduced throughout Japan in 1872. (The concept itself was not new.) The same word is used today, but as a result of a postwar reform, the basic unit is formed by a married couple rather than by the family itself. (See Fukuzawa's proposal below.) The basis of the system lies in Chinese methods of social organization.

19. When Fukuzawa wrote this, women kept their original surnames even after marriage into another family, but could use their husband's surname socially. Offspring took the father's surname. This practice continued until the establishment of the Meiji Civil Code in 1898, according to which wives were to assume the name of the husband's family.

20. The abolition of these status divisions had taken place in 1869. The three lower groups became 'commoners' (*heimin*), and Fukuzawa refers to them as such in the next sentence.

21. Work on Japan's first Civil Code was in progress at the time when Fukuzawa was writing.

22. Although the general trend in Europe and North America was definitely in the direction of equal divorce rights, they were not universal at this time. In particular, as Fukuzawa probably knew, in England and Wales adultery by wives was sufficient grounds for divorce, but husbands had to be guilty of "aggravated adultery"(cruelty, desertion, bigamy, incest or sodomy in addition to adultery). This did not change until 1923.

23. The Tokugawa government wanted husbands to produce a written statement of divorce. In colloquial speech it became known as *mikudarihan* (literally "three and a half lines") because this was the stock length. Divorce was certainly easier for men than for women in Japan at this time, but evidence produced by Harald Fuess suggests that women, including samurai wives, and their families of origin were in fact able to initiate divorces in the Tokugawa period. After the Meiji Restoration, state decrees of 1873 actually put this on the statute books. See *Divorce in Japan: Family, Gender and the State, 1600–2000*, Stanford: Stanford University Press, 2004, pp. 44, 76–78, 96–97, 100–102. *Mikudarihan* were still common in the early Meiji period, but gradually disappeared. While Fukuzawa implies here that the practice was an insult to women, Fuess suggests that women wanted the statements because they gave proof that they were able to remarry (*ibid.*, pp. 78–81).

24. Fukuzawa may have been aware that in 1863, the first British Minister to Japan, Rutherford Alcock, had rather condescendingly remarked on the use of "letters of divorce" rather than "the assistance of a court" as a sign of Japan's relative lack of civilization. See Fuess, *op.cit.*, p. 4, and Alcock's *The Capital of the Tycoon: A Narrative of a Three Years' Residence in Japan* I, New York: Greenwood Press, 1969, pp. 194–195 (originally published London: Longman, 1863).

25. Fukuzawa's argument about the relationship between custom and law, and the difficulty of changing the former, is similar to that of John Stuart Mill in *op cit*, pp. 1–6.

26. In *Fukuzawa Yukichi to josei* p. 40, Nishizawa Naoko suggests that Fukuzawa obtained the information about the position of women in Korea in *On Japanese Women* from Korean students at Keio or even from Park Yeong-hyo (1861–1939), who stayed

with Fukuzawa for a time after the failure of the Gapsin Coup in December 1884. However, the information given here may be the result of a misunderstanding. *Ingin*, the word that he uses for "go-between," was a Korean term for a prostitute.

On Japanese Women, Part Two

◆NOTES TO TEXT

1. *Nihon fujinron kōhen* (日本婦人論後編), 1885. This revised translation is based on the text in *Fukuzawa Yukichi chosakushū* 10, pp. 55–100. The preface has been newly translated since it did not appear in the original translation. The divisions between the installments were removed from the published version, but have been retained for clarity.

2. A draper's shop in the Nihonbashi district of Tokyo that was the precursor of the famous Mitsukoshi department store chain.

3. (1854–1901) Fukuzawa's nephew and at that time manager of *Jiji shinpō*.

4. In *Fukuzawa Yukichi to josei* (p. 7), Nishizawa Naoko points out that Fukuzawa had the opportunity to observe women working in a telegraph office in London in 1862, on his second trip outside Japan. He had probably made similar observations in the United States in 1860, on his first trip abroad. In *The Subjection of Women* (pp. 105–120 in the 1870 American edition), John Stuart Mill suggests areas where women are likely to perform better than men, for example in the practical application of theory and in what would today be called "multitasking." This may be what Fukuzawa means by "it is said."

5. See note 2, "A Message of Farewell to Nakatsu," p. 391.

6. As *Sources of Japanese Tradition 2, 1600–2000*, 2nd edn, points out (p. 267), this is a reference to *Shi jing* (*Book of Odes*, one of the Five Classics), no. 189: "And so he bears sons; they lay them on a bed, . . . [they will be] rulers of hereditary houses. And so he bears daughters; they lay them on the ground, . . . they shall have nothing but simplicity." (The translation is from Bernhard Karlgren, *The Book of Odes*, Stockholm: Museum of Far Eastern Antiquities, 1950, p. 131. *Sources* gives his first name as Bernard, but this is a misspelling.)

7. The translation used here is by Basil Hall Chamberlain, first printed in 1878 and included in his *Things Japanese*, London: Kegan Paul & Co., 1890, pp. 454–463.

8. Kiyohime, a symbol of female jealousy in traditional Japan, is the main character in a folktale that became the basis of the Kabuki drama known as *Musume Dōjōji*. Rejected by the young monk with whom she has become infatuated, Kiyohime turns into a huge serpent and pursues him by swimming across the Hidaka River.

9. By using the phrase "shūchaku jishi" here, Fukuzawa may be making an ironic reference to the "obsessed lion" in the Kabuki dance known as *Hanabusa shūchaku jishi*. In the first scene, a woman dances holding a miniature lion-dance lion (a "lion" mask attached to a sheet to cover the body of the dancer(s), still seen, for example, in Chinatown New Year dances) and gradually comes under its influence; in the second scene, she has actually been transformed into a dancing lion. The role was traditionally performed by a male actor specializing in female roles.

10. The relevant part of Chamberlain's translation of *The Great Learning for Women* has been adapted so that the genders are reversed.

11. *Jo* is often translated as "reciprocity." Huang prefers "like-hearted considerateness." His translation of *Analects* 15:24 is as follows (p. 156):

> Zi-gong asked: "Is there one single word that one can practice throughout one's life?" The Master said: "It is perhaps 'like-hearted considerateness.' What you do not wish for yourself, do not impose on others.'"

Although Fukuzawa had not necessarily realized the connection, it is worth noting that in *The Elements of Moral Science*, which greatly influenced his view of society, Wayland saw "the duties of reciprocity," including the "duties arising from the constitution of the sexes" as the first duties of men to each other, after the duties arising from love of God, with the "law of reciprocity" being the basis of civil society. See Wayland, pp. 190–366.

12. Here Fukuzawa is adapting the words of Buddha just after his birth according to the Pali canon: "Chief am I in the world, eldest am I in the world, foremost am I in the world" (E. H. Brewster, *The Life of Gotama the Buddha: Compiled Exclusively from the Pali*, London: Trübner, 1926, p. 11). Presumably his intent is ironic.

13. For example, this expression had been used by the People's Rights activist Numa Morikazu (1844–1890) in 1882 to argue that Japan could not have female Emperors. A child produced by a female emperor would be of doubtful provenance, since her womb had been "borrowed" by her husband, who was not of the imperial line. See Kano Mikiyo, "Boseishugi to nashonarizumu" pp. 196–197 in *Iwanami kōza: Gendai shakaigaku* 19, *"Kazoku" no shakaigaku*, Tokyo: Iwanami shoten, 1996, pp. 189–215.

14. Both before and after the Meiji Restoration, it was not unusual for poor parents in severe financial difficulties to sell their daughters into prostitution. See Amy Stanley, *Selling Women: Prostitution, Markets, and the Household in Early Modern Japan*, Berkeley: University of California Press, 2012. In an 1896 interview with a foreign reporter, prominent politician and womanizer Itō Hirobumi praised the "lofty" motives of those Japanese prostitutes who desired to "help" their families in this way ("The Japan of Today," *Daily News* (London), 2 July 1896, cited in Sheldon Garon, *Molding Japanese Minds: The State in Everyday Life*, Princeton, N.J.: Princeton University Press, 1997, p. 102).

15. According to his children, Fukuzawa himself disliked this custom. He would try to return home via the veranda in the back garden so that his wife could not give him a formal welcome home, until she finally gave up trying to. See Fukuzawa Daishirō, *Chichi, Fukuzawa Yukichi*, Tokyo: Tokyo shobō, 1959, p. 129 and Nishikawa Shunsaku, Nishizawa Naoko, eds., *Fudangi no Fukuzawa Yukichi*, pp. 11–12.

16. Fukuzawa is referring to one of the Five Relationships, as stated in *Mencius* Book III, Part A.4 (p. 120 in Lau's translation).

17. Here Fukuzawa is making a semi-serious reference to the popular Buddhist idea that one's behavior in this life has an effect on what happens in one's next life.

18. Fukuzawa is referring to *Analects* 13:18, where Confucius makes an implicit criticism of a righteous son who testified against his sheep-stealing father. He points out that "In my native place, straight people are different from this man: Father conceals for

son and son conceals for father. Straightness lies therein." See p. 136 in Chichung Huang's translation.

19. In the 1880s, the government was in the process of drawing up Japan's first Civil Code.

20. This is the traditional folk image of thunder in Japan. See, for example, the famous painting by Ogata Kōrin (1658–1716).

21. This is the sort of approach that Fukuzawa took towards his two eldest sons in their "Daily Lessons," especially with regard to the tale of Momotarō. See pp. 291–292 in this volume.

22. This (*gusai*) is the "polite (= deferential)" term that some husbands still use today when talking about their wives in formal situations.

23. In 1881, the government had tried to pacify the People's Rights Movement by issuing an imperial proclamation that announced the establishment of a National Diet in 1890.

24. Fukuzawa is probably referring to Kishida Toshiko (1864–1901), who caused a sensation in 1882 when she began giving speeches in favor of equality for women at meetings organized by the People's Rights Movement.

25. This is the Japanese pipe (*kiseru*) with its long slender stem and small bowl. Respectable women had smoked in the Tokugawa period, and older women were still doing so in the Meiji period. (See Fukuzawa Taki, "Nihon joshi no seikatsu," *Jiji shinpō*, 14 July 1892.) However, they presumably handled their pipes more elegantly.

On Moral Behavior

♦NOTE TO EDITOR'S INTRODUCTION

1. "The Equal Numbers of Men and Women," *Meiroku zasshi*, Issue Thirty-One, March 1875, pp. 385–386.

♦NOTES TO TEXT

1. *Hinkōron* (品行論), 1885. This revised translation is based on the text in *Fukuzawa Yukichi zenshū* 5, 2nd edn, Tokyo: Iwanami shoten, 1970, pp. 547–578. The preface has been newly translated since it did not appear in the original translation. The divisions between the installments were removed in the published version, but have been retained for clarity. The editor must thank Senior Lecturer Emerita Teruko Craig as well as Professor Nishizawa for help in revising Kiyooka's original. However, responsibility for any errors rests with the editor alone.

2. Fukuzawa must be referring to this passage (12.11) from *The Analects* regarding the nature of good government:

"When Duke Jing of Qi asked Master Kong about government, Master Kong replied: 'Let a sovereign act like a sovereign, a minister like a minister, a father like a father and a son like a son.'

The duke said: 'Well said! If indeed a sovereign acts unlike a sovereign, a minister unlike a minister, a father unlike a father and a son unlike a son, even though there was millet, how could I get to eat it?'" (translation by Chichung Huang, p. 128.)

3. Hideyoshi was of low birth but was able to take advantage of the situation during the civil war period, then in its closing stages, to fight his way to power, becoming the effective ruler of Japan in 1583.

4. The Catholic mission to Japan had begun with the arrival of Francis Xavier in 1549. Fukuzawa is probably referring to a visit to Hideyoshi's castle by Gaspar Coelho, at that time head of the mission, in 1586, although Hideyoshi's rejection of monogamy seems to have occurred on an earlier occasion. For details, see, for example, C. R. Boxer, *The Christian Century in Japan, 1549–1650*, London: Cambridge University Press, 1951, pp. 139–143. The issue of monogamy was an obstacle to the conversion of elite Japanese in general.

5. *The Analects* 11.24 (in Chichung Hang's translation, p. 123).

6. *The Analects* 12.11. (See footnote 2.)

7. These are all core Confucian values. The first four (*jingi reichi*) are expounded in *Mencius* Book 6, Part A.6, the second four (*kōtei chūshin*) in Book 1, Part A.5, pp. 163 and 53 respectively in D. C. Lau's translation.

8. "*Danson johi.*" Takahashi Yoshio, a *Jiji shinpō* reporter, claimed to have been the first to use the expression in this sense in "Danson johi no fūshū," a speech given at the Mita campus on 5 May 1885 that was later published as "A: Wagakuni ni wa danson johi ari" (*Jiji shinpō*, 20 May 1885).

9. This echoes a quotation from Confucius in *Mencius* Book IV, Part A.2: "Confucius said, 'There are two ways, and two ways only: benevolence and cruelty.'" For the context of this quotation, and Fukuzawa's criticisms of the attitude it reveals, see *On Relations Between Men and Women*, pp. 185–187 and note 4, p. 405.

10. For the source of this quotation, see "A Message of Farewell to Nakatsu," note 2.

11. *The Analects* 1.8, in Chichung Huang's translation, p. 48.

12. As was pointed out in the General Notes about the Translations, p. 57, the references to spring, flowers, willows, leaves and grass all have sexual connotations.

13. This is how the editor decided to translate "*bai'in.*"

14. Fukuzawa uses the word "*geigi,*" which was the official Meiji term for the Edo "geisha" (Kyoto/Osaka "*geiko*") of the Tokugawa period. For the changing role of geisha in the Tokugawa Yoshiwara (explained below), see Cecilia Segawa Seigle, *Yoshiwara: The Glittering World of the Japanese Courtesan*, Honolulu: University of Hawai'i, 1993, pp. 170–175, 217–218.

15. Shin Yoshiwara was established as the licensed brothel area for Tokyo in 1657, being located away from the center of Edo, near the famous Sensōji temple in Asakusa. It was surrounded by walls and a moat and had only one gate until more were added in the early Meiji period. The early Meiji period also saw the establishment of other licensed brothel areas in the city. Regular inspections of prostitutes for syphilis had been gradually introduced in Japan after the first opening of ports for trade with Western countries in 1859, along with lock hospitals for the compulsory treatment of those who were infected. Initially this was as a result of pressure from Western diplomats who wished to protect the health of their nationals, particularly those in military or naval

service. For the traumatic nature of the inspections and attempts to avoid them, see Fujime Yuki, "Kindai Nihon no kōshō seido to haishō undō," p. 465 in Wakita Haruko, Hanley, S. B., eds., *Jendā no Nihonshi 1, Shūkyō to minzoku, shintai to sei'ai*, Tokyo: Tokyo Daigaku shuppankai, 1994, pp. 461–491.

16. Boyi and his younger brother Shuqi were famous paragons of the Confucian virtues said to have lived around BCE 1500. Fukuzawa is referring to *Mencius* Book V, Part B.1, p. 149 in D. C. Lau's translation: "(Boyi) would neither look at improper sights with his eyes nor listen to improper sounds with his ears. He would only serve the right prince and rule over the right people. He could not bear to remain in a place where the government took outrageous measures and unruly people were to be found. To be in company with a fellow-villager was, for him, just like sitting in mud or pitch while wearing a court cap and gown."

17. Ancient Learning refers to the schools of Confucianism associated with Tokugawa period scholars such as Yamaga Sokō and Itō Jinsai (1627–1705) who rejected Neo-Confucian theories in favor of a return to the ancient texts themselves.

18. "Floating world" (*ukiyo*) was originally a Buddhist term referring to the illusory nature of "reality," but in the Tokugawa period it came to describe the fleeting pleasures that life had to offer, and in particular the pleasure quarters.

19. Liu Xiahui was a politician and sage who is mentioned in both *The Analects* and *Mencius*. Fukuzawa must be referring to the tale that he had been able to warm a woman with his body without incurring any stain on his character. See *K'ung Tzu Chia Yu: The School Sayings of Confucius*, translated and with an introduction by R. P. Kramers, Leiden: Brill, 1950, pp. 248–249.

20. Before the Meiji period, the most widespread general term for licensed prostitutes was *yūjo*, although other words, including *shōgi*, existed. In the Meiji period, *shōgi* became the standard term.

21. Kiyooka's translation in *Fukuzawa Yukichi on Japanese Women: Selected Writings* (p. 88), "the violation of lonely widows," is incorrect, as Fukuzawa uses *wakan* not *gōkan*.

22. Fukuzawa may be referring to the anonymous author of *The Elements of Social Science; or Physical, Sexual and Natural Religion: An Exposition of the True Cause and Only Cure of the Three Primary Social Ills: Poverty, Prostitution and Celibacy*, 3rd edn enlarged, London: E. Truelove, 1859. (He was posthumously revealed to be George Drysdale, 1824–1904.) This influential work, which aroused great controversy with its support for birth control and advocacy of regular sexual activity as essential for male and female health, refers to prostitutes as martyrs three times. For example, on p. 276 they are "martyrs to the sexual passions," and on p. 409 "sexual martyrs." Unlike Fukuzawa, Drysdale wanted society to give public recognition to the important role played by prostitutes. However, when he suggested that women had sexual needs just like men, and deserved equal opportunities to satisfy them, this anticipated one of the points made by Fukuzawa in "On Japanese Women."

23. Shinran accepted that it was impossible for people to gain enlightenment through their own efforts in the present state of the world. He taught that they should seek salvation through faith in the Buddha Amida, who had vowed that all who chanted his

name would be reborn in the Western Paradise, where it was easy to gain enlightenment. He was exiled to present-day Niigata in 1207 due to mainstream Buddhist opposition to his teacher, Hōnen, and spent five years preaching there. Fukuzawa's family belonged to the Jōdo Shinshū (True Pure Land) sect that developed as a result of Shinran's teachings. Nichiren taught that devotion to the Lotus sutra and the practice of invocating its title were the only way to obtain the Buddha nature. A fierce critic of all existing Buddhist sects, he was exiled twice, to Izu in 1261 and to the island of Sado in 1271, the year in which he was nearly executed. A number of sects developed from his teachings. Iwamoto Yoshiharu (1863–1942), a Christian intellectual and editor of the journal *Jogaku zasshi* who was often critical of Fukuzawa's approach (see the General Introduction pp. 46–47), claimed to have been so incensed by the idea that prostitutes could be compared to Shinran and Nichiren that before he realized what he was doing he had ripped the newspaper ("*Jiji shinpō* no shōgiron," p. 183, *Jogaku zasshi*, no. 10, 8 Dec.1885, pp. 183–184).

24. For example, in April, blossoming cherry trees were planted in the Yoshiwara and lit up at night; in August, large lanterns were displayed. For a description of the effects, see Joseph E. de Becker, *The Nightless City, or "The History of the Yoshiwara Yukwaku,"* Yokohama: Z. P. Maruya & Co., 1899, pp. 28–31, 325–334.

25. For de Becker's description of the Yoshiwara *niwaka*, see *op.cit*, pp. 334–348.

26. Edomachi and Kyōmachi were the names of blocks within the Yoshiwara. One song that mentions them is "Hokushu sennen no kotobuki" (The everlasting Yoshiwara). Composed in 1818, it describes various yearly events in the Yoshiwara. It was not unusual for poets, including residents of the Yoshiwara, to meet there to share their verses.

27. There is no evidence that such a ban had been issued.

28. Professor Nishizawa suggests that this is not because they are ashamed of having concubines, but because if the addresses are known, it will limit their ability to hold secret meetings at these places.

29. In the humid summer weather, for example, men engaged in physical labor had traditionally worn only their *fundoshi* (loin cloths). This was not regarded as a problem until the shocked reactions of Western visitors to Japan led concerned Japanese to see taboos about nakedness as an aspect of (Western) civilization. As a consequence, rules against public displays of undress were included in local ordinances of 1872 onwards that were designed to bring the public behavior of ordinary people up to "civilized" standards.

30. One of the "talented men" described here was surely Itō Hirobumi (1841–1909), a leader of the Chōshū faction within the Meiji political elite who became Japan's first prime minister soon after the serialization of *On Moral Behavior*. He was a notorious and unrepentant womanizer whose second wife was a former geisha.

31. Xie An's life of retreat with his "female entertainers" features in one of the anecdotes in *Shio shuo xin yu* (*A New Account of Tales of the World*), compiled in the 5th century by Liu Yiqing. See pp. 219–220 in the translation by Richard B. Mather (*Shih-shuo Hsin-yü: A New Account of Tales of the World*, 2nd edn, Ann Arbor: Centre for Chinese Studies, University of Michigan, 2002). It is also referred to in a poem by the famous 8th century poet Li Bai.

32. In "Fujo kōkōron" ("On Female Acts of Filial Piety") and its appendix, "Fujo kōkō yoron" (*Jiji shinpō*, 8 and 18 Oct., 1883), Fukuzawa had criticized contemporary newspapers for praising poor girls who sold themselves into prostitution in order to help their families. This was damaging not only because it encouraged high-minded girls in similar situations to see this as an honorable solution, but also because of the direct and indirect ways in which such attitudes created a favorable image of prostitution.

33. "Gozen" is a term indicating respect. Tokiwa Gozen was originally the wife or concubine of Minamoto no Yoshitomo, who began the unsuccessful Heiji Rebellion against Taira no Kiyomori in 1159. She is said to have agreed to become the concubine of Taira no Kiyomori in order to save the lives of her three sons by Yoshitomo. She features in *Heiji monogatari* (c. 1230–1250), a tale of this rebellion, and in many dramas. *Heiji monogatari* has been translated by Royall Tyler in *Before Heike and After: Hōgen, Heiji, Jōkyūki*, Lexington, KY: An Arthur Nettleton Book, 2013.

Shizuka Gozen is said to have been the favorite concubine of Tokiwa's youngest son, the tragic hero Minamoto no Yoshitsune, and to have remained loyal to him even after being captured by his elder brother and arch rival, Minamoto no Yoritomo. She is portrayed as a gifted female *shirabyōshi* (courtesan entertainers who sang and danced while dressed in male court robes). She features briefly in *Heike monogatari* (*The Tale of the Heike*), which focuses on the ultimate defeat of the Taira by the Minamoto; in *Azuma kagami* (c. 1300), an official history of the period 1180–1286; and in illustrated books and dramas about her tragic love affair with Yoshitsune. The most recent translation of *Heike monogatari* is by Royall Tyler (New York: Viking, 2012).

34. The two Soga brothers, Soga Sukenari and his younger brother Tokimune, are famous for the dedication with which they pursued their vendetta against Kudō Suketsune, the military leader responsible for the death of their birthfather, Kawazu Sukeyasu. In 1193 they succeeded in killing Kudō, but died as a result. *Soga monogatari* (*The Tale of the Soga Brothers*) contains several scenes between Tora and Sukenari and describes how she became a Buddhist nun after the deaths of the brothers and devoted herself to prayers for their salvation. Tora Gozen also appears in the account of the vendetta in *Azuma kagami*. The Shōshō who appears in the story and witnesses the killing of Kudō is not involved with Tokimune, but she is paired with him in later dramas based on the story. *Soga monogatari* has been translated by Thomas J. Cogan (Tokyo: University of Tokyo Press, 1987).

35. Fujiwara no Kagekiyo was a warrior on the Taira side who survived their final defeat in 1185. He is said to have had a wife and also a concubine, Akoya, who bore him two sons. In a play by the famous Tokugawa dramatist, Chikamatsu Monzaemon, Akoya's jealousy of his wife leads her to betray Kagekiyo. When an imprisoned Kagekiyo later refuses to accept Akoya's pleas for forgiveness, she kills first her sons and then herself in front of his cell.

36. Komurasaki sold herself to the Yoshiwara to provide money for her parents. Shirai Gonpachi (loosely based on a notorious mid-17th century criminal named Hirai Gonpachi), a masterless samurai whose life she has previously saved, is in love with her and becomes a criminal in order to earn enough money to continue to purchase her

services. After he is executed, she kills herself at his grave. The story was the basis for various dramas. For an English version, see A. B. Mitford, *Tales of Old Japan* 1, London: Macmillan and Co., 1871, pp. 47–57.

37. There seems to be more than one version of the tale of Miyagino and Shinobu, a favorite with Tokugawa dramatists. (It may have some basis in historical truth.) An expert swordsman kills the sisters' father, a farmer, for some trivial offence. Determined to avenge their father's death, the sisters devote some years to the study of sword fighting. Eventually they are able to challenge their enemy to a public fight and slay him, spending the rest of their lives as Buddhist nuns. In the Kabuki version, Miyagino is a famous Yoshiwara beauty and does not know of her father's murder until Shinobu seeks her out. For an extract from the play prefaced by an introduction, see James R. Brandon and Samuel L. Leiter, eds., *Kabuki Plays on Stage* 2, *Villainy and Vengeance, 1773–1789*, Honolulu: University of Hawai'i, 2002.

38. Okaru is a character in *Kanadehon Chūshingura*, the most well known of several dramas inspired by the famous vendetta of the forty-seven *rōnin*, who dedicated themselves to revenging the death of their lord, the daimyo of Akō, in 1701. Hayano Kanpei is in love with Okaru, and this causes him to neglect his duty to his lord, En'ya Hangan of Hakushū. Kanpei is with Okaru when Hangan makes the mistake that leads to his death. Full of guilt, Kanpei leaves Edo with Okaru, and they marry. It is Okaru's father Yo'ichibei, a farmer, who makes the arrangement to sell her. Okaru also appears in a famous scene set in the Gion pleasure quarters. See the translation by Donald Keene (New York: Columbia University Press, 1971).

39. For example, *Honchō retsujoden* (*Biographies of Notable Japanese Women*), published in 1668, included nine concubines (pp. 391–398) and ten prostitutes (pp. 399–411) in its 217 short biographies, alongside women of Imperial lineage, wives of ordinary people, and shrine priestesses. See the reproduction in Haga Noboru et al. eds., *Nihon jinbutsu jōhō taikei* 1, *Josei-hen: sōden-hen* 1, Tokyo: Kōseisha, 1999.

40. This had certainly been the fate of some daughters of impoverished ex-samurai families in the earlier part of the Meiji period. A famous example is the wife of Ōkuma Shigenobu, who came from a wealthy *hatamoto* family, the Saegusa, that had lost its privileged position after supporting the Bakufu side during the Meiji Restoration. See "Arashi no ato," pp. 223–224, in Imaizumi Mine, *Nagori no yume,* Tokyo: Heibonsha, 1963, cited in Kondō Tomie, *Rokumeikan kifujin kō*, Tokyo: Kōdansha, 1983, p. 43.

41. The sentences referring to *eta* were omitted from the original translation, presumably because the term itself, and the discrimination experienced by people regarded as having *eta* status, had become such a sensitive subject by the time when it was published (1988). In the Tokugawa period, *eta*, literally "much filth," was one of the words used to describe members of marginalized groups who were mainly found at the bottom of society. They tended to be engaged in occupations that were seen to be polluting, such as executing criminals or leatherwork, but included entertainers, whose role was more ambiguous. (The designation was legally removed in 1871, as part of the reforms of the early Meiji period, but attitudes did not change so easily.) See Timothy D. Amos, *Embodying Difference: The Making of Burakumin in Modern Japan*, Honolulu:

University of Hawai'i Press, 2011.

42. This was the position of Sheldon Amos, an acquaintance of Baba Tatsui, a former Keio student who studied in England from 1870 to 1878 and kept in touch with Fukuzawa during this time. Amos explained his opinion in *Difference of Sex as a Topic of Jurisprudence and Legislation*, London: Longmans, Green & Co., 1870, pp. 28–34. This book was translated into Japanese by Suzuki Yoshimune in 1878, with the title *Fujo hōritsuron*. It is possible that Fukuzawa was told about this text by Baba.

On Relations between Men and Women

◆NOTES TO TEXT

1. *Danjo kōsairon* (男女交際論), 1886. This revised translation is based on the text in *Fukuzawa Yukichi chosakushū* 10, pp. 101–136. The divisions between the installments were removed from the published version, but have been retained for clarity. The preface has been newly translated since it did not appear in the original translation.

2. See note 2 of "A Message of Farewell to Nakatsu," p. 391.

3. These women included the official wife of the daimyo, and his concubines, but the majority were servants.

4. This is D. C. Lau's translation of *Mencius*. After the quotation from Confucius, the text continues: "If one wishes to be a ruler, one must fulfill the duties proper to a ruler; if one wishes to be a subject, one must fulfill the duties proper to a subject ... If a ruler ill-uses his people to an extreme degree, he will be murdered and his state annexed; if he does it to a lesser degree, his person will be in danger and his territory reduced." See *Mencius* Book IV, Part A.2 (p. 118).

5. This phrase occurs in *Mencius* Book I, Part A.1. He is criticizing a king who hopes that Mencius' teachings will profit his kingdom. D. C. Lau translates the sentence in which the phrase occurs as follows: "if profit is put before righteousness, there is no satisfaction short of total usurpation" (p. 49).

6. Both Confucius and Mencius contrast the ideal man, the "gentleman" (*kunshi*) with his opposite, the "small man" (*shōnin*).

7. This is one of the five human relationships given in *Mencius* Book III, Part A.4, p. 102 in D. C. Lau's translation. Here Fukuzawa accepts the orthodox interpretation that this is a call for propriety. This is different from his interpretation in "A Message of Farewell to Nakatsu," p. 64.

8. This derives from *The Book of Rites, Summary of the Rules of Propriety*, Part 1, 38, but is not an exact translation.

9. Fukuzawa is referring to the "social Darwinism" of Herbert Spencer here, since he is talking about the inheritance of learnt behavior rather than natural selection through the inheritance of chance variations. In fact, Spencer's writings were attracting a lot of interest among intellectuals in Japan at this time.

10. See note 2 of "A Message of Farewell to Nakatsu," p. 391.

11. This expression is said to have originated with the seventh emperor of the Tang,

Xuanzong (685–762). He used it when describing how his beloved concubine, Yang Yuhuan, surpassed lotus blossoms in her beauty. As a result of his infatuation with Yang Yuhuan, who had originally been his daughter-in-law, he neglected his duties and the power of the Tang dynasty declined.

12. Fukuzawa printed these English words in parentheses after their Japanese equivalent, *shakai no assei*, presumably to clarify his meaning. His normal practice when using foreign words was to write them in *katakana*, as with "hysterie" in "On Japanese Women." Fukuzawa's source for this phrase is not clear, although John Stuart Mill uses "social tyranny" to express a very similar idea in Chapter 1 of *On Liberty*.

13. In *The Subjection of Women*, p. 153, Mill had also pointed out "the loss to the world, by refusing to make use of one-half of the whole quantity of talent it possesses."

14. See note 7.

15. Xi Que (d. 598 BCE) had to leave the court after his father plotted against Duke Wen of Jin. The story goes that an adviser to the Duke who was travelling on official business chanced to observe Xi Que's dignified behavior, and was able to use this story to convince a reluctant Duke Wen to employ him. He went on to become a renowned and loyal statesman.

16. Two states of China during the Spring and Autumn period (c. 771–476 BCE). There was a considerable geographical distance between them.

17. *Senryū* are 17-syllable poems about everyday life. They often have a comic or satirical edge.

18. In a letter to his eldest son, Ichitarō, dated 2 May 1886 Fukuzawa had already given a brief description of a successful experiment in holding a buffet-style party at his house for women and some single men. (See Letter No. 19, p. 334.)

One Husband, One Wife, Together Even in the Grave

♦NOTE TO EDITOR'S INTRODUCTION

1. This is pointed out by Matsuzawa Hiroaki in footnote 8, p. 381, *Fukuzawa Yukichi-shū, Shin Nihon kotenbungaku taikei, Meiji-hen* 10, Tokyo: Iwanami shoten, 2011.

♦NOTES TO TEXT

1. "Ippu ippu kairō dōketsu" (一夫一婦偕老洞穴), *Fukuo hyakuwa* (福翁百話) 20, 1896. This new translation is based on the text in *Fukuzawa chosakushū* 11, 2003, pp. 53–54.

2. *Mencius* Book 5, Part A.2, p. 139 in D. C. Lau's translation.

A Critique of *The Great Learning for Women*; A New Great Learning for Women

♦NOTES TO EDITOR'S INTRODUCTION

1. These pieces included a five-part series entitled "Nihon fujin mondai" by prominent figures including Kataoka Kenkichi, former leader of the People's Rights Movement and

at that time Speaker of the Lower House (3 April, 1889), and Shimoda Utako, a poet who was also a pioneer in women's education (12 and 15 April, 1899).

2. 3 June 1900 "Kyoto-fu jogakkō no *Shin onna daigaku* kinshi," *Jiji shinpō*, 3 June 1900. Referred to in Nishizawa Naoko, *Fukuzawa Yukichi to josei*, pp. 213–219.

♦NOTES TO TEXT (Preface [1], [2] A Critique of *The Great Learning for Women*)————

1. Onna daigaku hyoron (女大学評論); *Shin onna daigaku* (新女大学), 1899. This revised translation is based on the texts in *Fukuzawa Yukichi chosakushū*, 10, pp. 237–338. The first preface and the appendix have been newly translated since they did not appear in the original translation.

2. This was written in February 1899. In July of that year foreigners in Japan were due to lose the right of extraterritoriality, in other words, were to become subject to Japanese law. This was generally welcomed by public opinion as a sign that Japan was recognized as a "civilized nation." However, there was great anxiety about the consequences of what was a corollary to the end of extraterritoriality: the removal of limits on travel and residence by foreigners outside the foreign settlements in the treaty ports and open cities.

3. "Sensei," which literally means teacher, is also used both as a title after the names of teachers, doctors and so on, and as a term of respect. Later in the passage, it is used by itself to refer to Fukuzawa.

4. Ogata was a doctor who had studied Western medicine through the medium of Dutch texts. His pupils learnt to read the Dutch texts in his possession. Fukuzawa writes vividly of his experiences as a pupil in his autobiography.

5. Kaibara was a Confucian scholar who did write manuals about the education of children, but recent scholarly opinion suggests that he was not the author of *Onna daigaku*. (See the General Introduction for more details.)

6. In *A Critique*, Fukuzawa quotes *The Great Learning for Women* section by section, interspersed with his comments. The translation used here is by Basil Hall Chamberlain, first printed in 1878 and included in his *Things Japanese*, London: Kegan Paul & Co., 1890, pp. 454–463. Some revisions have been made by the editor, mainly for clarity, and in order to fit Fukuzawa's interpretation of the text. Each section has been numbered, again for clarity. For background information about *The Great Learning for Women*, see the General Introduction. (The translation can also be found in a version revised by W. T. de Bary in Wm Theodore de Bary et al, eds., *Sources of Japanese Tradition 2, 1600–2000*, 2nd ed., New York: Columbia University Press, 2005, pp. 261–268.)

7. Where Fukuzawa is following the actual wording of *The Great Learning for Women*, as here, the editor has used quotation marks.

8. These qualities are ascribed to Confucius in *The Analects* 1.4 (p. 49 in Chichung Huang's translation). However, Fukuzawa substitutes 謙 (*ken*: modesty) for 倹 (*ken*: frugality), and omits "deference."

9. *Shōgaku* (*Xiaoxue*), a straightforward introduction to the basic rules of etiquette and morality associated with Confucianism. It was compiled according to the instructions of Zhu Xi towards the end of the twelfth century and soon spread to Japan.

10. Ji Dan, a paragon of wisdom and virtue, who acted as regent to his young nephew, son of King Wu, in the 11th century BCE. He is also said to be author of two of the Five

Chinese Classics, the *I Ching* (*Book of Changes*) and the *Shijing* (*Book of Odes*).

11. The English text has been taken from *The Civil Code of Japan,* Part II, translated by John Harrington Gubbins, Tokio: Maruya & Co., 1899, p. 19. This is in fact Article 772, not 771. The Code was enacted in 1898 after a dispute that focused on the family section.

12. In the Tokugawa period, the Bakufu and individual *han* would make awards to ordinary people who had exhibited model behavior. *Kōfuden* (*Tales of Dutiful Women*) were published accounts of women who had received such recognition.

13. English text taken from *The Civil Code of Japan*, Part II, 35–36, with the addition of 'defrauding of property (*sagishuzai*),' that was missing from Gubbin's translation of sub-heading iv. This new Civil Code had come into effect in July 1898, just before Fukuzawa began *A Critique*, and may have been one reason for his decision to write it.

14. For *mikudarihan*, see "On Japanese Women," note 23, p. 397.

15. These warrior brothers of the late 12th century, who took revenge on their father's murderer and died themselves as a result, have been immortalized in Japanese literature, drama, and art. See also *On Moral Behavior*, note 34, p. 404.

16. See *Mencius* Book VII, Part A.22: "If there are five hens and two sows, and these do not miss their breeding seasons, then the aged will not be deprived of meat" (p. 186 in D. C. Lau's translation). This is part of Mencius' description of the empire under the benevolent rule of King Wen. Fukuzawa uses the phrase here because the passage implies that if one cock is supplied with five hens, or one boar with two sows, they will have enough offspring for a farmer to have adequate supplies of chicken and pork. In other words, men who are willing to have sexual relations with women other than their wives are behaving in exactly the same way as cocks or boars.

17. See "A Message of Farewell to Nakatsu," note 2, p. 391.

18. Since women's childbearing age was thought to end at forty, it was presumably safe for married women beyond this age to have more freedom outside the home. A footnote to the translation of *The Great Learning* in *Sources of Tradition* 2, p. 265, points out that during festivals, and on other occasions, many people would gather at shrines and temples in order to enjoy themselves.

19. In a speech to Keio students on 23 October 1892 (published in *Jiji shinpō*, 28, 29 October) in which he was advising them of the qualities they would need for a career in business. (I am indebted to Professor Nishizawa for this information.)

20. This era is regarded as the high point of culture during the Tokugawa period. Although Genroku culture is normally associated with the townspeople of Kyoto and Osaka, people of the samurai class — who were by then primarily bureaucrats — were also involved in its development. Chikamatsu Monzaemon, the famous dramatist, was of samurai birth, as were Confucian scholars such as Muro Kyūsō and Kumazawa Banzan.

21. Chamberlain makes the sentence more logical by changing "five" to "four": "The worst of them all, and the parent of the other four, is silliness." To fit Fukuzawa's commentary, however, it is necessary to use the original "five."

22. The reference is to poem no. 189 in the *Book of Odes* (*Shi Jing*), one of the five Chinese Classics. In Bernhard Karlgren's translation: "And so he bears sons; they lay them on a bed, . . . [they will be] rulers of hereditary houses. And so he bears daughters;

they lay them on the ground, . . . they shall have nothing but simplicity." See *The Book of Odes*, p. 131. The mention of three days may be linked to traditional Japanese beliefs about the time needed for the pollution associated with birth to clear away.

23. Presumably Fukuzawa is making a tongue-in-cheek reference to himself and his sisters. (See the General Introduction, p. 33.)

♦NOTES TO TEXT (A New Great Learning for Women)

1. This is the dagger carried by samurai women in the Tokugawa period that Fukuzawa has already referred to in Section 12 of *A Critique of* The Great Learning for Women, p. 243.

2. The *Hyakunin isshu* is a famous thirteenth-century anthology of 100 *waka* poems written by 100 different poets. In the game, cards containing only the second part of each poem are arranged on the floor. As one player reads out the words of one of the poems, the others compete to be the first to find the appropriate card. To play successfully it is necessary to know the words of the poems, but not to understand their meaning.

3. It was certainly not unusual for this to happen in the Meiji period. For example, as has already been mentioned in note 30 to *On Moral Behavior*, p. 403, it was widely known that Itō Hirobumi was married to a former geisha.

4. This term, which means "family feuds" or "strife within noble families," was originally used to refer to disputes within the daimyo families of Tokugawa Japan. It is relevant here because one factor leading to succession disputes was the existence of competing heirs who had different mothers.

5. See "On Japanese Women," note 11, p. 395.

Daily Lessons

♦NOTES TO EDITOR'S INTRODUCTION

1. Yamauchi Keita, "Fukuzawa Yukichi no kodomo-muke no hon" in Komuro Masamichi, ed., *Kindai Nihon to Fukuzawa Yukichi*, pp. 128–131, Tokyo: Keiogijuku Daigaku shuppankai, 2013, pp. 123–148.

2. *Fukuzawa zenshū chogen*, in *Fukuzawa Yukichi chosakushū* 12, pp. 476–478, Tokyo: Keiogijuku Daigaku shuppankai, 2003 (originally published in 1897).

3. See Koizumi Takashi, *Fukuzawa Yukichi no shūkyōkan*, Tokyo: Keiogijuku Daigaku shuppankai, 2002, pp. 47–55. Koizumi also points out that Christianity was still clearly a banned religion at this time (p. 51).

4. *On Japanese Women, Part Two*, p. 131 in this volume.

5. Preface to the original English translation of "Hibi no oshie" in *Fukuzawa Yukichi on Education: Selected Works*, translated and edited by Kiyooka Eiichi, Tokyo: University of Tokyo Press, 1985, p. 47.

6. Fukuzawa Ichitarō, first printed in *Shōnen* 28, January 1906, reprinted in Yamauchi, *op.cit*, pp. 125–126.

♦NOTES TO TEXT

1. "Hibi no oshie" (ひゞのをしへ), 1871. This revised translation is based on the text in *Fukuzawa Yukichi zenshū* 20, 2nd edn, Tokyo: Iwanami shoten, 1971, pp. 67–77, with a newly translated portion from *ibid.*, pp. 818–819.

2. This is clearly based on the introduction to the section on "Conduct towards Animals" in William and Robert Chambers, eds., *The Moral Class-Book*, Edinburgh: William and Robert Chambers, 1856, p. 11.

3. This is clearly based on the introduction to the section on "Self-Service and Self-Dependence" in *op.cit*, pp. 37–38.

4. In this and other parts where Fukuzawa uses the word "*kokoro*," I have endeavored to translate it as "inside" or "feelings," rather than decide whether he means "mind" or "heart."

5. Yamauchi Keita suggests that he wrote this passage partly to prepare the boys in the event of his assassination by opponents of Western learning, since this was still a possibility in late 1871. (See "Fukuzawa Yukichi no kodomo-muke no hon," pp. 126–127.) It is not clear why Fukuzawa chose to use the word "God" (in *hiragana*) here, however, especially since he claims elsewhere to have no religious beliefs. He could just as well have used "Heaven" (*Ten*), a more neutral and "Asian" concept, as he does, for example, in a similar context when writing to his only surviving sister about the death of their last remaining sibling. (See Letter No. 53 in this volume, p. 369.)

6. For the origin of this quotation, see note 2, "A Message of Farewell to Nakatsu."

7. In the original folk tale, Momotarō is treated as a brave hero, and the demons are assumed to be evil. Fukuzawa's condemnation of Momotarō calls to mind his controversial criticism of the vendetta carried out by the forty-seven *rōnin*, folk heroes of the Tokugawa period, in the sixth section of *An Encouragement of Learning*, published in 1874. See *The Thought of Fukuzawa* 2, pp. 44–48, 138.

8. This was the method being used in Japan at the time, until the complete introduction of the Western calendar in 1872. The length of the hours differed according to the seasons, with daytime hours being longest at midsummer, and nighttime hours being longest at midwinter.

9. 1 *shaku* (*kanejaku*) is 30 cm. (0.995 ft).

10. 1 *shaku* (*kujirajaku*) is 38 cm. (1.246 ft).

11. 1 *tsubo* is 3.3 m^2 (3.947 yd^2).

12. 1 *ken* is 1.818 m. (1.988 yd).

13. This is where Kiyooka's original translation ends. However, on pp. 818–819 of the appendix to volume 20 of *Fukuzawa Yukichi zenshū* there are three more sections from Sutejirō's version of the "Daily Lessons." The editor has translated these below.

14. This saying (*saru no chie*) refers to a Chinese tale of an island inhabited by 500 monkeys. The island provided everything that the monkeys needed, but one of them saw the glittering of the sea and was convinced that this must be the reflection of a wonderful place beyond the waters. He decided to swim there. Another monkey noticed him leave, and when he did not come back concluded that this was because he had indeed found a better place to live. This monkey therefore decided to follow his example. Eventually,

there were no monkeys left on the island.

Reasons for Sharing Some Old Coins with My Children

◆NOTES TO EDITOR'S INTRODUCTION

1. "Nakamura Ritsuen no shokan," p. 489, in *Fukuzawa Yukichi zenshū* 4, 2nd edn, Tokyo: Iwanami shoten, 1970, pp. 487–490, reprinted from *Fukuzawa bunshū* 2, vol. 1, 1879.

2. Letter dated 21 Jan 1878, in *Fukuzawa Yukichi shokanshū* 2, Tokyo: Iwanami, 2001, pp. 43–44. In a longer reply to Nakamura written a few days later, he expressed his agreement concerning the importance of filial piety. A translation of this reply can be found in *Fukuzawa Yukichi on Education: Selected works*, translated and edited by Kiyooka Eiichi, Tokyo: University of Tokyo Press, 1985, pp. 111–117. (The Japanese original is in *Fukuzawa Yukichi zenshū* 4, pp. 491–496, reprinted from *Fukuzawa bunshū* 2, vol. 1, 1879.)

3. *Onna no oi to otoko no oi*, Tokyo: Yoshikawa kōbunkan, 2005, pp. 11–14.

4. See p. 343 in this volume.

5. See p. 52 in this volume.

◆NOTES TO TEXT

1. "Fukuzawa-shi kosen haibun no ki" (福澤氏古銭配分之記), 1878, first published in *Jiji shinpō*, 11 March, 1896. This revised translation is based on the text in *Fukuzawa Yukichi zenshū* 15, 2nd edn, Tokyo: Iwanami shoten, 1971, pp. 394–397.

2. Nomoto was one of the first teachers at Shinshūkan, the academy set up by Okudaira Masataka, daimyo of Nakatsu, in 1796. Hoashi was invited to teach at Nakatsu. He was interested in science as well as in Chinese studies.

3. Itō Jinsai, one of the most influential Confucian scholars of the Tokugawa period, encouraged people to read the Chinese classics themselves for their insights about practical ethical issues instead of studying the interpretations of Neo-Confucian scholars.

Selected Letters from Fukuzawa

◆NOTES TO EDITOR'S INTRODUCTION

1. Interview of Kiyooka Shun by Kiyooka Eiichi in Nishikawa Shunsaku and Nishikawa Naoko, eds., *Fudangi no Fukuzawa Yukichi*, p. 11.

2. For Marion Saucier's analysis of the letters sent by Fukuzawa to his two eldest sons while they were studying abroad, see Marion Saucier, "Lettres d'un père à ses fils" in Galan and Lozerand eds., *La Famille Japonaise Moderne*, pp. 473–485.

3. "Chōnan Ichitarō kekkon hirō no sekijō ni okeru enzetsu," *Fukuzawa Yukichi zenshū* (hereinafter referred to as *Zenshū*) 19, 2nd edn, Tokyo: Iwanami shoten, 1971, pp. 174–177.

◆NOTES TO TEXTS

1. 築紀平 No. 69, *Fukuzawa Yukichi shokanshū* (hereinafter referred to as *Shokanshū*) 1, pp. 132–134.

2. Two days before the date of this letter, ownership of *han* had been "returned" to the government (*hanseki hōkan*). Daimyo were now known as *chihanji*, and there was no guarantee that their positions would still be hereditary. This was a preliminary to the complete disbanding of the feudal system two years later.

3. In a letter to Hattori Gorobei, Matashiro's father, on Sept. 29 [No. 73, pp. 138–40], he actually asks Hattori to persuade his mother to give up the idea of his entering Okudaira's service. She did not actually move to Tokyo until Fukuzawa went to fetch her around ten months later. (This was when he wrote "A Message of Farewell to Nakatsu.") Two of his sisters came to join their mother in 1872.

4. 九鬼隆義 No. 86, *Shokanshū* 1, pp. 161–162.

5. No. 558, *Zenshū* 17, pp. 552–553.

6. 一太郎 Fukuzawa's eldest son, then aged twenty.

7. 捨次郎 Fukuzawa's second son, then aged eighteen.

8. No. 748, *Shokanshū* 3, pp. 298–301.

9. Imaizumi Tō, elder sister of Fukuzawa's wife. She and her son were living in Fukuzawa's house.

10. Fukuzawa's three eldest daughters: Sato (aged fifteen), Fusa (aged thirteen), and Shun (aged ten).

11. Fukuzawa's third son, aged two.

12. Fukuzawa's youngest daughter, aged four. The remaining daughter, Taki, was aged seven at this time.

13. Terashima had been a friend since he and Fukuzawa were students at Ogata Kōan's academy of Dutch learning in Osaka in the mid 1850s. Sameshima was a former Keio student.

14. This was a trading company set up in 1876 by Morimura Ichitarō, an acquaintance of Fukuzawa, and his younger brother, Yutaka, who had studied at Keio. Yutaka went to New York and established Morimura Bros. in 1879.

15. No. 777, *Shokanshū* 3, pp. 333–336.

16. No. 798, *Shokanshū* 4, pp. 29–32.

17. No. 818, *ibid.*, pp. 65–66.

18. No. 823, *ibid.*, pp. 75–78.

19. No. 838, *ibid.*, pp. 100–103.

20. Simmons worked as a doctor, initially as a medical missionary, in Japan and had become friends with Fukuzawa after treating him for a severe case of typhoid in 1870. At this time, he was living in Poughkeepsie. Until returning to Japan in 1886 he acted as physician and general adviser to Ichitarō and Sutejirō, at Fukuzawa's request.

21. In his autobiography, Fukuzawa claimed that during his second voyage to the United States in 1867 he became drunk on board ship and criticized the Bakufu in a loud voice, and that on his return he received an official reprimand for "offensive acts" while abroad. He concluded that his remarks had been overheard and reported. See *The*

Autobiography of Yukichi Fukuzawa, pp. 172–174. However, Matsuzawa Hiroaki throws doubt on this incident. (See *Fukuzawa Yukichi-shū*, pp. 196–197, footnote 4.)

22. No. 853, *Shokanshū* 4, pp. 122–123.

23. No. 862, *ibid.*, pp. 131–133.

24. Remarks of this nature were a stock beginning of most of the letters Fukuzawa sent to his sons while they were away.

25. When conscription was introduced in Japan in 1873, pupils at government-funded educational institutions were exempted. For a short period, from January 1877 to October 1879, Keio students were exempted as well. Fukuzawa is referring here to revisions of December 1883 that prohibited exemptions for any school or college, but allowed deferments for students at government-funded institutions only. He had protested about this in January, but Keio students did not obtain similar privileges until 1899.

26. No. 883, *Shokanshū* 4, pp. 164–166.

27. No. 884, *ibid.*, pp. 167–168.

28. No. 907, *ibid.*, pp. 199–203.

29. Fukuzawa's fifth son and youngest child, then aged two.

30. No. 985, *Shokanshū* 4, pp. 306–308.

31. Fukuzawa is here referring to his first major writings about the need to improve the position of women in Japan. "On Japanese Women" and *On Japanese Women, Part Two* were both serialized in *Jiji shinpō* in 1885. The latter was also published in book form in the same year. Translations can be found in this volume, on pp. 75–103 and 107–138.

32. It appeared in *Jiji shinpō* on 6 October, 1885.

33. The British-style gentlemen's club that Fukuzawa had been instrumental in founding in Ginza in 1880.

34. Fukuzawa had been a major shareholder in the Maruya Bank, which had failed in 1884.

35. No. 995, *Shokanshū* 4, pp. 323–327.

36. Both former Keio students who were successful in setting up their own businesses after studying in the United States. For Morimura Yutaka, see also note 14, p. 413.

37. No. 998, *Shokanshū* 4, pp. 329–330.

38. No. 1036, *Shokanshū* 5, pp. 37–39.

39. No. 1055, *ibid.*, pp. 58–59.

40. This party is presumably an example of the sort of informal gatherings of men and women that Fukuzawa was to propose in the final installment of "On Relations between Men and Women," which appeared on 3 June 1886. (See p. 203 in this volume.)

41. No. 1076, *Shokanshū* 5, pp. 89–90.

42. No. 1116, *ibid.*, pp. 137–138.

43. Takashima appears to have married into the family of Ōkura Hachirō, a wealthy businessman, so whether this story is true or not, presumably no wedding actually took place.

44. 服部鐘 No. 1121, *Shokanshū* 5, p. 143.

45. No. 1126, *ibid.*, pp. 150–151.
46. No. 1130, *ibid.*, pp. 155–156.
47. The school was Yokohama Kyōritsu Jogakkō (The Doremus School), a boarding school for girls established by female missionaries of the Women's Union Missionary Society of the United States in 1871. However, they were withdrawn from the school after only two months. For the possible reasons, see the General Introduction, p. 38.
48. No. 1141, *Shokanshū* 5, pp. 170–173.
49. No. 1148, *ibid.*, pp. 180–182.
50. No. 1159, *ibid.*, pp. 192–195.
51. No. 1176, *ibid.*, pp. 212–215.
52. This is probably the letter that Kin refers to in her letter to Ichitarō, p. 370.
53. If Fukuzawa is following the traditional Japanese way of counting ages, according to which a baby is counted as one year old when born, this would mean that Ichitarō did not start to speak until the age of four by Western reckoning.
54. No. 1187, *Shokanshū* 5, pp. 231–233.
55. Fukuzawa Momosuke (1868–1938). He was adopted by the Fukuzawa family as a future husband for their second eldest daughter, Fusa, while a student at Keio in 1886. In 1887 Fukuzawa sent him to the United States, where he studied and then gained experience in railway management by working on the Pennsylvania Railway. He married Fusa on his return in 1889. Momosuke was a successful entrepreneur, but the marriage may not have been a happy one.
56. It appears that Dr. Yunghans was a believer in cold baths in winter and other Spartan-like practices. (See Terasaki Osamu and Nishikawa Shunsaku, "Kaidai," p. 400, *Shokanshū* 5.)
57. No. 1213, *ibid.*, pp. 267–269.
58. No. 1262, *ibid.*, pp. 333–334.
59. These would probably have included the children of contemporaries of Fukuzawa who, unlike Fukuzawa himself, had chosen to take government posts and subsequently been raised to the peerage as a reward.
60. No. 1264, *Shokanshū* 5, pp. 337–339.
61. No. 1286, *ibid.*, p. 367.
62. 小田部礼 No. 1295, *Shokanshū* 6, pp. 16–17.
63. 中上川彦次郎 No. 1363, *ibid.*, pp. 101–102.
64. In this letter, Fukuzawa assumes that all public officials were exempt from call-up but, as his next letter (translated here as No. 36) makes clear, he received a reply from Nakamigawa informing him that he had misunderstood the situation.
65. At this time, Nakamigawa (1854–1901) was President of the San'yō Railway Company. He had a very close relationship with Fukuzawa, who had paid for him to study in England in the mid 1870s.
66. No. 1364, *Shokanshū* 6, pp. 103–104.
67. According to letter no. 1390 to his adopted son Momosuke (27 May 1889, *Shokanshū* 6, p. 144), Sutejirō was indeed able to obtain a lifelong exemption from conscription because of his bad teeth.

68. A former Keio student who had a private practice in Yokohama, while also working at a hospital there. He acted as a physician for the Fukuzawas as well as for the Minoda family.

69. No. 1381, *Shokanshū* 6, pp. 128–130.

70. No. 1405, *ibid.*, pp. 168–170.

71. At this time, Sutejirō was working for the San'yō Railway Company in Kobe.

72. They set out on September 16th and returned to Tokyo on October 5th. A diary of this trip remains. It has been suggested that Fukuzawa wrote it to use as the basis for tales to amuse the younger participants afterwards. See Nishizawa, *Fukuzawa Yukichi to furī rabu*, pp. 57–58.

73. No. 1416, *Shokanshū* 6, pp. 182–183.

74. A former Keio student who played an important role in the development of the practice of Western medicine in Japan. He also acted as physician to the Fukuzawa family.

75. A former Keio student who taught medicine at Tokyo Imperial University and was also the head physician of Japan's first life insurance company, Meiji Seimei.

76. 近藤良薫 No. 1420, *Shokanshū* 6, pp. 187–190.

77. No. 1422, *ibid.*, pp. 192–195.

78. No. 1423, *ibid.*, pp. 196–197.

79. No. 1425, *ibid.*, pp. 199–201.

80. No. 1427, *ibid.*, pp. 205–206.

81. No. 1456, *ibid.*, p. 243.

82. Letter No. 1464 to Dr. Kondō, dated 31 March 1890, indicates that everything has been settled. See *Shokanshū* 6, p. 252.

83. No. 1490, *ibid.*, pp. 283–284.

84. A scholar of Western studies who became a friend of Fukuzawa before the Meiji Restoration and then played an important role in the development of Japan's chemical industry.

85. 福沢桃介／房 No. 1495, *Shokanshū* 6, p. 291.

86. 益田英次 No. 1498, *ibid.*, pp. 294–295.

87. According to Taki, Miss Fallot had three dogs. See "Fudangi no Yukichi to Eigo kyōiku," p. 9.

88. No. 1505, *Shokanshū* 6, pp. 303–304.

89. Shimada Hirosuke was a mid-sixteenth century swordsmith. Although Fukuzawa deliberately stopped wearing two swords in 1868, when it was still a sign of samurai rank, he practiced the art of drawing swords in preparation for combat (*iai*) throughout his life.

90. Muramasa was a famous sixteenth-century school of swordmaking. Muramasa swords were said to be particularly sharp.

91. No. 1549, *Shokanshū* 6, pp. 361–362.

92. No. 1568, *Shokanshū* 7, pp. 14–16.

93. 清岡邦之助／俊 No. 1942, *Shokanshū* 8, pp. 62–63.

94. This is the second of three letters that he writes to his third daughter O-Shun and her husband about the outbreak of cholera at Hiroshima. Presumably they were living in Hiroshima because Kuninosuke had business related to the Sino-Japanese War.

95. No. 2165, *Shokanshū* 8, pp. 307–308.

96. No. 910, *Zenshū* 18, pp. 129–130. This letter from Kin was in an envelope with a letter of the same date from Fukuzawa. I have not translated Fukuzawa's letter but, like Letter No. 28 of 29 June (pp. 340–341), it makes no reference to any worries about Ichitarō. For what seems to be, finally, a direct response to the letter of 20 May that Kin is probably talking about, see Fukuzawa's letter of 18 July (No. 29, pp. 342–344 in this volume).

97. No. 1121, *ibid.*, pp. 340–341. This letter seems to have been sent to Sutejirō with Letter No. 44, of 25 November 1889 (pp. 361–362 in this volume).

Index

civilization 62, 132, 142–143, 154, 155, 157, 165, 170, 173; levels / stages of 20, 41, 55, 119, 134, 141, 142–143, 147, 169, 180; Western 71, 76, 151–152, 153, 158, 163, 168, 179, 193–194

concubines 15–16, 18, 20, 21–22, 41, 64, 86, 87, 89, 92, 99–100, 112, 116, 118, 119, 125, 139–140, 144, 146, 148, 155, 166–175 passim, 200, 201, 219, 220, 221, 223, 234, 239, 240, 266, 275, 276, 382 (note 46)

Confucianism 20, 26, 28, 33, 65, 101, 105, 147, 185; Ancient Learning 古学 (*kogaku*) 158, 173, 203, 204, 255, 402 (note 17); and the family 11, 219–220; and women 15, 44–45, 86–87; constructed by men 29, 45, 110, 113, 115–116, 223, 225, 239, 255; Fukuzawa's criticisms of 9, 21, 29, 44–45, 52, 64–65, 76, 86–87, 89–90, 93, 111, 139, 147–149, 168, 177, 185–187, 202, 218, 219–220, 228–229, 278, 313; Fukuzawa's positive use of Confucianism / Confucian language 44–45, 63, 109; on husbands and wives 9, 15, 21, 44–45, 64–66, 124, 132, 149, 195–197; on parents and children 14, 21, 29, 64–65, 149, 227–229, 313; reciprocity 恕 115–116, 117; yin 陰 and yang 陽 29, 45, 105, 109–110, 119, 180, 249, 253–254. *See also* Confucian texts

Confucian texts: *Analects, The* 『論語』 64, 65, 79, 80, 115, 144, 146, 152, 186, 399–400 (note 18); *Mencius* 『孟子』 29, 44–45, 125, 147, 158, 186, 195, 206, 234, 401 (notes 7 and 9), 409 (note 16); *The Book of Documents* 『書経』 44, 63, 109, 119, 150, 181, 190, 234, 291; *The Book of Rites* 『礼記』 44–45, 186. *See also* Great Learning for Women, The

education 18, 42; and females 10–23 passim, 28, 30, 31, 42, 43–44, 54, 69–72, 76, 79–81, 130, 148, 237, 241–243, 253, 260–264, 273–275, 392–393 (note 1); and males 14, 18, 23, 28, 305–306, 363–364; and physical health 36, 313, 315, 320; of Fukuzawa's daughters 23, 37–38, 39, 54, 69, 337; of Fukuzawa's sons 38, 305–306; in Meiji Japan 28–29; in Tokugawa Japan 12, 14–15; moral education 29, 36, 263–264, 292–297 passim, 301, 302

equality: of men and women 9, 11, 16,

20–30 passim, 35, 41–42, 44, 52, 62, 64, 102, 108–109, 134, 148–149, 252–253, 259

family: adoption 13, 38, 95, 121, 210, 215, 222, 362, 363–364; and Confucianism. See Confucianism; family spirit / traditions 家風 33, 36, 39, 243–244, 263–264, 299, 301, 302–303, 343; Fukuzawa and his family: See under Fukuzawa Yukichi; Fukuzawa's ideal of 15, 42, 61, 122, 229, 244, 263–264, 269, 307–308, 332; hereditary family system 13–14, 20, 26, 52, 73, 74, 95, 96, 117–118, 121, 123, 299, 303; in Europe and America as opposed to Japan 41; in Meiji Japan 18, 20–21; in Tokugawa Japan 10, 13–16, 20, 41; nuclear family system 18, 52, 96, 122, 123, 129, 229, 266–269; relationships / roles within 10, 11, 15, 18, 19–20, 26–32 passim, 42, 64, 65–66, 197, 199–200, 215, 227–229, 231, 256, 264, 266–269, 393 (note 4); surnames 74, 96, 121, 397 (note 19)

fertility 13–14, 15, 22, 26, 77–78, 117–118, 119, 223

freedom: free love 30, 42, 205, 206–207; meaning of the word 20–21, 63–64, 391 (note 3); of family units 19, 268; of individuals 10, 19, 38, 65, 68, 85, 87, 91–94, 102, 103, 112, 115, 130, 133, 134, 145–146, 154, 171–172, 174, 192, 193, 199–200, 202–203, 225, 239, 243, 246, 256, 265, 311; of nations 19, 68

Fukuzawa Daishirō 福沢大四郎 (fourth son) 35, 37, 40, 327, 337

Fukuzawa Fusa 福沢房 (second daughter) 38, 315, 337, 362, 363, 364, 367

Fukuzawa Hyakusuke 福沢百助 (father) 33, 211, 213, 299–303

Fukuzawa Ichitarō 福沢一太郎 (eldest son) 35, 36. 37, 39–40, 48, 50, 211–212, 287–288, 305–307, 347–348, 362; Fukuzawa's advice to 313–347 passim; first marriage and divorce 40, 308, 350–351, 354–363 passim, 372–372, 397 (note 23); mental weakness 39, 324, 333, 342, 350; problems with alcohol 40, 306, 314, 325, 343, 355

Fukuzawa Kin 福沢錦 (wife) 34, 36, 38, 305, 308, 317, 367, 370–372; relationship with husband 34–35, 38–39, 317, 326, 334, 341, 355, 362, 370–371; Taki's portrayal of 36, 39

Fukuzawa Mitsu 福沢光 (fifth daughter) 315, 337, 364

Fukuzawa O-Jun 福沢於順 (mother) 33, 300, 301, 310, 370

Fukuzawa Sanpachi 福沢三八 (third son) 315, 317, 321–322, 327, 337

Fukuzawa Sato 福沢里 (eldest daughter) 35, 36, 315, 337; illness of 353–354, 356, 357

Fukuzawa Shun 福沢俊 (third daughter) 34, 35, 38, 315, 337, 362, 363–364, 367–369

Fukuzawa Sutejirō 福沢捨次郎 (second son) 36, 37, 39–40, 287, 305–306, 347, 349–350, 351–353, 361–362, 364, 365–368, 371–372; Fukuzawa's advice

to 313–321 passim, 340, 346–347
Fukuzawa Taki 福沢滝 (fourth daughter) 38–39, 337, 367
Fukuzawa Yukichi 福沢諭吉: and his family 32–39 passim, 61, 212, 299–303, 305, 307–308, 310–315 passim, 319, 341, 343, 351–352, 364–370 passim, 385–386 (note 105), 387 (note 127) *See also under* names of family members; consciousness of the Western eye 20, 31, 41, 43, 55, 126, 141–142, 155–156, 158–159, 165, 169, 240, 282; diachronic / evolutionary perspective of 20, 42, 52, 55–56, 91–94, 108, 123–124, 142–143, 144–149, 150–151, 160, 161, 166, 180, 181, 186, 190, 198–199, 206–207, 255, 258, 265, 266; influence of Dutch studies / science on 43, 78, 118–119, 120–121, 151–152, 181, 189–190, 206, 223; letters and letter-writing 9–10, 33, 36–40 passim, 54, 55, 305–370; motives for writing about women 19, 25–34 passim, 41, 123–124, 141–142, 211–212, 278, 282–283; on morality 17, 21, 28–32 passim, 36, 45, 53, 55, 143–144, 243–244, 287, 289–297 passim, 299, 300–301, 312–313 *See also* sex workers and the sex trade; on rights 28, 48 *See also under* women; on sexual fulfillment 10, 53, 151; organization of mixed-gender social gatherings by 26–28, 38, 334; possible gap between public and private personas 9, 35, 36, 39, 54–55, 305–306, 338–339, 342–343, 349–350; responses to his writings 45–55, 107, 327, 385 (notes 95 and 101) *For individual texts see under* Fukuzawa, writings

Fukuzawa, writings: "Answer to a Certain Gentleman's Inquiry about Female Education, An"「女子教育の事に付某氏に答」19, 69–72; *Autobiography of Fukuzawa Yukichi, The*『福翁自伝』31–33, 36, 37, 61, 205; *Critique of The Great Learning for Women, A*『女大学評論』10–11, 22–35 passim, 46, 47, 48, 49, 51–52, 209–258, 281–283; *Encouragement of Learning, An*『学問のすゝめ』10, 16, 19; "Equal Numbers of Men and Women, The"「男女同数論」19, 20–21; *Fukuzawa's Talks on Worldly Affairs*『福沢浮世談』28, 31; "Daily Lessons" 36, 287–297; "Message of Farewell to Nakatsu, A"「中津留別之書」19–20, 21, 44, 61–68, 305; *New Great Learning for Women, A*『新女大学』10–11, 28, 32, 46, 47, 48, 49, 55, 209–214, 259–283; "One Husband, One Wife, Together Even in the Grave"「一夫一婦偕老同穴」, *One Hundred Reflections by Fukuzawa*『福翁百話』28, 29–31, 42, 205–207; "On Female Acts of Filial Piety"「婦女孝行論」24, 27; *On Japanese Men*『日本男子論』24, 27, 28; "On Japanese Women"「日本婦人論」10, 24, 25, 26, 27, 43–44, 48, 73–103, 117, 124, 138, 327; 384 (note 80); *On Japanese Women, Part Two*『日本婦人論後編』11, 24–30 passim, 41, 48, 51, 105–138, 327–328; *On Moral Behavior*『品行論』16, 22, 24, 27, 41, 46, 53, 139–176; *On Relations* between Men and Women 『男女交際論』 13, 24, 27–28, 44–45, 46, 177–204; *Outline of a Theory of Civilization, An* 『文明論之概略』 42; *Popular Discussion of People's Rights, A* 『通俗国権論』 27; "Reasons for Sharing some Old Coins with My Children" 「福沢氏古銭配分之記」 33, 36, 299–303

geisha 芸者 21, 28, 139, 140, 156–159, 169, 172, 174, 175, 265, 273, 275
Great Learning for Women, The 『女大学』 11, 12, 14, 23, 49, 124; Fukuzawa on 10–11, 12, 17, 21, 32, 46, 51–52, 76, 105, 110–112, 113, 114, 117, 124, 135, 209–210, 215–258, 277–278, 280, 281–282, 313; other views of 12, 47, 49; updated versions of 23–24, 28, 45–46, 47–48

independence 20–21, 39; of individuals 19–21, 23–24, 32–42 passim, 48, 52, 55, 61, 62, 63, 65, 130, 154, 290, 305–306, 310, 319, 324, 338–339, 341, 387 (note 128); of family units 19, 42, 52, 62, 63, 129, 268, 342; of nations 9, 19, 28, 41, 55, 62, 63–64, 68
Itō Hirobumi 伊藤博文 25, 139, 399 (note 14), 403 (note 30)
Iwamoto Yoshiharu 巌本善治 25, 53, 403 (note 23)

jealousy 21, 43, 112, 113, 115, 193, 224, 225, 231–235, 250–251, 257, 276
Jogaku zasshi 『女学雑誌』 25, 46, 53–54

Kaibara Ekiken 貝原益軒 11, 214, 282
Keiogijuku 10, 29, 37, 39, 40, 318, 331, 339, 350; girl's education at 23; female teachers at 23, 364

love 18, 19–20, 29, 30, 36, 46, 65, 66, 99–100, 118, 123, 132–133, 148, 182, 189, 191, 196, 197–198, 201, 206–207, 227–229, 246, 267, 269, 279, 294, 343. *For* free love, *see under* freedom

marriage 18, 21–22, 29, 30, 31, 44, 55, 92–93, 153–155, 160–161, 194–197; adultery 20, 22, 31, 46, 54; and monogamy 15–16, 20, 22, 42, 45, 62, 63, 64–65, 145, 206–207; and women 11, 26, 29, 76, 78–79, 80, 118–119, 257, 266, 279; arranged marriages 38, 46, 48, 124–125, 194–195, 264–266, 276, 308, 341; as an equal / unequal partnership 9, 15, 20, 22, 26, 29, 52, 96–99, 105, 121–123, 129, 132–135, 195–196, 229–231, 240–241, 247–248, 255–256, 270, 275; as the basis of morality / society 62, 64, 168, 234, 312–313, 356, 360; between Japanese and foreigners 75, 307, 335–336, 338–339, 394 (note 2); divorce 22, 40, 42, 46, 49, 98, 100, 112, 221–226, 358, 397 (note 23) *See also under* Fukuzawa Ichitarō; free love: *See under* freedom; Fukuzawa's ideal of 31, 42–43, 44–45, 50, 54, 99–100, 118, 123, 129, 132, 133, 266, 275; marriages of Fukuzawa's children 38, 40, 341, 362, 363–364 *See also under* Fukuzawa Ichitarō; of

Fukuzawa 34–35, 54; remarriage 15, 36, 42, 86–87, 92–93, 102, 277, 308, 354, 363. *See also* family

Meiji Japan 9, 12, 18, 24, 42, 51, 55; and position of women 9, 42, 48–50, 156; Meiji Civil Code 22, 31, 52, 98, 220, 225–226, 236, 282, 283

men 27, 28, 32; and child–rearing 14, 18, 65–66, 259; and social gatherings involving women 26–28, 43, 45, 46–47, 169, 177–178, 179, 182, 189, 194, 202–203; as fathers of daughters 70–72, 130, 218–219, 243–244, 256–257; as husbands 15, 20, 22, 29, 42–43, 52, 77–79, 112–113, 125, 126, 132–133, 195–197, 230–231, 239; duties of 52, 130–131, 259; in Europe and America as opposed to Japan 17, 27, 31, 141, 151–152, 170; need to change 113, 123, 130, 133, 139, 141, 150–151, 165, 166, 169–170, 172, 174–175, 230. *See also* equality, family and promiscuity

Mill, John Stuart 21, 43, 52–53, 73, 105, 390 (note 177), 394 (note 6), 397 (note 25), 398 (note 4), 407 (notes 12 and 13)

pleasure quarters 遊郭 (*yūkaku*): *See* sex workers and the sex trade

promiscuity 16–17, 20, 21–22, 26, 27–28, 30, 31, 43, 45, 53, 87, 139, 144–149 passim, 163–169 passim, 200–201

prostitutes: *See* sex workers and the sex trade

respecting men and despising women 男尊女卑 (*danson johi*) 148, 149, 171, 180, 188, 195, 202, 211, 234, 255, 278, 401 (note 8)

sex workers and the sex trade 12, 16, 17, 46, 53–54, 125, 401 (note 15); Fukuzawa on 17, 21–22, 27, 31, 43, 46 52–53, 139–140, 154–166 passim, 170–172, 173–175, 176, 275; in Europe and America as opposed to Japan 17–18, 27, 31, 163, 175–176; licensing of 53, 140, 156–157, 176, 401–402 (note 15). *See also* concubines and geisha

social custom / oppression 10, 21, 25–26, 42, 74, 76, 81–82, 88, 90, 105, 152, 166, 177, 192–204 passim, 235, 257, 278

Tokugawa Japan 9, 44, 183, 310–311; and position of women 10–17, 18, 20, 41, 49, 50, 51, 145–149, 156, 184–185, 191–192, 257; and promiscuity 10, 15–16

treaty revision 条約改正 (*jōyaku kaisei*) 31, 209–210, 240, 282, 283

Ueki Emori 植木枝盛 53, 54

Wayland, Francis 20, 21, 62, 287, 312, 391–392 (notes 4 and 9), 399 (note 11)

Women: and assets / property 10, 26, 42, 77, 78, 81, 96–97, 99, 130, 131, 280–281; and child-rearing 12, 14, 18, 21, 65–66, 270–271; and Confucianism:

See Confucianism; and education: *See* education; and economic activity 11, 13, 17, 34, 42–43, 52, 77, 127–129, 130, 242, 252–253, 272–273, 280–281; and leisure 43, 54, 75, 85, 86, 271, 336; and marriage *See* marriage; and political activity 22, 24–25, 52, 136–137; and social gatherings involving men 26–28, 43, 45, 46–47, 177–178, 180, 182, 194, 202–203; as borrowed wombs 腹は借物 (*hara wa karimono*) 13–14, 43, 105, 118–120, 399 (note 13); as daughters-in-law 45, 46, 227–229, 266–270; as mothers 12, 22–23, 24, 28, 43, 73, 77–78, 259, 270–272, 279, 281; as widows 15, 42, 86–87, 127–131 passim, 252, 272–273, 277; as wives 10, 11, 14, 15, 21, 22, 26, 28, 29, 30, 32, 42, 52, 77–79, 112, 125–126, 171–172, 230–231, 241–242; duties of 276; in China and Korea as opposed to Japan 100–101; in Europe and America as opposed to Japan 16, 17, 21, 30, 31, 43, 47, 51, 55, 81, 108–109, 126, 131, 171, 193–194, 252–253, 271, 274, 281; Fukuzawa's ideal of 242–243, 262, 275–276, 279; menstruation 88, 190, 261; mental and physical health of 10, 53, 79, 81–82, 85, 88–89, 92, 93, 94, 124, 125, 126; of the middle class / middle levels of society and above 13, 22, 25, 26, 42, 51, 54, 73, 82, 85, 88, 91, 101, 124, 126; of the samurai class 10, 12–13, 14–15, 243; responsibilities of 10, 26, 28, 52, 77–78, 79, 81, 99, 210, 252; responses to Fukuzawa's writings 35, 48–50, 54, 107; rights of 22, 24, 30, 35, 42, 43 49, 52, 78, 99, 210, 232, 234–235, 240–241, 244, 245–246, 251, 276, 280; sexual frustration of 10, 53, 73, 85–87; unequal treatment of by men 20, 26, 86–87, 119, 121–122, 134–135, 136–137, 223, 225, 238–239, 257; work inside and outside the home 11–12, 13, 26, 42, 52, 81, 108, 130, 247–248, 251–253, 272–273, 275. *See also* equality, family, fertility, promiscuity, and sex workers and the sex trade

Yamakawa Kikue 山川菊栄 13; evaluation of Fukuzawa's writings on women 49–50; *Women of the Mito Domain* 『武士の女性』 13, 14–15, 16

Yoshiwara 吉原. *See* sex workers and the sex trade

TRANSLATOR
Helen Ballhatchet is a professor at Keio University. She has also taught at the School of Oriental and African Studies, University of London. Her research involves the intellectual history of Meiji Japan and she has written about missionary activity, Japanese responses to Christianity, and Baba Tatsui as well as working on Fukuzawa Yukichi.

About the series:

The Thought of Fukuzawa 1
An Outline of a Theory of Civilization, Revised Translation by David A. Dilworth and G. Cameron Hurst, III, with an Introduction by Inoki Takenori, Tokyo: Keio University Press, 2008.

The Thought of Fukuzawa 2
An Encouragement of Learning, Translated by David A. Dilworth, with an Introduction with Nishikawa Shunsaku, Tokyo: Keio University Press, 2012.

The Thought of Fukuzawa 3
Fukuzawa Yukichi on Women and the Family, Edited and with New and Revised Translations by Helen Ballhatchet, Tokyo: Keio University Press, 2017.

慶應義塾創立 150 年記念
THE THOUGHT OF FUKUZAWA

編集顧問 Advisory Board	編集委員 Editorial Committee
Albert M. Craig	Helen Ballhatchet
安西祐一郎 Anzai Yūichirō	池田幸弘 Ikeda Yukihiro
福澤武 Fukuzawa Takeshi	岩谷十郎 Iwatani Jūrō
服部禮次郎 Hattori Reijirō	小室正紀 Komuro Masamichi
坂本達哉 Sakamoto Tatsuya	西川俊作 Nishikawa Shunsaku
	西澤直子 Nishizawa Naoko
	山内慶太 Yamauchi Keita

The Thought of Fukuzawa, Volume 3
Fukuzawa Yukichi on Women and the Family

2017 年 3 月 30 日　初版第 1 刷発行

著　者――――福澤諭吉
編訳者――――Helen Ballhatchet
発行者――――古屋正博
発行所――――慶應義塾大学出版会株式会社
　　　　　〒108-8346　東京都港区三田 2-19-30
　　　　　TEL〔編集部〕03-3451-0931
　　　　　　〔営業部〕03-3451-3584〈ご注文〉
　　　　　　〔　〃　〕03-3451-6926
　　　　　FAX〔営業部〕03-3451-3122
　　　　　振替　00190-8-155497
　　　　　http://www.keio-up.co.jp/
装　丁――――耳塚有里
印刷・製本――萩原印刷株式会社

©2017 Keio University Press
Printed in Japan　ISBN 978-4-7664-2414-0

慶應義塾大学出版会

The Thought of Fukuzawa Vol. 1

An Outline of a Theory of Civilization

福澤諭吉 著
デヴィッド・A・ディルワース／G・キャメロン・ハースト, III 訳

福澤の思索が最も充実した壮年期の著作で最高傑作の一つと名高い『文明論之概略』（1875年刊行）の英訳。近代日本を啓蒙し、先導した福澤諭吉の著作を、国内外の読者に向けて英訳で刊行するシリーズの第1巻。＊年表・参考文献一覧・索引付き。

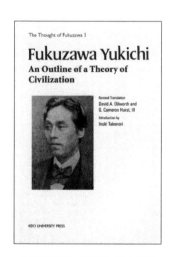

B5判変型／並製／320頁
ISBN 978-4-7664-1560-5
◎3,200円

表示価格は刊行時の本体価格（税別）です。

慶應義塾大学出版会

The Thought of Fukuzawa Vol. 2

An Encouragement of Learning

福澤諭吉 著
デヴィッド・A・ディルワース 訳

青少年に向けて新しい「知」のあり方を説いた福澤思想のエッセンスが凝縮された『学問のすゝめ』の英訳。福澤諭吉の著作を、国内外の読者に向けて英訳で刊行するシリーズの第2巻。＊年表・参考文献一覧・索引付き。

B5判変型／並製／192頁
ISBN 978-4-7664-1684-8
◎3,200円

表示価格は刊行時の本体価格（税別）です。